# JEFFERSON'S LETTERS

# JEFFERSON'S LETTERS

Selections from the private and political correspondence of Thomas Jefferson, telling the story of American independence and the founding of the American government

## Arranged by WILLSON WHITMAN

E. M. HALE AND COMPANY

*Eau Claire, Wisconsin*

# JEFFERSON'S LETTERS

# JEFFERSON'S LETTERS

## Romantic Young Man

### TO JOHN PAGE.

FAIRFIELD, *December 25, 1762.*

DEAR PAGE,—This very day, to others the day of greatest mirth and jollity, sees me overwhelmed with more and greater misfortunes than have befallen a descendant of Adam for these thousand years past, I am sure; and perhaps, after excepting Job, since the creation of the world. I think his misfortunes were somewhat greater than mine; for, although we may be pretty nearly on a level in other respects, yet, I thank my God, I have the advantage of brother Job in this, that Satan has not as yet put forth his hand to load me with bodily afflictions. You must know, dear Page, that I am now in a house surrounded with enemies, who take counsel together against my soul; and when I lay me down to rest, they say among themselves, come let us destroy him. I am sure if there is such a thing as a Devil in this world, he must have been here last night, and have had some hand in contriving what happened to me. Do you think the cursed rats (at his instigation, I suppose) did not eat up my pocket-book, which was in my pocket, within a foot of my head? And not contented with plenty for the present, they carried away my jemmy-worked silk garters, and half a dozen new minuets I had just got, to serve, I suppose, as provision for the winter. But of this I should not have accused the Devil, (because, you know rats will be rats, and hunger, without the addition of his instigations, might have urged them to do this,) if something worse, and from a different quarter, had not happened. You know it rained last night, or if you do not know it, I am sure I do. When I went to bed, I laid my watch in the usual place, and going to take her up after I arose this morning, I found her in the same place, it's true, but *Quantum mutatus ab illo!* all afloat in water, let in at a leak in the roof of the house, and as silent and still as the rats that had eat my pocket-book. Now, you know, if chance had had anything to do in this matter, there were a thousand other spots where it might have chanced to leak as well as at this one, which was perpendicularly over my watch. But I'll tell you, it's my opinion that the Devil came and bored the hole over it on purpose.

Well, as I was saying, my poor watch had lost her speech. I should not have cared much for this, but something worse attended it; the subtle particles of the water with which the case was filled, had, by their penetration, so overcome the cohesion of the particles of the paper, of which my dear picture and watch-paper were composed, that, in attempting to take them out to dry them, good God! *Mens horret referre!* My cursed fingers gave them such a rent, as I fear I never shall get over. This, cried I, was the last stroke Satan had in reserve for me; he knew I cared not for anything else he could do to me, and was determined to try his last most fatal expedient. *"Multis fortunæ vulneribus percussus, huic uni me imparem sensi, et penitus succubui!"* I would have cried bitterly, but I thought it beneath the dignity of a man, and a man too, who had read των οντων, τα μεν εφ'ημιν, τα δ εχ εφ'ημιν. However, whatever misfortunes may attend the picture or lover, my hearty prayers shall be, that all the health and happiness which Heaven can send may be the portion of the original, and that so much goodness may ever meet with what may be most agreeable in this world, as I am sure it must be in the next. And now, although the picture be defaced, there is so lively an image of her imprinted in my mind, that I shall think of her too often, I fear, for my peace of mind; and too often, I am sure, to get through old Coke this winter; for God knows I have not seen him since I packed him up in my trunk in Williamsburg. Well, Page, I do wish the Devil had old Coke, for I am sure I never was so tired of an old dull scoundrel in my life. What! are there so few inquietudes tacked to this momentary life of ours, that we must need be loading ourselves with a thousand more? Or, as brother Job says, (who, by-the-bye, I think began to whine a little under his afflictions,) "Are not my days few? Cease then, that I may take comfort a little before I go whence I shall not return, even to the land of darkness, and the shadow of death." But the old fellows say we must read to gain knowledge, and gain knowledge to make us happy and admired. *Mere jargon!* Is there any such thing as happiness in this world? No. And as for admiration, I am sure the man who powders most, perfumes most, embroiders most, and talks most nonsense, is most admired. Though to be candid, there are some who have too much good sense to esteem such monkey-like animals as these, in whose formation, as the saying is, the tailors and barbers go halves with God Almighty; and since these are the only persons whose esteem is worth a wish, I do not know but that, upon the whole, the advice of these old fellows may be worth following.

You cannot conceive the satisfaction it would give me to have a letter from you. Write me very circumstantially everything which happened at the wedding. Was she there? because, if she was, I ought to have been at the Devil for not being there too. If there is any news stirring in town or country, such as deaths, courtships, or marriages, in the circle of my acquaintance, let me know it. Remember me affectionately to all the young ladies of my acquaintance, particularly the Miss Burwells, and Miss Potters, and tell them that though that heavy earthly part of me, my body, be absent, the better half of me, my soul, is ever with them, and that my best

wishes shall ever attend them. Tell Miss Alice Corbin that I verily believe
the rats knew I was to win a pair of garters from her, or they never would
have been so cruel as to carry mine away. This very consideration makes
me so sure of the bet, that I shall ask everybody I see from that part of the
world what pretty gentleman is making his addresses to her. I would fain ask
the favor of Miss Becca Burwell to give me another watch-paper of her own
cutting, which I should esteem much more, though it were a plain round
one, than the nicest in the world cut by other hands; however, I am afraid
she would think this presumption, after my suffering the other to get spoiled.
If you think you can excuse me to her for this, I should be glad if you would
ask her. Tell Miss Sukey Potter that I heard, just before I came out of town,
that she was offended with me about something, what it is I do not know;
but this I know, that I never was guilty of the least disrespect to her in my
life, either in word or deed; as far from it as it has been possible for one to
be. I suppose when we meet next, she will be *endeavoring* to repay an
imaginary affront with a real one; but she may save herself the trouble, for
nothing that she can say or do to me shall ever lessen her in my esteem, and
I am determined always to look upon her as the same honest-hearted, good-
humored, agreeable lady I ever did. Tell—tell—in short, tell them all ten
thousand things more than either you or I can now or ever shall think of as
long as we live.

My mind has been so taken up with thinking of my acquaintances, that,
till this moment, I almost imagined myself in Williamsburg, talking to you in
our old unreserved way; and never observed, till I turned over the leaf, to
what an immoderate size I had swelled my letter; however, that I may not
tire your patience by further additions, I will make but this one more, that
I am sincerely and affectionately,

Dear Page, your friend and servant.

P. S. I am now within an easy day's ride of Shadwell, whither I shall
proceed in two or three days.

## Proposals and Plans

### TO JOHN PAGE.

SHADWELL, *Jan. 20, 1763.*

DEAR PAGE,—To tell you the plain truth, I have not a syllable to write to
you about. For I do not conceive that anything can happen in my world
which you would give a curse to know, or I either. All things here appear
to me to trudge on in one and the same round: we rise in the morning that
we may eat breakfast, dinner and supper, and go to bed again that we may
get up the next morning and do the same: so that you never saw two peas
more alike than our yesterday and to-day. Under these circumstances, what
would you have me say? Would you that I should write nothing but truth?

I tell you I know nothing that is true. Or would you rather that I should write you a pack of lies? Why, unless they were more ingenious than I am able to invent, they would furnish you with little amusement. What can I do then? nothing, but ask you the news in your world. How have you done since I saw you? How did Nancy look at you when you danced with her at Southall's? Have you any glimmering of hope? How does R. B. do? Had I better stay here and do nothing, or go down and do less? or, in other words, had I better stay here while I am here, or go down that I may have the pleasure of sailing up the river again in a full-rigged flat? Inclination tells me to go, receive my sentence, and be no longer in suspense; but reason says, if you go, and your attempt proves unsuccessful, you will be ten times more wretched than ever. In my last to you, dated Fairfield, Dec. 25, I wrote to you of the losses I had sustained; in the present I may mention one more, which is the loss of the whites of my eyes, in the room of which I have got reds, which gives me such exquisite pain that I have not attempted to read anything since a few days after Jack Walker went down, and God knows when I shall be able to do it. I have some thoughts of going to Petersburg, if the actors go there in May. If I do, I do not know but I may keep on to Williamsburg, as the birth night will be near. I hear that Ben Harrison has been to Wilton: let me know his success. Have you an inclination to travel, Page? because if you have, I shall be glad of your company. For you must know that as soon as the Rebecca (the name I intend to give the vessel above mentioned) is completely finished, I intend to hoist sail and away. I shall visit particularly England, Holland, France, Spain, Italy, (where I would buy me a good fiddle,) and Egypt, and return through the British provinces to the Northward home. This to be sure, would take us two or three years, and if we should not both be cured of love in that time, I think the devil would be in it. After desiring you to remember me to acquaintances below, male and female, I subscribe myself,

Dear Page, your friend and servant.

# Young Philosophy

## TO JOHN PAGE.

SHADWELL, *July 15th, 1763.*

DEAR PAGE,—Yours of May 30th came safe to hand. The rival you mentioned I know not whether to think formidable or not, as there has been so great an opening for him during my absence. I say *has been*, because I expect there is one no longer. Since you have undertaken to act as my attorney, you advise me to go immediately and lay siege *in form*. You certainly did not think, at the time you wrote this, of that paragraph in my letter wherein I mentioned to you my resolution of going to Britain. And to begin an affair of that kind now, and carry it on so long a time in form, is by no means a proper plan. No, no, Page; whatever assurances I may give her in private of my esteem for her, or whatever assurances I may ask in return from her, depend on it—they must be kept in private. Necessity will oblige me to proceed in a method which is not generally thought fair; that of treating with a ward before obtaining the approbation of her guardian. I say necessity will oblige me to it, because I never can bear to remain in suspense so long a time. If I am to succeed, the sooner I know it, the less uneasiness I shall have to go through. If I am to meet with a disappointment, the sooner I know it, the more of life I shall have to wear it off; and if I do meet with one, I hope in God, and verily believe, it will be the last. I assure you, that I almost envy you your present freedom; and if Belinda will not accept of my service, it shall never be offered to another. That she may, I pray most sincerely; but that she will, she never gave me reason to hope. With regard to my not proceeding in form, I do not know how she may like it. I am afraid not much. That her guardians would not, if they should know of it, is very certain. But I should think that if they were consulted after I return, it would be sufficient. The greatest inconvenience would be my not having the liberty of visiting so freely. This is a subject worth your talking over with her; and I wish you would, and would transmit to me your whole confab at length. I should be scared to death at making her so unreasonable a proposal as that of waiting until I return from Britain, unless she could first be prepared for it. I am afraid it will make my chance of succeeding considerably worse. But the event at last must be this, that if she consents, I shall be happy; if she does not, I must *endeavor* to be as much so as possible. I have thought a good deal on your case, and as mine may perhaps be similar, I must endeavor to look on it in the same light in which I have often advised you to look on yours. Perfect happiness, I believe, was never intended by the Deity to be the lot of one of his creatures in this world; but that he has very much put in our power the nearness of our approaches to it, is what I have steadfastly believed.

The most fortunate of us, in our journey through life, frequently meet with calamities and misfortunes which may greatly afflict us; and, to fortify our minds against the attacks of these calamities and misfortunes, should be one of the principal studies and endeavors of our lives. The only method of doing this is to assume a perfect resignation to the Divine will, to consider that whatever does happen, must happen; and that, by our uneasiness, we cannot prevent the blow before it does fall, but we may add to its force after it has fallen. These considerations, and others such as these, may enable us in some measure to surmount the difficulties thrown in our way; to bear up with a tolerable degree of patience under this burthen of life; and to proceed with a pious and unshaken resignation, till we arrive at our journey's end, when we may deliver up our trust into the hands of him who gave it, and receive such reward as to him shall seem proportioned to our merit. Such, dear Page, will be the language of the man who considers his situation in this life, and such should be the language of every man who would wish to render that situation as easy as the nature of it will admit. Few things will disturb him at all: nothing will disturb him much.

If this letter was to fall into the hands of some of our gay acquaintance, your correspondent and his solemn notions would probably be the subjects of a great deal of mirth and raillery, but to you, I think, I can venture to send it. It is in effect a continuation of the many conversations we have had on subjects of this kind; and I heartily wish we could now continue these conversations face to face. The time will not be very long now before we may do it, as I expect to be in Williamsburg by the first of October, if not sooner. I do not know that I shall have occasion to return, if I can rent rooms in town to lodge in; and to prevent the inconvenience of moving my lodgings for the future, I think to build: no castle though, I assure you; only a small house, which shall contain a room for myself and another for you, and no more, unless Belinda should think proper to favor us with her company, in which case I will enlarge the plan as much as she pleases. Make my compliments to her particularly, as also to Sukey Potter, Judy Burwell, and such others of my acquaintance as enquire after me. I am,

Dear Page, your sincere friend.

## Plea Denied

### TO JOHN PAGE.

WILLIAMSBURG, *October 7, 1763.*

DEAR PAGE,—In the most melancholy fit that ever any poor soul was, I sit down to write to you. Last night, as merry as agreeable company and dancing with Belinda in the Apollo could make me, I never could have thought the succeeding sun would have seen me so wretched as I now am! I was prepared to say a great deal: I had dressed up, in my own mind, such thoughts as occurred to me, in as moving a language as I knew how, and expected to have performed in a tolerably creditable manner. But, good God! When I had an opportunity of venting them, a few broken sentences, uttered in great disorder, and interrupted with pauses of uncommon length, were the too visible marks of my strange confusion! The whole confab I will tell you, word for word, if I can, when I see you, which God send may be soon. Affairs at W. and M. are in the greatest confusion. Walker, M'Clurg and Wat Jones are expelled *pro tempore*, or, as Horrox softens it, rusticated for a month. Lewis Burwell, Warner Lewis, and one Thompson, have fled to escape flagellation. I should have excepted Warner Lewis, who came off of his own accord. Jack Walker leaves town on Monday. The court is now at hand, which I must attend constantly, so that unless you come to town, there is little probability of my meeting with you anywhere else. For God sake come. I am, dear Page, your sincere friend.

subsequent atonement, and view with emulation a soul candidly acknowl-edging its fault and making a just reparation. Considering history as a moral exercise, her lessons would be too infrequent if confined to real life. Of those recorded by historians few incidents have been attended with such circumstances as to excite in any high degree this sympathetic emotion of virtue. We are, therefore, wisely framed to be as warmly interested for a fictitious as for a real personage. The field of imagination is thus laid open to our use and lessons may be formed to illustrate and carry home to the heart every moral rule of life. Thus a lively and lasting sense of filial duty is more effectually impressed on the mind of a son or daughter by reading King Lear, than by all the dry volumes of ethics, and divinity that ever were written. This is my idea of well written Romance, of Tragedy, Comedy and Epic poetry.—If you are fond of speculation the books under the head of Criticism will afford you much pleasure. Of Politics and Trade I have given you a few only of the best books, as you would probably choose to be not unacquainted with those commercial principles which bring wealth into our country, and the constitutional security we have for the enjoyment of that wealth. In Law I mention a few systematical books, as a knowledge of the minutiae of that science is not necessary for a private gentleman. In Religion, History, Natural philosophy, I have followed the same plan in general.— But whence the necessity of this collection? Come to the new Rowanty, from which you may reach your hand to a library formed on a more exten-sive plan. Separated from each other but a few paces the possessions of each would be open to the other. A spring centrically situated might be the scene of every evening's joy. There we should talk over the lessons of the day, or lose them in music, chess or the merriments of our family companions.

## Rumors of War

### TO DR. WILLIAM SMALL.

*May 7, 1775.*

DEAR SIR,—Within this week we have received the unhappy news of an action of considerable magnitude, between the King's troops and our brethren of Boston, in which it is said five hundred of the former, with the Earl of Percy, are slain. That such an action has occurred, is undoubted, though perhaps the circumstances may not have reached us with truth. This accident has cut off our last hope of reconciliation, and a phrensy of revenge seems to have seized all ranks. . . . When I saw Lord Chatham's bill, I entertained high hope that a reconciliation could have been brought about. The difference between his terms, and those offered by our Congress, might have been accommodated, if entered on, by both parties, with a disposition to accommodate. But the dignity of Parliament, it seems, can brook no opposition to its power. Strange, that a set of men, who have made sale of their virtue to the Minister, should yet talk of retaining dignity! But I am

## Sally in the Green Chair

### TO JOHN PAGE.

CHARLOTTESVILLE, *Feb. 21, 1770.*

Am I never more to have a letter from you? Why the devil don't you write? But I suppose you are always in the moon, or some of the planetary regions. I mean you are there in idea; and, unless you mend, you shall have my consent to be there *de facto*; at least, during the vacations of the Court and Assembly. If your spirit is too elevated to advert to sublunary subjects, depute my friend Mrs. Page to support your correspondences. Methinks I should, with wonderful pleasure, open and peruse a letter written by so fair, and (what is better) so friendly hands. If thinking much of you would entitle me to the civility of a letter, I assure you I merit a very long one. . . . apprehensive that if we were placed together, we should pull down the moon, or play some such devilish prank with their works. I reflect often with pleasure on the philosophical evenings I passed at Rosewell in my last visits there. I was always fond of philosophy, even in its drier forms; but from a ruby lip, it comes with charms irresistible. Such a feast of sentiment must exhilarate and lengthen life, at least as much as the feast of the sensualist shortens it in a word, I prize it so highly, that, if you will at any time collect the same *Belle Assemblée*, on giving me three days previous notice, I shall certainly repair to my place as a member of it. Should it not happen before I come down, I will carry Sally Nicholas in the green chair to New-quarter, where your periagua (how the —— should I spell that word?) will meet us, automaton-like, of its own accord. You know I had a wagon which moved itself—cannot we construct a boat then which shall row itself?

## Tobacco and Tea

### TO THOMAS ADAMS.

MONTICELLO, *Feb. 20, 1771.*

DEAR SIR,—Not expecting to have the pleasure of seeing you again before you leave the country, I inclose you an order on the inspectors at Shockoe for two hogsheads of tobacco which I consign to you, and give you also the trouble of shipping as I am too far from the spot to do it myself. They are to be laid out in the purchase of the articles on the back hereof. You will observe that part of these articles (such as are licensed by the association) are to be sent at any event. Another part (being prohibited) are only to be sent if the tea act should be repealed before you get home; if it is not, you will observe a third class to be sent instead of those which are prohibited. I am not without expectation that the repeal may take place. I believe the parliament want nothing but a colorable motive to adopt this measure. The conduct of our brethren of New York affords them this.

## Piano for a Lady

### TO THOMAS ADAMS.

MONTICELLO, *June 1, 1771.*

DEAR SIR,—As it was somewhat doubtful when you left the country how far my little invoice delivered you might be complied with till we should know the fate of the association, I desired you to withhold purchasing the things till you should hear farther from me. The day appointed for the meeting of the associates is not yet arrived; however from the universal sense of those who are likely to attend, it seems reduced to a certainty that the restrictions will be taken off everything but the dutied articles. I will, therefore, venture to desire that branch of my invoice may be complied with in which were some shoes and other prohibited articles; since if contrary to our expectations the restrictions should be continued, I can store, or otherwise dispose of them as our committees please. I must alter one article in the invoice. I wrote therein for a Clavichord. I have since seen a Forte-piano and am charmed with it. Send me this instrument then instead of the Clavichord: let the case be of fine mahogany, solid, not veneered, the compass from Double G. to F. in alt, a plenty of spare strings; and the workmanship of the whole very handsome and worthy the acceptance of a lady for whom I intend it. I must add also ½ dozen pair India cotton stockings for myself @ 10/ sterling per pair, ½ dozen pair best white silk do.; and a large umbrella with brass ribs, covered with green silk, and neatly finished. By this change of the Clavichord into a Forte-piano and addition of the other things, I shall be brought in debt to you, to discharge which I will ship you of the first tobacco I get to the warehouse in the fall. I expect by that time, and also from year to year afterwards, I must send you an invoice, with tobacco, somewhat enlarged, as I have it in prospect to become more regularly a paterfamilias.—I desired the favor of you to procure me an architect. I must repeat the request earnestly, and that you will send him in as soon as you can.—I shall conclude with one petition: that you send me the articles contained in my invoice and written for above as soon as you receive this, as I suppose they may be bought ready made; and particularly the Forte-piano, for which I shall be very impatient. By this means I may get them in October, which will prevent my being obliged to purchase as I must do if they do not come in time.

## Books and Friends

### TO ROBERT SKIPWITH.

MONTICELLO, *Aug. 3,*

I sat down with a design of executing your request to form a catalo books to the amount of about 50 lib. sterling. But could by no means myself with any partial choice I could make. Thinking, therefore, it mi as agreeable to you I have framed such a general collection as I thin would wish and might in time find convenient to procure. Out of th will choose for yourself to the amount you mentioned for the presen and may hereafter as shall be convenient proceed in completing the A view of the second column in this catalogue would I suppose ex smile from the face of gravity. Peace to its wisdom! Let me not awa A little attention however to the nature of the human mind evinces th entertainments of fiction are useful as well as pleasant. That they are pl when well written every person feels who reads. But wherein is its asks the reverend sage, big with the notion that nothing can be useful b learned lumber of Greek and Roman reading with which his head is st

I answer, everything is useful which contributes to fix in the prin and practices of virtue. When any original act of charity or of gratitud instance, is presented either to our sight or imagination, we are deepl pressed with its beauty and feel a strong desire in ourselves of doing table and grateful acts also. On the contrary when we see or read o atrocious deed, we are disgusted with its deformity, and conceive a horrence of vice. Now every emotion of this kind is an exercise of ou tuous dispositions, and dispositions of the mind, like limbs of the body a strength by exercise. But exercise produces habit, and in the instan which we speak the exercise being of the moral feelings produces a of thinking and acting virtuously. We never reflect whether the stor read be truth or fiction. If the painting be lively, and a tolerable pict nature, we are thrown into a reverie, from which if we awaken it fault of the writer. I appeal to every reader of feeling and sentiment wl the fictitious murder of Duncan by Macbeth in Shakespeare does not in him as great a horror of villainy, as the real one of Henry IV. by Ra as related by Davila? And whether the fidelity of Nelson and generos Blandford in Marmontel do not dilate his breast and elevate his senti as much as any similar incident which real history can furnish? Does in fact feel himself a better man while reading them, and privately co to copy the fair example? We neither know nor care whether Law Sterne really went to France, whether he was there accosted by the Fr can, at first rebuked him unkindly, and then gave him a peace offeri whether the whole be not fiction. In either case we equally are sorrov the rebuke, and secretly resolve *we* will never do so: we are pleased wl

# Sally in the Green Chair

TO JOHN PAGE.

CHARLOTTESVILLE, *Feb. 21, 1770.*

Am I never more to have a letter from you? Why the devil don't you write? But I suppose you are always in the moon, or some of the planetary regions. I mean you are there in idea; and, unless you mend, you shall have my consent to be there *de facto;* at least, during the vacations of the Court and Assembly. If your spirit is too elevated to advert to sublunary subjects, depute my friend Mrs. Page to support your correspondences. Methinks I should, with wonderful pleasure, open and peruse a letter written by so fair, and (what is better) so friendly hands. If thinking much of you would entitle me to the civility of a letter, I assure you I merit a very long one. . . . apprehensive that if we were placed together, we should pull down the moon, or play some such devilish prank with their works. I reflect often with pleasure on the philosophical evenings I passed at Rosewell in my last visits there. I was always fond of philosophy, even in its drier forms; but from a ruby lip, it comes with charms irresistible. Such a feast of sentiment must exhilarate and lengthen life, at least as much as the feast of the sensualist shortens it in a word, I prize it so highly, that, if you will at any time collect the same *Belle Assemblée,* on giving me three days previous notice, I shall certainly repair to my place as a member of it. Should it not happen before I come down, I will carry Sally Nicholas in the green chair to New-quarter, where your periagua (how the —— should I spell that word?) will meet us, automaton-like, of its own accord. You know I had a wagon which moved itself—cannot we construct a boat then which shall row itself?

# Tobacco and Tea

TO THOMAS ADAMS.

MONTICELLO, *Feb. 20, 1771.*

DEAR SIR,—Not expecting to have the pleasure of seeing you again before you leave the country, I inclose you an order on the inspectors at Shockoe for two hogsheads of tobacco which I consign to you, and give you also the trouble of shipping as I am too far from the spot to do it myself. They are to be laid out in the purchase of the articles on the back hereof. You will observe that part of these articles (such as are licensed by the association) are to be sent at any event. Another part (being prohibited) are only to be sent if the tea act should be repealed before you get home; if it is not, you will observe a third class to be sent instead of those which are prohibited. I am not without expectation that the repeal may take place. I believe the parliament want nothing but a colorable motive to adopt this measure. The conduct of our brethren of New York affords them this.

# Piano for a Lady

## TO THOMAS ADAMS.

MONTICELLO, *June 1, 1771.*

DEAR SIR,—As it was somewhat doubtful when you left the country how far my little invoice delivered you might be complied with till we should know the fate of the association, I desired you to withhold purchasing the things till you should hear farther from me. The day appointed for the meeting of the associates is not yet arrived; however from the universal sense of those who are likely to attend, it seems reduced to a certainty that the restrictions will be taken off everything but the duties articles. I will, therefore, venture to desire that branch of my invoice may be complied with in which were some shoes and other prohibited articles; since if contrary to our expectations the restrictions should be continued, I can store, or otherwise dispose of them as our committees please. I must alter one article in the invoice. I wrote therein for a Clavichord. I have since seen a Forte-piano and am charmed with it. Send me this instrument then instead of the Clavichord: let the case be of fine mahogany, solid, not veneered, the compass from Double G. to F. in alt, a plenty of spare strings; and the workmanship of the whole very handsome and worthy the acceptance of a lady for whom I intend it. I must add also ½ dozen pair India cotton stockings for myself @ 10/ sterling per pair, ½ dozen pair best white silk do.; and a large umbrella with brass ribs, covered with green silk, and neatly finished. By this change of the Clavichord into a Forte-piano and addition of the other things, I shall be brought in debt to you, to discharge which I will ship you of the first tobacco I get to the warehouse in the fall. I expect by that time, and also from year to year afterwards, I must send you an invoice, with tobacco, somewhat enlarged, as I have it in prospect to become more regularly a paterfamilias.—I desired the favor of you to procure me an architect. I must repeat the request earnestly, and that you will send him in as soon as you can.—I shall conclude with one petition: that you send me the articles contained in my invoice and written for above as soon as you receive this, as I suppose they may be bought ready made; and particularly the Forte-piano, for which I shall be very impatient. By this means I may get them in October, which will prevent my being obliged to purchase as I must do if they do not come in time.

## Books and Friends

TO ROBERT SKIPWITH.

MONTICELLO, *Aug. 3, 1771.*

I sat down with a design of executing your request to form a catalogue of books to the amount of about 50 lib. sterling. But could by no means satisfy myself with any partial choice I could make. Thinking, therefore, it might be as agreeable to you I have framed such a general collection as I think you would wish and might in time find convenient to procure. Out of this you will choose for yourself to the amount you mentioned for the present year and may hereafter as shall be convenient proceed in completing the whole. A view of the second column in this catalogue would I suppose extort a smile from the face of gravity. Peace to its wisdom! Let me not awaken it. A little attention however to the nature of the human mind evinces that the entertainments of fiction are useful as well as pleasant. That they are pleasant when well written every person feels who reads. But wherein is its utility asks the reverend sage, big with the notion that nothing can be useful but the learned lumber of Greek and Roman reading with which his head is stored?

I answer, everything is useful which contributes to fix in the principles and practices of virtue. When any original act of charity or of gratitude, for instance, is presented either to our sight or imagination, we are deeply impressed with its beauty and feel a strong desire in ourselves of doing charitable and grateful acts also. On the contrary when we see or read of any atrocious deed, we are disgusted with its deformity, and conceive an abhorrence of vice. Now every emotion of this kind is an exercise of our virtuous dispositions, and dispositions of the mind, like limbs of the body acquire strength by exercise. But exercise produces habit, and in the instance of which we speak the exercise being of the moral feelings produces a habit of thinking and acting virtuously. We never reflect whether the story we read be truth or fiction. If the painting be lively, and a tolerable picture of nature, we are thrown into a reverie, from which if we awaken it is the fault of the writer. I appeal to every reader of feeling and sentiment whether the fictitious murder of Duncan by Macbeth in Shakespeare does not excite in him as great a horror of villainy, as the real one of Henry IV. by Ravaillac as related by Davila? And whether the fidelity of Nelson and generosity of Blandford in Marmontel do not dilate his breast and elevate his sentiments as much as any similar incident which real history can furnish? Does he not in fact feel himself a better man while reading them, and privately covenant to copy the fair example? We neither know nor care whether Lawrence Sterne really went to France, whether he was there accosted by the Franciscan, at first rebuked him unkindly, and then gave him a peace offering: or whether the whole be not fiction. In either case we equally are sorrowful at the rebuke, and secretly resolve *we* will never do so: we are pleased with the

subsequent atonement, and view with emulation a soul candidly acknowl-
edging its fault and making a just reparation. Considering history as a moral
exercise, her lessons would be too infrequent if confined to real life. Of
those recorded by historians few incidents have been attended with such
circumstances as to excite in any high degree this sympathetic emotion of
virtue. We are, therefore, wisely framed to be as warmly interested for a
fictitious as for a real personage. The field of imagination is thus laid open
to our use and lessons may be formed to illustrate and carry home to the
heart every moral rule of life. Thus a lively and lasting sense of filial duty
is more effectually impressed on the mind of a son or daughter by reading
King Lear, than by all the dry volumes of ethics, and divinity that ever were
written. This is my idea of well written Romance, of Tragedy, Comedy and
Epic poetry.—If you are fond of speculation the books under the head of
Criticism will afford you much pleasure. Of Politics and Trade I have given
you a few only of the best books, as you would probably choose to be not
unacquainted with those commercial principles which bring wealth into our
country, and the constitutional security we have for the enjoyment of that
wealth. In Law I mention a few systematical books, as a knowledge of the
minutiae of that science is not necessary for a private gentleman. In Religion,
History, Natural philosophy, I have followed the same plan in general.—
But whence the necessity of this collection? Come to the new Rowanty,
from which you may reach your hand to a library formed on a more extensive plan. Separated from each other but a few paces the possessions of each
would be open to the other. A spring centrically situated might be the scene
of every evening's joy. There we should talk over the lessons of the day,
or lose them in music, chess or the merriments of our family companions.

# Rumors of War

## TO DR. WILLIAM SMALL.

*May 7, 1775.*

DEAR SIR,—Within this week we have received the unhappy news of an
action of considerable magnitude, between the King's troops and our
brethren of Boston, in which it is said five hundred of the former, with the
Earl of Percy, are slain. That such an action has occurred, is undoubted,
though perhaps the circumstances may not have reached us with truth. This
accident has cut off our last hope of reconciliation, and a phrensy of revenge
seems to have seized all ranks. . . . When I saw Lord Chatham's bill, I
entertained high hope that a reconciliation could have been brought about.
The difference between his terms, and those offered by our Congress, might
have been accommodated, if entered on, by both parties, with a disposition
to accommodate. But the dignity of Parliament, it seems, can brook no
opposition to its power. Strange, that a set of men, who have made sale of
their virtue to the Minister, should yet talk of retaining dignity! But I am

getting into politics, though I sat down only to ask your acceptance of the wine, and express my constant wishes for your happiness.

## On British Policy

TO JOHN RANDOLPH, ESQ.

MONTICELLO, *August 25, 1775.*

DEAR SIR,—I am sorry the situation of our country should render it not eligible to you to remain longer in it. I hope the returning wisdom of Great Britain will, ere long, put an end to this unnatural contest. There may be people to whose tempers and dispositions contention is pleasing, and who, therefore, wish a continuance of confusion, but to me it is of all states but one, the most horrid. My first wish is a restoration of our just rights; my second, a return of the happy period, when, consistently with duty, I may withdraw myself totally from the public stage, and pass the rest of my days in domestic ease and tranquillity, banishing every desire of ever hearing what passes in the world. Perhaps (for the latter adds considerably to the warmth of the former wish), looking with fondness towards a reconciliation with Great Britain, I cannot help hoping you may be able to contribute towards expediting this good work. I think it must be evident to yourself, that the Ministry have been deceived by their officers on this side of the water, who (for what purpose I cannot tell) have constantly represented the American opposition as that of a small faction, in which the body of the people took little part. This, you can inform them, of your own knowledge, is untrue. They have taken it into their heads, too, that we are cowards, and shall surrender at discretion to an armed force. The past and future operations of the war must confirm or undeceive them on that head. I wish they were thoroughly and minutely acquainted with every circumstance relative to America, as it exists in truth. I am persuaded, this would go far towards disposing them to reconciliation. Even those in Parliament who are called friends to America, seem to know nothing of our real determinations. I observe, they pronounced in the last Parliament, that the Congress of 1774 did not mean to insist rigorously on the terms they held out, but kept something in reserve, to give up; and, in fact, that they would give up everything but the article of taxation. Now, the truth is far from this, as I can affirm, and put my honor to the assertion. Their continuance in this error may, perhaps, produce very ill consequences. The Congress stated the lowest terms they thought possible to be accepted, in order to convince the world they were not unreasonable. They gave up the monopoly and regulation of trade, and all acts of Parliament prior to 1764, leaving to British generosity to render these, at some future time, as easy to America as the interest of Britain would admit. But this was before blood was spilt. I cannot affirm, but have reason to think, these terms would not now be accepted. I wish no false sense of honor, no ignorance of our real intentions, no vain hope that partial concessions of right will be accepted, may induce the Ministry to trifle with accommodation, till it shall be out of their power ever to accommodate. If, indeed, Great Britain, disjoined from her colonies, be a match for the most potent nations of Europe, with the colonies thrown into their scale, they may go on securely. But if they are not assured of this, it would be certainly unwise, by trying the event of another campaign, to risk our accepting a foreign aid, which, perhaps, may not be obtainable, but on condition of everlasting avulsion from Great Britain. This would be thought a hard condition, to those who still wish for re-union with their parent country. I am sincerely one of those, and would rather be in dependence on Great Britain, properly limited, than on any nation on earth, or than on no nation. But I am one of those, too, who, rather than submit to the rights of legislating for us, assumed by the British Parliament, and which late experience has shown they will so cruelly exercise, would lend my hand to sink the whole Island in the ocean.

If undeceiving the Minister, as to matters of fact, may change his disposition, it will, perhaps, be in your power, by assisting to do this, to render service to the whole empire, at the most critical time, certainly, that it has ever seen. Whether Britain shall continue the head of the greatest empire on earth, or shall return to her original station in the political scale of Europe, depends, perhaps, on the resolutions of the succeeding winter. God send they may be wise and salutary for us all.

## The Sword Is Drawn

### TO JOHN RANDOLPH, ESQ.

PHILADELPHIA, *November 29, 1775.*

I have it in my power to acquaint you, that the success of our arms has corresponded with the justice of our cause. Chambly and St. John's were taken some weeks ago, and in them the whole regular army in Canada, except about forty or fifty men. This day, certain intelligence has reached us, that our General, Montgomery, is received into Montreal; and we expect, every hour, to be informed that Quebec has opened its arms to Colonel Arnold, who, with eleven hundred men, was sent from Boston up the Kennebec, and down the Chaudière river to that place. He expected to be there early this month. Montreal acceded to us on the 13th, and Carleton set out, with the shattered remains of his little army, for Quebec, where we hope he will be taken up by Arnold. In a short time, we have reason to hope, the delegates of Canada will join us in Congress, and complete the American union, as far as we wish to have it completed. We hear that one of the British transports has arrived at Boston; the rest are beating off the coast, in very bad weather. You will have heard, before this reaches you, that Lord Dunmore has commenced hostilities in Virginia. That people bore with everything, till he attempted to burn the town of Hampton. They opposed

and repelled him, with considerable loss on his side, and none on ours. It has
raised our countrymen into a perfect phrensy. . . . Believe me, dear Sir,
there is not in the British empire a man who more cordially loves a union
with Great Britain than I do. But by the God that made me, I will cease
to exist before I yield to a connection on such terms as the British Parliament propose; and in this, I think I speak the sentiments of America.

## On Independence

### TO THOMAS NELSON.

PHILADELPHIA, *May 16, 1776.*

The last post carried you an account of the naval engagement in Delaware. I inclose a vote of yesterday on the subject of government as the
ensuing campaign is likely to require greater exertion than our unorganized
powers may at present effect. Should our Convention propose to establish
now a form of government perhaps it might be agreeable to recall for a
short time their delegates. It is a work of the most interesting nature and
such as every individual would wish to have his voice in. In truth it is the
whole object of the present controversy; for should a bad government be
instituted for us in future it had been as well to have accepted at first the bad
one offered to us from beyond the water without the risk and expense of
contest.
I am at present in our old lodgings though I think, as the excessive heats
of the city are coming on fast, to endeavor to get lodgings in the skirts of
the town where I may have the benefit of a freely circulating air. Tell Page
and McClurgh that I received their letters this morning and shall devote
myself to their contents. I am here in the same uneasy anxious state in which
I was the last fall without Mrs. Jefferson who could not come with me. I
wish much to see you here, yet hope you will contrive to bring on as early
as you can in convention the great questions of the session. I suppose they
will tell us what to say on the subject of independence, but hope respect will
be expressed to the right of opinion in other colonies who may happen
to differ from them. When at home I took great pains to enquire into the
sentiments of the people on that head, in the upper counties I think I may
safely say nine out of ten are for it. Adieu. My compliments to Mrs. Nelson.

## Congressional Record

### TO JOHN ADAMS.

WILLIAMSBURG, *16 May, 1777.*

I learn from our delegates that the confederation is again on the carpet,
a great and a necessary work, but I fear almost desperate. The point of rep-

resentation is what most alarms me, as I fear the great and small colonies are bitterly determined not to cede. Will you be so good as to collect the proposition I formerly made you in private, and try if you can work it into some good to save our union? It was, that any proposition might be negatived by the representatives of a majority of the people of America, or of a majority of the colonies of America. The former secures the larger, the latter, the smaller colonies. I have mentioned it to many here. The good whigs, I think, will so far cede their opinions for the sake of the Union, and others we care little for.

The journals of Congress not being printed earlier, gives more uneasiness than I would wish ever to see produced by any act of that body, from whom alone I know our salvation can proceed. In our Assembly, even the best affected think it an indignity to freemen to be voted away, life and fortune, in the dark. Our House have lately written for a manuscript copy of your journals, not meaning to desire a communication of any thing ordered to be kept secret. I wish the regulation of the post-office, adopted by Congress last September, could be put in practice. It was for the travel night and day, and to go their several stages three times a week. The speedy and frequent communication of intelligence is really of great consequence. So many falsehoods have been propagated that nothing now is believed unless coming from Congress or camp. Our people, merely for want of intelligence which they may rely on, are become lethargic and insensible of the state they are in.

## The Declaration

### TO RICHARD HENRY LEE.

PHILADELPHIA, *July 8, 1776.*

DEAR SIR,—For news, I refer you to your brother, who writes on that head. I enclose you a copy of the Declaration of Independence, as agreed to by the House, and also as originally framed. You will judge whether it is the better or worse for the critics. I shall return to *Virginia* after the 11th of *August.* I wish my successor may be certain to come before that time; in that case I shall hope to see you, and not *Wythe,* in Convention, that the business of Government, which is of everlasting concern, may receive your aid.

## Home Front

### TO DR. BENJAMIN FRANKLIN, PARIS.

VIRGINIA, *August 13, 1777.*

With respect to the State of Virginia in particular, the people seem to have laid aside the monarchical, and taken up the republican government, with as much ease as would have attended their throwing off an old, and putting on a new suit of clothes. Not a single throe has attended this important transformation. A half-dozen aristocratical gentlemen, agonizing under the loss of pre-eminence, have sometimes ventured their sarcasms on our political metamorphosis. They have been thought fitter objects of pity, than of punishment. We are, at present, in the complete and quiet exercise of well-organized government, save only that our courts of justice do not open till the fall. I think nothing can bring the security of our continent and its cause into danger, if we can support the credit of our paper. To do that, I apprehend, one of two steps must be taken. Either to procure free trade by alliance with some naval power able to protect it; or, if we find there is no prospect of that, to shut our ports totally, to all the world, and turn our colonies into manufactories. The former would be most eligible, because most conformable to the habits and wishes of our people. Were the British Court to return to their senses in time to seize the little advantage which still remains within their reach, from this quarter, I judge, that, on acknowledging our absolute independence and sovereignty, a commercial treaty beneficial to them, and perhaps even a league of mutual offence and defence, might, not seeing the expense or consequences of such a measure, be approved by our people, if nothing, in the mean time, done on your part, should prevent it. But they will continue to grasp at their desperate sovereignty, till every benefit short of that is forever out of their reach. I wish my domestic situation had rendered it possible for me to join you in the very honorable charge confided to you. Residence in a polite Court, society of literati of the first order, a just cause and an approving God, will add length to a life for which all men pray, and none more than

Your most obedient and humble servant.

## Threat to Virginia

TO HIS EXCELLENCY GENERAL WASHINGTON.

RICHMOND, *October 22, 1780.*

SIR,—I have this morning received certain information of the arrival of a hostile fleet in our bay, of about sixty sail. The debarkation of some light horse, in the neighborhood of Portsmouth, seems to indicate that as the first scene of action. We are endeavoring to collect as large a body to oppose them as we can arm; this will be lamentably inadequate, if the enemy be in any force. It is mortifying to suppose that a people, able and zealous to contend with their enemy, should be reduced to fold their arms for want of the means of defence. Yet no resources, that we know of, insure us against this event. It has become necessary to divert to this new object, a considerable part of the aids we had destined for General Gates. We are still, however, sensible of the necessity of supporting him, and have left that part of the country nearest him uncalled on, at present, that they may reinforce him as soon as arms can be received. We have called to the command of our forces Generals Weeden and Muhlenburg, of the line, and Nelson and Stevens of the militia. You will be pleased to make to these such additions as you may think proper. As to the aids of men, I ask for none, knowing that if the late detachment of the enemy shall have left it safe for you to spare aids of that kind, you will not await my application. Of the troops we shall raise, there is not a single man who ever saw the face of an enemy. Whether the Convention troops will be removed or not, is yet undetermined. This must depend on the force of the enemy, and the aspect of their movements.

## A Spy Is Caught

### TO HIS EXCELLENCY GENERAL WASHINGTON.

RICHMOND, *November 10, 1780.*

SIR,—I inclose your Excellency a copy of an intercepted letter from Major General Leslie, to Lord Cornwallis.[1] It was taken from a person endeavoring to pass through the country from Portsmouth towards Carolina. When apprehended, and a proposal made to search him, he readily consented to be searched, but, at the same time, was observed to put his hand into his pocket and carry something towards his mouth, as if it were a quid of tobacco; it was examined, and found to be a letter, of which the inclosed is a copy, written on silk paper, rolled up in gold-beater's skin, and nicely tied at each end, so as not to be larger than a goose-quill. As this is the first authentic disclosure of their purpose in coming here, and may serve to found, with somewhat more of certainty, conjectures respecting their future movements, while their disappointment in not meeting with Lord Cornwallis may occasion new plans at New York, I thought it worthy of communication to your Excellency.

## The Enemy Approaches

### TO HIS EXCELLENCY GENERAL WASHINGTON.

RICHMOND, *February 8, 1781.*

SIR,—I have just received intelligence, which, though from a private hand, I believe is to be relied on, that a fleet of the enemy's ships have entered

---

[1] TO LORD CORNWALLIS.

PORTSMOUTH, Virginia, November 4th, 1780.
MY LORD,—I have been here near a week, establishing a post. I wrote to you to Charleston, and by another messenger, by land. I cannot hear, for a certainty, where you are: I wait your orders. The bearer is to be handsomely rewarded, if he brings me any note or mark from your Lordship.          A. L.

Cape Fear river, that eight of them had got over the bar, and many others were laying off; and that it was supposed to be a reinforcement to Lord Cornwallis, under the command of General Prevost. This account, which had come through another channel, is confirmed by a letter from General Parsons at Halifax, to the gentleman who forwards it to me. I thought it of sufficient importance to be communicated to your Excellency by the stationed expresses. The fatal want of arms puts it out of our power to bring a greater force into the field, than will barely suffice to restrain the adventures of the pitiful body of men they have at Portsmouth. Should any more be added to them, this country will be perfectly open to them, by land as well as water.

## Virginia to Arms

### TO BARON STEUBEN.

RICHMOND, *February 18, 1781.*

SIR,—I have this moment received intelligence that Lord Cornwallis continues his rapid approach, and there is reason to believe he was at Roanoke on the 14th. This information is not authentic, yet it comes in such manner as to command some attention. I have, therefore, thought it expedient to order every man of the counties of Powhatan, Cumberland, Amelia, Lunenburg and Brunswick who has a firelock, or for whom one can be procured, to be embodied and marched immediately to join General Greene, and those of the counties of Chesterfield and Dinwiddie to be embodied, but not marched till further orders.

## Spirit of Opposition

### TO HIS EXCELLENCY GENERAL WASHINGTON.

RICHMOND, *February 26, 1781.*

SIR,—I gave you information in my last letter, that General Greene had crossed the Dan, at Boyd's ferry, and that Lord Cornwallis had arrived at the opposite shore. Large reinforcements of militia having embodied both in front and rear of the enemy, he is retreating with as much rapidity as he advanced; his route is towards Hillsborough. General Greene re-crossed the Dan on the 21st, in pursuit of him. I have the pleasure to inform you, that the spirit of opposition was as universal as could have been wished for. There was no restraint on the numbers that embodied, but the want of arms.

## Help from Abroad

TO MAJOR-GENERAL MARQUIS DE LAFAYETTE.

RICHMOND, *March 2d, 1781.*

SIR,—I was two days ago honored with your letter and that of General Washington on the same subject; I immediately transmitted by express the one accompanying it to the commanding officer of the naval force of his Christian Majesty in our bay and took measures for providing pilots. Baron Steuben will communicate to you the arrangements he proposes, which I shall have the pleasure of forwarding with every aid in my power. I hope that when you shall arrive at the point of action every thing will be found in readiness. I think the prospect flattering of lopping off this branch of the British force and of relieving the southern operations by pointing all their efforts to one object only. The relief of this State being the most immediate effect of the enterprise it gives me great pleasure that we shall be so far indebted for it to a nobleman who has already so much endeared himself to the citizens of these States by his past exertions and the very effectual aids he has been the means of procuring them. I have the honor to be with sentiments of the most perfect gratitude and respect, Sir, Your etc.

## Enemy Landing

TO HIS EXCELLENCY GENERAL WASHINGTON.

RICHMOND, *April 23, 1781.*

SIR,—On the 18th instant, the enemy came from Portsmouth up James river, in considerable force, though their numbers are not yet precisely known to us. They landed at Burwell's ferry, below Williamsburg, and also a short distance above the mouth of Chickahominy. This latter circumstance obliged Colonel Innis, who commanded a body of militia, stationed on that side the river to cover the country from depredation, to retire upwards, lest he should be placed between their two bodies. One of these entered Williamsburg on the 20th, and the other proceeded to a ship-yard we had on Chickahominy. What injury they did there, I am not yet informed. I take for granted, they have burned an unfinished twenty-gun ship we had there. Such of the stores, belonging to the yard as were movable, had been carried some miles higher up the river. Two small gallies also retired up the river. Whether by this, either the stores or gallies were saved, is yet unknown. I am just informed, from a private hand, that they left Williamsburg early yesterday morning. If this sudden departure was not in consequence of some circumstance of alarm unknown to us, their expedition to Williamsburg has been unaccountable. There were no public stores at that place, but those which were necessary for the daily subsistence of the men there. Where they mean to descend next, the event alone can determine. Besides harassing our militia with this kind of war, the taking them from their farms at the interesting season of planting their corn, will have an unfortunate effect on the crop of the ensuing year.

## Towards Yorktown

### TO HIS EXCELLENCY GENERAL WASHINGTON.

CHARLOTTESVILLE, *May 28, 1781.*

SIR,—I make no doubt you will have heard, before this shall have the honor of being presented to your Excellency, of the junction of Lord Cornwallis with the force at Petersburg under Arnold, who had succeeded to the command on the death of Major-general Phillips. I am now advised that they have evacuated Petersburg, joined at Westover a reinforcement of two thousand men just arrived from New York, crossed James River, and on the 26th instant, were three miles advanced on their way towards Richmond; at which place, Major-General the Marquis Fayette lay with three thousand men, regulars and militia: these being the whole number we could arm, until the arrival of the eleven hundred arms from Rhode Island, which are, about this time, at the place where our public stores are deposited. The whole force of the enemy within this State, from the best intelligence I have been able to get, is, I think, about seven thousand men, infantry and cavalry, including, also, the small garrison left at Portsmouth. A number of privateers, which are constantly ravaging the shores of our rivers, prevent us from receiving any aid from the counties lying on navigable waters; and powerful operations meditated against our western frontier, by a joint force of British and Indian savages, have, as your Excellency before knew, obliged us to embody between two and three thousand men in that quarter. Your Excellency will judge from this state of things, and from what you know of our country, what it may probably suffer during the present campaign.

## Famous Victory

### TO GENERAL WASHINGTON.

MONTICELLO, *October 28th, 1781.*

SIR,—I hope it will not be unacceptable to your Excellency to receive the congratulations of a private individual on your return to your native country, and, above all things, on the important success which has attended it.[1]

[1][The battle of Yorktown.]

Great as this has been, however, it can scarcely add to the affection with which we have looked up to you. And if, in the minds of any, the motives of gratitude to our good allies were not sufficiently apparent, the part they have borne in this action must amply evince them.

## Peace Mission

### TO GEORGE WASHINGTON.

PHILADELPHIA, *January 22d, 1783.*

SIR,—Having lately received a call from Congress to pass the Atlantic in the character of their minister for negotiating peace, I cannot leave the continent without separating myself for a moment from the general gratitude of my country, to offer my individual tribute to your Excellency for all you have suffered and all you have effected for us. Were I to indulge myself in those warm effusions which this subject forever prompts, they would wear an appearance of adulation very foreign to my nature; for such is become the prostitution of language that sincerity has no longer distinct terms in which to express her own truths. Should you give me occasion, during the short mission on which I go, to render you any service beyond the water, I shall, for a proof of my gratitude, appeal from language to the zeal with which I shall embrace it. The negotiations to which I am joined may perhaps be protracted beyond our present expectations, in which case, though I know you must receive much better intelligence from the gentlemen whose residence there has brought them into a more intimate acquaintance with the characters and views of the European courts, yet I shall certainly presume to add my mite, should it only serve to convince you of the warmth of those sentiments of respect and esteem with which I have the honor to be, your Excellency's most obedient, and most humble servant.

## Planning a Constitution

### TO JAMES MADISON.

MONTICELLO, *June 17, 1783.*

A convention for the amendment of our Constitution having been much the topic of conversation for some time, I have turned my thoughts to the amendments necessary. The result I enclose to you. You will have opportunities during your stay in Philadelphia of enquiring into the success of some of the parts of it which though new to us have been tried in other States.

# Fatherly Advice

TO MARTHA JEFFERSON.

ANNAPOLIS, *Nov. 28, 1783.*

DEAR PATSY,—After four days' journey, I arrived here without any accident, and in as good health as when I left Philadelphia. The conviction that you would be more improved in the situation I have placed you than if still with me, has solaced me on my parting with you, which my love for you has rendered a difficult thing. The acquirements which I hope you will make under the tutors I have provided for you will render you more worthy of my love; and if they cannot increase it, they will prevent its diminution. Consider the good lady who has taken you under her roof, who has undertaken to see that you perform all your exercises, and to admonish you in all those wanderings from what is right or what is clever, to which your inexperience would expose you: consider her, I say, as your mother, as the only person to whom, since the loss with which Heaven has pleased to afflict you, you can now look up; and that her displeasure or disapprobation, on any occasion, will be an immense misfortune, which should you be so unhappy as to incur by any unguarded act, think no concession too much to regain her good-will. With respect to the distribution of your time, the following is what I should approve:

From 8 to 10, practice music.

From 10 to 1, dance one day and draw another.

From 1 to 2, draw on the day you dance, and write a letter next day.

From 3 to 4, read French.

From 4 to 5, exercise yourself in music.

From 5 till bed-time, read English, write, etc.

Communicate this plan to Mrs. Hopkinson, and if she approves of it, pursue it. As long as Mrs. Trist remains in Philadelphia, cultivate her affection. She has been a valuable friend to you, and her good sense and good heart make her valued by all who know her, and by nobody on earth more than me. I expect you will write me by every post. Inform me what books you read, what tunes you learn, and enclose me your best copy of every lesson in drawing. Write also one letter a week either to your Aunt Eppes, your Aunt Skipwith, your Aunt Carr, or the little lady from whom I now enclose a letter, and always put the letter you so write under cover to me. Take care that you never spell a word wrong. Always before you write a word, consider how it is spelt, and, if you do not remember it, turn to a dictionary. It produces great praise to a lady to spell well. I have placed my happiness on seeing you good and accomplished; and no distress this world can now bring on me would equal that of your disappointing my hopes. If you love me, then strive to be good under every situation and to all living creatures, and to acquire those accomplishments which I have put in your power, and which will go far towards ensuring you the warmest love of your affectionate father.

P. S.  Keep my letters and read them at times, that you may always have present in your mind those things which will endear you to me.

## Off to Paris

### TO BENJAMIN FRANKLIN.

BOSTON, *June 19, 1784.*

DEAR SIR,—Supposing that Congress would communicate to you directly the powers committed to yourself, Mr. Adams and myself, I have delayed from day to day the honor of writing to you, in hopes that every day would open to me a certainty of the time and place at which I might sail. A French packet will leave New York early in the month. By her I mean to take my passage, and may, therefore, expect, in the ordinary course of things, to have the pleasure of joining you at Paris in the middle or latter part of August, and of communicating the commissions and instructions under which we are to act. The latter are more special than those heretofore sent. I shall then also have the pleasure of giving you more particular information of the situation of our affairs than I could do by letter; in general, I may observe to you that their aspect is encouraging.

## Degenerate America

### TO GENERAL CHASTELLUX.

PARIS, *June 7, 1785.*

I will beg leave to say here a few words on the general question of the degeneracy of animals in America. 1. As to the degeneracy of the man of Europe transplanted to America, it is no part of Monsieur de Buffon's system. He goes, indeed, within one step of it, but he stops there. The Abbé Raynal alone has taken that step. Your knowledge of America enables you to judge this question, to say, whether the lower class of people in America are less informed and less susceptible of information, than the lower class in Europe; and whether those in America, who have received such an education as that country can give, are less improved by it than Europeans of the same degree of education. 2. As to the aboriginal man of America, I know of no respectable evidence on which the opinion of his inferiority of genius has been founded, but that of Don Ulloa. As to Robertson, he never was in America, he relates nothing on his own knowledge, he is a compiler only of the relations of others, and a mere translator of the opinions of

Monsieur de Buffon. I should as soon, therefore, add the translators of Robertson to the witnesses of this fact, as himself. Paw, the beginner of this charge, was a compiler from the works of others; and of the most unlucky description; for he seems to have read the writings of travellers, only to collect and republish their lies. It is really remarkable, that in three volumes 12mo, of small print, it is scarcely possible to find one truth, and yet, that the author should be able to produce authority for every fact he states, as he says he can. Don Ulloa's testimony is the most respectable. He wrote of what he saw, but he saw the Indian of South America only, and that after he had passed through ten generations of slavery. It is very unfair, from this sample, to judge of the natural genius of this race of men; and, after supposing that Don Ulloa had not sufficiently calculated the allowance which should be made for this circumstance, we do him no injury in considering the picture he draws of the present Indians of South America, as no picture of what their ancestors were three hundred years ago. It is in North America we are to seek their original character. And I am safe in affirming, that the proofs of genius given by the Indians of North America place them on a level with whites in the same uncultivated state. The North of Europe furnishes subjects enough for comparison with them, and for a proof of their equality. I have seen some thousands myself, and conversed much with them, and have found in them a masculine, sound understanding. I have had much information from men who had lived among them, and whose veracity and good sense were so far known to me, as to establish a reliance on their information. They have all agreed in bearing witness in favor of the genius of this people. As to their bodily strength, their manners rendering it disgraceful to labor, those muscles employed in labor will be weaker with them, than with the European laborer; but those which are exerted in the chase, and those faculties which are employed in the tracing an enemy or a wild beast, in contriving ambuscades for him, and in carrying them through their execution, are much stronger than with us, because they are more exercised. I believe the Indian, then, to be, in body and mind, equal to the white man. I have supposed the black man, in his present state, might not be so; but it would be hazardous to affirm, that, equally cultivated for a few generations, he would not become so. 3. As to the inferiority of the other animals of America, without more facts, I can add nothing to what I have said in my Notes.

As to the theory of Monsieur de Buffon, that heat is friendly, and moisture adverse to the production of large animals, I am lately furnished with a fact by Dr. Franklin, which proves the air of London and of Paris to be more humid than that of Philadelphia, and so creates a suspicion that the opinion of the superior humidity of America may, perhaps, have been too hastily adopted. And, supposing that fact admitted, I think the physical reasonings urged to show, that in a moist country animals must be small, and that in a hot one they must be large, are not built on the basis of experiment. These questions, however, cannot be decided, ultimately, at this day.

More facts must be collected, and more time flow off, before the world will be ripe for decision. In the meantime, doubt is wisdom.

I have been fully sensible of the anxieties of your situation, and that your attentions were wholly consecrated, where alone they were wholly due, to the succor of friendship and worth. However much I prize your society, I wait with patience the moment when I can have it without taking what is due to another. In the meantime, I am solaced with the hope of possessing your friendship, and that it is not ungrateful to you to receive assurances of that with which I have the honor to be, dear Sir,

Your most obedient, and most humble servant.

## Tobacco Trade

### TO THE GOVERNOR OF MARYLAND.

PARIS, *June 16, 1785.*

SIR,—I have the honor of enclosing to your Excellency some propositions which have been made from London to the Farmers General to furnish them with the tobaccos of Maryland and Virginia. For this paper, I am indebted to the zeal of the M. de La Fayette. I take the liberty of troubling you with it on a supposition that it may be possible to have this article furnished from those States to this country immediately without its passing through the entrepôt of London, and the returns for it being made, of course, in London merchandise. Twenty thousand hogsheads of tobacco a year delivered here in exchange for the produce and manufacture of this country, many of which are as good and cheaper than in England, would establish a rivalship for our commerce which would have happy effects upon both countries.

## Trade Regulation

### TO COLONEL MONROE.

PARIS, *June 17, 1785.*

I like your removal to New York, and hope Congress will continue there, and never execute the idea of building their Federal town. Before it could be finished, a change of members in Congress, or the admission of new States, would remove them somewhere else. It is evident that when a sufficient number of the western States come in, they will remove it to Georgetown. In the meantime, it is our interest that it should remain where it is, and give no new pretensions to any other place. I am also much pleased with the proposition to the States to invest Congress with the regulation of their trade, reserving its revenue to the States. I think it a happy idea, removing the only objection which could have been justly made to the proposition.

The time, too, is the present, before the admission of the western States. I am very differently affected towards the new plan of opening our land office, by dividing the lands among the States, and selling them at vendue. It separates still more the interests of the States, which ought to be made joint in every possible instance, in order to cultivate the idea of our being one nation, and to multiply the instances in which the people shall look up to Congress as their head. And when the States get their portions, they will either fool them away, or make a job of it to serve individuals. Proofs of both these practices have been furnished, and by either of them that invaluable fund is lost, which ought to pay our public debt. To sell them at vendue, is to give them to the bidders of the day, be they many or few. It is ripping up the hen which lays golden eggs. If sold in lots at a fixed price, as first proposed, the best lots will be sold first; as these become occupied, it gives a value to the interjacent ones, and raises them, though of inferior quality, to the price of the first. I send you by Mr. Otto a copy of my book.[1] Be so good as to apologize to Mr. Thompson for my not sending him one by this conveyance. I could not burthen Mr. Otto with more on so long a road as that from here to L'Orient. I will send him one by a Mr. Williams, who will go ere long. I have taken measures to prevent its publication. My reason is, that I fear the terms in which I speak of slavery, and of our constitution, may produce an irritation which will revolt the minds of our countrymen against reformation in these two articles, and thus do more harm than good. I have asked of Mr. Madison to sound this matter as far as he can, and, if he thinks it will not produce that effect, I have then copies enough printed to give one to each of the young men at the College, and to my friends in the country. . . .

I will take the liberty of hazarding to you some thoughts on the policy of entering into treaties with the European nations, and the nature of them. . . . My primary object in the formation of treaties is to take the commerce of the States out of the hands of the States, and to place it under the superintendence of Congress, so far as the imperfect provisions of our constitutions will admit, and until the States shall, by new compact, make them more perfect. I would say, then, to every nation on earth, *by treaty*, your people shall trade freely with us, and ours with you, paying no more than the most favored nation, in order to put an end to the right of individual States, acting by fits and starts, to interrupt our commerce, or to embroil us with any nation. As to the terms of these treaties, the question becomes more difficult. I will mention three different plans. 1. That no duty shall be laid by either party on the productions of the other. 2. That each may be permitted to equalize their duties to those laid by the other. 3. That each shall pay in the ports of the other, such duties only as the most favored nations pay.

1. Were the nations of Europe as free and unembarrassed of established systems as we are, I do verily believe they would concur with us in the first plan. But it is impossible. These establishments are fixed upon them; they

[1] "Notes on Virginia." See excerpts following.

are interwoven with the body of their laws and the organization of their government, and they make a great part of their revenue; they cannot then, get rid of them.

2. The plan of equal imposts presents difficulties insurmountable. For how are the equal imposts to be effected? Is it by laying, in the ports of A, an equal per cent. on the goods of B, with that which B has laid in his ports on the goods of A? But how are we to find what is that per cent.? For this is not the usual form of imposts. They generally pay by the ton, by the measure, by the weight, and not by the value. Besides, if A sends a million's worth of goods to B, and takes back but the half of that, and each pays the same per cent., it is evident that A pays the double of what he recovers in the same way from B: this would be our case with Spain. Shall we endeavor to effect equality, then, by saying A may levy so much on the sum of B's importations into his ports, as B does on the sum of A's importations into the ports of B? But how find out that sum? Will either party lay open their custom-house books candidly to evince this sum? Does either keep their books so exactly as to be able to do it? This proposition was started in Congress when our instructions were formed, as you may remember, and the impossibility of executing it occasioned it to be disapproved. Besides, who should have a right of deciding, when the imposts were equal? A would say to B, my imposts do not raise so much as yours: I raise them therefore. B would then say, you have made them greater than mine, I will raise mine; and thus a kind of auction would be carried on between them, and a mutual irritation, which would end in anything, sooner than equality and right.

3. I confess then to you, that I see no alternative left but that which Congress adopted, of each party placing the other on the footing of the most favored nation. If the nations of Europe, from their actual establishments, are not at liberty to say to America, that she shall trade in their ports duty free, they may say she may trade there paying no higher duties than the most favored nation; and this is valuable in many of these countries, where a very great difference is made between different nations. There is no difficulty in the execution of this contract, because there is not a merchant who does not know, or may not know, the duty paid by every nation on every article. This stipulation leaves each party at liberty to regulate their own commerce by general rules, while it secures the other from partial and oppressive discriminations.

Shall I send you so much of the Encyclopedia as is already published, or reserve it here till you come? It is about forty volumes, which probably is about half the work. Give yourself no uneasiness about the money; perhaps I may find it convenient to ask you to pay trifles occasionally for me in America. I sincerely wish you may find it convenient to come here; the pleasure of the trip will be less than you expect, but the utility greater. It will make you adore your own country, its soil, its climate, its equality, liberty, laws, people, and manners. My God! how little do my countrymen know what precious blessings they are in possession of, and which no other people on earth enjoy. I confess I had no idea of it myself. While we shall see multiplied instances of Europeans going to live in America, I will venture to say, no man now living will ever see an instance of an American removing to settle in Europe, and continuing there. Come, then, and see the proofs of this, and on your return add your testimony to that of every thinking American, in order to satisfy our countrymen how much it is their interest to preserve, uninfected by contagion, those peculiarities in their governments and manners, to which they are indebted for those blessings.

P. S.   June 19.   Since writing the above, we have received the following account: Monsieur Pilatre de Roziere, who had been waiting for some months at Boulogne for a fair wind to cross the channel, at length took his ascent with a companion. The wind changed after awhile, and brought him back on the French coast. Being at a height of about six thousand feet, some accident happened to his balloon of inflammable air; it burst, they fell from that height, and were crushed to atoms. There was a Montgolfier combined with the balloon of inflammable air. It is suspected the heat of the Montgolfier rarefied too much the inflammable air of the other, and occasioned it to burst. The Montgolfier came down in good order.

# From "Notes on Virginia"

Excerpts dealing with the slavery problem, publication of which Jefferson thought might "do more harm than good," follow.

". . . There must doubtless be an unhappy influence on the manners of our people produced by the existence of slavery among us. The whole commerce between master and slave is a perpetual exercise of the most boisterous passions, the most unremitting despotism on the one part, and degrading submissions on the other. . . .

"And with what execration should the statesman be loaded, who, permitting one half the citizens thus to trample on the rights of the other, transforms those into despots, and these into enemies, destroys the morals of the one part, and the *amor patriae* of the other. For if a slave can have a country in this world, it must be any other in preference to that in which he is born to live and labor for another; in which he must lock up the faculties of his nature, contribute as far as depends on his individual endeavors to the evanishment of the human race, or entail his own miserable condition on the endless generations proceeding from him. With the morals of the people, their industry also is destroyed. For in a warm climate, no man will labor for himself who can make another labor for him. This is so true, that of the proprietors of slaves a very small proportion indeed are ever seen to labor. And can the liberties of a nation be thought secure when we have removed their only firm basis, a conviction in the minds of the people that these liberties are of the gift of God? That they are not to be violated but with His wrath? Indeed I tremble for my country when I reflect that God is just; that his justice cannot sleep forever; that considering numbers, nature and natural means only, a revolution of the wheel of fortune, an exchange of situation is among possible events; that it may become probably by supernatural interference! The Almighty has no attribute which can take side with us in such a contest. But it is impossible to be temperate and to pursue this subject through the various considerations of policy, of morals, of history natural and civil. We must be contented to hope they will force their way into every one's mind. I think a change already perceptible, since the origin of the present revolution. The spirit of the master is abating, that of the slave rising from the dust, his condition mollifying, the way I hope preparing, under the auspices of heaven, for a total emancipation, and that this is disposed, in the order of events, to be with the consent of the masters, rather than by their extirpation."

## Cities Compared

TO ABIGAIL ADAMS (MRS. JOHN ADAMS) IN LONDON.

PARIS, *June 21, 1785.*

Dear Madam,

I have received duly the honour of your letter and am now to return you thanks for your condescension in having taken the first steps for settling a correspondence which I so much desired; for I now consider it as *settled* and proceed accordingly. I have always found it best to remove obstacles first. I will do so therefore in the present case by telling you that I consider your boasts of the splendour of your city and of its superb hackney coaches as a flout, and declaring I would not give the polite, self-denying, feeling, hospitable, good-humored people of this country & their amiability in every point of view (though it must be confessed our streets are somewhat dirty, & our fiacres rather indifferent) for ten such races of rich, proud, hectoring, swearing, squibbing, carnivorous animals as those among whom you are; and that I do *love* this people with all my heart, and think that with a better religion, a better form of Government, and their present governors their condition and Country would be most enviable. I pray you to observe that I have used the term *people* and that this is a noun of the masculine as well as feminine gender. I must add too that we are about reforming our fiacres, and that I expect soon an ordnance that all the drivers should wear breeches unless any difficulty should arise whether this is a subject for the police or for the general legislature of the country to take care of.

. . . I took a trip yesterday to Saurois and commenced an acquaintance with the old Countess d'Hocquetout. I received much pleasure from it and hope it has opened a door of admission for me to the circle of the literati with which she is environed. I heard there the nightingale in all its perfection: and I do not hesitate to pronounce that in America it would be deemed a bird of the third rank only, our mocking bird, & fox-coloured thrush being unquestionably superior to it.

. . . In stating my accounts with the United States I am at a loss whether to charge house rent or not. It has always been allowed to Dr. Franklin. Does Mr. Adams mean to charge this for Auteuil and London? Because if he does, I certainly will, being convinced that my expenses here will otherwise exceed my allowance. I ask this information of you, Madam, because I think you know better than Mr. Adams what may be necessary and right for him to do in occasions of this class. . . .

# Trade Treaties

### TO JOHN ADAMS.

PARIS, *July* 7, *1785*.

DEAR SIR,—This will accompany a joint letter enclosing the draft of a treaty, and my private letter of June 23d, which has waited so long for a private conveyance.

A late conversation with an English gentleman here makes me believe, what I did not believe before, that his nation thinks seriously that Congress have no power to form a treaty of commerce. As the explanations of this matter, which you and I may separately give, may be handed to their minister, it would be well that they should agree. For this reason, as well as for the hope of your showing me wherein I am wrong, and confirming me where I am right, I will give you my creed on the subject. It is contained in these four principles. By the Confederation, Congress have no power given them, in the first instance, over the commerce of the States. But they have a power given them of entering into treaties of commerce, and these treaties may cover the whole field of commerce, with two restrictions only. 1. That the States may impose equal duties on foreigners as natives: and 2. That they may prohibit the exportation or importation of any species of goods whatsoever. . . . I own to you that my wish to enter into treaties with the other powers of Europe arises more from a desire of bringing all our commerce under the jurisdiction of Congress, than for any other views.

P. S. Monsieur Houdon has agreed to go to America to take the figure of General Washington. In case of his death, between his departure from Paris, and his return to it, we may lose twenty thousand livres. I ask the favor of you to enquire what it will cost to ensure that sum, on his life, in London, and to give me as early an answer as possible, that I may order the insurance if I think the terms easy enough. He is, I believe, between thirty and thirty-five years of age, healthy enough, and will be absent about six months.

## Screw Propellers

TO DR. STYLES.

PARIS, *July 17, 1785.*

The researches of the natural philosophers of Europe seem mostly in the field of chemistry, and here, principally, on the subjects of air and fire. The analysis of these two subjects, presents to us very new ideas. When speaking of the "Bibliothéque Physico-œconomique," I should have observed, that since its publication, a man in this city has invented a method of moving a vessel on the water, by a machine worked within the vessel. I went to see it. He did not know himself the principle of his own invention. It is a screw with a very broad thin worm, or rather it is a thin plate with its edge applied spirally round an axis. This being turned, operates on the air, as a screw does, and may be literally said to screw the vessel along; the thinness of the medium, and its want of resistance, occasion a loss of much of the force. The screw, I think, would be more effectual if placed below the surface of the water. I very much suspect that a countryman of ours, Mr. Bushnel of Connecticut, is entitled to the merit of a prior discovery of this use of the screw. I remember to have heard of his submarine navigation during the war, and, from what Colonel Humphreys now tells me, I conjecture that the screw was the power he used. He joined to this a machine for exploding under water at a given moment. If it were not too great a liberty for a stranger to take, I would ask from him a narration of his actual experiments, with or without a communication of his principle, as he should choose. If he thought proper to communicate it, I would engage never to disclose it, unless I could find an opportunity of doing it for his benefit. I thank you for your information as to the great bones found on the Hudson river. I suspect that they must have been of the same animal with those found on the Ohio; and, if so, they could not have belonged to any human figure, because they are accompanied with tusks of the size, form and substance, of those of the elephant. I have seen a part of the ivory, which was very good. The animal itself must have been much larger than an elephant. Mrs. Adams gives me an account of a flower found in Connecticut, which vegetates when suspended in the air. She brought one to Europe. What can be this flower? It would be a curious present to this continent.

# On Slavery

### TO DR. PRICE.

PARIS, *August* 7, *1785.*

SIR,—Your favor of July the 2d came duly to hand. The concern you therein express as to the effect of your pamphlet in America, induces me to trouble you with some observations on that subject.

From my acquaintance with that country, I think I am able to judge, with some degree of certainty, of the manner in which it will have been received. Southward of the Chesapeake, it will find but few readers concurring with it in sentiment, on the subject of slavery. From the mouth to the head of the Chesapeake, the bulk of the people will approve it in theory, and it will find a respectable minority ready to adopt it in practice; a minority, which for weight and worth of character, preponderates against the greater number, who have not the courage to divest their families of a property, which, however, keeps their conscience unquiet. Northward of the Chesapeake, you may find, here and there, an opponent to your doctrine, as you may find, here and there, a robber and murderer; but in no greater number. In that part of America, there being but few slaves, they can easily disencumber themselves of them; and emancipation is put into such a train, that in a few years there will be no slaves northward of Maryland. In Maryland, I do not find such a disposition to begin the redress of this enormity, as in Virginia. This is the next State to which we may turn our eyes for the interesting spectacle of justice, in conflict with avarice and oppression; a conflict wherein the sacred side is gaining daily recruits, from the influx into office of young men grown, and growing up. These have sucked in the principles of liberty, as it were, with their mother's milk; and it is to them I look with anxiety to turn the fate of this question. Be not therefore discouraged. What you have written will do a great deal of good.

# On Life in France

### TO MRS. TRIST.

PARIS, *August 18, 1785.*

I am much pleased with the people of this country. The roughness of the human mind is so thoroughly rubbed off with them, that it seems as if one might glide through a whole life among them without a jostle. Perhaps, too, their manners may be the best calculated for happiness to a people in their situation, but I am convinced they fall far short of effecting a happiness so temperate, so uniform, and so lasting as is generally enjoyed with us. The domestic bonds here are absolutely done away, and where can their compensation be found? Perhaps they may catch some moments of transport above the level of the ordinary tranquil joy we experience, but they are separated by long intervals, during which all the passions are at sea without rudder or compass. Yet, fallacious as the pursuits of happiness are, they seem on the whole to furnish the most effectual abstraction from a contemplation of the hardness of their government. Indeed, it is difficult to conceive how so good a people, with so good a King, so well-disposed rulers in general, so genial a climate, so fertile a soil, should be rendered so ineffectual for producing human happiness by one single curse,—that of a bad form of government. But it is a fact, in spite of the mildness of their governors, the people are ground to powder by the vices of the form of government. Of twenty millions of people supposed to be in France, I am of opinion there are nineteen millions more wretched, more accursed in every circumstance of human existence than the most conspicuously wretched individual of the whole United States. I beg your pardon for getting into politics. I will add only one sentiment more of that character, that is, nourish peace with their persons, but war against their manners. Every step we take towards the adoption of their manners is a step to perfect misery. I pray you to write to me often. Do not you turn politician too; but write me all the small news—the news about persons and about states; tell me who dies, that I may meet these disagreeable events in detail, and not all at once when I return; who marry, who hang themselves because they cannot marry, &c. Present me in the most friendly terms to Mrs. House and Browse, and be assured of the sincerity with which I am, dear Madam,

Your affectionate friend and servant.

# To a Student

## TO PETER CARR.

PARIS, *August 19, 1785.*

DEAR PETER,—I received, by Mr. Mazzei, your letter of April the 20th. I am much mortified to hear that you have lost so much time; and that, when you arrived in Williamsburg, you were not at all advanced from what you were when you left Monticello. Time now begins to be precious to you. Every day you lose will retard a day your entrance on that public stage whereon you may begin to be useful to yourself. However, the way to repair the loss is to improve the future time. I trust, that with your dispositions, even the acquisition of science is a pleasing employment. I can assure you, that the possession of it is, what (next to an honest heart) will above all things render you dear to your friends, and give you fame and promotion in your own country. When your mind shall be well improved with science, nothing will be necessary to place you in the highest points of view, but to pursue the interests of your country, the interests of your friends, and your own interests also, with the purest integrity, the most chaste honor. The defect of these virtues can never be made up by all the other acquirements of body and mind. Make these, then, your first object. Give up money, give up fame, give up science, give the earth itself and all it contains, rather than do an immoral act. And never suppose, that in any possible situation, or under any circumstances, it is best for you to do a dishonorable thing, however slightly so it may appear to you. Whenever you are to do a thing, though it can never be known but to yourself, ask yourself how you would act were all the world looking at you, and act accordingly. Encourage all your virtuous dispositions, and exercise them whenever an opportunity arises; being assured that they will gain strength by exercise, as a limb of the body does, and that exercise will make them habitual. From the practice of the purest virtue, you may be assured you will derive the most sublime comforts in every moment of life, and in the moment of death. If ever you find yourself environed with difficulties and perplexing circumstances, out of which you are at a loss how to extricate yourself, do what is right, and be assured that that will extricate you the best out of the worst situations. Though you cannot see, when you take one step, what will be the next, yet follow truth, justice, and plain dealing, and never fear their leading you out of the labyrinth, in the easiest manner possible. The knot which you thought a Gordian one, will untie itself before you. Nothing is so mistaken as the supposition, that a person is to extricate himself from a difficulty, by intrigue, by chicanery, by dissimulation, by trimming, by an untruth, by an injustice. This increases the difficulties tenfold; and those, who pursue these methods, get themselves so involved at length, that they can turn no way but their infamy becomes more exposed. It is of great importance to set a resolution, not to be shaken, never to tell an untruth. There is no vice so mean, so pitiful, so contemptible; and he who permits himself to tell a lie once, finds it much easier to do it a second and third time, till at length it becomes habitual; he tells lies without attending to it, and truths without the world's believing him. This falsehood of the tongue leads to that of the heart, and in time depraves all its good dispositions.

An honest heart being the first blessing, a knowing head is the second. It is time for you now to begin to be choice in your reading; to begin to pursue a regular course in it; and not to suffer yourself to be turned to the right or left by reading anything out of that course. I have long ago digested a plan for you, suited to the circumstances in which you will be placed. This I will detail to you, from time to time, as you advance. For the present, I advise you to begin a course of ancient history, reading everything in the original and not in translations. First read Goldsmith's history of Greece. This will give you a digested view of that field. Then take up ancient history in the detail, reading the following books, in the following order: Herodotus, Thucydides, Xenophontis Anabasis, Arrian, Quintus Curtius, Diodorus Siculus, Justin. This shall form the first stage of your historical reading, and is all I need mention to you now. The next will be of Roman history.[1] From that, we will come down to modern history. In Greek and Latin poetry, you have read or will read at school, Virgil, Terence, Horace, Anacreon, Theocritus, Homer, Euripides, Sophocles. Read also Milton's "Paradise Lost," Shakspeare, Ossian, Pope's and Swift's works, in order to form your style in your own language. In morality, read Epictetus, Xenophontis Memorabilia, Plato's Socratic dialogues, Cicero's philosophies, Antoninus, and Seneca. In order to assure a certain progress in this reading, consider what hours you have free from the school and the exercises of the school. Give about two of them, every day, to exercise; for health must not be sacrificed to learning. A strong body makes the mind strong. As to the species of exercise, I advise the gun. While this gives a moderate exercise to the body, it gives boldness, enterprise, and independence to the mind. Games played with the ball, and others of that nature, are too violent for the body, and stamp no character on the mind. Let your gun, therefore, be the constant companion of your walks. Never think of taking a book with you. The object of walking is to relax the mind. You should therefore not permit yourself even to think while you walk; but divert yourself by the objects surrounding you. Walking is the best possible exercise. Habituate yourself to walk very far. The Europeans value themselves on having subdued the horse to the uses of man; but I doubt whether we have not lost more than we have gained, by the use of this animal. No one has occasioned so much the degeneracy of the human body. An Indian goes on foot nearly as far in a day, for a long journey, as an enfeebled white does on his horse; and he will tire the best horses. There is no habit you will value so much as that of walking far without fatigue. I would advise you to take your exercise in the afternoon: not because it is the best time for exercise, for certainly it is not; but because it is the best time to spare from your studies; and habit will soon reconcile it to health, and render it nearly as useful as if you gave to that the more precious hours of the day. A little walk of half an hour, in the morning, when you first rise, is advisable also. It shakes off sleep, and produces other good effects in the animal economy. Rise at a fixed and an early hour, and go to bed at a fixed and early hour also. Sitting up late at night is injurious to the health, and not useful to the mind. Having ascribed proper hours to exercise, divide what remain (I mean of your vacant hours) into three portions. Give the principal to History, the other two, which should be shorter, to Philosophy and Poetry. Write to me once every month or two, and let me know the progress you make. Tell me in what manner you employ every hour in the day. The plan I have proposed for you is adapted to your present situation only. When that is changed, I shall propose a corresponding change of plan. I have ordered the following books to be sent to you from London, to the care of Mr. Madison: Herodotus, Thucydides, Xenophon's Hellenics, Anabasis and Memorabilia, Cicero's works, Baretti's Spanish and English Dictionary, Martin's Philosophical Grammar, and Martin's Philosophia Britannica. I will send you the following from hence: Bezout's Mathematics, De la

[1] Livy, Sallust, Cæsar, Cicero's epistles, Suetonius, Tacitus, Gibbon.

Lande's Astronomy, Muschenbrock's Physics, Quintus Curtius, Justin, a Spanish Grammar, and some Spanish books. You will observe that Martin, Bezout, De la Lande, and Muschenbrock, are not in the preceding plan. They are not to be opened till you go to the University. You are now, I expect, learning French. You must push this; because the books which will be put into your hands when you advance into Mathematics, Natural philosophy, Natural history, &c., will be mostly French, these sciences being better treated by the French than the English writers. Our future connection with Spain renders that the most necessary of the modern languages, after the French. When you become a public man, you may have occasion for it, and the circumstance of your possessing that language, may give you a preference over other candidates. I have nothing further to add for the present, but husband well your time, cherish your instructors, strive to make everybody your friend; and be assured that nothing will be so pleasing as your success to, Dear Peter,

Yours affectionately.

# On Sea Power

## TO JOHN JAY.

### (Private.)

PARIS, *August 23, 1785.*

DEAR SIR,—I shall sometimes ask your permission to write you letters, not official, but private. The present is of this kind, and is occasioned by the question proposed in yours of June the 14th; "whether it would be useful to us, to carry all our own productions, or none?"

Were we perfectly free to decide this question, I should reason as follows. We have now lands enough to employ an infinite number of people in their cultivation. Cultivators of the earth are the most valuable citizens. They are the most vigorous, the most independent, the most virtuous, and they are tied to their country, and wedded to its liberty and interests, by the most lasting bonds. As long, therefore, as they can find employment in this line, I would not convert them into mariners, artisans, or anything else. But our citizens will find employment in this line, till their numbers, and of course their productions, become too great for the demand, both internal and foreign. This is not the case as yet, and probably will not be for a considerable time. As soon as it is, the surplus of hands must be turned to something else. I should then, perhaps, wish to turn them to the sea in preference to manufactures; because, comparing the characters of the two classes, I find the former the most valuable citizens. I consider the class of artificers as the panders of vice, and the instruments by which the liberties of a country are generally overturned. However, we are not free to decide this question on principles of theory only. Our people are decided in the opinion, that it is necessary for us to take a share in the occupation of the ocean, and their established habits induce them to require that the sea be kept open to them, and that that line of policy be pursued, which will render the use of that element to them as great as possible. I think it a duty in those entrusted with the administration of their affairs, to conform themselves to the decided choice of their constituents; and that therefore, we should, in every instance, preserve an equality of right to them in the transportation of commodities, in the right of fishing, and in the other uses of the sea.

But what will be the consequence? Frequent wars without a doubt. Their property will be violated on the sea, and in foreign ports, their persons will be insulted, imprisoned, &c., for pretended debts, contracts, crimes, contraband, &c., &c. These insults must be resented, even if we had no feelings, yet to prevent their eternal repetition; or, in other words, our commerce on the ocean and in other countries, must be paid for by frequent war. The justest dispositions possible in ourselves, will not secure us against it. It would be necessary that all other nations were just also. Justice indeed, on our part, will save us from those wars which would have been produced by a contrary disposition. But how can we prevent those produced by the wrongs of other nations? By putting ourselves in a condition to punish them. Weakness provokes insult and injury, while a condition to punish, often prevents them. This reasoning leads to the necessity of some naval force; that being the only weapon by which we can reach an enemy. I think it to our interest to punish the first insult; because an insult unpunished is the parent of many others. We are not, at this moment, in a condition to do it, but we should put ourselves into it, as soon as possible. If a war with England should take place, it seems to me that the first thing necessary would be a resolution to abandon the carrying trade, because we cannot protect it. Foreign nations must, in that case, be invited to bring us what we want, and to take our productions in their own bottoms.

# Growing Pains

### TO COLONEL MONROE.

PARIS, *August 28, 1785.*

I am much pleased with your land ordinance, and think it improved from the first, in the most material circumstances. I had mistaken the object of the division of the lands among the States. I am sanguine in my expectations of lessening our debts by this fund, and have expressed my expectations to the minister and others here. I see by the public papers, you have adopted the dollar as your money unit. In the arrangement of coins I proposed, I ought to have inserted a gold coin of five dollars, which, being within two shillings of the value of a guinea, would be very convenient. The English papers are so incessantly repeating their lies about the tumults, the anarchy, the bankruptcies and distresses of America, that these ideas prevail very generally in Europe. At a large table where I dined the other day, a gentleman from Switzerland expressed his apprehensions for the fate of Dr. Franklin, as he said he had been informed, that he would be received with stones by the people, who were generally dissatisfied with the Revolution, and incensed against all those who had assisted in bringing it about. I told him his apprehensions were just, and that the people of America would probably salute Dr. Franklin with the same stones they had thrown at the Marquis Fayette. The reception of the Doctor is an object of very general attention, and will weigh in Europe, as an evidence of the satisfaction or dissatisfaction of America, with their Revolution.

## Mass Production

### TO JOHN JAY.

PARIS, *August 30, 1785.*

An improvement is made here in the construction of muskets, which it may be interesting to Congress to know, should they at any time propose to procure any. It consists in the making every part of them so exactly alike, that what belongs to any one, may be used for every other musket in the magazine. The government here has examined and approved the method, and is establishing a large manufactory for the purpose of putting it into execution. As yet, the inventor has only completed the lock of the musket, on this plan. He will proceed immediately to have the barrel, stock, and other parts, executed in the same way. Supposing it might be useful in the United States, I went to the workman. He presented me the parts of fifty locks taken to pieces, and arranged in compartments. I put several together myself, taking pieces at hazard as they came to hand, and they fitted in the most perfect manner. The advantages of this, when arms need repair, are evident. He effects it by tools of his own contrivance, which, at the same time, abridge the work, so that he thinks he shall be able to furnish the musket two livres cheaper than the common price. But it will be two or three years before he will be able to furnish any quantity. I mention it now, as it may have an influence on the plan for furnishing our magazines with this arm.

## European Views

### TO JAMES MADISON.

PARIS, *September 1, 1785.*

I am well informed that the late proceedings in America, have produced a wonderful sensation in England in our favor. I mean the disposition which seems to be becoming general, to invest Congress with the regulation of our commerce, and, in the meantime, the measures taken to defeat the avidity of the British government grasping at our carrying business. I can add with truth, that it was not till these symptoms appeared in America that I have been able to discover the smallest token of respect towards the United States in any part of Europe. There was an enthusiasm towards us all over Europe at the moment of the peace. The torrent of lies published unremittingly in every day's London paper first made an impression and produced a coolness. The republication of these lies in most of the papers of Europe, (done probably by authority of the governments to discourage emigrations,) carried them home to the belief of every mind. They supposed everything in America was anarchy, tumult, and civil war. The reception of the Marquis Fayette gave a check to these ideas. The late proceedings seem to be producing a decisive vibration in our favor.

# Paris Shopping

## TO ABIGAIL ADAMS.

Paris, *September 25, 1785.*

Dear Madam,

Mr. Short's return the night before last availed me of your favor of Aug. 12. I immediately ordered the shoes you desired which will be ready tomorrow. . . . I have also procured for you three plateaux de dessert with a silvered ballustrade round them, and four figures. Of Biscuit, the former cost 192#, the latter 12# each, making together 240 livres or 10 louis. . . . With respect to the figures I could only find three of those you named, matched in size. These were Minerva, Diana and Apollo. I was obliged to add a fourth, unguided by your choice. They offered me a fine Venus; but I thought it out of taste to have two at table at the same time. . . . At length a fine Mars was offered, calm, bold, his faulchion not drawn but ready to be drawn. This will do, thinks I, for the table of the American Minister in London, where those whom it may concern may look and learn that though Wisdom is our guide, and the Song and Chase our supreme delight, yet we offer adoration to that tutelar God also who rocked the cradle of our birth, who has accepted our infant offerings & has shown himself the patron of our rights & avenger of our wrongs. The group then was closed, and your party formed. Envy & malice will never be quiet. I hear it already whispered to you that in admitting Minerva to your table I have departed from the principle which made me reject Venus; in plain English that I have paid a just respect to the daughter but failed to the mother. No, Madam, my respect to both is sincere. Wisdom, I know, is social. She seeks her fellows, but Beauty is jealous, and illy bears the presence of a rival.

But, Allons, let us turn over another leaf, & begin the next chapter. I received by Mr. Short a budget of London papers, they teem with every horror of which human nature is capable, assassinations, suicide, theft, or robbery, the blackest slanders! indeed the man must be a rock who can stand all this; to Mr. Adams it will be but one victory the more. It would have illy suited me. I do not love difficulties. I am fond of quiet, willing to do my duty, but irritable by slander & apt to be forced by it to abandon my post. These are weaknesses from which reason & your counsels will preserve Mr. Adams. I fancy it must be the quantity of animal food eaten by the English which renders their characters insusceptible of civilization. I suspect it is in their kitchens & not in their churches that their reformation must be worked, and that Missionaries of that description from hence would avail more than those who should endeavor to tame them by precepts of religion or philosophy. But what do the foolish printers of America mean by retailing all this stuff in our papers? As if it was not enough to be slandered by one's enemies without circulating the slanders among his friends also.

To show you how willingly I shall ever receive & execute your commissions, I venture to impose one on you. From what I recollect of the diaper & damask we used to import from England I think they were better and cheaper than here, you are well acquainted with those of both countries, if you are of the same opinion I would trouble you to send me two sets of tablecloths and napkins for 20 covers each. . . .

## American View

### TO MR. BELLINI.

PARIS, *September 30, 1785.*

Behold me at length on the vaunted scene of Europe! It is not necessary for your information, that I should enter into details concerning it. But you are, perhaps, curious to know how this new scene has struck a savage of the mountains of America. Not advantageously, I assure you. I find the general fate of humanity here most deplorable. The truth of Voltaire's observation, offers itself perpetually, that every man here must be either the hammer or the anvil. It is a true picture of that country to which they say we shall pass hereafter, and where we are to see God and his angels in splendor, and crowds of the damned trampled under their feet. While the great mass of the people are thus suffering under physical and moral oppression, I have endeavored to examine more nearly the condition of the great, to appreciate the true value of the circumstances in their situation, which dazzle the bulk of spectators, and, especially, to compare it with that degree of happiness which is enjoyed in America, by every class of people. Intrigues of love occupy the younger, and those of ambition, the elder part of the great. Conjugal love having no existence among them, domestic happiness, of which that is the basis, is utterly unknown. In lieu of this, are substituted pursuits which nourish and invigorate all our bad passions, and which offer only moments of ecstasy, amidst days and months of restlessness and torment. Much, very much inferior, this, to the tranquil, permanent felicity with which domestic society in America blesses most of its inhabitants; leaving them to follow steadily those pursuits which health and reason approve, and rendering truly delicious the intervals of those pursuits.

In science, the mass of the people are two centuries behind ours; their literati, half a dozen years before us. Books, really good, acquire just reputation in that time, and so become known to us, and communicate to us all their advances in knowledge. Is not this delay compensated, by our being placed out of the reach of that swarm of nonsensical publications which issues daily from a thousand presses, and perishes almost in issuing? With respect to what are termed polite manners, without sacrificing too much the sincerity of language, I would wish my countrymen to adopt just so much of European politeness, as to be ready to make all those little sacrifices of self, which really render European manners amiable, and relieve society from the disagreeable scenes to which rudeness often subjects it. Here, it seems that a man might pass a life without encountering a single rudeness. In the pleasures of the table, they are far before us, because, with good taste they unite temperance. They do not terminate the most sociable meals by transforming themselves into brutes. I have never yet seen a man drunk in France, even among the lowest of the people. Were I to proceed to tell you how much I enjoy their architecture, sculpture, painting, music, I should want words. It is in these arts they shine. The last of them, particularly, is an enjoyment, the deprivation of which with us, cannot be calculated. I am almost ready to say, it is the only thing which from my heart I envy them, and which, in spite of all the authority of the Decalogue, I do covet.

# On Fire Engines

## TO JAMES MADISON, OF WILLIAM AND MARY COLLEGE.

PARIS, *October 2, 1785.*

DEAR SIR,—I have duly received your favor of April the 10th, by Mr. Mazzei. You therein speak of a new method of raising water by steam, which you suppose will come into general use. I know of no new method of that kind, and suppose (as you say the account you have received of it is very imperfect) that some person has represented to you, as new, a fire engine erected at Paris, and which supplies the greater part of the town with water. But this is nothing more than the fire engine you have seen described in the books of hydraulics, and particularly in the "Dictionary of Arts and Sciences," published in 8vo, by Owen, the idea of which was first taken from Papin's "Digester." It would have been better called the steam engine. The force of the steam of water, you know, is immense. In this engine, it is made to exert itself towards the working of pumps. That of Paris is, I believe, the largest known, raising four hundred thousand cubic feet (French) of water, in twenty-four hours; or rather, I should have said, *those* of Paris, for there are two under one roof, each raising that quantity. . . .

Herschel has pushed his discoveries of double stars, now, to upwards of nine hundred, being twice the number of those communicated in the "Philosophical Transactions." You have probably seen, that a Mr. Pigott had discovered periodical variations of light in the star Algol. He has observed the same in the $\eta$ of Antinous, and makes the period of variation seven days, four hours, and thirty minutes, the duration of the increase sixty-three hours, and of the decrease thirty-six hours. What are we to conclude from this? That there are suns which have their orbits of revolution too? But this would suppose a wonderful harmony in their planets, and present a new scene, where the attracting powers should be without, and not within the orbit. The motion of our sun would be a miniature of this. But this must be left to you astronomers.

I went some time ago to see a machine which offers something new. A man had applied to a light boat a very large screw, the thread of which was a thin plate, two feet broad, applied by its edge spirally around a small axis. It somewhat resembled a bottle brush, if you will suppose the hairs of the bottle brush joining together, and forming a spiral plane. This, turned on its axis in the air, carried the vessel across the Seine. It is, in fact, a screw which takes hold of the air and draws itself along by it; losing, indeed, much of its effort by the yielding nature of the body it lays hold of to pull itself on by. I think it may be applied in the water with much greater effect, and to very useful purposes. Perhaps it may be used also for the balloon.

It is impossible but you must have heard long ago of the machine for copying letters at a single stroke, as we had received it in America before I left there.

## On Education Abroad

TO J. BANNISTER, JUNIOR.

PARIS, *October 15, 1785.*

DEAR SIR,—I should sooner have answered the paragraph in your letter, of September the 19th, respecting the best seminary for the education of youth in Europe, but that it was necessary for me to make inquiries on the subject. The result of these has been, to consider the competition as resting between Geneva and Rome.

But why send an American youth to Europe for education? What are the objects of an useful American education? Classical knowledge, modern languages, chiefly French, Spanish, and Italian; Mathematics, Natural philosophy, Natural history, Civil history, and Ethics. In Natural philosophy, I mean to include Chemistry and Agriculture, and in Natural history, to include Botany, as well as the other branches of those departments. It is true that the habit of speaking the modern languages cannot be so well acquired in America; but every other article can be as well acquired at William and Mary college, as at any place in Europe. When college education is done with, and a young man is to prepare himself for public life, he must cast his eyes (for America) either on Law or Physics. For the former, where can he apply so advantageously as to Mr. Wythe? For the latter, he must come to Europe: the medical class of students, therefore, is the only one which need come to Europe.

Let us view the disadvantages of sending a youth to Europe. To enumerate them all, would require a volume. I will select a few. If he goes to England, he learns drinking, horse racing, and boxing. These are the peculiarities of English education. The following circumstances are common to education in that, and the other countries of Europe. He acquires a fondness for European luxury and dissipation, and a contempt for the simplicity of his own country; he is fascinated with the privileges of the European aristocrats, and sees, with abhorrence, the lovely equality which the poor enjoy with the rich, in his own country; he contracts a partiality for aristocracy or monarchy; he forms foreign friendships which will never be useful to him, and loses the seasons of life for forming, in his own country, those friendships which, of all others, are the most faithful and permanent; he is led, by the strongest of all the human passions, into a spirit for female intrigue, destructive of his own and others' happiness, or a passion for whores, destructive of his health, and, in both cases, learns to consider fidelity to the marriage bed as an ungentlemanly practice, and inconsistent with happiness; he recollects the voluptuary dress and arts of the European women, and pities and despises the chaste affections and simplicity of those of his own country; he retains, through life, a fond recollection, and a hankering after those places, which were the scenes of his first pleasures and of his first connections; he returns to his own country, a foreigner, unacquainted with the practices of domestic economy, necessary to preserve him from ruin, speaking and writing his native tongue as a foreigner, and therefore unqualified to obtain those distinctions, which eloquence of the pen and tongue ensures in a free country; for I would observe to you, that what is called style in writing or speaking is formed very early in life, while the imagination is warm, and impressions are permanent. I am of opinion, that there never was an instance of a man's writing or speaking his native tongue with elegance, who passed from fifteen to twenty years of age out of the country where it was spoken. Thus, no instance exists of a person's writing two languages perfectly. That will always appear to be his native language, which was most familiar to him in his youth.

It appears to me, then, that an American, coming to Europe for education, loses in his knowledge, in his morals, in his health, in his habits, and in his happiness. I had entertained only doubts on this head before I came to

Europe: what I see and hear, since I came here, proves more than I had even suspected. Cast your eye over America: who are the men of most learning, of most eloquence, most beloved by their countrymen and most trusted and promoted by them? They are those who have been educated among them, and whose manners, morals, and habits, are perfectly homogeneous with those of the country.

Did you expect by so short a question, to draw such a sermon on yourself? I dare say you did not. But the consequences of foreign education are alarming to me, as an American. I sin, therefore, through zeal, whenever I enter on the subject.

## On Unemployment

### TO REVEREND JAMES MADISON.

FONTAINEBLEAU, *Oct. 28, 1785.*

DEAR SIR,—Seven o'clock, and retired to my fireside, I have determined to enter into conversation with you. This is a village of about 15,000 inhabitants when the court is not here, and 20,000 when they are, occupying a valley through which runs a brook and on each side of it a ridge of small mountains, most of which are naked rock. The King comes here, in the fall always, to hunt. His court attend him, as do also the foreign diplomatic corps; but as this is not indispensably required and my finances do not admit the expense of a continued residence here, I propose to come occasionally to attend the King's levees, returning again to Paris, distant forty miles. This being the first trip, I set out yesterday morning to take a view of the place. For this purpose I shaped my course towards the highest of the mountains in sight, to the top of which was about a league.

As soon as I had got clear of the town I fell in with a poor woman walking at the same rate with myself and going the same course. Wishing to know the condition of the laboring poor I entered into conversation with her, which I began by enquiries for the path which would lead me into the mountain: and thence proceeded to enquiries into her vocation, condition and circumstances. She told me she was a day laborer at 8 sous or 4d. sterling the day: that she had two children to maintain, and to pay a rent of 30 livres for her house (which would consume the hire of 75 days), that often she could get no employment and of course was without bread. As we had walked together near a mile and she had so far served me as a guide, I gave her, on parting, 24 sous. She burst into tears of a gratitude which I could perceive was unfeigned because she was unable to utter a word. She had probably never before received so great an aid. This little *attendrissement*, with the solitude of my walk, led me into a train of reflections on that unequal division of property which occasions the numberless instances of wretchedness which I had observed in this country and is to be observed all over Europe.

The property of this country is absolutely concentred in a very few hands, having revenues of from half a million of guineas a year downwards. These employ the flower of the country as servants, some of them having as many as 200 domestics, not laboring. They employ also a great number of manufacturers and tradesmen, and lastly the class of laboring husbandmen. But after all there comes the most numerous of all classes, that is, the poor who cannot find work. I asked myself what could be the reason so many should be permitted to beg who are willing to work, in a country where there is a very considerable proportion of uncultivated lands? These lands are undisturbed only for the sake of game. It should seem then that it must be because of the enormous wealth of the proprietors which places them above attention to the increase of their revenues by permitting these lands to be labored. I am conscious that an equal division of property is impracticable, but the consequences of this enormous inequality producing so much misery to the bulk of mankind, legislators cannot invent too many devices for subdividing property, only taking care to let their subdivisions go hand in hand with the natural affections of the human mind. The descent of property of every kind therefore to all the children, or to all the brothers and sisters, or other relations in equal degree, is a politic measure and a practicable one.

Another means of silently lessening the inequality of property is to exempt all from taxation below a certain point, and to tax the higher portions or property in geometrical progression as they rise. Whenever there are in any country uncultivated lands and unemployed poor, it is clear that the laws of property have been so far extended as to violate natural right. The earth is given as a common stock for man to labor and live on. If for the encouragement of industry we allow it to be appropriated, we must take care that other employment be provided to those excluded from the appropriation. If we do not, the fundamental right to labor the earth returns to the unemployed. It is too soon yet in our country to say that every man who cannot find employment, but who can find uncultivated land, shall be at liberty to cultivate it, paying a moderate rent. But it is not too soon to provide by every possible means that as few as possible shall be without a little portion of land. The small landholders are the most precious part of a state.

The next object which struck my attention in my walk was the deer with which the wood abounded. They were of the kind called "Cerfs," and not exactly of the same species with ours. They are blackish indeed under the belly, and not white as ours, and they are more of the chestnut red; but these are such small differences as would be sure to happen in two races from the same stock breeding separately a number of ages. Their hares are totally different from the animals we call by that name; but their rabbit is almost exactly like him. The only difference is in their manners; the land on which I walked for some time being absolutely reduced to a honeycomb by their burrowing. I think there is no instance of ours burrowing. After descending the hill again I saw a man cutting fern. I went to him under pretence of asking the shortest road to town, and afterwards asked for what use he was cutting fern. He told me that this part of the country furnished a great deal of fruit to Paris. That when packed in straw it acquired an ill taste, but that dry fern preserved it perfectly without communicating any taste at all.

I treasured this observation for the preservation of my apples on my return to my own country. They have no apples here to compare with our Redtown pippin. They have nothing which deserves the name of a peach; there being not sun enough to ripen the plum-peach and the best of their soft peaches being like our autumn peaches. Their cherries and strawberries are fair, but I think lack flavor. Their plums I think are better; so also their gooseberries, and the pears infinitely beyond anything we possess. They have nothing better than our sweet-water; but they have a succession of as good from early in the summer till frost. I am to-morrow to get (to) M. Malsherbes (and uncle of the Chevalier Luzerne's) about seven leagues from hence, who is the most curious man in France as to his trees. He is making for me a collection of the vines from which the Burgundy, Champagne, Bordeaux, Frontignac, and other of the most valuable wines of this country are made. Another gentleman is collecting for me the best eating grapes, including what we call the raisin. I propose also to endeavor to colonize their hare, rabbit, red and grey partridge, pheasants of different kinds, and some other birds. But I find that I am wandering beyond the limits of my walk and will therefore bid you adieu. Yours affectionately.

## Pirate Threats

### TO FRANCIS EPPES.

PARIS, *December 11, 1785.*

DEAR SIR,—I wrote you by Mr. Fitzhugh Aug. 30 and to Mrs. Eppes by the same conveyance Sept. 22; in those as in my former letters I had troubled you on the subject of sending my daughter to me. To the cautions then suggested I am obliged to add another, which our situation with respect to the Barbary powers calls for. You have doubtless heard loose stories as to their captures on us without being able to know the certainty. The truth is that the Emperor of Morocco took one vessel from us the last winter, but he did it merely to induce us to treat. He took care of the crew, vessel and cargo and delivered the whole up for us to the Spanish coast, clothing the crew well. There is nothing further to be feared from him, as I think he will settle matters with us on tolerable terms.

But the Algerines this fall took two vessels from us and now have twentytwo of our citizens in slavery. Their dispositions are more hostile and they very possibly will demand a higher tribute than America will pay. In this event they will commit depredations on our trade next summer. I do not think the insurance against them on vessels coming to France will be worth one-half per cent, but who can estimate the value of a half per cent on the fate of a child? My mind revolts at the possibility of a capture, so that unless you hear from myself—not trusting the information of any other person on earth—that peace is made with the Algerines, do not send her but in a vessel of French or English property; for these vessels alone are safe from prize by the barbarians. Mr. Barclay, our consul here, expects to go to Philadelphia in the spring and to return again here. He offers to take charge of her. She would be then in the best hands possible and should the time of his return become well ascertained I will write you on the subject. In the meantime it need not prevent your embracing any opportunity which occurs of a sound French or English ship, neither new nor old, sailing in the months of April, May, June or July, under the care of a trusty person. You see how much trouble I give you till I get this little charge out of your hands.

P. S. I saw in a Virginia paper that somebody gave me as the author of information that we had nothing to fear from the Algerines. No such information ever went from me. The writer probably had not distinguished between the pirates of Algiers and Morocco. Of the peaceful disposition of the latter I have written, but never of the former.

# On Waterways

### TO GEORGE WASHINGTON.

PARIS, *January 4, 1786.*

SIR,—I have been honored with your letter of September 26, which was delivered me by Mr. Houdon, who is safely returned. He has brought with him a mould of the face only, having left the other parts of his work with his workmen to come by some other conveyance. Doctor Franklin, who was joined with me in the superintendence of this just monument, having left us before what is called the costume of the statue was decided on, I cannot so well satisfy myself as I am persuaded I should not so well satisfy the world as by consulting your own wish or inclination as to this arrangement. Permit me, therefore, to ask you whether there is any particular dress or any particular attitude which you would rather wish to be adopted? . . .

I sincerely rejoice that three such works as the opening the Potomac, the James river, Virginia canal from the Dismal, are like to be carried through. There is still a fourth, however, which I had the honor, I believe, of mentioning to you in a letter of March 15, 1784, from Annapolis. It is the cutting a canal which shall unite the heads of Cayahoga and the Beaver creek. The utility of this and even the necessity of it, if we mean to aim at the trade of the lakes, will be palpable to you. The only question is its practicability. The best information I could get as to this was from General Hand, who described the country as champaign and these waters as heading in lagoons which would be easily united. Maryland and Pennsylvania are both interested to concur with us in this work.

The institutions you propose to establish by the shore in the Potomac and

James river companies, given you by the assembly, and the particular objects of these institutions are most worthy. It occurs to me, however, that if the bill for the more general diffusion of knowledge which is in the revisal should be passed, it would supersede the use and obscure the existence of the charity schools you have thought of. I suppose in fact that that bill, or some other like it, will be passed. I never saw one received with more enthusiasm than that was by the House of Delegates in the year 1778 and ordered to be printed and it seemed afterwards that nothing but the extreme distress of our resources prevented it being carried into execution even during the war. It is an axiom in my mind that our liberty can never be safe but in the hands of the people themselves, and that, too, of the people with a certain degree of instruction. This it is the business of the state to effect, and on a general plan.

## Buffon's Mistake

### TO A. CARY.

PARIS, *January* 7, *1786.*

. . . In my conversations with the Count de Buffon on the subjects of natural history, I find him absolutely unacquainted with our elk and our deer. He has hitherto believed that our deer never had horns more than a foot long; and has, therefore, classed them with the roe buck, which I am sure you know them to be different from. I have examined some of the red deer of this country at the distance of about sixty yards, and I find no other difference between them and ours than a shade or two in the color. Will you take the trouble to procure for me the largest pair of buck's horns you can, and a large skin of each color, that is to say, a red and a blue? If it were possible to take these from a buck just killed, to leave all the bones of the head in the skin, with the horns on, to leave the bones of the legs in the skin also, and the hoofs to it, so that, having only made an incision all along the belly and neck, to take the animal out at, we could, by sewing up that incision, and stuffing the skin, present the true size and form of the animal, it would be a most precious present. Our deer have been often sent to England and Scotland. Do you know (with certainty) whether they have ever bred with the red deer of those countries? With respect to the elk, I despair of your being able to get for me anything but the horns of it. David Ross, I know, has a pair; perhaps he would give them to us. It is useless to ask for the skin and skeleton, because I think it not in your power to get them, otherwise, they would be most desirable. A gentleman, fellow passenger with me from Boston to England, promised to send to you, in my name, some hares, rabbits, pheasants, and partridges, by the return of the ship, which was to go to Virginia, and the captain promised to take great care of them. My friend procured the animals, and the ship changing her destination, he kept them in hopes of finding some other conveyance, till they all perished. I do not despair, however, of finding some opportunity still of sending a colony of useful animals. I am making a collection of vines for wine and for the table; also of some trees, such as the cork oak, &c., &c.

## Scientific Speculations

### TO MR. RITTENHOUSE.

PARIS, *January 25, 1786.*

DEAR SIR,—Your favor of September 28th, came to hand a few days ago. I thank you for the details on the subject of the southern and western lines. There remains thereon, one article, however, which I will still beg you to inform me of, viz., how far is the western boundary beyond the meridian of Pittsburg? This information is necessary to enable me to trace that boundary in my map. I shall be much gratified, also, with a communication of your observations on the curiosities of the western country. It will not be difficult to induce me to give up the theory of the growth of shells, without their being the nidus of animals. It is only an idea, and not an opinion with me. In the Notes with which I troubled you, I had observed that there were three opinions as to the origin of these shells. 1. That they have been deposited, even in the highest mountains, by an universal deluge. 2. That they, with all the calcareous stones and earths, are animal remains. 3. That they grow or shoot as crystals do. I find that I could swallow the last opinion, sooner than either of the others; but I have not yet swallowed it. Another opinion might have been added, that some throe of nature has forced up parts which had been the bed of the ocean. But have we any better proof of such an effort of nature, than of her shooting a lapidific juice into the form of a shell? No such convulsion has taken place in our time, nor within the annals of history; nor is the distance greater between the shooting of the lapidific juice into the form of a crystal or a diamond, which we see, and into the form of a shell, which we do not see, than between the forcing volcanic matter a little above the surface, where it is in fusion, which we see, and the forcing the bed of the sea fifteen thousand feet above the ordinary surface of the earth, which we do not see. It is not possible to believe any of these hypotheses; and, if we lean towards any of them, it should be only till some other is produced, more analogous to the known operations of nature. In a letter to Mr. Hopkinson, I mentioned to him that the Abbé Rochon, who discovered the double refracting power in some of the natural crystals, had lately made a telescope with the metal called platina, which, while it is as susceptible of as perfect a polish as the metal heretofore used for the specula of telescopes, is insusceptible of rust, as gold and silver are. There is a person here, who has hit on a new method of engraving. He gives you an ink of his composition. Write on copper plates anything of which you would wish to take several copies, and, in an hour, the plate will be ready to strike them off;

so of plans, engravings, &c. This art will be amusing to individuals, if ne
should make it known.


# English Views

## TO RICHARD HENRY LEE.

LONDON, *April 22, 1786.*

With respect to a commercial treaty with this country, be assured that this
government not only has it not in contemplation at present to make any, but
that they do not conceive that any circumstances will arise which shall
render it expedient for them to have any political connection with us. They
think we shall be glad of their commerce on their own terms. There is no
party in our favor here, either in power or out of power. Even the opposition concur with the ministry and the nation in this.

I dined the other day in a company of the ministerial party. A General
Clark, a Scotchman and ministerialist, sat next to me. He introduced the subject of American affairs, and in the course of the conversation told me that
were America to petition Parliament to be again received on their former
footing, the petition would be very generally rejected. He was serious in
this, and I think it was the sentiment of the company, and is the sentiment
perhaps of the nation. In this they are wise, but for a foolish reason. They
think they lost more by suffering us to participate of their commercial
privileges, at home and abroad, than they lose by our political severance.
The true reason, however, why such an application should be rejected is,
that in a very short time, we should oblige them to add another hundred
millions to their debt in unsuccessful attempts to retain the subjection offered
to them.


# The Steam Engine

## TO CHARLES THOMSON.

LONDON, *April 22, 1786.*

DEAR SIR,—In one of your former letters, you expressed a wish to have
one of the newly-invented lamps. I find them made here much better than at
Paris, and take the liberty of asking your acceptance of one, which will accompany this letter. It is now found that any tolerable oil may be used in
them. The spermaceti oil is best, of the cheap kind.

I could write you volumes on the improvements which I find made, and
making here, in the arts. One deserves particular notice, because it is simple,
great, and likely to have extensive consequences. It is the application of
steam, as an agent for working grist mills. I have visited the one lately made

here. It was, at that time, turning eight pair of stones. It consumes one hundred bushels of coal a day. It is proposed to put up thirty pair of stones. I do not know whether the quantity of fuel, is to be increased. I hear you are applying the same agent in America, to navigate boats, and I have little doubt, but that it will be applied generally to machines, so as to supersede the use of water ponds, and of course to lay open all the streams for navigation. We know that steam is one of the most powerful engines we can employ; and in America, fuel is abundant.

# National Barriers

## TO JAMES ROSS.

PARIS, *May 8, 1786.*

I am of opinion that twenty-three thousand hogsheads of tobacco, the annual consumption of this country, do not exceed the amount of those commodities which it is more advantageous to us to buy here than in England, or elsewhere; and such a commerce would powerfully reinforce the motives for a friendship from this country towards ours. This friendship we ought to cultivate closely, considering the present dispositions of England towards us.

I am lately returned from a visit to that country. The spirit of hostility to us has always existed in the mind of the King, but it has now extended itself through the whole mass of the people, and the majority in the public councils. In a country, where the voice of the people influence so much the measures of administration, and where it coincides with the private temper of the King, there is no pronouncing on future events. It is true they have nothing to gain, and much to lose by a war with us. But interest is not the strongest passion in the human breast. There are difficult points, too, still unsettled between us. They have not withdrawn their armies out of our country, nor given satisfaction for the property they brought off. On our part, we have not paid our debts, and it will take time to pay them. In conferences with some distinguished mercantile characters, I found them sensible of the impossibility of our paying these debts at once, and that an endeavor to force universal and immediate payment, would render debts desperate, which are good in themselves. I think we should not have differed in the term necessary. We differed essentially in the article of interest. For while the principal, and interest preceding and subsequent to the war, seem justly due from us, that which accrued during the war does not. Interest is a compensation for the use of money. Their money, in our hands, was in the form of lands and negroes. Tobacco, the produce of these lands and negroes (or as I may call it, the interest of them), being almost impossible of conveyance to the markets of consumption, because taken by themselves in its way there, sold during the war, at five or six shillings the hundred. This did not pay taxes, and for tools and other plantation charges. A man who should have attempted to remit to his creditor tobacco, for either principal or interest, must have remitted it three times before one cargo would have arrived safe; and this from the depredations of their own nation, and often of the creditor himself; for some of the merchants entered deeply into the privateering business. The individuals, who did not, say they have lost this interest; the debtor replies, that he has not gained it, and that it is a case, where a loss having been incurred, every one tries to shift it from himself. The known bias of the human mind from motives of interest should lessen the confidence of each party in the justice of their reasoning; but it is difficult to say, which of them should make the sacrifice, both of reason and interest. Our conferences were intended as preparatory to some arrangement. It is uncertain how far we should have been able to accommodate our opinions. But the absolute aversion of the government to enter into any arrangement prevented the object from being pursued. Each country is left to do justice to itself and to the other, according to its own ideas, as to what is past; and to scramble for the future, as well as they can; to regulate their commerce by duties and prohibitions, and perhaps by cannons and mortars; in which event, we must abandon the ocean, where we are weak, leaving to neutral nations the carriage of our commodities; and measure with them on land, where they alone can lose. Farewell, then, all our useful improvements of canals and roads, reformations of laws, and other rational employments.

## Justice for the Indians

### TO MR. HAWKINS.

PARIS, *August 13, 1786.*

DEAR SIR,—Your favor of June the 14th, is come to hand, and I am to thank you for your attention to my queries on the subject of the Indians. I have sent many copies to other correspondents, but as yet have heard nothing from them. I shall proceed, however, in my endeavors, particularly with respect to their language, and shall take care so to dispose of what I collect thereon, as that it shall not be lost. The attention which you pay to their rights, also, does you great honor, as the want of that is a principal source of dishonor to the American character. The two principles on which our conduct towards the Indians should be founded, are justice and fear. After the injuries we have done them, they cannot love us, which leaves us no alternative but that of fear to keep them from attacking us. But justice is what we should never lose sight of, and in time it may recover their esteem. Your attention to one burthen I laid on you, encourages me to remind you of another, which is the sending me some of the seeds of the Dionæa Muscipula, or Venus fly-trap, called also with you, I believe, the Sensitive Plant. This can come folded in a letter.

## American Advantages

TO MR. WYTHE.

PARIS, *August 13, 1786.*

The European papers have announced, that the Assembly of Virginia were occupied on the revisal of their code of laws. This, with some other similar intelligence, has contributed much to convince the people of Europe, that what the English papers are constantly publishing of our anarchy, is false; as they are sensible that such a work is that of a people only, who are in perfect tranquillity. Our act for freedom of religion is extremely applauded. The ambassadors and ministers of the several nations of Europe, resident at this Court, have asked of me copies of it, to send to their sovereigns, and it is inserted at full length in several books now in the press; among others, in the new "Encyclopédie." I think it will produce considerable good even in these countries, where ignorance, superstition, poverty, and oppression of body and mind, in every form, are so firmly settled on the mass of the people, that their redemption from them can never be hoped. If all the sovereigns of Europe were to set themselves to work, to emancipate the minds of their subjects from their present ignorance and prejudices, and that, as zealously as they now endeavor the contrary, a thousand years would not place them on that high ground, on which our common people are now setting out. Ours could not have been so fairly placed under the control of the common sense of the people, had they not been separated from their parent stock, and kept from contamination, either from them, or the other people of the old world, by the intervention of so wide an ocean. To know the worth of this, one must see the want of it here. I think by far the most important bill in our whole code, is that for the diffusion of knowledge among the people. No other sure foundation can be devised, for the preservation of freedom and happiness. If anybody thinks that kings, nobles, or priests are good conservators of the public happiness, send him here. It is the best school in the universe to cure him of that folly. He will see here, with his own eyes, that these descriptions of men are an abandoned confederacy against the happiness of the mass of the people. The omnipotence of their effect cannot be better proved, than in this country particularly, where, notwithstanding the finest soil upon earth, the finest climate under heaven, and a people of the most benevolent, the most gay and amiable character of which the human form is susceptible; where such a people, I say, surrounded by so many blessings from nature, are loaded with misery, by kings, nobles, and priests, and by them alone. Preach, my dear Sir, a crusade against ignorance; establish and improve the law for educating the common people. Let our countrymen know, that the people alone can protect us against these evils, and that the tax which will be paid for this purpose, is not more than the thousandth part of what will be paid to kings, priests and nobles, who will rise up among us if we leave the people in ignorance. The people of England, I think, are less oppressed than here. But it needs but half an eye to see, when among them, that the foundation is laid in their dispositions for the establishment of a despotism. Nobility, wealth, and pomp are the objects of their admiration. They are by no means the free-minded people we suppose them in America. Their learned men, too, are few in number, and are less learned, and infinitely less emancipated from prejudice, than those of this country.

## Prices and Markets

### TO DR. FRANKLIN.

PARIS, *August 14, 1786.*

I had been alarmed with the general cry that our commerce was in distress, and feared it might be for the want of markets. But the high price of commodities shows that markets are not wanting. Is it not yet possible, however, that these high prices may proceed from the smallness of the quantity made, and that from the want of laborers? It would really seem as if we did not make produce enough for home consumption, and, of course, had none superfluous to exchange for foreign articles. The price of wheat, for instance, shows it is not exported, because it could not, at such a price, enter into competition at a foreign market with the wheat of any other nation.

Your friends here, within the circle of my acquaintance, are well, and often enquire after you. No interesting change that I recollect has taken place among them. Houdon has just received the block of marble for General Washington's statue. He is married since his return. Trumbull, our young American painter, is come here to have his Death of Montgomery and Battle of Bunker's Hill engraved.

## Head vs. Heart

### TO MRS. COSWAY.

PARIS, *October 14, 1786.*

MY DEAR MADAM,—Having performed the last sad office of handing you into your carriage, at the pavillon de St. Denis, and seen the wheels get actually into motion, I turned on my heel and walked, more dead than alive, to the opposite door, where my own was awaiting me. Mr. Danquerville was missing. He was sought for, found, and dragged down stairs. We were crammed into the carriage, like recruits for the Bastille, and not having soul enough to give orders to the coachman, he presumed Paris our destination, and drove off. After a considerable interval, silence was broke, with a *"Je suis vraiment affligé du départ de ces bons gens."* This was a signal for a mutual confession of distress. We began immediately to talk of Mr. and Mrs. Cosway, of their goodness, their talents, their amiability; and, though we spoke of nothing else, we seemed hardly to have entered into the matter, when the coachman announced the rue St. Denis, and that we were opposite Mr. Danquerville's. He insisted on descending there, and traversing a short passage to his lodgings. I was carried home. Seated by my fireside, solitary and sad, the following dialogue took place between my Head and my Heart.

*Head.* Well, friend, you seem to be in a pretty trim.

*Heart.* I am indeed the most wretched of all earthly beings. But they told me they would come back again, the next year.

*Head.* But, in the meantime, see what you suffer. Perhaps you flatter yourself they may come to America?

*Heart.* God only knows what is to happen. I see nothing impossible in that supposition; and I see things wonderfully contrived sometimes, to make us happy. Where could they find such objects as in America, for the exercise of their enchanting art? especially the lady, who paints landscapes so inimitably. She wants only subjects worthy of immortality, to render her pencil immortal. The Falling Spring, the Cascade of Niagara, the passage of the Potomac through the Blue Mountains, the Natural Bridge; it is worth a voyage across the Atlantic to see these objects; much more to paint, and make them, and thereby ourselves, known to all ages. And our own dear Monticello; where has nature spread so rich a mantle under the eye? mountains, forests, rocks, rivers. With what majesty do we there ride above the storms! How sublime to look down into the workhouse of nature, to see her clouds, hail, snow, rain, thunder, all fabricated at our feet! and the glorious sun, when rising as if out of a distant water, just gilding the tops of the mountains, and giving life to all nature!

*Head.* Well. Let us put this possibility to trial then, on another point. When you consider the character which is given of our country, by the lying newspapers of London, and their credulous copiers in other countries; when you reflect that all Europe is made to believe we are a lawless banditti, in a state of absolute anarchy, cutting one another's throats, and plundering without distinction, how could you expect that any reasonable creature would venture among us?

*Heart.* But you and I know that all this is false: that there is not a country on earth, where there is greater tranquillity; where the laws are milder, or better obeyed; where every one is more attentive to his own business, or meddles less with that of others; where strangers are better received, more hospitably treated, and with a more sacred respect.

*Head.* True, you and I know this, but your friends do not know it.

*Heart.* But they are sensible people, who think for themselves. They will ask of impartial foreigners, who have been among us, whether they saw or heard on the spot, any instance of anarchy. They will judge, too, that a people, occupied as we are, in opening rivers, digging navigable canals, making roads, building public schools, establishing academies, erecting busts and statues to our great men, protecting religious freedom, abolishing sanguinary punishments, reforming and improving our laws in general; they will judge, I say, for themselves, whether these are not the occupations of a people at their ease; whether this is not better evidence of our true state, than a London newspaper, hired to lie, and from which no truth can ever be extracted but by reversing everything it says.

*Head.* I did not begin this lecture, my friend, with a view to learn from you what America is doing. Let us return, then, to our point. I wish to make you sensible how imprudent it is to place your affections, without reserve, on objects you must so soon lose, and whose loss, when it comes, must cost you such severe pangs.

*Heart.* I know, indeed, that you pretend authority to the sovereign control of our conduct, in all its parts; and a respect for your grave saws and maxims, a desire to do what is right, has sometimes induced me to conform to your counsels. A few facts, however, which I can readily recall to your memory, will suffice to prove to you, that nature has not organized you for our moral direction. When the poor, wearied soldier whom we overtook at Chickahominy, with his pack on his back, begged us to let him get up behind our chariot, you began to calculate that the road was full of soldiers, and that if all should be taken up, our horses would fail in their journey. We drove on therefore. But, soon becoming sensible you had made me do wrong, that, though we cannot relieve all the distressed, we should relieve as many as we can, I turned about to take up the soldier; but he had entered a bye-path, and was no more to be found; and from that moment to this, I could never find him out, to ask his forgiveness. Again, when the poor woman came to ask a charity in Philadelphia, you whispered that she looked like a drunkard, and that half a dollar was enough to give her for the ale-house. Those who want the dispositions to give, easily find reasons why they ought not to give. When I sought her out afterwards, and did what I should have done at first, you know that she employed the money immediately towards placing her child at school. If our country, when pressed with wrongs at the point of the bayonet, had been governed by its heads instead of its hearts, where should we have been now? Hanging on a gallows as high as Haman's. You began to calculate, and to compare wealth and numbers: we threw up a few pulsations of our blood; we supplied enthusiasm against wealth and numbers; we put our existence to the hazard, when the hazard seemed against us, and we saved our country: justifying, at the same time, the ways of Providence, whose precept is, to do always what is right, and leave the issue to Him. In short, my friend, as far as my recollection serves me, I do not know that I ever did a good thing on your suggestion, or a dirty one without it. I do forever, then, disclaim your interference in my province. Fill paper as you please with triangles and squares: try how many ways you can hang and combine them together. I shall never envy nor control your sublime delights. But leave me to decide, when and where friendships are to be contracted. You say, I contract them at random. So you said the woman at Philadelphia was a drunkard. I receive none into my esteem, till I know they are worthy of it. Wealth, title, office, are no recommendations to my friendship. On the contrary, great good qualities are requisite to make amends for their having wealth, title, and office.

# On the Gulf Stream

### M. LE ROY DE L'ACADÉMIE DES SCIENCES.

PARIS, *November 13, 1786.*

SIR,—I received the honor of yours of September the 18th, a day or two after the accident of a dislocated wrist had disabled me from writing. I have waited thus long in constant hope of recovering its use. But finding that this hope walks before me like my shadow, I can no longer oppose the desire and duty of answering your polite and learned letter. I therefore employ my left hand in the office of scribe, which it performs indeed slowly, awkwardly and badly.

The information given by me to the Marquis de Chastellux, and alluded to in his book and in your letter was, that the sea breezes which prevail in the lower parts of Virginia during the summer months, and in the warm parts of day, had made a sensible progress into the interior country: that formerly, within the memory of persons living, they extended but little above Williamsburg; that afterwards they became sensible as high as Richmond; and that, at present, they penetrate sometimes as far as the first mountains, which are above an hundred miles further from the sea coast than Williamsburg is. It is very rare, indeed, that they reach those mountains, and not till the afternoon is considerably advanced. A light north-westerly breeze is, for the most part, felt there, while an easterly or north-easterly wind is blowing strongly in the lower country. How far northward and southward of Virginia this easterly breeze takes place, I am not informed. I must, therefore, be understood as speaking of that State only, which extends on the sea coast from 36½° to 38° of latitude.

Having had occasion to mention the course of the tropical winds from east to west, I will add some observations connected with them. They are known to occasion a strong current in the ocean, in the same direction. This current breaks on that wedge of land of which Saint Roque is the point; the southern column of it *probably* turning off and washing the coast of Brazil. I say *probably*, because I have never heard of the fact, and conjecture it from reason only. The northern column having its western motion diverted towards the north, and reinforced by the currents of the great rivers Orinoko, Amazons and Tocantin, has probably been the agent which formed the Gulf of Mexico, cutting the American continent nearly in two, in that part. It re-issues into the ocean at the northern end of the Gulf, and passes by the name of the Gulf Stream, all along the coast of the United States, to its northern extremity. There it turns off eastwardly, having formed by its eddy at this turn the Banks of Newfoundland. Through the whole of its course, from the Gulf to the Banks, it retains a very sensible warmth. The Spaniards are, at this time, desirous of trading to the Philippine islands, by the way of the Cape of Good Hope; but opposed in it by the Dutch, under authority of the treaty of Munster, they are examining the practicability of a common passage through the Straits of Magellan or round Cape Horn. Were they to make an opening through the Isthmus of Panama, a work much less difficult than some even of the inferior canals of France, however small this opening should be in the beginning, the tropical current, entering it with all its force, would soon widen it sufficiently for its own passage, and thus complete, in a short time, that work which otherwise will still employ it for ages. Less country, too, would be destroyed by it in this way. These consequences would follow: 1. Vessels from Europe or the western coast of Africa, by entering the tropics, would have a steady wind and tide to carry them through the Atlantic, through America and the Pacific Ocean, to every part of the Asiatic coast, and of the eastern coast of Africa; thus performing with speed and safety the tour of the whole globe, to within about twenty-four degrees of longitude, or one fifteenth part of its circumference; the African continent, under the line, occupying about that space. 2. The Gulf of Mexico, now the most dangerous navigation in the world on account of its currents and movable sands, would become stagnant and safe. 3. The Gulf Stream on the coast of the United States would cease, and with that those derangements of course and reckoning, which now impede and endanger the intercourse with those States. 4. The fogs on the Banks of Newfoundland,[1] supposed to be the vapors of the Gulf Stream, rendered turbid by cold air, would disappear. 5. Those Banks ceasing to receive supplies of sand, weeds, and warm water, by the Gulf Stream, it might become problematical what effect changes of pasture and temperature would have on the fisheries. However, it is time to relieve you from this long lecture. I wish its subject may have been sufficiently interesting, to make amends for its details. These are submitted with entire deference to your better judgment. I will only add to them, by assuring you of the sentiments of perfect esteem and respect with which I have the honor to be, Sir, your most obedient, and most humble servant.

# Checks and Balances

## TO JAMES MADISON.

Paris, *December 16, 1786.*

To make us one nation as to foreign concerns, and keep us distinct in domestic ones, gives the outline of the proper division of powers between

[1] This ingenious and probable conjecture, I found in a letter from Dr. Franklin to yourself, published in the late volume of the American Philosophical Transactions.

the general and particular governments. But, to enable the federal head to exercise the powers given it to best advantage, it should be organized as the particular ones are, into legislative, executive, and judiciary. The first and last are already separated. The second should be. When last with Congress, I often proposed to members to do this, by making of the committee of the States, an executive committee during the recess of Congress, and, during its sessions, to appoint a committee to receive and despatch all executive business, so that Congress itself should meddle only with what should be legislative. But I question if any Congress (much less all successively) can have self-denial enough to go through with this distribution. The distribution, then, should be imposed on them. . . .

The Virginia act for religious freedom has been received with infinite approbation in Europe, and propagated with enthusiasm. I do not mean by the governments, but by the individuals who compose them. It has been translated into French and Italian, has been sent to most of the courts of Europe, and has been the best evidence of the falsehood of those reports which stated us to be in anarchy. It is inserted in the new "Encyclopédie," and is appearing in most of the publications respecting America. In fact, it is comfortable to see the standard of reason at length erected, after so many ages, during which the human mind has been held in vassalage by kings, priests, and nobles; and it is honorable for us, to have produced the first legislature who had the courage to declare, that the reason of man may be trusted with the formation of his own opinions. . . .

I thank you for your communications in Natural History. The several instances of trees, &c., found far below the surface of the earth, as in the case of Mr. Hay's well, seem to set the reason of man at defiance.

# The New Steam Power

## TO CHARLES THOMSON.

PARIS, *December 17, 1786.*

DEAR SIR,—I take the first moment I can to acknowledge the receipt of your letters of April the 6th, July the 8th and 30th. In one of these, you say, you have not been able to learn, whether, in the new mills in London, steam is the immediate mover of the machinery, or raises water to move it? It is the immediate mover. The power of this agent, though long known, is but now beginning to be applied to the various purposes of which it is susceptible. . . .

P. S. Since writing the preceding, I have had a conversation on the subject of the steam mills, with the famous Boulton, to whom those of London belong, and who is here at this time. He compares the effect of steam with that of horses, in the following manner: Six horses, aided with the most advantageous combination of the mechanical powers hitherto tried, will grind six bushels of flour in an hour; at the end of which time they are all in a foam, and must rest. They can work thus, six hours in the twenty-four, grinding thirty-six bushels of flour, which is six to each horse, for the twenty-four hours. His steam mill in London consumes one hundred and twenty bushels of coal in twenty-four hours, turns ten pair of stones, which grind eight bushels of flour an hour each, which is nineteen hundred and twenty bushels in the twenty-four hours. This makes a peck and a half of coal perform exactly as much as a horse, in one day, can perform.

## Notes on Science

### TO MR. HOPKINSON.

PARIS, *December 23, 1786.*

I thank you for the volume of the Philadelphia transactions, which came safely to hand, and is, in my opinion, a very valuable volume, and contains many precious papers. The paccan-nut is, as you conjecture, the Illinois nut. The former is the vulgar name south of the Potomac, as also with the Indians and Spaniards, and enters also into the Botanical name which is Juglano Paccan. I have many volumes of the "Encyclopédie" for yourself and Dr. Franklin; but, as a winter passage is bad for books, and before the spring the packets will begin to sail from Havre to New York, I shall detain them till then. You must not presume too strongly that your comb-footed bird is known to M. de Buffon. He did not know our panther. I gave him the stripped skin of one I bought in Philadelphia, and it presents him a new species, which will appear in his next volumes. . . .

## Yankee Invention

### TO MONSIEUR DE CREVE-COEUR.

PARIS, *January 15, 1787.*

DEAR SIR,—I see by the Journal of this morning, that they are robbing us of another of our inventions to give it to the English. The writer, indeed, only admits them to have revived what he thinks was known to the Greeks, that is, the making the circumference of a wheel of one single piece. The farmers in New Jersey were the first who practiced it, and they practiced it commonly. Dr. Franklin, in one of his trips to London, mentioned this practice to the man now in London, who has the patent for making those wheels. The idea struck him. The Doctor promised to go to his shop, and assist him in trying to make the wheel of one piece. The Jersey farmers do it by cutting a young sapling, and bending it, while green and juicy, into a circle;

and leaving it so until it becomes perfectly seasoned. But in London there are no saplings. The difficulty was, then, to give to old wood the pliancy of young. The Doctor and the workman labored together some weeks, and succeeded; and the man obtained a patent for it, which has made his fortune. I was in his shop in London, he told me the whole story himself, and acknowledged, not only the origin of the idea, but how much the assistance of Dr. Franklin had contributed to perform the operation on dry wood. He spoke of him with love and gratitude. I think I have had a similar account from Dr. Franklin, but cannot be quite certain. I know, that being in Philadelphia when the first set of patent wheels arrived from London, and were spoken of by the gentleman (an Englishman) who brought them, as a wonderful discovery, the idea of its being a new discovery was laughed at by the Philadelphians, who, in their Sunday parties across the Delaware, had seen every farmer's cart mounted on such wheels. The writer in the paper, supposes the English workman got his idea from Homer. But it is more likely the Jersey farmer got his idea from thence, because ours are the only farmers who can read Homer; because, too, the Jersey practice is precisely that stated by Homer: the English practice very different. Homer's words are (comparing a young hero killed by Ajax to a poplar felled by a workman) literally thus: "He fell on the ground, like a poplar, which has grown smooth, in the west part of a great meadow; with its branches shooting from its summit. But the chariot maker, with the sharp axe, has felled it, that he may bend a wheel for a beautiful chariot. It lies drying on the banks of the river." Observe the circumstances which coincide with the Jersey practice. 1. It is a tree growing in a moist place, full of juices and easily bent. 2. It is cut while green. 3. It is bent into the circumference of a wheel. 4. It is left to dry in that form. You, who write French well and readily, should write a line for the Journal, to reclaim the honor of our farmers.

## Sense of the People

### TO COLONEL EDWARD CARRINGTON.

PARIS, *January 16, 1787.*

The tumults in America I expected would have produced in Europe an unfavorable opinion of our political state. But it has not. On the contrary, the small effect of these tumults seems to have given more confidence in the firmness of our governments. The interposition of the people themselves on the side of government has had a great effect on the opinion here. I am persuaded myself that the good sense of the people will always be found to be the best army. They may be led astray for a moment, but will soon correct themselves. The people are the only censors of their governors; and even their errors will tend to keep these to the true principles of their institution. To punish these errors too severely would be to suppress the only safeguard of the public liberty. The way to prevent these irregular interpositions of the people, is to give them full information of their affairs through the channel of the public papers, and to contrive that those papers should penetrate the whole mass of the people. The basis of our governments being the opinion of the people, the very first object should be to keep that right; and were it left to me to decide whether we should have a government without newspapers, or newspapers without a government, I should not hesitate a moment to prefer the latter. But I should mean that every man should receive those papers, and be capable of reading them.

I am convinced that those societies (as the Indians) which live without government, enjoy in their general mass an infinitely greater degree of happiness than those who live under the European governments. Among the former, public opinion is in the place of law, and restrains morals as powerfully as laws ever did anywhere. Among the latter, under pretence of governing, they have divided their nations into two classes, wolves and sheep. I do not exaggerate. This is a true picture of Europe. Cherish, therefore, the spirit of our people, and keep alive their attention. Do not be too severe upon their errors, but reclaim them by enlightening them. If once they become inattentive to the public affairs, you and I, and Congress and Assemblies, Judges and Governors, shall all become wolves. It seems to be the law of our general nature, in spite of individual exceptions; and experience declares that man is the only animal which devours his own kind; for I can apply no milder term to the governments of Europe, and to the general prey of the rich on the poor.

The want of news has led me into disquisition instead of narration, forgetting you have every day enough of that. I shall be happy to hear from you sometimes, only observing that whatever passes through the post is read, and that when you write what should be read by myself only, you must be so good as to confide your letter to some passenger, or officer of the packet.

## Varieties of Government

### TO JAMES MADISON.[1]

PARIS, *January 30, 1787.*

DEAR SIR,—My last to you was of the 16th of December; since which, I have received yours of November the 25th, and December the 4th, which afforded me, as your letters always do, a treat on matters public, individual and economical. I am impatient to learn your sentiments on the late troubles in the Eastern States. So far as I have yet seen, they do not appear to threaten serious consequences. Those States have suffered by the stoppage of the channels of their commerce, which have not yet found other issues. This must render money scarce, and make the people uneasy. This uneasiness has

[1]The end of this letter is in cipher.

produced acts absolutely unjustifiable; but I hope they will provoke no severities from their governments. A consciousness of those in power that their administration of the public affairs has been honest, may, perhaps, produce too great a degree of indignation; and those characters, wherein fear predominates over hope, may apprehend too much from these instances of irregularity. They may conclude too hastily, that nature has formed man insusceptible of any other government than that of force, a conclusion not founded in truth nor experience. Societies exist under three forms, sufficiently distinguishable. 1. Without government, as among our Indians. 2. Under governments, wherein the will of every one has a just influence; as is the case in England, in a slight degree, and in our States, in a great one. 3. Under governments of force; as is the case in all other monarchies, and in most of the other republics. To have an idea of the curse of existence under these last, they must be seen. It is a government of wolves over sheep. It is a problem, not clear in my mind, that the first condition is not the best. But I believe it to be inconsistent with any great degree of population. The second state has a great deal of good in it. The mass of mankind under that, enjoys a precious degree of liberty and happiness. It has its evils, too; the principal of which is the turbulence to which it is subject. But weigh this against the oppressions of monarchy, and it becomes nothing. *Malo periculosam libertatem quam quietam servitutem.* Even this evil is productive of good. It prevents the degeneracy of government, and nourishes a general attention to the public affairs. I hold it, that a little rebellion, now and then, is a good thing, and as necessary in the political world as storms in the physical. Unsuccessful rebellions, indeed, generally establish the encroachments on the rights of the people, which have produced them. An observation of this truth should render honest republican governors so mild in their punishment of rebellions, as not to discourage them too much. It is a medicine necessary for the sound health of government.

If these transactions give me no uneasiness, I feel very differently at another piece of intelligence, to wit, the possibility that the navigation of the Mississippi may be abandoned to Spain. I never had any interest westward of the Alleghany; and I never will have any. But I have had great opportunities of knowing the character of the people who inhabit that country; and I will venture to say, that the act which abandons the navigation of the Mississippi is an act of separation between the eastern and western country. It is a relinquishment of five parts out of eight, of the territory of the United States; an abandonment of the fairest subject for the payment of our public debts. . . .

The Marquis de La Fayette is a most valuable auxiliary to me. His zeal is unbounded, and his weight with those in power, great. His education having been merely military, commerce was an unknown field to him. But his good sense enabling him to comprehend perfectly whatever is explained to him, his agency has been very efficacious. He has a great deal of sound genius, is well remarked by the King, and rising in popularity. He has nothing against him, but the suspicion of republican principles.

## Pleasures of Paris

TO MRS. BINGHAM.

PARIS, *February* 7, *1787.*

I know, Madam, that the twelve month is not yet expired; but it will be, nearly, before this will have the honor of being put into your hands. You are then engaged to tell me, truly and honestly, whether you do not find the tranquil pleasures of America, preferable to the empty bustle of Paris. For, to what does that bustle tend? At eleven o'clock, it is day, *chez madame.* The curtains are drawn. Propped on bolsters and pillows, and her head scratched into a little order, the bulletins of the sick are read, and the billets of the well. She writes to some of her acquaintance, and receives the visits of others. If the morning is not very thronged, she is able to get out and hobble round the cage of the Palais Royal; but she must hobble quickly, for the *coiffeur's* turn is come; and a tremendous turn it is! Happy, if he does not make her arrive when dinner is half over! The torpitude of digestion a little passed, she flutters half an hour through the streets, by way of paying visits, and then to the spectacles. These finished, another half hour is devoted to dodging in and out of the doors of her very sincere friends, and away to supper. After supper, cards; and after cards, bed; to rise at noon the next day, and to tread, like a mill horse, the same trodden circle over again. Thus the days of life are consumed, one by one, without an object beyond the present moment; ever flying from the ennui of that, yet carrying it with us; eternally in pursuit of happiness, which keeps eternally before us. If death or bankruptcy happen to trip us out of the circle, it is matter for the buzz of the evening, and is completely forgotten by the next morning. In America, on the other hand, the society of your husband, the fond cares for the children, the arrangements of the house, the improvements of the grounds, fill every moment with a healthy and an useful activity. Every exertion is encouraging, because, to present amusement, it joins the promise of some future good. The intervals of leisure are filled by the society of real friends, whose affections are not thinned to cob-web, by being spread over a thousand objects. This is the picture, in the light it is presented to my mind; now let me have it in yours. If we do not concur this year, we shall the next; or if not then, in a year or two more. You see I am determined not to suppose myself mistaken.

To let you see that Paris is not changed in its pursuits, since it was honored with your presence, I send you its monthly history. But this relating only to the embellishments of their persons, I must add, that those of the city go on well also. A new bridge, for example, is begun at the Place Louis Quinze; the old ones are clearing off the rubbish which encumbered them in the form of houses; new hospitals erecting; magnificent walls of inclosure, and Customhouses at their entrances, &c., &c., &c. I know of no interesting change among those whom you honored with your acquaintance, unless Monsieur de Saint James was of that number. His bankruptcy, and taking asylum in the Bastile, have furnished matter of astonishment. His garden, at the Pont de Neuilly, where, on seventeen acres of ground, he had laid out fifty thousand louis, will probably sell for somewhat less money. The workmen of Paris are making rapid strides towards English perfection. Would you believe, that in the course of the last two years, they have learned even to surpass their London rivals in some articles? Commission me to have you a phaeton made, and, if it is not as much handsomer than a London one, as that is than a *Fiacre*, send it back to me. Shall I fill the box with caps, bonnets, &c.? Not of my own choosing, but—I was going to say, of Mademoiselle Bertin's, forgetting, for the moment, that she too is a bankrupt. They shall be chosen then by whom you please; or, if you are altogether nonplused by her eclipse, we will call an *Assemblée des Notables* to help you out of the difficulty, as is now the fashion. In short, honor me with your commands of any kind, and they shall be faithfully executed. The packets now established from Havre to New York, furnish good opportunities of sending whatever you wish.

I shall end where I began, like a Paris day, reminding you of your engagement to write me a letter of respectable length, an engagement the more precious to me, as it has furnished the occasion, after presenting my respects to Mr. Bingham, of assuring you of the sincerity of those sentiments of esteem and respect with which I have the honor to be, dear Madam, your most obedient, and most humble servant.

## Congressional Diplomacy

### TO HIS EXCELLENCY MR. ADAMS.

PARIS, *February 23, 1787.*

I have read your book with infinite satisfaction and improvement. It will do great good in America. Its learning and its good sense will, I hope, make it an institute for our politicians, old as well as young. There is one opinion in it, however, which I will ask you to reconsider, because it appears to me not entirely accurate, and not likely to do good. Page 362, "Congress is not a legislative, but a diplomatic assembly." Separating into parts the whole sovereignty of our States, some of these parts are yielded to Congress. Upon these I should think them both legislative and executive, and that would have been judiciary also, had not the confederation required them for certain purposes to appoint a judiciary. It has accordingly been the decision of our courts that the confederation is a part of the law of the land, and superior in authority to the ordinary laws, because it cannot be altered by the legislature of any one State. I doubt whether they are at all a diplomatic assembly.

## Classic Architecture

TO MADAME LA COMTESSE DE TESSE.

NISMES, *March 20, 1787.*

Here I am, Madam, gazing whole hours at the Maison Quarrée, like a lover at his mistress. The stocking weavers and silk spinners around it consider me a hypochondriac Englishman, about to write with a pistol the last chapter of his history. This is the second time I have been in love since I left Paris. The first was with a Diana at the Chateau de Laye-Epinaye in Beaujolois, a delicious morsel of sculpture, by M. A. Slodtz. This, you will say, was in rule, to fall in love with a female beauty; but with a house! it is out of all precedent. No, Madam, it is not without a precedent in my own history. While in Paris, I was violently smitten with the Hotel de Salm, and used to go to the Tuileries almost daily, to look at it. The *loueuse des chaises*, inattentive to my passion, never had the complaisance to place a chair there, so that, sitting on the parapet, and twisting my neck round to see the object of my admiration, I generally left it with a *torti-colli*.

From Lyons to Nismes I have been nourished with the remains of Roman grandeur. They have always brought you to my mind, because I know your affection for whatever is Roman and noble. At Vienna I thought of you. But I am glad you were not there; for you would have seen me more angry than, I hope, you will ever see me. The Prætorian Palace, as it is called, comparable, for its fine proportions, to the Maison Quarrée, defaced by the barbarians who have converted it to its present purpose, its beautiful fluted Corinthian columns cut out, in part, to make space for Gothic windows, and hewed down, in the residue, to the plane of the building, was enough, you must admit, to disturb my composure. At Orange, too, I thought of you. I was sure you had seen with pleasure the sublime triumphal arch of Marius at the entrance of the city. I went then to the Arenæ. Would you believe, Madam, that in this eighteenth century, in France, under the reign of Louis XVI, they are at this moment pulling down the circular wall of this superb remain, to pave a road? And that, too, from a hill which is itself an entire mass of stone, just as fit, and more accessible? A former intendant, a M. de Basville, has rendered his memory dear to the traveller and amateur, by the pains he took to preserve and restore these monuments of antiquity. The present one (I do not know who he is) is demolishing the object, to make a good road to it. I thought of you again, and I was then in great good humor, at the Pont du Gard, a sublime antiquity, and well preserved. But most of all here, where Roman taste, genius, and magnificence, excite ideas analogous to yours at every step. I could no longer oppose the inclination to avail myself of your permission to write to you, a permission given with too much complaisance by you, and used by me with too much indiscretion. Madame de Tott did me the same honor. But she, being only the descendant of some of those puny heroes who boiled their own kettles before the walls of Troy, I shall write to her from a Grecian, rather than a Roman canton; when I shall find myself, for example, among her Phocæan relations at Marseilles.

Loving, as you do Madam, the precious remains of antiquity, loving architecture, gardening, a warm sun and a clear sky, I wonder you have never thought of moving Chaville to Nismes. This, as you know, has not always been deemed impracticable; and, therefore, the next time a *Sur-intendant des batiments du roi*, after the example of M. Colbert, sends persons to Nismes to move the Maison Quarrée to Paris, that they may not come empty handed, desire them to bring Chaville with them, to replace it. . . .

From a correspondent at Nismes, you will not expect news. Were I to attempt to give you news, I should tell you stories one thousand years old. I should detail to you the intrigues of the courts of the Cæsars, how they affect us here, the oppressions of their prætors, prefects, &c. I am immersed in antiquities from morning to night. For me, the city of Rome is actually existing in all the splendor of its empire. I am filled with alarms for the event of the irruptions daily making on us, by the Goths, the Visigoths, Ostrogoths, and Vandals, lest they should re-conquer us to our original barbarism. If I am sometimes induced to look forward to the eighteenth century, it is only when recalled to it by the recollection of your goodness and friendship.

# Travel Notes

## TO THE MARQUIS DE LA FAYETTE.

NICE, *April 11, 1787.*

Your head, my dear friend, is full of notable things; and being better employed, therefore, I do not expect letters from you. I am constantly roving about, to see what I have never seen before, and shall never see again. In the great cities, I go to see what travellers think alone worthy of being seen; but I make a job of it, and generally gulp it all down in a day. On the other hand, I am never satiated with rambling through the fields and farms, examining the culture and cultivators, with a degree of curiosity which makes some take me to be a fool, and others to be much wiser than I am. I have been pleased to find among the people a less degree of physical misery than I had expected. They are generally well clothed, and have a plenty of food, not animal indeed, but vegetable, which is as wholesome. Perhaps they are over-worked, the excess of the rent required by the landlord obliging them to too many hours of labor in order to produce that, and wherewith to feed and clothe themselves. . . . From the first olive fields of Pierrelatte, to the orangeries of Hieres, . . . I have often wished for you. I think you have not made this journey. It is a pleasure you have to come, and an improvement to be added to the many you have already made. It will be a great comfort to you, to know, from your own inspection, the condition of all the provinces of your own country, and it will be interesting to them at some future day, to be known to you. This is, perhaps, the only moment of your life in which you can acquire that knowledge. And to do it most effectually, you must be absolutely incognito, you must ferret the people out of their hovels as I have done, look into their kettles, eat their bread, loll on their beds under pretence of resting yourself, but in fact, to find if they are soft. You will feel a sublime pleasure in the course of this investigation, and a sublimer one hereafter, when you shall be able to apply your knowledge to the softening of their beds, or the throwing a morsel of meat into their kettle of vegetables.

## On Latin America

### TO JOHN JAY.

MARSEILLES, *May 4, 1787.*

My journey into this part of the country has procured me information which I will take the liberty of communicating to Congress. In October last I received a letter dated Montpelier, October the 2d, 1786, announcing to me that the writer was a foreigner, who had a matter of very great consequence to communicate to me, and desired I would indicate the channel through which it might pass safely. I did so.

I received soon after a letter in the following words, omitting only the formal parts. [*A translation of it is here given.*]

"I am a native of Brazil. You are not ignorant of the frightful slavery under which my country groans. This continually becomes more insupportable since the epoch of your glorious independence, for the cruel Portuguese omit nothing which can render our condition more wretched, from an apprehension that we may follow your example. The conviction, that these usurpers against the laws of nature and humanity only meditate new oppressions, has decided us to follow the guiding light which you have held out to us, to break our chains, to revive our almost expiring liberty, which is nearly overwhelmed by that force, which is the sole foundation of the authority that Europeans exercise over American. But it is necessary that some power should extend assistance to the Brazilians, since Spain would certainly unite herself with Portugal; and in spite of our advantages for defence, we could not make it effectual, or, at least, it would be imprudent to hazard the attempt without some assurance of success. In this state of affairs, Sir, we can with propriety look only to the United States, not only because we are following her example, but, moreover, because nature, in making us inhabitants of the same continent, has in some sort united us in the bonds of a common patriotism. On our part, we are prepared to furnish the necessary supplies of money, and at all times to acknowledge the debt of gratitude due to our benefactors. I have thus, Sir, laid before you a sum-

mary of my views. It is in discharge of this commission that I have come to
France, since I could not effect it in America without exciting suspicion. It
now remains for you to decide whether those views can be accomplished.
Should you desire to consult your nation on them, it is in my power to give
you all the information you may require."

As, by this time, I had been advised to try the waters of Aix, I wrote to
the gentleman my design, and that I would go off my road as far as Nismes,
under the pretext of seeing the antiquities of that place, if he would meet
me there. He met me, and the following is the sum of the information I
received from him: "Brazil contains as many inhabitants as Portugal. They
are, 1. Portuguese. 2. Native whites. 3. Black and mulatto slaves. 4. Indians,
civilized and savage. 1. The Portuguese are few in number, mostly married
there, have lost sight of their native country, as well as the prospect of
returning to it, and are disposed to become independent. 2. The native
whites form the body of their nation. 3. The slaves are as numerous as the
free. 4. The civilized Indians have no energy, and the savage would not
meddle. There are twenty thousand regular troops. Originally these were
Portuguese. But as they died off, they were replaced by natives, so that
these compose at present the mass of the troops, and may be counted on
by their native country. The officers are partly Portuguese, partly Brazilians;
their bravery is not doubted, and they understand the parade, but not the
science of their profession. They have no bias for Portugal, but no energy
either for anything. The priests are partly Portuguese, partly Brazilians,
and will not interest themselves much. The Noblesse are scarcely known as
such. They will, in no manner, be distinguished from the people. The men
of letters are those most desirous of a revolution. The people are not much
under the influence of their priests, most of them read and write, possess
arms, and are in the habit of using them for hunting. The slaves will take
the side of their masters. In short, as to the question of revolution, there is
but one mind in that country. But there appears no person capable of conducting a revolution, or willing to venture himself at its head, without the
aid of some powerful nation, as the people of their own might fail them.
There is no printing press in Brazil. They consider the North American
revolution as a precedent for theirs. They look to the United States as most
likely to give them honest support, and, from a variety of considerations,
have the strongest prejudices in our favor. This informant is a native and
inhabitant of Rio Janeiro, the present metropolis. . . ."

I took care to impress on him, through the whole of our conversation,
that I had neither instructions nor authority to say a word to anybody on
this subject, and that I could only give him my own ideas, as a single individual; which were, that we were not in a condition at present to meddle
nationally in any war; that we wished particularly to cultivate the friendship
of Portugal, with whom we have an advantageous commerce. That yet a
successful revolution in Brazil could not be uninteresting to us. That prospects of lucre might possibly draw numbers of individuals to their aid, and
purer motives our officers, among whom are many excellent. That our

citizens being free to leave their own country individually, without the consent of their governments, are equally free to go to any other.

A little before I received the first letter of the Brazilian, a gentleman informed me there was a Mexican in Paris, who wished to have some conversation with me. He accordingly called on me. The substance of the information I drew from him was as follows. He is himself a native of Mexico, where his relations are, principally. He left it at about seventeen years of age, and seems now to be about thirty-three or thirty-four. He classes and characterizes the inhabitants of that country, as follows: 1. The natives of Old Spain, possessed of most of the offices of government, and firmly attached to it. 2. The clergy, equally attached to the government. 3. The natives of Mexico, generally disposed to revolt, but without instruction, without energy, and much under the dominion of their priests. 4. The slaves, mulatto and black; the former enterprising and intelligent, the latter brave, and of very important weight, into whatever scale they throw themselves; but he thinks they will side with their masters. 5. The conquered Indians, cowardly, not likely to take any side, nor important which they take. 6. The free Indians, brave and formidable, should they interfere, but not likely to do so, as being at a great distance. I asked him the numbers of these several classes, but he could not give them. The first, he thought very inconsiderable; that the second formed the body of the freemen; the third equal to the two first; the fourth, to all the preceding; and, as to the fifth, he could form no idea of their proportion. Indeed, it appeared to me, that his conjectures as to the others, were on loose grounds. He said he knew from good information, there were three hundred thousand inhabitants in the city of Mexico. I was still more cautious with him than with the Brazilian, mentioning it as my private opinion (unauthorized to say a word on the subject otherwise) that a successful revolution was still at a distance with them; that I feared they must begin by enlightening and emancipating the minds of their people; that, as to us, if Spain should give us advantageous terms of commerce, and remove other difficulties, it was not probable that we should relinquish certain and present advantages, though smaller, for uncertain and future ones, however great. I was led into this caution by observing that this gentleman was intimate at the Spanish ambassador's, and that he was then at Paris, employed by Spain to settle her boundaries with France, on the Pyrenees. He had much the air of candor, but that can be borrowed; so that I was not able to decide about him in my own mind.

Led by a unity of subject, and a desire to give Congress as general a view of the disposition of our southern countrymen, as my information enables me, I will add an article which, old and insulated, I did not think important enough to mention at the time I received it. You will remember, Sir, that during the late war, the British papers often gave details of a rebellion in Peru. The character of those papers discredited the information. But the truth was, that the insurrections were so general, that the event was long on the poise. Had Commodore Johnson, then expected on that coast, touched and landed there two thousand men, the dominion of Spain in that country would have been at an end. They only wanted a point of union, which this body would have constituted. Not having this, they acted without concert, and were at length subdued separately. This conflagration was quenched in blood; two hundred thousand souls, on both sides, having perished; but the remaining matter is very capable of combustion. I have this information from a person who was on the spot at the time, and whose good faith, understanding, and means of information, leave no doubt of the facts. He observed, however, that the numbers above supposed to have perished, were on such conjectures only as he could collect.

I trouble Congress with these details, because, however distant we may be, both in condition and dispositions, from taking an active part in any commotions in that country, nature has placed it too near us, to make its movements altogether indifferent to our interests, or to our curiosity.

## On Doing Good

### TO MARTHA JEFFERSON.

MARSEILLES, *May 5, 1787.*

My Dear Patsy,
. . . When I left Paris I wrote to London to desire that your harpsichord might be sent during the months of April and May, so that I am in hopes it will arrive a little before I shall, and give me an opportunity of judging whether you have got the better of that want of industry which I began to fear would be the rock on which you would split. Determine never to be idle. No person will have occasion to complain of the want of time who never loses any. It is wonderful how much may be done if we are always doing. And that you may always be doing good, my dear, is the ardent prayer of, yours affectionately . . .

## Nightingales vs. Mocking-Birds

### TO MARTHA JEFFERSON.

*May 21, 1787.*

I write you, my dear Patsy, from the canal of Languedoc, on which I am at present sailing, as I have been for a week past, cloudless skies above, limpid waters below, and on each hand a row of nightingales in full chorus. . . . I think you told me that you had not yet noticed this bird. As you have trees in the garden of the convent, there might be nightingales in them, and this is the season of their song. Endeavor, my dear, to make yourself acquainted with the music of this bird, that when you return to your own country, you may be able to estimate its merit in comparison with that of the mocking-bird. The latter has the advantage of singing through a great part of the year, whereas the nightingale sings about five or six weeks in the spring, and a still shorter time, and with a more feeble voice, in the fall. . . .

# Walking Tour

## TO J. BANNISTER, JUNIOR.

PARIS, *June 19, 1787.*

I had a letter from Ledyard lately, dated at St. Petersburg. He had but two shirts, and yet more shirts than shillings. Still he was determined to obtain the palm of being the first circumambulator of the earth. He says, that having no money, they kick him from place to place, and thus he expects to be kicked round the globe. Are you become a great walker? You know I preach up that kind of exercise. Shall I send you a *conte-pas?* It will cost you a dozen louis, but be a great stimulus to walking, as it will record your steps. I finished my tour a week or ten days ago. I went as far as Turin, Milan, Genoa; and never passed three months and a half more delightfully. I returned through the canal of Languedoc, by Bordeaux, Nantes, L'Orient, and Rennes; then returned to Nantes and came up the Loire to Orleans. I was alone through the whole, and think one travels more usefully when alone, because he reflects more.

# Study of Languages

## TO T. M. RANDOLPH, JUNIOR.

PARIS, *July 6, 1787.*

DEAR SIR,—Your favor of April the 14th, came here during my absence on a journey through the southern parts of France and northern of Italy, from which I am but lately returned. This cause alone has prevented your receiving a more early answer to it. I am glad to find, that among the various branches of science presenting themselves to your mind, you have fixed on that of politics as your principal pursuit. Your country will derive from this a more immediate and sensible benefit. She has much for you to do. For, though we may say with confidence, that the worst of the American constitutions is better than the best which ever existed before, in any other country, and that they are wonderfully perfect for a first essay, yet every human essay must have defects. It will remain, therefore, to those now coming on the stage of public affairs, to perfect what has been so well begun by those going off it. Mathematics, Natural Philosophy, Natural History, Anatomy, Chemistry, Botany, will become amusements for your hours of relaxation, and auxiliaries to your principal studies. Precious and delightful ones they will be. As soon as such a foundation is laid in them, as you may build on as you please, hereafter, I suppose you will proceed to your main objects, Politics, Law, Rhetoric, and History. As to these, the place where you study them is absolutely indifferent. I should except Rhetoric, a very essential member of them, and which I suppose must be taught to advantage where you are. You would do well, therefore, to attend the public exercises in this branch also, and to do it with very particular diligence. This being done, the question arises, where you shall fix yourself for studying Politics, Law, and History? I should not hesitate to decide in favor of France, because you will, at the same time, be learning to speak the language of that country, become absolutely essential under our present circumstances.

The best method of doing this, would be to fix yourself in some family where there are women and children, in Passy, Auteuil, or some other of the little towns in reach of Paris. The principal hours of the day, you will attend to your studies, and in those of relaxation, associate with the family. You will learn to speak better from women and children in three months, than from men in a year. Such a situation, too, will render more easy a due attention to economy of time and money. Having pursued your main studies here, about two years, and acquired a facility in speaking French, take a tour of four or five months through this country and Italy, return then to Virginia, and pass a year in Williamsburg, under the care of Mr. Wythe; and you will be ready to enter on the public stage, with superior advantages. I have proposed to you, to carry on the study of the law with that of politics and history. Every political measure will, forever, have an intimate connection with the laws of the land; and he, who knows nothing of these, will always be perplexed, and often foiled by adversaries having the advantage of that knowledge over him. Besides, it is a source of infinite comfort to reflect, that under every chance of fortune, we have a resource in ourselves from which we may be able to derive an honorable subsistence. I would, therefore, propose not only the study, but the practice of the law for some time, to possess yourself of the habit of public speaking.

With respect to modern languages, French, as I have before observed, is indispensable. Next to this, the Spanish is most important to an American. Our connection with Spain is already important, and will become daily more so. Besides this, the ancient part of American history is written chiefly in Spanish.

## On Tree Crops

### TO WILLIAM DRAYTON.

PARIS, *July 30, 1787.*

I was induced, in the course of my journey through the south of France, to pay very particular attention to the objects of their culture, because the resemblance of their climate to that of the southern parts of the United States, authorizes us to presume we may adopt any of their articles of culture, which we would wish for. We should not wish for their wines, though they are good and abundant. The culture of the vine is not desirable in lands capable of producing anything else. It is a species of gambling, and of desperate gambling too, wherein, whether you make much or nothing, you are equally ruined. The middling crop alone is the saving point, and that the seasons seldom hit. Accordingly, we see much wretchedness among this class of cultivators. Wine, too, is so cheap in these countries, that a laborer with us, employed in the culture of any other article, may exchange it for wine, more and better than he could raise himself. It is a resource for a country, the whole of whose good soil is otherwise employed, and which still has some barren spots, and surplus of population to employ on them. There the vine is good, because it is something in the place of nothing. It may become a resource to us at a still earlier period; when the increase of population shall increase our productions beyond the demand for them, both at home and abroad. Instead of going on to make an useless surplus of them, we may employ our supernumerary hands on the vine. But that period is not yet arrived.

The almond tree is also so precarious, that none can depend for subsistence on its produce, but persons of capital.

The caper, though a more tender plant, is more certain in its produce, because a mound of earth of the size of a cucumber hill, thrown over the plant in the fall, protects it effectually against the cold of winter. When the danger of frost is over in the spring, they uncover it, and begin its culture. There is a great deal of this in the neighborhood of Toulon.

The fig and mulberry are so well known in America, that nothing need be said of them. . . .

The olive is a tree the least known in America, and yet the most worthy of being known. Of all the gifts of heaven to man, it is next to the most precious, if it be not the most precious. Perhaps it may claim a preference even to bread, because there is such an infinitude of vegetables, which it renders a proper and comfortable nourishment. In passing the Alps at the Col de Tende, where they are mere masses of rock, wherever there happens to be a little soil, there are a number of olive trees, and a village supported by them. Take away these trees, and the same ground in corn would not support a single family. A pound of oil, which can be bought for three or four pence sterling, is equivalent to many pounds of flesh, by the quantity of vegetables it will prepare, and render fit and comfortable food. Without this tree, the country of Provence and territory of Genoa would not support one-half, perhaps not one-third, their present inhabitants. The nature of the soil is of little consequence if it be dry. The trees are planted from fifteen to twenty feet apart, and when tolerably good, will yield fifteen or twenty pounds of oil yearly . . . This is an article, the consumption of which will always keep pace with its production. Raise it, and it begets its own demand. Little is carried to America, because Europe has it not to spare. We, therefore, have not learned the use of it. But cover the southern States with it, and every man will become a consumer of oil, within whose reach it can be brought in point of price. If the memory of other persons is held in great respect in South Carolina who introduced there the culture of rice, a plant which sows life and death with almost equal hand, what obligations would be due to him who should introduce the olive tree, and set the example of its culture! Were the owner of slaves to view it only as the means of bettering their condition, how much would he better that by planting one of those trees for every slave he possessed! Having been myself an eye witness to the blessings which this tree sheds on the poor, I never had my wishes so kindled for the introduction of any article of new culture into our own country. South Carolina and Georgia appear to me to be the States, wherein its success, in favorable positions at least, could not be doubted, and I flattered myself it would come within the views of the society for agriculture to begin the experiments which are to prove its practicability. Carcassonne is the place from which the plants may be most certainly and cheaply obtained. They can be sent from thence by water to Bordeaux, where they may be embarked on vessels bound for Charleston. There is too little intercourse between Charleston and Marseilles to propose this as the port of exportation. I offer my services to the society for the obtaining and forwarding any number of plants which may be desired. . . .

I had the honor of sending you, the last year, some seeds of the sulla of Malta, or Spanish St. Foin. Lest they should have miscarried, I now pack with the rice a canister of the same kind of seed, raised by myself. By Colonel Franks, in the month of February last, I sent a parcel of acorns of the cork oak, which I desired him to ask the favor of the Delegates of South Carolina in Congress to forward to you.

## On Monarchy

### TO DR. DAVID RAMSAY.

PARIS, *August 4, 1787.*

I am sensible that there are defects in our federal government, yet they are so much lighter than those of monarchies, that I view them with much indulgence. I rely, too, on the good sense of the people for remedy, whereas the evils of monarchical government are beyond remedy. If any of our countrymen wish for a King, give them Æsop's fable of the frogs who asked a King; if this does not cure them, send them to Europe. They will go back good republicans.

## Powers of Congress

### TO EDWARD CARRINGTON.

PARIS, *August 4, 1787.*

I am happy to find that the States have come so generally into the schemes of the federal convention, from which, I am sure, we shall see wise propositions. I confess, I do not go as far in the reforms thought necessary, as some of my correspondents in America; but if the convention should adopt such propositions, I shall suppose them necessary. My general plan would be, to make the States one as to everything connected with foreign nations, and several as to everything purely domestic. But with all the imperfections of our present government, it is without comparison the best existing, or that ever did exist. Its greatest defect is the imperfect manner in which matters of commerce have been provided for. It has been so often said, as to be generally believed, that Congress have no power by the Confederation to enforce anything; for example, contributions of money. It was not necessary to give them that power expressly; they have it by the law of nature. When two parties make a compact, there results to each a power of compelling the other to execute it. Compulsion was never so easy as in our case, where a single frigate would soon levy on the commerce of any State the deficiency of its contributions; nor more safe than in the hands of Congress, which has always shown that it would wait, as it ought to do, to the last extremities, before it would execute any of its powers which are disagreeable. I think it very material, to separate, in the hands of Congress, the executive and legislative powers, as the judiciary already are, in some degree. This, I hope, will be done. The want of it has been the source of more evil than we have experienced from any other cause. Nothing is so embarrassing nor so mischievous, in a great assembly, as the details of execution. The smallest trifle of that kind occupies as long as the most important act of legislation, and takes place of everything else. Let any man recollect, or look over, the files of Congress; he will observe the most important propositions hanging over, from week to week, and month to month, till the occasions have passed them, and the things never done. I have ever viewed the executive details as the greatest cause of evil to us, because they in fact place us as if we had no federal head, by diverting the attention of that head from great to small subjects; and should this division of power not be recommended by the convention, it is my opinion Congress should make it itself, by establishing an executive committee.

## On a Liberal Education

### TO PETER CARR.

Paris, *August 10, 1787.*

Dear Peter,—I have received your two letters of December the 30th and April the 18th, and am very happy to find by them, as well as by letters from Mr. Wythe, that you have been so fortunate as to attract his notice and good will; I am sure you will find this to have been one of the most fortunate events of your life, as I have ever been sensible it was of mine. I enclose you a sketch of the sciences to which I would wish you to apply, in such order as Mr. Wythe shall advise; I mention, also, the books in them worth your reading, which submit to his correction. Many of these are among your father's books, which you should have brought to you. As I do not recollect those of them not in his library, you must write to me for them, making out a catalogue of such as you think you shall have occasion for, in eighteen months from the date of your letter, and consulting Mr. Wythe on the subject. To this sketch, I will add a few particular observations:

1. Italian. I fear the learning this language will confound your French and Spanish. Being all of them degenerated dialects of the Latin, they are apt to mix in conversation. I have never seen a person speaking the three languages, who did not mix them. It is a delightful language, but late events having rendered the Spanish more useful, lay it aside to prosecute that.

2. Spanish. Bestow great attention on this, and endeavor to acquire an accurate knowledge of it. Our future connections with Spain and Spanish America, will render that language a valuable acquisition. The ancient history of that part of America, too, is written in that language. I send you a dictionary.

3. Moral Philosophy. I think it lost time to attend lectures on this branch. He who made us would have been a pitiful bungler, if he had made the rules of our moral conduct a matter of science. For one man of science, there are thousands who are not. What would have become of them? Man was destined for society. His morality, therefore, was to be formed to this object. He was endowed with a sense of right and wrong, merely relative to this. This sense is as much a part of his nature, as the sense of hearing, seeing, feeling; it is the true foundation of morality, and not the το καλον, truth, &c., as fanciful writers have imagined. The moral sense, or conscience, is as much a part of man as his leg or arm. It is given to all human beings in a stronger or weaker degree, as force of members is given them in a greater or less degree. It may be strengthened by exercise, as may any particular limb of the body. This sense is submitted, indeed, in some degree, to the guidance of reason; but it is a small stock which is required for this: even a less one than what we call common sense. State a moral case to a ploughman and a professor. The former will decide it as well, and often better than the latter, because he has not been led astray by artificial rules. In this branch, therefore, read good books, because they will encourage, as well as direct your feelings. The writings of Sterne, particularly, form the best course of morality that ever was written. Besides these, read the books mentioned in the enclosed paper; and, above all things, lose no occasion of exercising your dispositions to be grateful, to be generous, to be charitable, to be humane, to be true, just, firm, orderly, courageous, &c. Consider every act of this kind, as an exercise which will strengthen your moral faculties and increase your worth.

4. Religion. Your reason is now mature enough to examine this object. In the first place, divest yourself of all bias in favor of novelty and singularity of opinion. Indulge them in any other subject rather than that of

religion. It is too important, and the consequences of error may be too serious. On the other hand, shake off all the fears and servile prejudices, under which weak minds are servilely crouched. Fix reason firmly in her seat, and call to her tribunal every fact, every opinion. Question with boldness even the existence of a God; because, if there be one, he must more approve of the homage of reason, than that of blindfolded fear. You will naturally examine first, the religion of your own country. Read the Bible, then, as you would read Livy or Tacitus. The facts which are within the ordinary course of nature, you will believe on the authority of the writer, as you do those of the same kind in Livy and Tacitus. The testimony of the writer weighs in their favor, in one scale, and their not being against the laws of nature, does not weigh against them. But those facts in the Bible which contradict the laws of nature, must be examined with more care, and under a variety of faces. Here you must recur to the pretensions of the writer to inspiration from God. Examine upon what evidence his pretensions are founded, and whether that evidence is so strong, as that its falsehood would be more improbable than a change in the laws of nature, in the case he relates. For example, in the book of Joshua, we are told, the sun stood still several hours. Were we to read that fact in Livy or Tacitus, we should class it with their showers of blood, speaking of statues, beasts, etc. But it is said, that the writer of that book was inspired. Examine, therefore, candidly, what evidence there is of his having been inspired. The pretension is entitled to your inquiry, because millions believe it. On the other hand, you are astronomer enough to know how contrary it is to the law of nature that a body revolving on its axis, as the earth does, should have stopped, should not, by that sudden stoppage, have prostrated animals, trees, buildings, and should after a certain time have resumed its revolution, and that without a second general prostration. Is this arrest of the earth's motion, or the evidence which affirms it, most within the law of probabilities? You will next read the New Testament. It is the history of a personage called Jesus. Keep in your eye the opposite pretensions: 1, of those who say he was begotten by God, born of a virgin, suspended and reversed the laws of nature at will, and ascended bodily into heaven; and 2, of those who say he was a man of illegitimate birth, of a benevolent heart, enthusiastic mind, who set out without pretensions to divinity, ended in believing them, and was punished capitally for sedition, by being gibbeted, according to the Roman law, which punished the first commission of that offence by whipping, and the second by exile, or death *in furea*. See this law in the Digest, Lib. 48. tit. 19. § 28. 3. and Lipsius Lib. 2. de cruce. cap. 2. These questions are examined in the books I have mentioned, under the head of Religion, and several others. They will assist you in your inquiries; but keep your reason firmly on the watch in reading them all. Do not be frightened from this inquiry by any fear of its consequences. If it ends in a belief that there is no God, you will find incitements to virtue in the comfort and pleasantness you feel in its exercise, and the love of others which it will procure you. If you find reason to believe there is a God, a consciousness that you are acting under his eye, and that he approves you, will be a vast additional incitement; if that there be a future state, the hope of a happy existence in that increases the appetite to deserve it; if that Jesus was also a God, you will be comforted by a belief of his aid and love. In fine, I repeat, you must lay aside all prejudice on both sides, and neither believe nor reject anything, because any other persons, or description of persons, have rejected or believed it. Your own reason is the only oracle given you by heaven, and you are answerable, not for the rightness, but uprightness of the decision. I forgot to observe, when speaking of the New Testament, that you should read all the histories of Christ, as well of those whom a council of ecclesiastics have decided for us, to be Pseudo-evangelists, as those they named Evangelists. Because these Pseudo-evangelists pretended to inspiration, as much as the others, and you are to judge their pretensions by your own reason, and not by the reason of those ecclesiastics. Most of these are lost. There are some, however, still extant, collected by Fabricius, which I will endeavor to get and send you.

5. Travelling. This makes men wiser, but less happy. When men of sober age travel, they gather knowledge, which they may apply usefully for their country; but they are subject ever after to recollections mixed with regret; their affections are weakened by being extended over more objects; and they learn new habits which cannot be gratified when they return home. Young men, who travel, are exposed to all these inconveniences in a higher degree, to others still more serious, and do not acquire that wisdom for which a previous foundation is requisite, by repeated and just observations at home. The glare of pomp and pleasure is analogous to the motion of the blood; it absorbs all their affection and attention, they are torn from it as from the only good in this world, and return to their home as to a place of exile and condemnation. Their eyes are forever turned back to the object they have lost, and its recollection poisons the residue of their lives. Their first and most delicate passions are hackneyed on unworthy objects here, and they carry home the dregs, insufficient to make themselves or anybody else happy. Add to this, that a habit of idleness, an inability to apply themselves to business is acquired, and renders them useless to themselves and their country. These observations are founded in experience. There is no place where your pursuit of knowledge will be so little obstructed by foreign objects, as in your own country, nor any, wherein the virtues of the heart will be less exposed to be weakened. Be good, be learned, and be industrious, and you will not want the aid of travelling, to render you precious to your country, dear to your friends, happy within yourself. I repeat my advice, to take a great deal of exercise, and on foot. Health is the first requisite after morality. Write to me often, and be assured of the interest I take in your success, as well as the warmth of those sentiments of attachment with which I am, dear Peter, your affectionate friend.

# Life Preserver

## TO THE REVEREND JAMES MADISON.

PARIS, *August 13, 1787.*

The genius of invention and improvement in Europe seems to be absolutely taking a nap. We have nothing to communicate to you but of the small kind, such as making the axletree turn with the wheel, which has been proposed here, adopted by some, and thought to be proved best by experiment, though theory has nothing to urge in its favor. A hydrostatic waistcoat is lately announced, which a person puts on either above or below his clothes in a minute, and fills with air by blowing with the mouth in twelve seconds. It is not yet shown, however, so I cannot tell you either the manner or matter of its construction. It may be useful when the loss of a vessel is foreseen.

# On Statuary

## TO GENERAL WASHINGTON.

PARIS, *August 14, 1787.*

DEAR SIR,—I am happy to find, by the letter of August the 1st, 1786, which you did me the honor to write to me, that the modern dress for your statue would meet your approbation. I found it strongly the sentiment of West, Copley, Trumbull, and Brown, in London; after which, it would be ridiculous to add, that it was my own. I think a modern in an antique dress as just an object of ridicule as a Hercules or Marius with a periwig and a chapeau bras.

# Constitutional Convention

## TO MONSIEUR DUMAS.

PARIS, *September 10, 1787.*

Our Federal Convention is likely to sit till October; there is a general disposition through the States to adopt what they shall propose, and we may be assured their propositions will be wise, as a more able assembly never sat in America. Happily for us, that when we find our constitutions defective and insufficient to secure the happiness of our people, we can assemble with all the coolness of philosophers, and set it to rights, while every other nation on earth must have recourse to arms to amend or to restore their constitutions.

# World Politics

## TO MR. GEORGE WYTHE.

PARIS, *Sept. 16, 1787.*

This world is going all to war. I hope ours will remain clear of it. It is already declared between the Turks and Russians, and considering the present situation of Holland, it cannot fail to spread itself all over Europe. Perhaps it may not be till next spring, that the other powers will be engaged in it: nor is it as yet clear how they will arrange themselves. . . .

You ask me in your letter, what ameliorations I think necessary in our federal constitution. It is now too late to answer the question, and it would always have been presumption in me to have done it. Your own ideas, and those of the great characters who were to be concerned with you in these discussions, will give the law, as they ought to do, to us all. My own general idea was, that the States should severally preserve their sovereignty in whatever concerns themselves alone, and that whatever may concern another State, or any foreign nation, should be made a part of the federal sovereignty; that the exercise of the federal sovereignty should be divided among three several bodies, legislative, executive, and judiciary, as the State sovereignties are; and that some peaceable means should be contrived, for the federal head to force compliance on the part of the States.

# Indian Migration

## TO CHARLES THOMSON.

PARIS, *Sept. 20, 1787.*

I thank you for the extract of the letter you were so kind as to communicate to me, on the antiquities found in the western country. I wish that the persons who go thither would make very exact descriptions of what they see of that kind, without forming any theories. The moment a person forms a theory, his imagination sees, in every object, only the traits which favor that theory. But it is too early to form theories on those antiquities. We must wait with patience till more facts are collected. I wish your Philosophical Society would collect exact descriptions of the several monuments as yet known, and insert them naked in their Transactions, and continue their attention to those hereafter to be discovered. Patience and observation may enable us in time, to solve the problem, whether those who formed the scattering monuments in our western country, were colonies sent off from Mexico, or the founders of Mexico itself? Whether both were the descendants or the progenitors of the Asiatic red men?

I remember you asked me, in a former letter, whether the steam mill in London was turned by the steam immediately, or by the intermediate agency of water raised by the steam. When I was in London, Boulton made a secret of his mill. Therefore, I was permitted to see it only superficially. I saw no water wheels, and, therefore, supposed none. I answered you, accordingly, that there were none. But when I was at Nismes, I went to see the steam mill there, and they showed it to me in all the parts. I saw that their steam raised water, and that this water turned a wheel. I expressed my doubts of the necessity of the inter-agency of water, and that the London mill was without it. But they supposed me mistaken; perhaps I was so; I have had no opportunity since of clearing up the doubt.

## English Manners

### TO COLONEL SMITH.

PARIS, *September 28, 1787.*

I really think, and had taken the liberty some time ago of hinting to Congress, that they would do well to have a diplomatic character at Lisbon. There is no country whose commerce is more interesting to us. I wish Congress would correspond to the wishes of that court, in sending a person there, and to mine, in sending yourself. For I confess, I had rather see you there than at London, because I doubt whether it be honorable for us to keep anybody at London, unless they keep some person at New York. Of all nations on earth, they require to be treated with the most hauteur. They require to be kicked into common good manners.

## Here Is a Moose

### TO MONSIEUR LE COMTE DE BUFFON.

PARIS, *October 3, 1787.*

SIR,—I had the honor of informing you, some time ago, that I had written to some of my friends in America, desiring they would send me such of the spoils of the moose, caribou, elk and deer, as might throw light on that class of animals; but more particularly, to send me the complete skeleton, skin and horns of the moose, in such condition as that the skin might be sewed up and stuffed, on its arrival here. I am happy to be able to present to you at this moment, the bones and skin of a moose, the horns of another individual of the same species, the horns of the caribou, the elk, the deer, the spiked horned buck, and the roebuck of America. They all come from New Hampshire and Massachusetts and were received by me yesterday. I give you their popular names, as it rests with yourself to decide their real names. The skin of the moose was dressed with the hair on, but a great deal of it has come off, and the rest is ready to drop off. The horns of the elk are remarkably small. I have certainly seen some of them which would have weighed five or six times as much. . . . I must observe also, that the horns of the deer, which accompany these spoils, are not of the fifth or sixth part of the weight of some that I have seen. This individual has been of three years of age, according to our method of judging. I have taken measures, particularly, to be furnished with large horns of our elk and our deer, and therefore beg of you not to consider those now sent, as furnishing a specimen of their ordinary size. I really suspect you will find that the moose, the round-horned elk, and the American deer, are species not existing in Europe. The moose is, perhaps, of a new class.

# Tree of Liberty

## TO COLONEL SMITH.

PARIS, *November 13, 1787.*

I do not know whether it is to yourself or Mr. Adams, I am to give my thanks for the copy of the new constitution. I beg leave through you to place them where due. It will yet be three weeks before I shall receive them from America. There are very good articles in it, and very bad. I do not know which preponderate. What we have lately read, in the history of Holland, in the chapter on the Stadtholder, would have sufficed to set me against a chief magistrate, eligible for a long duration, if I had ever been disposed towards one; and what we have always read of the elections of Polish Kings should have forever excluded the idea of one continuable for life. Wonderful is the effect of impudent and persevering lying. The British ministry have so long hired their gazetteers to repeat, and model into every form, lies about our being in anarchy, that the world has at length believed them, the English nation has believed them, the ministers themselves have come to believe them, and what is more wonderful, we have believed them ourselves. Yet where does this anarchy exist? Where did it ever exist, except in the single instance of Massachusetts? And can history produce an instance of rebellion so honorably conducted? I say nothing of its motives. They were founded in ignorance, not wickedness. God forbid we should ever be twenty years without such a rebellion. The people cannot be all, and always, well informed. The part which is wrong will be discontented, in proportion to the importance of the facts they misconceive. If they remain quiet under such misconceptions, it is a lethargy, the forerunner of death to the public liberty. We have had thirteen States independent for eleven years. There has been one rebellion. That comes to one rebellion in a century and a half, for each State. What country before, ever existed a century and a half without a rebellion? And what country can preserve its liberties, if its rulers are not warned from time to time, that this people preserve the spirit of resistance? Let them take arms. The remedy is to set them right as to facts, pardon and pacify them. What signify a few lives lost in a century or two? The tree of liberty must be refreshed from time to time, with the blood of patriots and tyrants. It is its natural manure. Our convention has been too much impressed by the insurrection of Massachusetts; and on the spur of the moment, they are setting up a kite to keep the hen yard in order. I hope in God, this article will be rectified before the new constitution is accepted. You ask me if anything transpires here on the subject of South America? Not a word. I know that there are combustible materials there, and that they wait the torch only.

## New Constitution

### TO WILLIAM CARMICHAEL.

Paris, *December 11, 1787.*

Our new Constitution is powerfully attacked in the American newspapers. The objections are, that its effect would be to form the thirteen States into one; that, proposing to melt all down into one general government, they have fenced the people by no declaration of rights; they have not renounced the power of keeping a standing army; they have not secured the liberty of the press; they have reserved the power of abolishing trials by jury in civil cases; they have proposed that the laws of the federal legislatures shall be paramount to the laws and constitutions of the States; they have abandoned rotation in office; and particularly, their President may be re-elected from four years to four years, for life, so as to render him a King for life, like a King of Poland; and they have not given him either the check or aid of a council. To these they add calculations of expense, etc., etc., to frighten the people. You will perceive that these objections are serious, and some of them not without foundation. The Constitution, however, has been received with a very general enthusiasm. . . .

I have been told, that the cutting through the Isthmus of Panama, which the world has so often wished, and supposed practicable, has at times been thought of by the government of Spain, and that they once proceeded so far, as to have a survey and examination made of the ground; but that the result was, either impracticability or too great difficulty. Probably the Count de Campomanes, or Don Ulloa, can give you information on this head. I should be exceedingly pleased to get as minute details as possible on it, and even copies of the survey, report, etc., if they could be obtained at a moderate expense. I take the liberty of asking your assistance in this.

# Bill of Rights

TO JAMES MADISON.

PARIS, *December 20, 1787.*

I like much the general idea of framing a government, which should go on of itself, peaceably, without needing continual recurrence to the State legislatures. I like the organization of the government into legislative, judiciary and executive. I like the power given the legislature to levy taxes, and for that reason solely, I approve of the greater House being chosen by the people directly. For though I think a House so chosen, will be very far inferior to the present Congress, will be very illy qualified to legislate for the Union, for foreign nations, etc., yet this evil does not weigh against the good, of preserving inviolate the fundamental principle, that the people are not to be taxed but by representatives chosen immediately by themselves. I am captivated by the compromise of the opposite claims of the great and little States, of the latter to equal, and the former to proportional influence. I am much pleased, too, with the substitution of the method of voting by person, instead of that of voting by States; and I like the negative given to the Executive, conjointly with a third of either House; though I should have liked it better, had the judiciary been associated for that purpose, or invested separately with a similar power. There are other good things of less moment. I will now tell you what I do not like. First, the omission of a bill of rights, providing clearly, and without the aid of sophism, for freedom of religion, freedom of the press, protection against standing armies, restriction of monopolies, the eternal and unremitting force of the habeas corpus laws, and trials by jury in all matters of fact triable by the laws of the land, and not by the laws of nations. . . .

The second feature I dislike, and strongly dislike, is the abandonment, in every instance, of the principle of rotation in office, and most particularly in the case of the President. Reason and experience tell us, that the first magistrate will always be re-elected if he may be re-elected. He is then an officer for life. This once observed, it becomes of so much consequence to certain nations, to have a friend or a foe at the head of our affairs, that they will interfere with money and with arms. A Galloman, or an Angloman, will be supported by the nation he befriends. If once elected, and at a second or third election outvoted by one or two votes, he will pretend false votes, foul play, hold possession of the reins of government, be supported by the States voting for him, especially if they be the central ones, lying in a compact body themselves, and separating their opponents; and they will be aided by one nation in Europe, while the majority are aided by another. The election of a President of America, some years hence, will be much more interesting to certain nations of Europe, than ever the election of a King of Poland was. . . . Smaller objections are, the appeals on matters of fact as well as laws; and the binding all persons, legislative, executive, and judiciary by oath, to maintain that constitution. I do not pretend to decide, what would be the best method of procuring the establishment of the manifold good things in this constitution, and of getting rid of the bad. Whether by adopting it, in hopes of future amendment; or after it shall have been duly weighed and canvassed by the people, after seeing the parts they generally dislike, and those they generally approve, to say to them, "We see now what you wish. You are willing to give to your federal government such and such powers; but you wish, at the same time, to have such and such fundamental rights secured to you, and certain sources of convulsion taken away. Be it so. Send together deputies again. Let them establish your fundamental rights by a sacrosanct declaration, and let them pass the parts of the Constitution you have approved. These will give powers to your federal government sufficient for your happiness."

This is what might be said, and would probably produce a speedy, more perfect and more permanent form of government. At all events, I hope you will not be discouraged from making other trials, if the present one should fail. We are never permitted to despair of the commonwealth. I have thus told you freely what I like, and what I dislike, merely as a matter of curiosity; for I know it is not in my power to offer matter of information to your judgment, which has been formed after hearing and weighing everything which the wisdom of man could offer on these subjects. I own, I am not a friend to a very energetic government. It is always oppressive. It places the governors indeed more at their ease, at the expense of the people. The late rebellion in Massachusetts has given more alarm, than I think it should have done. Calculate that one rebellion in thirteen States in the course of eleven years, is but one for each State in a century and a half. No country should be so long without one. Nor will any degree of power in the hands of government, prevent insurrections. . . . And say, finally, whether peace is best preserved by giving energy to the government, or information to the people. This last is the most certain, and the most legitimate engine of government. Educate and inform the whole mass of the people. Enable them to see that it is their interest to preserve peace and order, and they will preserve them. And it requires no very high degree of education to convince them of this. They are the only sure reliance for the preservation of our liberty. After all, it is my principle that the will of the majority should prevail. If they approve the proposed constitution in all its parts, I shall concur in it cheerfully, in hopes they will amend it, whenever they shall find it works wrong. This reliance cannot deceive us, as long as we remain virtuous; and I think we shall be so, as long as agriculture is our principal object, which will be the case, while there remain vacant lands in any part of America. When we get piled upon one another in large cities, as in Europe, we shall become corrupt as in Europe, and go to eating one another as they do there.

# Ratification

## TO MR. WILLIAM RUTLEDGE.

PARIS, *Feb. 2, 1788.*

I am glad to hear that our new Constitution is pretty sure of being accepted by States enough to secure the good it contains, and to meet with such opposition in some others, as to give us hopes it will be accommodated to them, by the amendment of its most glaring faults, particularly the want of a declaration of rights.

# Abolition

## TO MR. WARVILLE.

PARIS, *February 12, 1788.*

SIR,—I am very sensible of the honor you propose to me, of becoming a member of the society for the abolition of the slave trade. You know that nobody wishes more ardently to see an abolition, not only of the trade, but of the condition of slavery; and certainly, nobody will be more willing to encounter every sacrifice for that object. But the influence and information of the friends to this proposition in France will be far above the need of my association. I am here as a public servant, and those whom I serve, having never yet been able to give their voice against the practice, it is decent for me to avoid too public a demonstration of my wishes to see it abolished. Without serving the cause here, it might render me less able to serve it beyond the water. I trust you will be sensible of the prudence of those motives, therefore, which govern my conduct on this occasion, and be assured of my wishes for the success of your undertaking, and the sentiments of esteem and respect, with which I have the honor to be, Sir, your most obedient humble servant.

# American Admiral

## TO GENERAL WASHINGTON.

PARIS, *May 2, 1788.*

The war between the Russians and Turks, has made an opening for our Commodore Paul Jones. The Empress has invited him into her service. She insures to him the rank of rear admiral; will give him a separate command, and, it is understood, that he is never to be commanded. I think she means to oppose him to the Captain Pacha, on the Black Sea. He is by this time, probably, at St. Petersburg. The circumstances did not permit his await-ing the permission of Congress, because the season was close at hand for opening the campaign. But he has made it a condition, that he shall be free at all times to return to the orders of Congress, whenever they shall please to call for him; and also, that he shall not in any case be expected to bear arms against France. I believe Congress had it in contemplation, to give him the grade of admiral, from the date of his taking the Serapis. Such a measure now would greatly gratify him, second the efforts of fortune in his favor, and better the opportunities of improving him for our service, whenever the moment shall come in which we may want him.

I had intended to have written a word to your Excellency on the subject of the new Constitution, but I have already spun out my letter to an im-moderate length. I will just observe, therefore, that according to my ideas, there is a great deal of good in it. There are two things, however, which I dislike strongly. 1. The want of a declaration of rights. I am in hopes the opposition of Virginia will remedy this, and produce such a declaration. 2. The perpetual re-eligibility of the President. This, I fear, will make that an office for life, first, and then hereditary. I was much an enemy to mon-archies before I came to Europe. I am ten thousand times more so, since I have seen what they are. There is scarcely an evil known in these coun-tries, which may not be traced to their king, as its source, nor a good, which is not derived from the small fibres of republicanism existing among them. I can further say, with safety, there is not a crowned head in Europe, whose talents or merits would entitle him to be elected a vestryman, by the people of any parish in America. However, I shall hope, that before there is danger of this change taking place in the office of President, the good sense and free spirit of our countrymen, will makes the changes necessary to prevent it.

## New Pedometer

### TO MR. JAMES MADISON.

PARIS, *May 3, 1788.*

You remember the report, drawn by Governor Randolph, on the naviga-tion of the Mississippi. When I came to Europe, Mr. Thompson was so kind as to have me a copy of it made out. I lent it to Dr. Franklin, and he mislaid it, so that it could never be found. Could you make interest with him to have me another copy made, and send it to me? By Mr. Warville I send your pedometer. To the loop at the bottom of it, you must sew a tape, and at the other end of the tape, a small hook, (such as we use under the name of hooks and eyes) cut a little hole in the bottom of your left watch pocket, pass the hook and tape through it, and down between the breeches and drawers, and fix the hook on the edge of your knee band, an inch from the knee buckle; then hook the instrument itself by its swivel hook, on the upper edge of the watch pocket. Your tape being well adjusted in length, your double steps will be exactly counted by the instrument, the shortest hand pointing out the thousands, the flat hand the hundreds, and the long hand the tens and units. Never turn the hands backward; indeed, it is best not to set them to any given place, but to note the number they stand at when you begin to walk. The adjusting the tape to its exact length is a critical business, and will cost you many trials. But once done, it is done for ever. The best way is, to have a small buckle fixed on the middle of the tape, by which you can take it up, and let it out at pleasure. When you choose it should cease to count, unhook it from the top of the watch pocket, and let it fall down to the bottom of the pocket.

## Pirate Claims

### TO JOHN JAY.

PARIS, *May 4, 1788.*

I had taken measures to have it believed at Algiers, that our government withdrew its attention from our captives there. This was to prepare their captors for the ransoming them at a reasonable price. I find, however, that Captain O'Bryan is apprized that I have received some authority on this subject. He writes me a cruel letter, supposing me the obstacle to their redemption. Their own interest requires that I should leave them to think thus hardly of me. Were the views of government communicated to them, they could not keep their own secret, and such a price would be demanded for them, as Congress, probably, would think ought not to be given, lest it should be the cause of involving thousands of others of their citizens in the same condition. The moment I have money, the business shall be set in motion. . . .

This country still pursues its line of peace. The ministry seem now all united in it; some from a belief of their inability to carry on a war; others from a desire to arrange their internal affairs, and improve their constitution. The differences between the King and parliaments, threaten a serious issue. Many symptoms indicate that the government has in contemplation some act of high-handed authority. An extra number of printers have, for several days, been employed, the apartment wherein they are at work being surrounded by a body of guards, who permit nobody either to come out or go in. The commanders of the provinces, civil and military, have been ordered to be at their stations on a certain day of the ensuing week. They are accordingly gone; so that the will of the King is probably to be announced through the whole kingdom, on the same day. The parliament of Paris, apprehending that some innovation is to be attempted, which may take from them the opportunity of deciding on it after it shall be made known, came last night to the resolution, of which I have the honor to enclose you a manuscript copy. This you will perceive to be, in effect, a declaration of rights.

## Santee Project

### TO MONSIEUR TERRASSON.

PARIS, *May* 7, *1788.*

SIR,—I have read with attention the papers on the subject of the canal of the Santee and Cooper rivers, and shall be glad to do anything I can to promote it. But I confess I have small expectations for the following reason: General Washington sent me a copy of the Virginia act for opening the Potomac. As that canal was to unite the commerce of the whole western country almost, with the eastern, it presented a great view. The General detailed the advantages of it, and it had the weight of his name, and was known to be under his immediate direction. It was pushed here among the monied men to obtain subscriptions, but not a single one could be obtained. The stockjobbing in this city offered greater advantages than to buy shares in the canal. I tried whether they would lend money on the security of the canal, but they answered they could get as good an interest by lending to their own government, with a douceur in the outset, and would have their money under their own eye, more at their command, and more sure as to the payment of interest. However, if you find any opening, and can point out to me how I may be useful in promoting it, I shall do it with infinite pleasure.

## Home Affairs

### TO WILLIAM CARMICHAEL.

PARIS, *May* 27, *1788.*

The conduct of Massachusetts has been noble. She accepted the constitution, but voted that it should stand as a perpetual instruction to her Delegates, to endeavor to obtain such and such reformations; and the minority, though very strong both in numbers and abilities, declared *viritim* and *seriatim,* that acknowledging the principle that the majority must give the law, they would now support the new constitution with their tongues, and with their blood, if necessary. I was much pleased with many and essential parts of this instrument, from the beginning. But I thought I saw in it many faults, great and small. What I have read and reflected has brought me over from several of my objections of the first moment, and to acquiesce under some others. Two only remain, of essential consideration, to wit, the want of a bill of rights, and the expunging the principle of necessary rotation in the offices of President and Senator. At first, I wished that when nine States should have accepted the constitution, so as to insure us what is good in it, the other four might hold off till the want of the bill of rights, at least, might be supplied. But I am now convinced that the plan of Massachusetts is the best, that is, to accept, and to amend afterwards.

. . . There is no doubt that General Washington will accept the presidentship; though he is silent on the subject. He would not be chosen to the Virginia convention. A riot has taken place in New York, which I will state to you from an eye witness. It has long been a practice with the surgeons of that city, to steal from the grave bodies recently buried. A citizen had lost his wife: he went the first or second evening after her burial, to pay a visit to her grave. He found that it had been disturbed, and suspected from what quarter. He found means to be admitted to the anatomical lecture of that day, and on his entering the room, saw the body of his wife, naked and under dissection. He raised the people immediately. The body, in the meantime, was secreted. They entered into, and searched the houses of the physicians whom they most suspected, but found nothing. One of them, however, more guilty or more timid than the rest, took asylum in the prison. The mob considered this an acknowledgment of guilt. They attacked the prison. The Governor ordered militia to protect the culprit, and suppress the mob. The militia, thinking the mob had just provocation, refused to turn out. Hereupon the people of more reflection, thinking it more dangerous that even a guilty person should be punished without the forms of law, than that he should escape, armed themselves, and went to protect the physician. They were received by the mob with a volley of stones, which wounded several of them. They hereupon fired on the mob, and killed four. By this time, they received a reinforcement of other citizens of the militia horse, the appearance of which, in the critical moment, dispersed the mob. So ended this chapter of history, which I have detailed to you, because it may be represented as a political riot, when politics had nothing to do with it. Mr. Jay and Baron Steuben were both grievously wounded in the head by stones. The former still kept his bed, and the latter his room, when the packet sailed, which was the 24th of April.

## The States Accept

### TO T. LEE SHIPPEN, ESQ.

PARIS, *June 19, 1788.*

General Washington writes me word he thinks Virginia will accept of the new Constitution. It appears to me, in fact, from all information, that its rejection would drive the States to despair and bring on events which cannot be foreseen; and that its adoption is become absolutely necessary. It will be easier to get the assent of nine States to correct what is wrong in the way pointed out by the Constitution itself, than to get thirteen to concur in a new convention and another plan of confederation. I therefore sincerely pray that the remaining States may accept it, as Massachusetts has done, with standing instructions to their delegates to press for amendments till they are obtained. They cannot fail of being obtained when the delegates of eight States shall be under such perpetual instructions.

. . . Mr. Barlow, the American poet, is arrived in Paris.

## On the War in Virginia

### TO DOCTOR GORDON.

PARIS, *July 16, 1788.*

You ask, in your letter of April the 24th, details of my sufferings by Colonel Tarleton. I did not suffer by him. On the contrary, he behaved very genteelly with me. On his approach to Charlottesville, which is within three miles of my house at Monticello, he despatched a troop of his horse, under Captain McLeod, with the double object of taking me prisoner, with the two Speakers of the Senate and Delegates, who then lodged with me, and of remaining there in *vidette*, my house commanding a view of ten or twelve miles round about. He gave strict orders to Captain McLeod to suffer nothing to be injured. The troop failed in one of their objects, as we had notice of their coming, so that the two Speakers had gone off about two hours before their arrival at Monticello, and myself, with my family, about five minutes. But Captain McLeod preserved everything with sacred care, during about eighteen hours that he remained there. Colonel Tarleton was just so long at Charlottesville, being hurried from thence by the news of the rising of the militia, and by a sudden fall of rain, which threatened to swell the river, and intercept his return. In general, he did little injury to the inhabitants, on that short and hasty excursion, which was of about sixty miles from their main army, then in Spottsylvania; and ours in Orange. It was early in June, 1781. Lord Cornwallis then proceeded to the Point of Fork, and encamped his army from thence all along the main James River, to a seat of mine called Elk-hill, opposite to Elk Island, and a little below the mouth of the Byrd Creek. (You will see all these places exactly laid down in the map annexed to my notes on Virginia, printed by Stockdale.) He remained in this position ten days, his own head quarters being in my house, at that place. I had time to remove most of the effects out of the house. He destroyed all my growing crops of corn and tobacco; he burned all my barns, containing the same articles of the last year, having first taken what corn he wanted; he used, as was to be expected, all my stock of cattle, sheep and hogs, for the sustenance of his army, and carried off all the horses capable of service; of those too young for service he cut the throats; and he burned all the fences on the plantation, so as to leave it an absolute waste. He carried off also about thirty slaves. Had this been to give them freedom, he would have done right; but it was to consign them to inevitable death from the small pox and putrid fever, then raging in his camp. This I knew afterwards to be the fate of twenty-seven of them. I never had news of the remaining three, but presume they shared the same fate. When I say that Lord Cornwallis did all this, I do not mean that he carried about the torch in his own hands, but that it was all done under his eye; the situation of the house in which he was, commanding a view of every part of the plantation, so that he must have seen every fire. I relate these things on my own knowledge, in a great degree, as I was on the ground soon after he left it. He treated the rest of the neighborhood somewhat in the same style, but not with that spirit of total extermination with which he seemed to rage over my possessions. Wherever he went, the dwelling houses were plundered of everything which could be carried off. Lord Cornwallis' character in England, would forbid the belief that he shared in the plunder; but that his table was served with the plate thus pillaged from private houses, can be proved by many hundred eye-witnesses. From an estimate I made at that time, on the best information I could collect, I supposed the State of Virginia lost, under Lord Cornwallis' hands, that year, about thirty thousand slaves; and that of these, about twenty-seven thousand died of the small pox and camp fever, and the rest were partly sent to the West Indies, and exchanged for rum, sugar, coffee and fruit, and partly sent to New York, from whence they went, at the peace, either to Nova Scotia or England. From this last place, I believe they have been lately sent to Africa. History will never relate the horrors committed by the British army in the *southern* States of America. They raged in Virginia six months only, from the middle of April to the middle of October, 1781, when they were all taken prisoners; and I give you a faithful specimen of their transactions for ten days of that time, and on one spot only. *Ex pede Herculem.* I suppose their whole devastations during those six months, amounted to about three millions sterling. The copiousness of this subject has only left me space to assure you of the sentiments of esteem and respect, with which I am, Sir, your most obedient humble servant.

## On Reasonable Change

### TO MR. IZARD.

PARIS, *July 17, 1788.*

I have hoped this country would settle her internal disputes advantageously and without bloodshed. As yet none has been spilt, though the British newspapers give the idea of a general civil war. Hitherto, I had supposed both the King and parliament would lose authority, and the nation gain it, through the medium of its States General and provincial Assemblies, but the arrest of the deputies of Bretagne two days ago, may kindle a civil war. Its issue will depend on two questions. 1. Will other provinces rise? 2. How will the army conduct itself? A stranger cannot predetermine these questions. Happy for us that abuses have not yet become patrimonies, and that every description of interest is in favor of national and moderate government. That we are yet able to send our wise and good men together to talk over our form of government, discuss its weaknesses and establish its remedies with the same *sang-froid* as they would a subject of agriculture. The example we have given to the world is single, that of changing our form of government under the authority of reason only, without bloodshed.

## Progress of Science

TO JAMES MADISON, OF WILLIAM AND MARY COLLEGE.

PARIS, *July 19, 1788.*

Herschel's volcano in the moon you have doubtless heard of, and placed among the other vagaries of a head, which seems not organized for sound induction. The wildness of the theories hitherto proposed by him, on his own discoveries, seems to authorize us to consider his merit as that of a good optician only. You know also, that Dr. Ingenhouse had discovered, as he supposed, from experiment, that vegetation might be promoted by occasioning streams of the electrical fluid to pass through a plant, and that other physicians had received and confirmed this theory. He now, however, retracts it, and finds by more decisive experiments, that the electrical fluid can neither forward nor retard vegetation. Uncorrected still of the rage of drawing general conclusions from partial and equivocal observations, he hazards the opinion that *light* promotes vegetation. I have heretofore supposed from observation, that light affects the color of living bodies, whether vegetable or animal; but that either the one or the other receives *nutriment* from that fluid, must be permitted to be doubted of, till better confirmed by observation. It is always better to have no ideas, than false ones; to believe nothing, than to believe what is wrong. In my mind, theories are more easily demolished than rebuilt.

An Abbé here has shaken, if not destroyed, the theory of de Dominis, Descartes and Newton, for explaining the phenomenon of the rainbow. According to that theory, you know, a cone of rays issuing from the sun, and falling on a cloud in the opposite part of the heavens, is reflected back in the form of a smaller cone, the apex of which is the eye of the observer; so that the eye of the observer must be in the axis of both cones, and equally distant from every part of the bow. But he observes, that he has repeatedly seen bows, the one end of which has been very near to him, and the other at a very great distance. I have often seen the same thing myself. I recollect well to have seen the end of a rainbow between myself and a house, or between myself and a bank, not twenty yards distant; and this repeatedly. But I never saw, what he says he has seen, different rainbows at the same time intersecting each other. I never saw coexistent bows, which were not concentric also. Again, according to the theory, if the sun is in the horizon, the horizon intercepts the lower half of the bow, if above the horizon, that intercepts more than the half, in proportion. So that generally, the bow is less than a semi-circle, and never more. He says he has seen it more than a semi-circle. I have often seen the leg of the bow below my level. My situation at Monticello admits this, because there is a mountain there in the opposite direction of the afternoon's sun, the valley between which and Monticello, is five hundred feet deep. I have seen a leg of a rainbow plunge down on the river running through the valley. But I do not recollect to have remarked at any time, that the bow was more than half a circle. It appears to me, that these facts demolish the Newtonian hypothesis, but they do not support that erected in its stead by the Abbé. He supposes a cloud between the sun and the observer, and that through some opening in that cloud, the rays pass, and form an iris on the opposite part of the heavens, just as a ray passing through a hole in the shutter of a darkened room, and falling on a prism there, forms the prismatic colors on the opposite wall. According to this, we might see bows of more than the half circle, as often as of less. A thousand other objections occur to this hypothesis, which need not be suggested to you. The result is, that we are wiser than we were, by having an error the less in our catalogue; but the blank occasioned by it, must remain for some happier hypothesist to fill up.

The dispute about the conversion and re-conversion of water and air, is still stoutly kept up. The contradictory experiments of chemists, leave us at liberty to conclude what we please. My conclusion is, that art has not yet invented sufficient aids, to enable such subtle bodies to make a well-defined impression on organs as blunt as ours; that it is laudable to encourage investigation, but to hold back conclusion. Speaking one day with Monsieur de Buffon, on the present ardor of chemical inquiry, he affected to consider chemistry but as cookery, and to place the toils of the laboratory on a footing with those of the kitchen. I think it, on the contrary, among the most useful of sciences, and big with future discoveries for the utility and safety of the human race. . . .

Having seen announced in a gazette, that some person had found in a library of Sicily, an Arabic translation of Livy, which was thought to be complete, I got the chargé des affaires of Naples here, to write to Naples to inquire into the fact. He obtained in answer, that an Arabic translation was found, and that it would restore to us seventeen of the books lost, to wit, from the sixtieth to the seventy-seventh, inclusive: that it was in possession of an Abbé Vella, who, as soon as he shall have finished a work he has on hand, will give us an Italian, and perhaps a Latin translation of this Livy. There are persons, however, who doubt the truth of this discovery. . . .

A countryman of ours, a Mr. Ledyard of Connecticut, set out from hence some time ago for St. Petersburg, to go thence to Kamtschatka, thence to cross over to the western coast of America, and penetrate through the continent, to the other side of it. He had got within a few days' journey of Kamtschatka, when he was arrested by order of the Empress of Russia, sent back, and turned adrift in Poland. He went to London; engaged under the auspices of a private society, formed there for pushing discoveries into

Africa; passed by this place, which he left a few days ago for Marseilles, where he will embark for Alexandria and Grand Cairo; thence explore the Nile to its source; cross the head of the Niger, and descend that to its mouth. He promises me, if he escapes through his journey, he will go to Kentucky, and endeavor to penetrate westwardly to the South Sea.

## Origin of the Indians

### TO E. RUTLEDGE.

PARIS, *July 18, 1788.*

You promise, in your letter of October the 23d, 1787, to give me in your next, at large, the conjectures of your philosopher on the descent of the Creek Indians from the Carthaginians, supposed to have been separated from Hanno's fleet, during his periplus. I shall be very glad to receive them, and see nothing impossible in his conjecture. I am glad he means to appeal to similarity of language, which I consider as the strongest kind of proof it is possible to adduce. I have somewhere read, that the language of the ancient Carthaginians is still spoken by their descendants, inhabiting the mountainous interior parts of Barbary, to which they were obliged to retire by the conquering Arabs. If so, a vocabulary of their tongue can still be got, and if your friend will get one of the Creek languages, the comparison will decide. He probably may have made progress in this business; but if he wishes any enquiries to be made on this side the Atlantic, I offer him my services cheerfully; my wish being like his, to ascertain the history of the American aborigines.

## Safeguards of Freedom

### TO JAMES MADISON.

PARIS, *July 31, 1788.*

I sincerely rejoice at the acceptance of our new constitution by nine States. It is a good canvass, on which some strokes only want retouching. What these are, I think are sufficiently manifested by the general voice from north to south, which calls for a bill of rights. It seems pretty generally understood, that this should go to juries, habeas corpus, standing armies, printing, religion and monopolies. I conceive there may be difficulty in finding general modifications of these, suited to the habits of all the States. But if such cannot be found, then it is better to establish trials by jury, the right of habeas corpus, freedom of the press and freedom of religion, in all cases, and to abolish standing armies in time of peace, and monopolies in all cases, than not to do it in any. The few cases wherein these things may do evil, cannot be weighed against the multitude wherein the want of them will do evil. In disputes between a foreigner and a native, a trial by jury may be improper. But if this exception cannot be agreed to, the remedy will be to model the jury, by giving the *mediatas linguæ*, in civil as well as criminal cases. Why suspend the habeas corpus in insurrections and rebellions? The parties who may be arrested, may be charged instantly with a well-defined crime; of course, the judge will remand them. If the public safety requires that the government should have a man imprisoned on less probable testimony, in those than in other emergencies, let him be taken and tried, retaken and retried, while the necessity continues, only giving him redress against the government, for damages. Examine the history of England. See how few of the cases of the suspension of the habeas corpus law, have been worthy of that suspension. They have been either real treason, wherein the parties might as well have been charged at once, or sham plots, where it was shameful they should ever have been suspected. Yet for the few cases wherein the suspension of the habeas corpus has done real good, that operation is now become habitual, and the minds of the nation almost prepared to live under its constant suspension. A declaration, that the federal government will never restrain the presses from printing anything they please, will not take away the liability of the printers for false facts printed. The declaration, that religious faith shall be unpunished, does not give impunity to criminal acts, dictated by religious error. The saying there shall be no monopolies, lessens the incitements to ingenuity, which is spurred on by the hope of a monopoly for a limited time, as of fourteen years; but the benefit of even limited monopolies is too doubtful, to be opposed to that of their general suppression. If no check can be found to keep the number of standing troops within safe bounds, while they are tolerated as far as necessary, abandon them altogether, discipline well the militia, and guard the magazines with them. More than magazine guards will be useless, if few, and dangerous, if many. No European nation can ever send against us such a regular army as we need fear, and it is hard, if our militia are not equal to those of Canada or Florida. My idea then, is, that though proper exceptions to these general rules are desirable, and probably practicable, yet if the exceptions cannot be agreed on, the establishment of the rules, in all cases, will do ill in very few. I hope, therefore, a bill of rights will be formed, to guard the people against the federal government, as they are already guarded against their State governments, in most instances. The abandoning the principle of necessary rotation in the Senate, has, I see, been disapproved by many; in the case of the President, by none. I readily, therefore, suppose my opinion wrong, when opposed by the majority, as in the former instance, and the totality, as in the latter. In this, however, I should have done it with more complete satisfaction, had we all judged from the same position.

Solicitations, which cannot be directly refused, oblige me to trouble you often, with letters recommending and introducing to you, persons who go from hence to America. I will beg the favor of you, to distinguish the letters wherein I appeal to recommendations from other persons, from those which

I write on my own knowledge. In the former, it is never my intention to compromit myself or you. In both instances, I must beg you to ascribe the trouble I give you, to circumstances which do not leave me at liberty to decline it.

## American Election

TO WILLIAM CARMICHAEL,

PARIS, *August 12, 1788.*

My latest American intelligence is of the 24th of June, when nine certainly, and probably ten States, had accepted the new Constitution, and there was no doubt of the eleventh (North Carolina), because there was no opposition there. In New York, two-thirds of the State were against it, and certainly, if they had been called to the decision in any other stage of the business, they would have rejected it; but before they put it to the vote, they would certainly have heard that eleven States had joined in it, and they would find it safer to go with those eleven, than put themselves into opposition, with Rhode Island only. Though I am much pleased with this successful issue of the new Constitution, yet I am more so, to find that one of its principal defects (the want of a declaration of rights) will pretty certainly be remedied. I suppose this, because I see that both people and conventions, in almost every State, have concurred in demanding it. Another defect, the perpetual re-eligibility of the same President, will probably not be cured during the life of General Washington. His merit has blinded our countrymen to the danger of making so important an officer re-eligible. I presume there will not be a vote against him in the United States. It is more doubtful who will be Vice-President. The age of Dr. Franklin, and the doubt whether he would accept it, are the only circumstances that admit a question, but that he would be the man. After these two characters of first magnitude, there are so many which present themselves equally, on the second line, that we cannot see which of them will be singled out. John Adams, Hancock, Jay, Madison, Rutledge, will all be voted for. Congress has acceded to the prayer of Kentucky, to become an independent member of the Union. A committee was occupied in settling the plan of receiving them, and their government is to commence on the 1st day of January next.

You are, I dare say, pleased, as I am, with the promotion of our countryman, Paul Jones. He commanded the right wing, in the first engagement between the Russian and Turkish galleys; his absence from the second proves his superiority over the Captain Pacha, as he did not choose to bring his ships into the shoals in which the Pacha ventured, and lost those entrusted to him. I consider this officer as the principal hope of our future efforts on the ocean. You will have heard of the action between the Swedes and Russians, on the Baltic; as yet, we have only the Swedish version of it. I apprehend this war must catch from nation to nation, till it becomes general.

## "Rennedeer"

### TO MR. RUTLEDGE.

PARIS, *September 9, 1788.*

DEAR SIR,—I have duly received your favors of August 30th and September 4th. The animal, whose skin you saw here, is called the Moose. Monsieur de Buffon had well known it by name; but he has supposed it to be the same as the Rennedeer of Lapland, in his history. Being satisfied myself that it was a different animal, I asked the favor of General Sullivan to have one killed for me, and to send me the skin and skeleton. This is what you saw, it is found only eastward of the Hudson river. M. de Buffon describes the Renne to be about three feet high, and truly, the Moose you saw here was seven feet high, and there are some of them ten feet high. The experiment was expensive to me, having cost me hunting, curing, and transporting, sixty guineas. The animal whose enormous bones are found on the Ohio, is supposed by M. de Buffon and M. Daubenton to have been an Elephant. Dr. Hunter demonstrated it not to have been an Elephant. Similar bones are found in Siberia, where it is called the Mammoth. The Indians of America say it still exists very far north in our continent. I suppose there is no such thing at Geneva as a copy of my notes on Virginia, or you might see the subject treated there somewhat at length, as also some short notice of the Moose.

## The Federalist

### TO JAMES MADISON.

PARIS, *November 18, 1788.*

Mr. Carrington was so kind as to send me the second volume of the American Philosophical Transactions, the Federalist, and some other interesting pamphlets; and I am to thank you for another copy of the Federalist, and the report of the instructions to the ministers, for negotiating peace. The latter, unluckily, omitted exactly the passage I wanted, which was what related to the navigation of the Mississippi. With respect to the Federalist, the three authors had been named to me. I read it with care, pleasure and improvement, and was satisfied there was nothing in it by one of those hands, and not a great deal by a second. It does the highest honor to the third, as being, in my opinion, the best commentary on the principles of government, which ever was written. In some parts, it is discoverable that the author means only to say what may be best said in defence of opinions, in which he did not concur. But in general, it establishes firmly the plan of government. I confess, it has rectified me on several points. As to the bill of rights,

however, I still think it should be added; and I am glad to see, that three
States have at length considered the perpetual re-eligibility of the President,
as an article which should be amended. I should deprecate with you, indeed,
the meeting of a new convention. I hope they will adopt the mode of
amendment by Congress and the Assemblies, in which case, I should not fear
any dangerous innovation in the plan. But the minorities are too respectable,
not to be entitled to some sacrifice of opinion, in the majority; especially,
when a great proportion of them would be contented with a bill of rights.

# War and Taxes

## TO GENERAL WASHINGTON.

PARIS, *December 4, 1788.*

SIR,—Your favor of August the 31st came to hand yesterday; and a confidential conveyance offering, by the way of London, I avail myself of it, to
acknowledge the receipt.

I have seen, with infinite pleasure, our new Constitution accepted by eleven
States, not rejected by the twelfth; and that the thirteenth happens to be
a State of the least importance. It is true, that the minorities in most of the
accepting States have been very respectable; so much so as to render it
prudent, were it not otherwise reasonable, to make some sacrifice to them.
I am in hopes, that the annexation of a bill of rights to the Constitution will
alone draw over so great a proportion of the minorities as to leave little
danger in the opposition of the residue; and that this annexation may be made
by Congress and the Assemblies, without calling a convention, which might
endanger the most valuable parts of the system. Calculation has convinced
me that circumstances may arise, and probably will arise, wherein all the
resources of taxation will be necessary for the safety of the State. For
though I am decidedly of opinion we should take no part in European quarrels, but cultivate peace and commerce with all, yet who can avoid seeing
the source of war, in the tyranny of those nations, who deprive us of the
natural right of trading with our neighbors? The produce of the United
States will soon exceed the European demand; what is to be done with the
surplus, when there shall be one? It will be employed, without question, to
open, by force, a market for itself, with those placed on the same continent
with us, and who wish nothing better. Other causes, too, are obvious, which
may involve us in war; and war requires every resource of taxation and
credit. The power of making war often prevents it, and in our case would
give efficacy to our desire of peace. If the new government wears the front
which I hope it will, I see no impossibility in the availing ourselves of the
wars of others, to open the other parts of America to our commerce, as the
price of our neutrality.

## Rights and Gunpowder

### TO DOCTOR CURRIE.

PARIS, *December 20, 1788.*

I have asked of Congress a leave of five or six months' absence this year to carry my family back to America, and hope to obtain it in time to sail in April from Havre for James river directly. In this case I shall have the pleasure of seeing you at Richmond and Eppington a few days. This country is seriously meditating the establishment of a constitution, and the distress of the court for money, with the real good intentions of the King, will produce their concurrence in it. All the world is occupied at present in framing, every one his own plan, of a bill of rights. The States General will meet probably in March, (the day not being yet known). They will probably establish their own periodical meetings, their right to participate of the legislation, their sole right to tax. So far the court will not oppose. Some will endeavor to procure, at the same time, a habeas corpus law and free press. I doubt if the latter can be obtained yet, and as for the former, I hardly think the nation itself ripe to accept it. . . . There is a vast improvement in the composition of gunpowder, not yet communicated to the public. We are now at the twenty-ninth livraison of the Encyclopedia.

## On Bridge Building

### TO THOMAS PAINE.

PARIS, *December 23, 1788.*

DEAR SIR,—It is true that I received, very long ago, your favors of September the 9th and 15th, and that I have been in daily intention of answering them, fully and confidentially; but you know, such a correspondence between you and me cannot pass through the post, nor even by the couriers of ambassadors. The French packet boats being discontinued, I am now obliged to watch opportunities by Americans going to London, to write my letters to America. Hence it has happened, that these, the sole opportunities by which I can write to you without fear, have been lost, by the multitude of American letters I had to write. I now determine, without foreseeing any such conveyance, to begin my letter to you, so that when a conveyance occurs, I shall only have to add recent occurrences. Notwithstanding the interval of my answer which has taken place, I must beg a continuance of your correspondence; because I have great confidence in your communications, and since Mr. Adams' departure, I am in need of authentic information from that country.

I will begin with the subject of your bridge, in which I feel myself interested; and it is with great pleasure that I learn, by your favor of the 16th, that the execution of the arch of experiment exceeds your expectations. In your former letter, you mention, that instead of arranging your tubes and bolts as ordinates to the cord of the arch, you had reverted to your first idea, of arranging them in the direction of the radii. I am sure it will gain, both in beauty and strength. It is true that the divergence of those radii recurs as a difficulty, in getting the rails on upon the bolts; but I thought this fully removed by the answer you first gave me, when I suggested that difficulty, to wit, that you should place the rails first, and drive the bolts through them, and not, as I had imagined, place the bolts first, and put the rails on them. I must doubt whether what you now suggest, will be as good as your first idea; to wit, to have every rail split into two pieces longitudinally, so that there shall be but the halves of the holes in each, and then to clamp the two halves together. The solidity of this method cannot be equal to that of the solid rail, and it increases the suspicious part of the whole machine, which, in a first experiment, ought to be rendered as few as possible. But of all this, the practical iron men are much better judges than we theorists. . . .

## Affairs in France

TO MR. THOMAS PAINE.

PARIS, *December 23, 1788.*

DEAR SIR,—As to the affairs of this country, they have hitherto gone on well. The Court being decided to call the States General, know that the form of calling and constituting them would admit of cavil. They asked the advice of the Notables. These advised that the form of the last States General of 1614 be observed. In that, the commons had but about one-third of the whole number of members, and they voted by orders. The Court wished now that they should have one-half of the whole number of members, and that they should form but one house, not three. The parliament have taken up the subject, and given the opinion which the Court would have wished. We are, therefore, in hopes that, availing themselves of these contrary opinions, they will follow that which they wished. The priests and nobles threaten schism; and we do not know yet what form will ultimately be adopted. If no schism of this kind prevents it, the States will meet about March or April, and will obtain, without opposition from the Court, 1. Their own periodical convocation; 2. A share in the legislation; 3. The exclusive right to tax and appropriate the public money. They will attempt also to obtain a habeas corpus law and free press; but it does not appear to me that the nation is ripe to accept of these, if offered.

# American Influence

TO DR. PRICE.

PARIS, *January 8, 1789.*

I concur with you strictly in your opinion of the comparative merits of atheism and demonism, and really see nothing but the latter in the Being worshipped by many who think themselves Christians. Your opinions and writings will have effect in bringing others to reason on this subject. Our new Constitution, of which you speak also, has succeeded beyond what I apprehended it would have done. I did not at first believe that eleven States out of thirteen would have consented to a plan consolidating them as much into one. A change in their dispositions, which had taken place since I left them, had rendered this consolidation necessary, that is to say, had called for a federal government which could walk upon its own legs, without leaning for support on the State legislatures. A sense of necessity, and a submission to it, is to me a new and consolatory proof that, whenever the people are well-informed, they can be trusted with their own government; that, whenever things get so far wrong as to attract their notice, they may be relied on to set them to rights. You say you are not sufficiently informed about the nature and circumstances of the present struggle here. Having been on the spot from its first origin, and watched its movements as an uninterested spectator, with no other bias than a love of mankind, I will give you my ideas of it. Though celebrated writers of this and other countries had already sketched good principles on the subject of government, yet the American war seems first to have awakened the thinking part of this nation in general from the sleep of despotism in which they were sunk. The officers too who had been to America, were mostly young men, less shackled by habit and prejudice, and more ready to assent to the dictates of common sense and common right. They came back impressed with these. The press, notwithstanding its shackles, began to disseminate them; conversation, too, assumed new freedom; politics became the theme of all societies, male and female, and a very extensive and zealous party was formed, which may be called the Patriotic party, who, sensible of the abusive government under which they lived, longed for occasions of reforming it. This party comprehended all the honesty of the kingdom, sufficiently at its leisure to think; the men of letters, the easy bourgeois, the young nobility, partly from reflection, partly from mode; for those sentiments became a matter of mode, and as such united most of the young women to the party. . . .

# Report on Europe

## TO JOHN JAY.

PARIS, *January 11, 1789.*

As the character of the Prince of Wales is becoming interesting, I have endeavored to learn what it truly is. This is less difficult in his case, than in that of other persons of his rank, because he has taken no pains to hide himself from the world. The information I most rely on, is from a person here with whom I am intimate, who divides his time between Paris and London, an Englishman by birth, of truth, sagacity and science. He is of a circle, when in London, which has had good opportunities of knowing the Prince; but he has also, himself, had special occasions of verifying their information, by his own personal observation. He happened, when last in London, to be invited to a dinner of three persons. The Prince came by chance, and made the fourth. He ate half a leg of mutton; did not taste of small dishes, because small; drank Champagne and Burgundy, as small beer during dinner, and Bordeaux after dinner, as the rest of the company. Upon the whole, he ate as much as the other three, and drank about two bottles of wine without seeming to feel it. My informant sat next him, and being till then unknown to the Prince, personally, (though not by character,) and lately from France, the Prince confined his conversation almost entirely to him. Observing to the Prince that he spoke French without the least foreign accent, the Prince told him, that when very young, his father had put only French servants about him, and that it was to that circumstance he owed his pronunciation. He led him from this to give an account of his education, the total of which was the learning a little Latin. He has not a single element of Mathematics, of Natural or Moral Philosophy, or of any other science on earth, nor has the society he has kept been such as to supply the void of education. It has been that of the lowest, the most illiterate and profligate persons of the kingdom, without choice of rank or mind, and with whom the subjects of conversation are only horses, drinking-matches, bawdy houses, and in terms the most vulgar. The young nobility, who begin by associating with him, soon leave him, disgusted with the insupportable profligacy of his society; and Mr. Fox, who has been supposed his favorite, and not over-nice in the choice of company, would never keep his company habitually. In fact, he never associated with a man of sense. He has not a single idea of justice, morality, religion, or of the rights of men, or any anxiety for the opinion of the world. He carries that indifference for fame so far, that he would probably not be hurt were he to lose his throne, provided he could be assured of having always meat, drink, horses, and women. In the article of women, nevertheless, he is become more correct, since his connection with Mrs. Fitzherbert, who is an honest and worthy woman: he is even less crapulous than he was. He had a fine person, but it is becoming coarse. He possesses good native common sense; is affable, polite, and very good humored. Saying to my informant, on another occasion, "your friend, such a one, dined with me yesterday, and I made him damned drunk;" he replied, "I am sorry for it; I had heard that your royal highness had left off drinking:" the Prince laughed, tapped him on the shoulder very good naturedly, without saying a word, or ever after showing any displeasure. The Duke of York, who was for some time cried up as the prodigy of the family, is as profligate, and of less understanding. To these particular traits, from a man of sense and truth, it would be superfluous to add the general terms of praise or blame, in which he is spoken of by other persons, in whose impartiality and penetration I have less confidence. A sample is better than a description. For the peace of Europe, it is best that the King should give such gleamings of recovery, as would prevent the regent or his ministry from thinking themselves firm, and yet, that he should not recover.

This country advances with a steady pace towards the establishment of a constitution, whereby the people will resume the great mass of those powers, so fatally lodged in the hands of the King. During the session of the Notables, and after their votes against the rights of the people, the parliament of Paris took up the subject, and passed a vote in opposition to theirs (which I send you). This was not their genuine sentiment; it was a manœuvre of the young members, who are truly well disposed, taking advantage of the accidental absence of many old members, and bringing others over. . . . You are not to suppose that these dispositions of the court proceed from any love of the people, or justice towards their rights. Courts love the people always, as wolves do the sheep. The fact is this. The court wants money. From the Tiers État they cannot get it, because they are already squeezed to the last drop. The clergy and the nobles, by their privileges and their influence, have hitherto screened their property in a great degree, from public contribution. That half of the orange then, remains yet to be squeezed, and for this operation there is no agent powerful enough, but the people. They are, therefore, brought forward as the favorites of the court, and will be supported by them. The moment of crisis will be the meeting of the States; because their first act will be, to decide whether they shall vote by persons or by orders. The clergy will leave nothing unattempted to obtain the latter; for they see that the spirit of reformation will not confine itself to the political, but will extend to the ecclesiastical establishment also. With respect to the nobles, the younger members are generally for the people, and the middle aged are daily coming over to the same side; so that by the time the States meet, we may hope there will be a majority of that body also in favor of the people, and consequently for voting by persons, and not by orders.

# Fears for La Fayette

## TO JAMES MADISON.

PARIS, *January 12, 1789.*

DEAR SIR,—My last to you was of the 18th of November; since which, I have received yours of the 21st of September and October the 8th, with the pamphlet on the Mohican language, for which, receive my thanks. I endeavor to collect all the vocabularies I can, of the American Indians, as of those of Asia, persuaded, that if they ever had a common parentage, it will appear in their languages.

I was pleased to see the vote of Congress, of September the 16th, on the subject of the Mississippi, as I had before seen, with great uneasiness, the pursuits of other principles, which I could never reconcile to my own ideas of probity or wisdom, and from which, and my knowledge of the character of our western settlers, I saw that the loss of that country was a necessary consequence. I wish this return to true policy, may be in time to prevent evil. There has been a little foundation for the reports and fears relative to the Marquis de La Fayette. He has, from the beginning, taken openly part with those who demand a constitution; and there was a moment that we apprehended the Bastile; but they ventured on nothing more, than to take from him a temporary service, on which he had been ordered; and this, more to save appearances for their own authority, than anything else; for at the very time they pretended that they had put him into disgrace, they were constantly conferring and communicating with him. Since this, he has stood on safe ground, and is viewed as among the foremost of the patriots. Everybody here is trying their hand at forming declarations of rights. As something of that kind is going on with you also, I send you two specimens from hence. The one is by our friend of whom I have just spoken. You will see that it contains the essential principles of ours, accommodated as much as could be, to the actual state of things here. The other is from a very sensible man, a pure theorist, of the sect called the economists, of which Turgot was considered as the head. The former is adapted to the existing abuses, the latter goes to those possible, as well as to those existing.

# Bread Riots

## TO JOHN JAY.

PARIS, *March 1, 1789.*

A note of the Chargé des Affaires of France at Warsaw shows a concert between France and Russia; it is a prognostication that Russia will interfere in the affairs of Poland, and if she does it is most probable that the King of Poland must be drawn into the war.

The revolution which has taken place in Geneva is a remarkable and late event. With the loss of only two or three lives, and in the course of one week, riots begun at first on account of a rise in the price of bread were improved and pointed to a reformation of their constitution, and their ancient constitution has been almost completely re-established. Nor do I see any reason to doubt of the permanence of the re-establishment.

There has been a riot in Brittany begun on account of the price of bread but converted into a quarrel between the noblesse and Tiers-État. Some few lives were lost in it. All is quieted for the present moment. In Burgundy and Franchecompte the opposition of the nobles to the views of government is very warm. Everywhere else, however, the revolution is going on quietly and steadily and the public mind ripening so fast that there is great reason to hope a good result from the States-General. Their numbers—about twelve hundred—give room to fear, indeed, that they may be turbulent.

Having never heard of Admiral Paul Jones since the action in which he took part before Oczahow, I began to be a little uneasy. But I have now received a letter from him dated at St. Petersburg, the 31st of January, where he had just arrived at the desire of the Empress. He has hitherto commanded on the Black Sea. He does not know whether he shall be employed there, or where, the ensuing campaign.

## On Party Alignment

### TO FRANCIS HOPKINSON.

PARIS, *March 13, 1789.*

DEAR SIR,—Since my last, which was of December the 21st, yours of December the 9th and 21st are received. Accept my thanks for the papers and pamphlets which accompanied them, and mine and my daughter's, for the book of songs. I will not tell you how much they have pleased us, nor how well the last of them merits praise for its pathos, but relate a fact only, which is, that while my elder daughter was playing it on the harpsichord, I happened to look towards the fire, and saw the younger one all in tears. I asked her if she was sick? She said "no; but the tune was so mournful."

You say that I have been dished up to you as an anti-federalist, and ask me if it be just. My opinion was never worthy enough of notice to merit citing; but since you ask it, I will tell it to you. I am not a federalist, because I never submitted the whole system of my opinions to the creed of any party of men whatever, in religion, in philosophy, in politics or in anything else, where I was capable of thinking for myself. Such an addiction, is the last degradation of a free and moral agent. If I could not go to heaven but with a party, I would not go there at all. Therefore, I am not of the party of federalists. But I am much farther from that of the anti-federalists. I approved, from the first moment, of the great mass of what is in the new Constitution; the consolidation of the government; the organization into executive, legislative, and judiciary; the subdivision of the legislative; the happy compromise of interests between the great and little States, by the different manner of voting in the different Houses; the voting by persons instead of States; the qualified negative on laws given to the executive, which, however, I should have liked better if associated with the judiciary also, as in New York; and the power of taxation. I thought at first that the latter might have been limited. A little reflection soon convinced me it ought not to be. What I disapproved from the first moment also, was the want of a bill of rights, to guard liberty against the legislative as well as the executive branches of the government; that is to say, to secure freedom in religion, freedom of the press, freedom from monopolies, freedom from unlawful imprisonment, freedom from a permanent military, and a trial by jury, in all cases determinable by the laws of the land. I disapproved, also, the perpetual re-eligibility of the President. To these points of disapprobation I adhere. My first wish was, that the nine first conventions might accept the constitution, as the means of securing to us the great mass of good it contained, and that the four last might reject it, as the means of obtaining amendments. But I was corrected in this wish, the moment I saw the much better plan of Massachusetts, and which had never occurred to me. With respect to the declaration of rights, I suppose the majority of the United States are of my opinion; for I apprehend, all the anti-federalists and a very respectable proportion of the federalists, think that such a declaration should now be annexed. The enlightened part of Europe have given us the greatest credit for inventing the instrument of security for the rights of the people, and have been not a little surprised to see us so soon give it up. With respect to the re-eligibility of the President, I find myself differing from the majority of my countrymen; for I think there are but three States out of the eleven which have desired an alteration of this. And indeed, since the thing is established, I would wish it not to be altered during the life of our great leader, whose executive talents are superior to those, I believe, of any man in the world, and who, alone, by the authority of his name and the confidence reposed in his perfect integrity, is fully qualified to put the new government so under way, as to secure it against the efforts of opposition. But, having derived from our error all the good there was in it, I hope we shall correct it, the moment we can no longer have the same name at the helm.

These, my dear friend, are my sentiments, by which you will see I was right in saying I am neither federalist nor anti-federalist; that I am of neither party, nor yet a trimmer between parties. These, my opinions, I wrote within a few hours after I had read the Constitution, to one or two friends in America. I had not then read one single word printed on the subject. I never had an opinion in politics or religion, which I was afraid to own. A costive reserve on these subjects might have procured me more esteem from some people, but less from myself.

## "Tyranny of Legislatures"

### TO JAMES MADISON.

PARIS, *March 15, 1789.*

Your thoughts on the subject of the declaration of rights, in the letter of October the 17th, I have weighed with great satisfaction. Some of them had not occurred to me before, but were acknowledged just in the moment they were presented to my mind. In the arguments in favor of a declaration of rights, you omit one which has great weight with me; the legal check which it puts into the hands of the judiciary. This is a body, which, if rendered independent and kept strictly to their own department, merits great confidence for their learning and integrity. In fact, what degree of confidence would be too much, for a body composed of such men as Wythe, Blair and Pendleton? On characters like these, the *"civium ardor prava jubentium"* would make no impression. I am happy to find that, on the whole, you are a friend to this amendment. The declaration of rights is, like all other human blessings, alloyed with some inconveniences, and not accomplishing fully its object. But the good in this instance, vastly overweighs the evil. . . . The executive, in our government, is not the sole, it is scarcely the principal object of my jealousy. The tyranny of the legislatures is the most formidable dread at present, and will be for many years. That of the executive will come in its turn; but it will be at a remote period. I know there are some among us, who would now establish a monarchy. But they are inconsiderable in number and weight of character. The rising race are all republicans. We were educated in royalism; no wonder, if some of us retain that idolatry still. Our young people are educated in republicanism; an apostasy from that to royalism, is unprecedented and impossible. I am much pleased with the prospect that a declaration of rights will be added; and I hope it will be done in that way, which will not endanger the whole frame of government, or any essential part of it.

## The Right to Think

### TO COLONEL HUMPHREYS.

PARIS, *March 18, 1789.*

The operations which have taken place in America lately, fill me with pleasure. In the first place, they realize the confidence I had, that whenever our affairs go obviously wrong, the good sense of the people will interpose, and set them to rights. The example of changing a constitution, by assembling the wise men of the State, instead of assembling armies, will be worth as much to the world as the former examples we had given them. The Constitution, too, which was the result of our deliberations, is unquestionably the wisest ever yet presented to men, and some of the accommodations of interest which it has adopted, are greatly pleasing to me, who have before had occasions of seeing how difficult those interests were to accommodate. A general concurrence of opinion seems to authorize us to say, it has some defects. I am one of those who think it a defect, that the important rights, not placed in security by the frame of the Constitution itself, were not explicitly secured by a supplementary declaration. There are rights which it is useless to surrender to the government, and which governments have yet always been found to invade. These are the rights of thinking, and publishing our thoughts by speaking or writing; the right of free commerce; the right of personal freedom. . . . I hope to receive soon permission to visit America this summer, and to possess myself anew, by conversation with my countrymen, of their spirit and their ideas. I know only the Americans of the year 1784. They tell me this is to be much a stranger to those of 1789. This renewal of acquaintance is no indifferent matter to one, acting at such a distance, as that instructions cannot be received hot and hot. One of my pleasures, too, will be that of talking over the old and new with you. In the meantime, and at all times, I have the honor to be, with great and sincere esteem, dear Sir, your friend and servant.

# New Discoveries

### TO DOCTOR WILLARD.

Paris, *March 24, 1789.*

In the arts, I think two of our countrymen have presented the most important inventions. Mr. Paine, the author of "Common Sense," has invented an iron bridge, which promises to be cheaper by a great deal than stone, and to admit of a much greater arch. He supposed it may be ventured for an arch of five hundred feet. He has obtained a patent for it in England, and is now executing the first experiment with an arch of between ninety and one hundred feet. Mr. Rumsey has also obtained a patent for his navigation by the force of steam, in England, and is soliciting a similar one here. His principal merit is in the improvement of the boiler, and, instead of the complicated machinery of oars and paddles, proposed by others, the substitution of so simple a thing as the reaction of a stream of water on his vessel. He is building a sea vessel at this time in England, and she will be ready for an experiment in May. He has suggested a great number of mechanical improvements in a variety of branches; and upon the whole, is the most original and the greatest mechanical genius I have ever seen. The return of La Peyrouse (whenever that shall happen) will probably add to our knowledge in Geography, Botany, and Natural History. What a field have we at our doors to signalize ourselves in! The Botany of America is far from being exhausted, its Mineralogy is untouched, and its Natural History or

Zoology, totally mistaken and misrepresented. As far as I have seen, there is not one single species of terrestrial birds common to Europe and America, and I question if there be a single species of quadrupeds. (Domestic animals are to be excepted.) It is for such institutions as that over which you preside so worthily, Sir, to do justice to our country, its productions and its genius. It is the work to which the young men, whom you are forming, should lay their hands. We have spent the prime of our lives in procuring them the precious blessing of liberty. Let them spend theirs in showing that it is the great parent of *science* and of virtue; and that a nation will be great in both, always in proportion as it is free.

# Advice to a Friend

## TO THE MARQUIS DE LA FAYETTE.

PARIS, *May 6, 1789.*

MY DEAR FRIEND,—As it becomes more and more possible that the Noblesse will go wrong, I become uneasy for you. Your principles are decidedly with the Tiers État, and your instructions against them. A complaisance to the latter on some occasions, and an adherence to the former on others, may give an appearance of trimming between the two parties, which may lose you both. You will, in the end, go over wholly to the Tiers État, because it will be impossible for you to live in a constant sacrifice of your own sentiments to the prejudices of the Noblesse. But you would be received by the Tiers État at any future day, coldly, and without confidence. This appears to me the moment to take at once that honest and manly stand with them which your own principles dictate. This will win their hearts forever, be approved by the world, which marks and honors you as the man of the people, and will be an eternal consolation to yourself. The Noblesse, and especially the Noblesse of Auvergne, will always prefer men who will do their dirty work for them. You are not made for that. They will, therefore, soon drop you, and the people, in that case, will perhaps not take you up. Suppose a scission should take place. The Priests and Nobles will secede, the nation will remain in place, and, with the King, will do its own business. If violence should be attempted, where will you be? You cannot then take side with the people in opposition to your own vote, that very vote which will have helped to produce the scission. Still less can you array yourself against the people. That is impossible. Your instructions are, indeed, a difficulty. But to state this at its worst it is only a single difficulty, which a single effort surmounts. Your instructions can never embarrass you a second time, whereas an acquiescence under them will reproduce greater difficulties every day, and without end. Besides, a thousand circumstances offer as many justifications of your departure from your instructions. Will it be impossible to persuade all parties that (as for good legislation two Houses are necessary) the placing the privileged classes together in one House, and the unprivileged in another, would be better for both than a scission? I own, I think it would. People can never agree without some sacrifices; and it appears but a moderate sacrifice in each party, to meet on this middle ground. The attempt to bring this about might satisfy your instructions, and a failure in it would justify your siding with the people, even to those who think instructions are laws of conduct. Forgive me, my dear friend, if my anxiety for you makes me talk of things I know nothing about. You must not consider this as advice. I know you and myself too well to presume to offer advice. Receive it merely as the expression of my uneasiness, and the effusion of that sincere friendship with which I am, my dear Sir, yours affectionately.

## Riot in Paris

### TO WILLIAM CARMICHAEL.

PARIS, *May 8, 1789.*

DEAR SIR,—Your favor of January the 26th, to March the 27th, is duly received, and I thank you for the interesting papers it contained. The answer of Don Ulloa, however, on the subject of the canal through the American isthmus, was not among them, though mentioned to be so. If you have omitted it through accident, I shall thank you for it at some future occasion, as I wish much to understand that subject thoroughly. Our American information comes down to the 16th of March. There had not yet been members enough assembled of the new Congress to open the tickets. They expected to do it in a day or two. In the meantime, it was said from all the States, that their vote had been unanimous for General Washington, and a good majority in favor of Mr. Adams, who is certainly, therefore, Vice-President. The new government would be supported by very cordial and very general dispositions in its favor from the people. I have not yet seen a list of the new Congress. This delay in the meeting of the new government, has delayed the determination on my petition for leave of absence. However, I expect to receive it every day, and am in readiness to sail the instant I receive it, so that this is probably the last letter I shall write you hence till my return.

We have had, in this city, a very considerable riot, in which about one hundred people have been probably killed. It was the most unprovoked, and is, therefore, justly, the most unpitied catastrophe of that kind I ever knew. Nor did the wretches know what they wanted, except to do mischief. It seems to have had no particular connection with the great national question now in agitation. The want of bread is very seriously dreaded through the whole kingdom. Between twenty and thirty ship loads of wheat and flour has already arrived from the United States, and there will be about the same quantity of rice sent from Charleston to this country directly, of which about half has arrived. I presume that between wheat and rice, one hundred ship loads may be counted on in the whole from us. Paris consumes about a ship load a day (say two hundred and fifty tons). The total supply of the West Indies for this year, rests with us, and there is almost a famine in Canada and Nova Scotia. The States General were opened the day before yesterday. Viewing it as an opera, it was imposing; as a scene of business, the King's speech was exactly what it should have been, and very well delivered; not a word of the Chancellor's was heard by anybody, so that, as yet, I have never heard a single guess at what it was about. . . .

The Noblesse, on coming together, show that they are not as much reformed in their principles as we had hoped they would be. In fact, there is real danger of their totally refusing to vote by persons. Some found hopes on the lower clergy, which constitute four-fifths of the deputies of that order. If they do not turn the balance in favor of the Tiers État, there is real danger of a scission. But I shall not consider even that event as rendering things desperate. If the King will do business with the Tiers État, which constitutes the nation, it may be well done without Priests or Nobles.

# Home Concerns

## TO GENERAL WASHINGTON.

PARIS, *May 10, 1789.*

SIR,—I am now to acknowledge the honor of your two letters of Nov. the 27th and Feb. the 13th, both of which have come to hand since my last to you of Dec. the 4th and 5th. The details you are so good as to give me on the subject of the navigation of the waters of the Potomac and Ohio, are very pleasing to me, as I consider the union of these two rivers, as among the strongest links of connection between the eastern and western sides of our confederacy. It will, moreover, add to the commerce of Virginia, in particular, all the upper parts of the Ohio and its waters. Another vast object, and of much less difficulty, is to add, also, all the country on the lakes and their waters. This would enlarge our field immensely, and would certainly be effected by a union of the upper waters of the Ohio and Lake Erie The Big Beaver and Cuyahoga offer the most direct line, and according to information I received from General Hand, and which I had the honor of writing you in the year 1783, the streams in that neighborhood head in lagoons, and the country is flat. With respect to the doubts which you say are entertained by some, whether the upper waters of Potomac can be rendered capable of navigation on account of the falls and rugged banks, they are answered, by observing, that it is reduced to a maxim, that whenever there is water enough to float a batteau, there may be navigation for a batteau. Canals and locks may be necessary, and they are expensive; but I hardly know what expense would be too great, for the object in question. Probably, negotiations with the Indians, perhaps even settlement, must precede the execution of the Cuyahoga canal. The States of Maryland and Virginia should make a common object of it. The navigation, again, between

Elizabeth River and the Sound, is of vast importance, and in my opinion, it is much better that these should be done at public than private expense.

Though we have not heard of the actual opening of the new Congress, and consequently, have not official information of your election as President of the United States, yet, as there never could be a doubt entertained of it, permit me to express here my felicitations, not to yourself, but to my country. Nobody who has tried both public and private life, can doubt but that you were much happier on the banks of the Potomac than you will be at New York. But there was nobody so well qualified as yourself, to put our new machine into a regular course of action; nobody, the authority of whose name could have so effectually crushed opposition at home, and produced respect abroad. I am sensible of the immensity of the sacrifice on your part. Your measure of fame was full to the brim; and, therefore, you have nothing to gain. But there are cases wherein it is a duty to risk all against nothing, and I believe this was exactly the case. We may presume, too, according to every rule of probability, that after doing a great deal of good, you will be found to have lost nothing but private repose.

In a letter to Mr. Jay, of the 19th of Nov., I asked a leave of absence to carry my children back to their own country, and to settle various matters of a private nature, which were left unsettled, because I had no idea of being absent so long. I expected that letter would have been received in time to be decided on by the Government then existing. I know now that it would arrive when there was no Congress, and consequently, that it must have awaited your arrival at New York. I hope you found the request not an unreasonable one. I am excessively anxious to receive the permission without delay, that I may be able to get back before the winter sets in. Nothing can be so dreadful to me, as to be shivering at sea for two or three months in a winter passage. Besides, there has never been a moment at which the presence of a minister here could be so well dispensed with, from certainty of no war this summer, and that the government will be so totally absorbed in domestic arrangements, as to attend to nothing exterior. Mr. Jay will, of course, communicate to you some ciphered letters lately written, and one of this date. My public letter to him contains all the interesting public details. I enclose with the present, some extracts of a letter from Mr. Paine, which he desired me to communicate; your knowledge of the writer will justify my giving you the trouble of these communications, which their interesting nature and his respectability, will jointly recommend to notice. I am in great pain for the Marquis de La Fayette. His principles, you know, are clearly with the people; but having been elected for the Noblesse of Auvergne, they have laid him under express instructions, to vote for the decision by orders and not persons. This would ruin him with the Tiers État, and it is not possible he could continue long to give satisfaction to the Noblesse. I have not hesitated to press on him to burn his instructions, and follow his conscience as the only sure clue, which will eternally guide a man clear of all doubts and inconsistencies. If he cannot effect a conciliatory plan, he will surely take his stand manfully at once, with the Tiers État.

He will in that case be what he pleases with them, and I am in hopes that base is now too solid to render it dangerous to be mounted on it. In hopes of being able in the course of the summer, to pay my respects to you personally, in New York, I have the honor to be, with sentiments of the most perfect respect and attachment, Sir, your most obedient, and most humble servant.

## Crisis in France

### TO JAMES MADISON.

PARIS, *May 11, 1789.*

The revolution of France has gone on with the most unexampled success, hitherto. There have been some mobs, occasioned by the want of bread, in different parts of the kingdom, in which there may have been some lives lost; perhaps a dozen or twenty. These had no professed connection, *generally,* with the constitutional revolution. A more serious riot happened lately in Paris, in which about one hundred of the mob were killed. This execution has been universally approved, as they seemed to have no view but mischief and plunder. But the meeting of the States General presents serious difficulties, which it had been hoped the progress of reason would have enabled them to get over. The nobility of and about Paris, have come over, as was expected, to the side of the people, in the great question of voting by persons or orders. This had induced a presumption that those of the country were making the same progress, and these form the great mass of the deputies of that order. But they are found to be where they were centuries ago, as to their disposition to keep distinct from the people, and even to tyrannize over them. They agree, indeed, to abandon their pecuniary privileges. The clergy seem, at present, much divided. Five-sixths of that representation consists of the lower clergy, who, being the sons of the peasantry, are very well with the Tiers État. But the Bishops are intriguing, and drawing them over daily. The Tiers État is so firm to vote by persons or to go home, that it is impossible to conjecture what will be the result.

## Paris Deadlock

### TO THOMAS PAINE.

PARIS, *May 19, 1789.*

You know that the States General have met, and probably have seen the speeches at the opening of them. The three orders sit in distinct chambers. The great question, whether they shall vote by orders or persons can never be surmounted amicably. It has not yet been proposed in form; but the votes which have been taken on the outworks of that question show that the Tiers

État are unanimous, a good majority of the Clergy (consisting of the Curés) disposed to side with the Tiers État, and in the chamber of the Noblesse, there are only fifty-four in that sentiment, against one hundred and ninety, who are for voting by orders. Committees to find means of conciliation are appointed by each chamber; but conciliation is impossible. Some think the Nobles could be induced to unite themselves with the *higher Clergy* into one House, the lower Clergy and Tiers État forming another. But the Tiers État are immovable. They are not only firm, but a little disdainful. The question is, what will ensue? One idea is to separate, in order to consult again their constituents, and to take new instructions. This would be doing nothing, for the same instructions would be repeated; and what, in the mean-time, is to become of a government, absolutely without money, and which cannot be kept in motion with less than a million of livres a day? The more probable expectation is as follows. As soon as it shall become evident that no amicable determination of the manner of voting can take place, the Tiers État will send an invitation to the two other orders to come and take their places in the common chamber. A majority of the Clergy will go, and the minority of the Noblesse. The chamber thus composed will declare that the States General are constituted, will notify it to the King, and that they are ready to proceed to business. If the King refuses to do business with them, and adheres to the Nobles, the common chamber will declare all taxes at an end, will form a declaration of rights, and do such other acts as circumstances will permit, and go home. The tax-gatherers will then be resisted, and it may well be doubted whether the soldiery and their officers will not divide, as the Tiers État and Nobles. But it is more likely that the King will agree to do business with the States General . . .

# Home Relief

## TO THE MARQUIS DE LA FAYETTE.

PARIS, *June 12, 1789.*

With respect to the utility, or inutility of your minority's joining the Commons, I am unable to form an opinion for myself. I know too little of the subject to see what may be its consequences.

I never knew an instance of the English parliament's undertaking to relieve the poor, by a distribution of bread in time of scarcity. In fact, the English commerce is so extensive and so active, that though bread may be a little more or less plenty, there can never be an absolute failure. This island is so narrow, that corn can be readily carried from the seaports to its interior parts. But were an absolute want to happen, and were the parliament to undertake a distribution of corn, I think, that according to the principles of their government, they would only vote a sum of money, and address the King to employ it for the best. The business is, in its nature, executive, and would require too great a variety of detail to be managed by an act of parliament. However, I repeat it, that I never heard or read of an instance of the parliament's interfering to give bread. If I see you at Versailles to-day, I can be more particular.

# Verge of Revolution

## TO JAMES MADISON.

PARIS, *June 18, 1789.*

We shall know, I think, within a day or two, whether the government will risk a bankruptcy and civil war, rather than see all distinction of orders done away, which is what the Commons will push for. If the fear of the former alternative prevails, they will spin the matter into negotiation. The Commons have in their chamber almost all the talents of the nation; they are firm and bold, yet moderate. There is, indeed, among them, a number of very hot-headed members; but those of most influence are cool, temperate and sagacious. Every step of this House has been marked with caution and wisdom. The Noblesse, on the contrary, are absolutely out of their senses. They are so furious, they can seldom debate at all. They have few men of moderate talents, and not one of great, in the majority. Their proceedings have been very injudicious. The Clergy are waiting to profit by every incident to secure themselves, and have no other object in view. Among the Commons there is an entire unanimity on the great question of voting by persons. Among the Noblesse there are about sixty for the Commons, and about three times that number against them. Among the Clergy, about twenty have already come over and joined the Commons, and in the course of a few days they will be joined by many more, not, indeed, making the majority of that House, but very near it. The Bishops and Archbishops have been very successful by bribes and intrigues, in detaching the Curés from the Commons, to whom they were at first attached to a man. The Commons are about five hundred and fifty-four in number, of whom three hundred and forty-four are of the law. These do not possess an influence founded in property; but in their habits of business and acquaintance with the people, and in their means of exciting them as they please. The Curés throughout the kingdom, form the mass of the Clergy; they are the only part favorably known to the people, because solely charged with the duties of baptism, burial, confession, visitation of the sick, instruction of the children, and aiding the poor; they are themselves of the people, and united with them. The carriages and equipage only of the higher Clergy, not their persons, are known to the people, and are in detestation with them. The soldiers will follow their officers, that is to say, their captains, lieutenants and ensigns. These are of the lower nobility, and, therefore, much divided. The colonels and higher officers are of the higher nobility, are seldom with the soldiers, little known to them, not possessing their attachment. These circumstances give them little weight in the partition of the army.

## Eyewitness Account

TO JOHN JAY.

PARIS, *June 24, 1789.*

On the 19th, a Council was held at Marly, in the afternoon. It was there proposed, that the King should interpose by a declaration of his sentiments in a *séance royale*. The declaration prepared by Mr. Neckar, while it censured in general the proceedings both of the Nobles and Commons, announced the King's views, such as substantially to coincide with the Commons. It was agreed to in Council, as also that the *séance royale* should be held on the 22d, and the meetings till then be suspended. While the Council was engaged in this deliberation at Marly, the Chamber of the Clergy was in debate, whether they should accept the invitation of the Tiers to unite with them in the common chamber. On the first question, to unite simply and unconditionally, it was decided in the negative by a very small majority. As it was known, however, that some members who had voted in the negative, would be for the affirmative with some modifications, the question was put with these modifications, and it was determined by a majority of eleven members, that their body should join the Tiers. These proceedings of the Clergy were unknown to the Council at Marly, and those of the Council were kept secret from everybody. The next morning (the 20th), the members repaired to the House as usual, found the doors shut and guarded, and a proclamation posted up for holding a *séance royale* on the 22d, and a suspension of their meetings till then. They presumed, in the first moment, that their dissolution was decided, and repaired to another place, where they proceeded to business. They there bound themselves to each other by an oath, never to separate of their own accord, till they had settled a constitution for the nation on a solid basis, and if separated by force, that they would re-assemble in some other place. It was intimated to them, however, that day, privately, that the proceedings of the *séance royale* would be favorable to them. The next day they met in a church, and were joined by a majority of the Clergy. The heads of the aristocracy saw that all was lost without some violent exertion. The King was still at Marly. Nobody was permitted to approach him but their friends. He was assailed by lies in all shapes. He was made to believe that the Commons were going to absolve the army from their oath of fidelity to him, and to raise their pay. . . . The nobility were in triumph, the people in consternation. When the King passed the next day through the lane they formed from the Château to the Hotel des États (about half a mile), there was a dead silence. He was about an hour in the House, delivering his speech and declaration, copies of which I enclose you. On his coming out, a feeble cry of "*vive le roy*" was raised by some children, but the people remained silent and sullen. When the Duke d'Orleans followed, however, their applauses were excessive. This must have been sensible to the King. He had ordered, in the close of his speech, that the members should follow him, and resume their deliberations the next day. The Noblesse followed him, and so did the Clergy, except about thirty, who, with the Tiers, remained in the room, and entered into deliberation. They protested against what the King had done, adhered to all their former proceedings, and resolved the inviolability of their own persons. An officer came twice to order them out of the room, in the King's name, but they refused to obey. In the afternoon, the people, uneasy, began to assemble in great numbers in the courts and vicinities of the palace. The Queen was alarmed. . . .

June 25. Just returned from Versailles, I am enabled to continue my narration. On the 24th, nothing remarkable passed, except an attack by the mob of Versailles on the Archbishop of Paris, who had been one of the instigators of the court, to the proceedings of the *séance royale*. They threw mud and stones at his carriage, broke the windows of it, and he in a fright promised to join the Tiers.

This day (the 25th) forty-eight of the Nobles have joined the Tiers. Among these, is the Duke d'Orleans. The Marquis de La Fayette could not be of the number, being restrained by his instructions. He is writing to his constituents, to change his instructions or to accept his resignation. There are with the Tiers now, one hundred and sixty-four members of the Clergy, so that the common chamber consists of upwards of eight hundred members. The minority of the Clergy, however, call themselves the chamber of the Clergy, and pretend to go on with business. I found the streets of Versailles much embarrassed with soldiers. There was a body of about one hundred horse drawn up in front of the Hotel of the States, and all the avenues and doors guarded by soldiers. Nobody was permitted to enter but the members, and this was by order of the King; for till now, the doors of the common room have been open, and at least two thousand spectators attending their debates constantly. They have named a deputation to wait on the King, and desire a removal of the soldiery from their doors, and seem determined, if this is not complied with, to remove themselves elsewhere.

Instead of being dismayed with what has passed, they seem to rise in their demands, and some of them to consider the erasing every vestige of a difference of order as indispensable to the establishment and preservation of a good constitution. I apprehend there is more courage than calculation in this project.

## Revolt of the Troops

### TO JOHN JAY.

PARIS, *June 29, 1789.*

SIR,—My letter of the 25th gave you the transactions of the States General to the afternoon of that day. On the next, the Archbishop of Paris joined the Tiers, as did some others of the Clergy and Noblesse. On the 27th, the question of the St. Domingo deputation came on, and it was decided that it should be received. I have before mentioned to you the ferment into which the proceedings at the *séance royale* of the 23d, had thrown the people. The soldiery also were affected by it. It began in the French guards, extended to those of every other denomination, (except the Swiss) and even to the body guards of the King. They began to quit their barracks, to assemble in squads, to declare they would defend the life of the King, but would not cut the throats of their fellow-citizens. They were treated and caressed by the people, carried in triumph through the streets, called themselves the soldiers of the nation, and left no doubt on which side they would be, in case of a rupture. Similar accounts came in from the troops in other parts of the kingdom, as well those which had not heard of the *séance royale*, as those which had, and gave good reason to apprehend that the soldiery, in general, would side with their fathers and brothers, rather than with their officers. The operation of this medicine, at Versailles, was as sudden as it was powerful. The alarm there was so complete, that in the afternoon of the 27th, the King wrote . . . to the President of the Clergy, the Cardinal de La Rochefoucault, in these words:[1]

"I pass my word that my faithful Clergy will, without delay, unite themselves with the other two orders, to hasten the accomplishment of my paternal views."

A like letter was written to the Duke de Luxemburgh, President of the Noblesse. The two chambers entered into debate on the question, whether they should obey the letter of the King. There was a considerable opposition; when notes written by the Count d'Artois to sundry members, and handed about among the rest, decided the matter, and they went in a body and took their seats with the Tiers, and thus rendered the union of the orders in one chamber complete. As soon as this was known to the people of Versailles, they assembled about the palace, demanded the King and Queen, who came and showed themselves in a balcony. They rent the skies with cries of *"vive le roy," "vive la reine."* They called for the Dauphin, who was also produced, and was the subject of new acclamations. After feasting themselves and the royal family with this tumultuary reconciliation, they went to the house of Mr. Neckar and M. de Montmorin, with shouts of thankfulness and affection. Similar emotions of joy took place in Paris, and at this moment, the triumph of the Tiers is considered as complete. To-morrow they will recommence business, voting by persons on all questions; and whatever difficulties may be opposed in debate by the malcontents of the Clergy and Nobility, everything must be finally settled at the will of the Tiers. It remains to see whether they will leave to the Nobility anything but their titulary appellations.

[1][A literal translation]

# Insecure Victory

## TO THOMAS PAINE.

PARIS, *July 11, 1789.*

DEAR SIR,—Since my last, which was of May the 19th, I have received yours of June the 17th and 18th. I am struck with the idea of the geometrical wheelbarrow, and will beg of you a farther account, if it can be obtained. I have no news yet of my *congé.*

Though you have doubtless heard most of the proceedings of the States General since my last, I will take up the narration where that left it, that you may be able to separate the true from the false accounts you have heard. A good part of what was conjectured in that letter, is now become true history. . . . The *National Assembly* then (for that is the name they take), having shown through every stage of these transactions a coolness, wisdom, and resolution to set fire to the four corners of the kingdom and to perish with it themselves, rather than to relinquish an iota from their plan of a total change of government, are now in complete and undisputed possession of the sovereignty. The executive and aristocracy are at their feet; the mass of the nation, the mass of the clergy, and the army are with them; they have prostrated the old government, and are now beginning to build one from the foundation. A committee, charged with the arrangement of their business, gave in, two days ago, the following order of proceedings.

"1. Every government should have for its only end, the preservation of the rights of man; whence it follows, that to recall constantly the government to the end proposed, the constitution should begin by a declaration of the natural and imprescriptible rights of man.

"2. Monarchical government being proper to maintain those rights, it has been chosen by the French nation. It suits especially a great society; it is necessary for the happiness of France. The declaration of the principles of this government, then, should follow immediately the declaration of the rights of man.

"3. It results from the principles of monarchy, that the nation, to assure its own rights, has yielded particular rights to the monarch; the constitution, then, should declare, in a precise manner, the rights of both. It should begin by declaring the rights of the French nation, and then it should declare the rights of the King.

"4. The rights of the King and nation not existing but for the happiness of the individuals who compose it, they lead to an examination of the rights of citizens.

"5. The French nation not being capable of assembling individually, to exercise all its rights, it ought to be represented. It is necessary, then, to declare the form of its representation and the rights of its representatives.

"6. From the union of the powers of the nation and King, should result the enacting and execution of the laws; thus, then, it should first be determined how the laws shall be established, afterwards should be considered, how they shall be executed.

"7. Laws have for their object the general administration of the kingdom, the property and the actions of the citizens. The execution of the laws which concern the general administration, requires Provincial and Municipal Assemblies. It is necessary to examine, therefore, what should be the organization of the Provincial Assemblies, and what of the Municipal.

"8. The execution of the laws which concern the property and actions of the citizens, call for the judiciary power. It should be determined how that should be confided, and then its duties and limits.

"9. For the execution of the laws and the defence of the kingdom, there exists a public force. It is necessary, then, to determine the principles which should direct it, and how it should be employed.

*"Recapitulation.*

"Declaration of the rights of man. Principles of the monarchy. Rights of the nation. Rights of the King. Rights of the citizens.

"Organization and rights of the National Assembly. Forms necessary for the enaction of laws. Organization and functions of the Provincial and Municipal Assemblies. Duties and limits of the judiciary power. Functions and duties of the military power."

You see that these are the materials of a superb edifice, and the hands which have prepared them, are perfectly capable of putting them together, and of filling up the work of which these are only the outlines. While there are some men among them of very superior abilities, the mass possess such a degree of good sense, as enables them to decide well. I have always been afraid their numbers might lead to confusion. Twelve hundred men in one room are too many. I have still that fear. Another apprehension is, that a majority cannot be induced to adopt the trial by jury; and I consider that as the only anchor ever yet imagined by man, by which a government can be held to the principles of its constitution.

# Fighting in the Streets

### TO THOMAS PAINE.

Paris, *July 13, 1789.*

Dear Sir,—I wrote you the day before yesterday by Mr. Paradise. I write now by post. . . . Mr. Neckar was dismissed from office the evening of the 11th and set out for Geneva. This was not generally known in Paris till yesterday afternoon. The mobs immediately shut up all the playhouses. The foreign troops were advanced into the city, engagements took place between some of them and the people. The first was in the Place St. Louis XV,

where a body of German cavalry being drawn up the people posted themselves upon and behind the piles of stones collected there for bridges,
attacked and drove off the cavalry with stones. I suspect the cavalry rallied
and returned, as I heard shortly after in the same spot a considerable firing.
This was a little before dusk and it is now early in the morning, so I have
not ascertained any particulars.

## Bastille Day

### TO JOHN JAY.

PARIS, *July 19, 1789.*

The scarcity of bread begins to lessen in the southern parts of France,
where the harvest has commenced. Here it is still threatening, because we
have yet three weeks to the beginning of harvest, and I think there has not
been three days' provision beforehand in Paris, for two or three weeks past.
Monsieur de Mirabeau, who is very hostile to Mr. Neckar, wished to find
a ground for censuring him, in a proposition to have a great quantity of
flour furnished from the United States, which he supposed me to have made
to Mr. Neckar, and to have been refused by him; and he asked time of the
States General to furnish proofs. The Marquis de La Fayette immediately
gave me notice of this matter, and I wrote him a letter to disavow having
ever made any such proposition to Mr. Neckar, which I desired him to
communicate to the States.

My letter of the 29th of June, brought down the proceedings of the States
and government to the re-union of the orders, which took place on the 27th.
Within the Assembly, matters went on well. But it was soon observed, that
troops, and particularly the foreign troops, were on their march towards
Paris from various quarters, and that this was against the opinion of Mr.
Neckar. The King was probably advised to this, under pretext of preserving
peace in Paris and Versailles, and saw nothing else in the measure. That his
advisers are supposed to have had in view, when he should be secured and
inspirited by the presence of the troops, to take advantage of some favorable
moment, and surprise him into an act of authority for establishing the
declaration of the 23d of June, and perhaps dispersing the States General,
is probable. The Marshal de Broglio was appointed to command all the
troops within the isle of France, a high flying aristocrat, cool and capable
of everything. Some of the French guards were soon arrested under other
pretexts, but in reality, on account of their dispositions in favor of the
national cause. The people of Paris forced the prison, released them, and
sent a deputation to the States General, to solicit a pardon. The States,
by a most moderate and prudent Arreté, recommended these prisoners to
the King, and peace to the people of Paris. Addresses came in to them from
several of the great cities, expressing sincere allegiance to the King, but a

determined resolution to support the States General. On the 8th of July, they voted an address to the King to remove the troops. This piece of masculine eloquence, written by Monsieur de Mirabeau, is worth attention on account of the bold matter it expresses and discovers through the whole. The King refused to remove the troops, and said they might remove themselves, if they pleased, to Noyons or Soissons. They proceeded to fix the order in which they will take up the several branches of their future constitution, from which it appears, they mean to build it from the bottom, confining themselves to nothing in their ancient form, but a King. A declaration of rights, which forms the first chapter of their work, was then proposed by the Marquis de La Fayette. This was on the 11th.

in the meantime, troops, to the number of about twenty-five or thirty thousand, had arrived, and were posted in and between Paris and Versailles. The bridges and passes were guarded. At three o'clock in the afternoon, the Count de La Luzerne was sent to notify Mr. Neckar of his dismission, and to enjoin him to retire instantly, without saying a word of it to anybody. . . . This change, however sudden it may have been in the mind of the King, was, in that of his advisers, only one chapter of a great plan, of which the bringing together the foreign troops had been the first. He was now completely in the hands of men, the principal among whom, had been noted through their lives, for the Turkish despotism of their characters, and who were associated about the King, as proper instruments for what was to be executed.

The news of this change began to be known in Paris about one or two o'clock. In the afternoon, a body of about one hundred German cavalry were advanced and drawn up in the Place Louis XV. and about two hundred Swiss posted at a little distance in their rear. This drew the people to that spot, who naturally formed themselves in front of the troops, at first merely to look at them. But as their numbers increased their indignation arose; they retired a few steps, posted themselves on and behind large piles of loose stone, collected in that place for a bridge adjacent to it, and attacked the horse with stones. The horse charged, but the advantageous position of the people, and the showers of stones, obliged them to retire, and even to quit the field altogether, leaving one of their number on the ground. The Swiss in their rear were observed never to stir. This was the signal for universal insurrection, and this body of cavalry, to avoid being massacred, retired towards Versailles. The people now armed themselves with such weapons as they could find in armorers' shops and private houses, and with bludgeons, and were roaming all night through all parts of the city, without any decided practicable object.

The next day, the States pressed on the King to send away the troops, to permit the Bourgeoise of Paris to arm for the preservation of order in the city, and offered to send a deputation from their body to tranquillize them. He refused all their propositions. A committee of magistrates and electors of the city were appointed by their bodies, to take upon them its government. The mob, now openly joined by the French guards, forced the prison of St. Lazare, released all the prisoners, and took a great store of corn, which they carried to the corn market. Here they got some arms, and the French guards began to form and train them. The committee determined to raise forty-eight thousand Bourgeoise, or rather to restrain their numbers to forty-eight thousand. On the 14th, they sent one of their members (Monsieur de Corny, whom we knew in America) to the Hotel des Invalides, to ask arms for their Garde Bourgeoise. He was followed by, or he found there, a great mob. The Governor of the Invalides came out, and represented the impossibility of his delivering arms, without the orders of those from whom he received them. De Corny advised the people then to retire, and retired himself; and the people took possession of the arms. It was remarkable, that not only the Invalides themselves made no opposition, but that a body of five thousand foreign troops, encamped within four hundred yards, never stirred. Monsieur de Corny and five others were then sent to ask arms of Monsieur de Launai, Governor of the Bastile. They found a great collection of people already before the place, and they immediately planted a flag of truce, which was answered by a like flag hoisted on the parapet. The deputation prevailed on the people to fall back a little, advanced themselves to make their demand of the Governor, and in that instant a discharge from the Bastile killed four people of those nearest to the deputies. The deputies retired; the people rushed against the place, and almost in an instant were in possession of a fortification, defended by one hundred men, of infinite strength, which in other times had stood several regular sieges, and had never been taken. How they got in, has, as yet, been impossible to discover. Those who pretend to have been of the party tell so many different stories, as to destroy the credit of them all. They took all the arms, discharged the prisoners, and such of the garrison as were not killed in the first moment of fury, carried the Governor and Lieutenant Governor to the Gréve, (the place of public execution,) cut off their heads, and sent them through the city in triumph to the Palais Royal. About the same instant, a treacherous correspondence having been discovered in Monsieur de Flesselles, Prevost des Marchands, they seized him in the Hotel de Ville, where he was in the exercise of his office, and cut off his head.

These events, carried imperfectly to Versailles, were the subject of two successive deputations from the States to the King, to both of which he gave dry and hard answers; for it has transpired, that it had been proposed and agitated in Council, to seize on the principal members of the States General, to march the whole army down upon Paris, and to suppress its tumults by the sword. But at night, the Duke de Liancourt forced his way into the King's bed chamber, and obliged him to hear a full and animated detail of the disasters of the day in Paris. He went to bed deeply impressed. The decapitation of de Launai worked powerfully through the night on the whole aristocratical party, insomuch, that in the morning, those of the greatest influence on the Count d'Artois, represented to him the absolute necessity that the King should give up everything to the States. This according well enough with the dispositions of the King, he went about eleven o'clock, accompanied only by his brothers, to the States General, and there read to them a speech, in which he asked their interposition to re-establish order. Though this be couched in terms of some caution, yet the manner in which it was delivered, made it evident that it was meant as a surrender at discretion.

He returned to the château a foot, accompanied by the States. They sent off a deputation, the Marquis de La Fayette at their head, to quiet Paris. He had, the same morning, been named Commandant-in-Chief of the Milice Bourgeoise, and Monsieur Bailly, former President of the States General, was called for as Prevost des Marchands. The demolition of the Bastile was now ordered, and begun. A body of the Swiss guards of the regiment of Ventimille, and the city horse guards, joined the people. The alarm at Versailles increased instead of abating. They believed that the aristocrats of Paris were under pillage and carnage, that one hundred and fifty thousand men were in arms, coming to Versailles to massacre the royal family, the court, the ministers, and all connected with them. . . .

The King came to Paris, leaving the Queen in consternation for his return. Omitting the less important figures of the procession, I will only observe, that the King's carriage was in the centre, on each side of it the States General, in two ranks, a foot, and at their head the Marquis de La Fayette, as Commander-in-Chief, on horseback, and Bourgeoise guards before and behind. About sixty thousand citizens of all forms and colors, armed with the muskets of the Bastile and Invalides, as far as they would go, the rest with pistols, swords, pikes, pruning hooks, scythes, etc., lined all the streets through which the procession passed, and, with the crowds of people in the streets, doors and windows, saluted them everywhere with cries of *"vive la nation;"* but not a single *"vive le roy"* was heard. The King stopped at the Hotel de Ville. There Monsieur Bailly presented and put into his hat the popular cockade, and addressed him. The King being unprepared and unable to answer, Bailly went to him, gathered from him some scraps of sentences, and made out an answer, which he delivered to the audience as from the King. On their return, the popular cries were *"vive le roy et la nation."* He was conducted by a Garde Bourgeoise to his palace at Versailles, and thus concluded such an *amende honorable*, as no sovereign ever made, and no people ever received. Letters written with his own hand to the Marquis de La Fayette, remove the scruples of his position.

Tranquillity is now restored to the capital: the shops are again opened; the people resuming their labors, and if the want of bread does not disturb our peace, we may hope a continuance of it. The demolition of the Bastile is going on, and the Milice Bourgeoise organizing and training. The ancient police of the city is abolished by the authority of the people, the introduction of the King's troops will probably be proscribed, and a watch or city guards substituted, which shall depend on the city alone. But we cannot suppose this paroxysm confined to Paris alone. The whole country must pass successfully through it, and happy if they get through it as soon and as well as Paris has done.

I went yesterday to Versailles, to satisfy myself what had passed there; for nothing can be believed but what one sees, or has from an eye witness. They believe there still, that three thousand people have fallen victims to the tumults of Paris. Mr. Short and myself have been every day among them, in order to be sure what was passing. We cannot find, with certainty, that anybody has been killed but the three before mentioned, and those who fell in the assault or defence of the Bastile. How many of the garrison were killed, nobody pretends to have ever heard. Of the assailants, accounts vary from six to six hundred. The most general belief is, that there fell about thirty. There have been many reports of instantaneous executions by the mob, on such of their body as they caught in acts of theft or robbery. Some of these may perhaps be true. There was a severity of honesty observed, of which no example has been known. Bags of money offered on various occasions through fear or guilt, have been uniformly refused by the mobs. The churches are now occupied in singing "*De profundis*" and "*Requiems*" "for the repose of the souls of the brave and valiant citizens who have sealed with their blood the liberty of the nation."

# Paris Mob

## TO MR. JAMES MADISON.

PARIS, *July 22, 1789.*

DEAR SIR,—My last to you was of the 18th of June. Within a day or two after, yours of May the 9th came to hand. In the rest of Europe nothing remarkable has happened; but in France such events as will be forever memorable in history.

. . . The tumults in the city had pretty well subsided, but to-day they have been revived by a new incident. Foulon, one of the fugitive ministers, was taken in the country, (it is said by his own tenants,) and brought to Paris. Every possible effort of persuasion was exerted in vain to save him. He was forced from the hands of the Gardes Bourgeoises by the mob, was hung, and after severing his head, the body was dragged by the enraged populace through the principal streets of Paris. The Intendant of Paris (de Chauvigny), accused of having been in the plots with the late ministry, and who had fled, was taken at Compiegne, and a party of two hundred militia horse are now gone for him. If they bring him to Paris it will be impossible to save him. Monsieur de La Luzerne was reappointed minister of marine yesterday. Your last letter says nothing of my leave of absence. The season is so far advanced towards the Equinox, that if it comes to hand I shall not leave Europe till that be over. Indeed this scene is too interesting to be left at present. But if the permission does not come in time for my passage in the fall, the necessity of my going is so imperious, that I shall be in a most distressing dilemma.

I am, with sincere esteem and respect, dear Sir, your affectionate friend and servant.

P. S. *July 23.* I just learn that Bretier de Chauvigny was brought to town in the night and massacred immediately.

## Royalty at Home

### TO MR. WILLIAM CARMICHAEL.

PARIS, *August 9, 1789.*

The Senate and Representatives differed about the title of the President. The former wanted to style him "His Highness, George Washington, President of the United States, and Protector of their liberties." The latter insisted and prevailed, to give no title but that of office, to wit, "George Washington, President of the United States." I hope the terms of Excellency, Honor, Worship, Esquire, forever disappear from among us, from that moment: I wish that of Mr. would follow them.

## No Money, No Bread

### TO JOHN JAY.

PARIS, *August 27, 1789.*

No act of violence has taken place in Paris since my last, except on account of the difference between the French and Swiss guards, which gave rise to occasional single combats, in which five or six were killed. The difference is made up. Some misunderstandings had arisen between the committees of the different districts of Paris, as to the form of the future municipal government. These gave uneasiness for awhile, but have been also reconciled. Still there is such a leaven of fermentation remaining in the body of the people, that acts of violence are always possible, and are quite unpunishable; there being, as yet, no judicature which can venture to act in any case, however small or great. The country is becoming more calm. The embarrassments of the government, for want of money, are extreme. The loan of thirty millions proposed by Mr. Neckar, has not succeeded at all. No taxes are paid. A total stoppage of all payment to the creditors of the State is possible every moment. These form a great mass in the city as well as country, and among the lower class of people, too, who have been used to carry their little savings of their service into the public funds upon life rents of five, ten, twenty guineas a year, and many of whom have no other dependence for daily subsistence. A prodigious number of servants are now also thrown out of employ by domestic reforms, rendered necessary by the late events. Add to this, the want of bread, which is extreme. For several days past, a considerable proportion of the people have been without bread altogether; for though the new harvest is begun, there is neither water nor wind to grind the grain. For some days past the people have besieged the doors of the bakers, scrambled with one another for bread, collected in squads all over the city, and need only some slight incident to lead them to excesses which may end in, nobody can tell what. The danger from the want of bread, however, which is the most imminent, will certainly lessen in a few days. What turn that may take which arises from the want of money, is difficult to be foreseen.

## On National Morals

### TO JAMES MADISON.

PARIS, *August 28, 1789.*

It is impossible to desire better dispositions towards us than prevail in this Assembly. Our proceedings have been viewed as a model for them on every occasion; and though in the heat of debate, men are generally disposed to contradict every authority urged by their opponents, ours has been treated like that of the Bible, open to explanation, but not to question. I am sorry that in the moment of such a disposition, anything should come from us to check it. The placing them on a mere footing with the English, will have this effect. When of two nations, the one has engaged herself in a ruinous war for us, has spent her blood and money to save us, has opened her bosom to us in peace, and received us almost on the footing of her own citizens, while the other has moved heaven, earth, and hell to exterminate us in war, has insulted us in all her councils in peace, shut her doors to us in every part where her interests would admit it, libelled us in foreign nations, endeavored to poison them against the reception of our most precious commodities; to place these two nations on a footing, is to give a great deal more to one than to the other, if the maxim be true, that to make unequal quantities equal, you must add more to one than the other. To say, in excuse, that gratitude is never to enter into the motives of national conduct, is to revive a principle which has been buried for centuries with its kindred principles of the lawfulness of assassination, poison, perjury, etc. All of these were legitimate principles in the dark ages which intervened between ancient and modern civilization, but exploded and held in just horror in the eighteenth century. I know but one code of morality for men, whether acting singly or collectively. He who says I will be a rogue when I act in company with a hundred others, but an honest man when I act alone, will be believed in the former assertion, but not in the latter. I would say with the poet, "*hic niger est, hunc tu Romane cavato.*" If the morality of one man produces a just line of conduct in him, acting individually, why should not the morality of one hundred men produce a just line of conduct in them, acting together?

I must now say a word on the declaration of rights, you have been so good as to send me. I like it, as far as it goes; but I should have been for going further. For instance, the following alterations and additions would have pleased me: Article 4. "The people shall not be deprived of their right to speak, to write, or *otherwise* to publish anything but false facts affecting injuriously the life, liberty, property or reputation of others, or affecting the peace of the confederacy with foreign nations. Article 7. All facts put in issue before any judicature, shall be tried by jury, except, 1, in cases of admiralty jurisdiction, wherein a foreigner shall be interested; 2, in cases cognizable before a court martial, concerning only the regular officers and soldiers of the United States, or members of the militia in actual service in time of war or insurrection; and 3, in impeachments allowed by the constitution. Article 8. No person shall be held in confinement more than —— days after he shall have demanded and been refused a writ of habeas corpus by the judge appointed by law, nor more than —— days after such a writ shall have been served on the person holding him in confinement, and no order given on due examination for his remandment or discharge, nor more than —— hours in any place at a greater distance than —— miles from the usual residence of some judge authorized to issue the writ of habeas corpus; nor shall that writ be suspended for any term exceeding one year, nor in any place more than —— miles distant from the State or encampment of enemies or of insurgents. Article 9. Monopolies may be allowed to persons for their own productions in literature, and their own inventions in the arts, for a term not exceeding —— years, but for no longer term, and no other purpose. Article 10. All troops of the United States shall stand *ipso facto* disbanded, at the expiration of the term for which their pay and subsistence shall have been last voted by Congress, and all officers and soldiers, not natives of the United States, shall be incapable of serving in their armies by land, except during a foreign war." These restrictions I think are so guarded, as to hinder evil only. However, if we do not have them now, I have so much confidence in my countrymen, as to be satisfied that we shall have them as soon as the degeneracy of our government shall render them necessary.

I have no certain news of Paul Jones. I understand only, in a general way, that some persecution on the part of his officers occasioned his being called to St. Petersburg, and that though protected against them by the Empress, he is not yet restored to his station. . . . I propose to sail from Havre as soon after the first of October as I can get a vessel; and shall consequently leave this place a week earlier than that. As my daughters will be with me, and their baggage somewhat more than that of mere *voyageures*, I shall endeavor, if possible, to obtain a passage for Virginia directly. Probably I shall be there by the last of November. If my immediate attendance at New York should be requisite for any purpose, I will leave them with a relation near Richmond, and proceed immediately to New York. But as I do not foresee any pressing purpose for that journey immediately on my arrival, and as it will be a great saving of time, to finish at once in Virginia, so as to have no occasion to return there after having once gone to the northward, I expect to proceed to my own house directly. Staying there two months (which I believe will be necessary), and allowing for the time I am on the road, I may expect to be at New York in February, and to embark from thence or some eastern port.

You ask me if I would accept any appointment on that side of the water? You know the circumstances which led me from retirement, step by step, and from one nomination to another, up to the present. My object is a return to the same retirement; whenever, therefore, I quit the present, it will not be to engage in any other office, and most especially any one which would require a constant residence from home. The books I have collected for you will go off for Havre in three or four days, with my baggage. From that port, I shall try to send them by a direct occasion to New York. I am, with great and sincere esteem, dear Sir, your affectionate friend and servant.

# To Whom the Earth Belongs

### TO JAMES MADISON.

PARIS, *September 6, 1789.*

The question, whether one generation of men has a right to bind another, seems never to have been started either on this or our side of the water. Yet it is a question of such consequences as not only to merit decision, but place also among the fundamental principles of every government. The course of reflection in which we are immersed here, on the elementary principles of society, has presented this question to my mind; and that no such obligation can be transmitted, I think very capable of proof. I set out on this ground, which I suppose to be self-evident, that the *earth belongs in usufruct to the living;* that the dead have neither powers nor rights over it. The portion occupied by any individual ceases to be his when himself ceases to be, and reverts to the society. If the society has formed no rules for the appropriation of its lands in severalty, it will be taken by the first occupants, and these will generally be the wife and children of the decedent. If they have formed rules of appropriation, those rules may give it to the wife and children, or to some one of them, or to the legatee of the deceased. So they may give it to its creditor. But the child, the legatee or creditor, takes it, not by natural right, but by a law of the society of which he is a member, and to which he is subject. Then, no man can, by *natural right,* oblige the lands he occupied, or the persons who succeed him in that occupation, to the payment of debts contracted by him. For if he could, he might during his own life, eat up the usufruct of the lands for several generations to come; and then the lands would belong to the dead, and not to the living, which is the reverse of our principle.

What is true of every member of the society, individually, is true of them all collectively; since the rights of the whole can be no more than the sum of the rights of the individuals. To keep our ideas clear when applying them to a multitude, let us suppose a whole generation of men to be born on the same day, to attain mature age on the same day, and to die on the same day, leaving a succeeding generation in the moment of attaining their mature age, all together. Let the ripe age be supposed of twenty-one years, and their period of life thirty-four years more, that being the average term given by the bills of mortality to persons of twenty-one years of age. Each successive generation would, in this way, come and go off the stage at a fixed moment, as individuals do now. Then I say, the earth belongs to each of these generations during its course, fully and in its own right. The second generation receives it clear of the debts and incumbrances of the first, the third of the second, and so on. For if the first could charge it with a debt, then the earth would belong to the dead and not to the living. . . .

To render this conclusion palpable, suppose that Louis the XIV. and XV. had contracted debts in the name of the French nation, to the amount of ten thousand milliards, and that the whole had been contracted in Holland. The interest of this sum would be five hundred milliards, which is the whole rent-roll or net proceeds of the territory of France. Must the present generation of men have retired from the territory in which nature produces them, and ceded it to the Dutch creditors? No; they have the same rights over the soil on which they were produced, as the preceding generations had. They derive these rights not from them, but from nature. They, then, and their soil are, by nature, clear of the debts of their predecessors. To present this in another point of view, suppose Louis XV. and his contemporary generation, had said to the money lenders of Holland, give us money, that we may eat, drink, and be merry in our day; and on condition you will demand no interest till the end of thirty-four years, you shall then, forever after, receive an annual interest of fifteen per cent. The money is lent on these conditions, is divided among the people, eaten, drunk, and squandered. Would the present generation be obliged to apply the produce of the earth and of their labor, to replace their dissipations? Not at all.

I suppose that the received opinion, that the public debts of one generation devolve on the next, has been suggested by our seeing, habitually, in private life, that he who succeeds to lands is required to pay the debts of his predecessor; without considering that this requisition is municipal only, not moral, flowing from the will of the society, which has found it convenient to appropriate the lands of a decedent on the condition of a payment of his debts; but that between society and society, or generation and generation, there is no municipal obligation, no umpire but the law of nature.

On similar ground it may be proved, that no society can make a perpetual constitution, or even a perpetual law. The earth belongs always to the living generation: they may manage it, then, and what proceeds from it, as they please, during their usufruct. They are masters, too, of their own persons, and consequently may govern them as they please. But persons and property make the sum of the objects of government. The constitution and the laws of their predecessors are extinguished then, in their natural course, with those whose will gave them being. This could preserve that being, till it ceased to be itself, and no longer. Every constitution, then, and every law, naturally expires at the end of thirty-four years. If it be enforced longer, it is an act of force, and not of right. It may be said, that the succeeding generation exercising, in fact, the power of repeal, this leaves them as free as if the constitution or law had been expressly limited to thirty-four years only. In the first place, this objection admits the right, in proposing an equivalent. But the power of repeal is not an equivalent. It might be, indeed, if every form of government were so perfectly contrived, that the will of the majority could always be obtained, fairly and without impediment. But this is true of no form. The people cannot assemble themselves; their representation is unequal and vicious. Various checks are opposed to every legislative proposition. Factions get possession of the public councils, bribery corrupts them, personal interests lead them astray from the general interests of their constituents; and other impediments arise, so as to prove to every practical man, that a law of limited duration is much more manageable than one which needs a repeal.

This principle, that the earth belongs to the living and not to the dead, is of very extensive application and consequences in every country, and most especially in France. It enters into the resolution of the questions, whether the nation may change the descent of lands holden in tail; whether they may change the appropriation of lands given anciently to the church, to hospitals, colleges, orders of chivalry, and otherwise in perpetuity; whether they may abolish the charges and privileges attached on lands, including the whole catalogue, ecclesiastical and feudal; it goes to hereditary offices, authorities and jurisdictions, to hereditary orders, distinctions and appellations, to perpetual monopolies in commerce, the arts or sciences, with a long train of *et ceteras*. . . .

# Mass Production

### TO GENERAL HENRY KNOX.

Paris, *September 12, 1789.*

Sir,—In a letter which I had the honor of writing to the Secretary for Foreign Affairs some three or four years ago I informed him that a workman had undertaken by the help of moulds and other means to make all the parts of the musket so exactly alike as that mixed together promiscuously any one part would serve equally for every musket. He had then succeeded as to the lock both of the officers' fusil and the soldiers' musket, from a promiscuous collection of parts. I put together myself half a dozen locks taking the first pieces which came to hand. He has now completed the barrels, stock and mounting of the officers' fusil and is proceeding on those of the soldiers' musket. This method of forming the fire-arm appears to me so advantageous when repairs become necessary that I have thought it my duty not only to mention to you the progress of this artist but to purchase and send you a half dozen of his officers' fusils. They are packed in a box marked TI no. 36, are sent to Havre, from whence they shall be forwarded to New York. The barrels and furniture are to their stocks, to protect the warping of the wood. The locks are in pieces. You will find them, tools for putting them together, also a single specimen of his soldiers' lock. He formerly told me, and still tells me, that he will be able, after a while, to furnish them cheaper than the common musket of the same quality, but at first they will not be so cheap in the first cost though economy in repairs will make them so in the end. He cannot tell me exactly at what price he can furnish them, nor will he be able immediately to furnish any great quantity annually; but with the aid of the government he expects to enlarge his establishment greatly.

# Trade Winds

## TO E. RUTLEDGE.

PARIS, *September 18, 1789.*

The conjecture that inhabitants may have been carried from the coast of Africa to that of America, by the trade winds, is possible enough; and its probability would be greatly strengthened by ascertaining a similarity of language, which I consider as the strongest of all proofs of consanguinity among nations. Still a question would remain between the red men of the eastern and western sides of the Atlantic, which is the stock, and which the shoot? If a fact be true, which I suspect to be true, that there is a much greater number of radical languages among those of America than among those of the other hemisphere, it would be a proof of superior antiquity, which I can conceive no arguments strong enough to overrule.

When I received your letter, the time of my departure was too near, to permit me to obtain information from Constantinople, relative to the demand and price of rice there. I, therefore, wrote to a merchant at Versailles, concerned in the Levant trade, for the prices current of rice at Constantinople and at Marseilles for several years past. He has sent me only the present price at Marseilles, and that of a particular cargo at Constantinople. I send you a copy of his letter. The Algerines form an obstacle; but the object of our commerce in the Mediterranean is so immense, that we ought to surmount that obstacle, and I believe it could be done by means in our power, and which, instead of fouling us with the dishonorable and criminal baseness of France and England, will place us in the road to respect with all the world.

# Revolutionary Factions

## TO JOHN JAY.

PARIS, *September 19, 1789.*

The sloth of the Assembly (unavoidable from their number) has done the most sensible injury to the public cause. The patience of a people who have less of that quality than any other nation in the world, is worn threadbare. Time has been given to the aristocrats to recover from their panic, to cabal, to sow dissensions in the Assembly, and distrust out of it. . . .

This being the face of things, troubled as you will perceive, civil war is much talked of and expected; and this talk and expectation has a tendency to beget it. What are the events which may produce it? 1. The want of bread, were it to produce a commencement of disorder, might ally itself to more permanent causes of discontent, and thus continue the effect beyond its first cause. The scarcity of bread, which continues very great amidst a plenty of corn, is an enigma which can be solved only by observing, that the furnishing the city is in the new municipality, not yet masters of their trade. 2. A public bankruptcy. Great numbers of the lower as well as higher classes of the citizens, depend for subsistence on their property in the public funds. 3. The absconding of the King from Versailles. This has for some time been apprehended as possible. In consequence of this apprehension, a person whose information would have weight, wrote to the Count de Montmorin, adjuring him to prevent it by every possible means, and assuring him that the flight of the King would be the signal of a St. Bartholomew against the aristocrats in Paris, and perhaps through the kingdom. M. de Montmorin showed the letter to the Queen, who assured him solemnly that no such thing was in contemplation. His showing it to the Queen, proves he entertained the same mistrust with the public. It may be asked, what is the Queen disposed to do in the present situation of things? Whatever rage, pride and fear can dictate in a breast which never knew the presence of one moral restraint.

Upon the whole, I do not see it as yet probable that any actual commotion will take place; and if it does take place, I have strong confidence that the patriotic party will hold together, and their party in the nation be what I have described it. In this case, there would be against them the aristocracy and the faction of Orleans. This consists, at this time, of only the Catilines of the Assembly, and some of the lowest description of the mob. Its force, *within the kingdom,* must depend on how much of this last kind of people it can debauch with money from its present bias to the right cause. This bias is as strong as any one can be, in a class which must accept its bread from him who will give it. Its resources *out of the kingdom* are not known. Without doubt, England will give money to produce and to feed the fire which should consume this country; but it is not probable she will engage in open war for that. If foreign troops should be furnished, it would be most probably by the King of Prussia, who seems to offer himself as the bull-dog of tyranny to all his neighbors.

# Working Drawings

## TO THE BARON DE GEISMER.

PARIS, *November 20, 1789.*

You have had great reason, my dear Sir, to wonder that you have been so long receiving an answer to your request relative to the drawing of a cabriolet and phaeton. Your object was to have such drawings as that a workman could work by them. A painter's eye draught would not have answered this purpose, and, indeed, to be sure of having them done with the accuracy necessary to guide a workman, I could depend on nobody but myself. But the work was to be done principally in an open court and there came on between two and three months of such intense cold as rendered this impossible. Since the season has become milder I have devoted such little scraps of time to this object as I was master of, and I now enclose you the drawings. They are made with such scrupulous exactness in every part that your workman may safely rely on them. . . .

Our late informations from America are that our new Constitution will begin [in] March and with an almost universal approbation. In order to reconcile those who still remain opposed to it a declaration of rights will be added. General Washington will undoubtedly be President. I have asked leave to pay a short visit to my own country. I expect to go out in the ensuing spring and to return in autumn. I shall pass two months at Monticello. The revolution in this country—for such we may call it—is going on smoothly and will, I think, end in rendering the nation more free and more powerful.

# State Department

## TO THE PRESIDENT.

CHESTERFIELD, *December 15, 1789.*

SIR,—I have received at this place the honor of your letters of October the 13th and November the 30th, and am truly flattered by your nomination of me to the very dignified office of Secretary of State; for which, permit me here to return you my humble thanks. Could any circumstance seduce me to overlook the disproportion between its duties and my talents, it would be the encouragement of your choice. But when I contemplate the extent of that office, embracing as it does the principal mass of domestic administration, together with the foreign, I cannot be insensible of my inequality to it; and I should enter on it with gloomy forebodings from the criticisms and censures of a public, just indeed in their intentions, but sometimes misinformed and misled, and always too respectable to be neglected. I cannot but foresee the possibility that this may end disagreeably for me, who, having no motive to public service but the public satisfaction, would certainly retire the moment that satisfaction should appear to languish. On the other hand, I feel a degree of familiarity with the duties of my present office, as far at least as I am capable of understanding its duties. The ground I have already passed over, enables me to see my way into that which is before me. The change of government too, taking place in a country where it is exercised, seems to open a possibility of procuring from the new rulers, some new advantages in commerce, which may be agreeable to our countrymen. So that as far as my fears, my hopes, or my inclinations might enter into this question, I confess they would not lead me to prefer a change.

But it is not for an individual to choose his post. You are to marshal us as may best be for the public good; and it is only in the case of its being indifferent to you, that I would avail myself of the option you have so kindly offered in your letter. If you think it better to transfer me to another post, my inclination must be no obstacle; nor shall it be, if there is any desire to suppress the office I now hold, or to reduce its grade. In either of these cases, be so good only as to signify to me by another line your ultimate wish, and I shall conform to it cordially. If it should be to remain at New York, my chief comfort will be to work under your eye, my only shelter the authority of your name, and the wisdom of measures to be dictated by you and implicitly executed by me. Whatever you may be pleased to decide, I do not see that the matters which have called me hither, will permit me to shorten the stay I originally asked; that is to say, to set out on my journey northward till the month of March. As early as possible in that month, I shall have the honor of paying my respects to you in New York. In the meantime, I have that of tendering you the homage of those sentiments of respectful attachment with which I am, Sir, your most obedient, and most humble servant.

## Gains by Inches

### TO THE REV. CHARLES CLAY.

MONTICELLO, *January 27, 1790.*

DEAR SIR,—I had hoped that during my stay here I could have had the pleasure of seeing you in Bedford, but I find it will be too short for that. Besides views of business in that country, I had wished again to visit that greatest of our curiosities, the Natural Bridge, and did not know but you might have the same desire. I do not know yet how I am to be disposed of, whether kept at New York, or sent back to Europe. If the former, one of my happinesses would be the possibility of seeing you there; for I understand you are a candidate for the representation of your district in Congress. I cannot be with you to give you my vote, nor do I know who are to be the competitors, but I am sure I shall be contented with such a representative as you will make; because I know you are too honest a patriot not to wish to see our country prosper by any means, though they be not exactly those you would have preferred; and that you are too well informed a politician, too good a judge of men, not to know, that the ground of liberty is to be gained by inches, that we must be contented to secure what we can get, from time to time, and eternally press forward for what is yet to get. It takes time to persuade men to do even what is for their own good.

## On National Interests

### TO THE MARQUIS DE LA FAYETTE.

NEW YORK, *April 2, 1790.*

Behold me, my dear friend, elected Secretary of State, instead of returning to the far more agreeable position which placed me in the daily participation of your friendship. I found the appointment in the newspapers the day of my arrival in Virginia. I had indeed been asked while in France, whether I would accept of any appointment at home, and I had answered that, not meaning to remain long where I was, I meant it to be the last office I should ever act in. Unfortunately this letter had not arrived at the time of arranging the new Government. I expressed freely to the President my desire to return. He left me free, but still showing his own desire. This, and the concern of others, more general than I had a right to expect, induced, after three months parleying, to sacrifice my own inclinations. I have been here, then, ten days harnessed in new gear. Wherever I am, or ever shall be, I shall be sincere in my friendship to you and to your nation. I think with others, that nations are to be governed with regard to their own interests, but I am convinced that it is their interest, in the long run, to be grateful, faithful to their engagements, even in the worst of circumstances, and honorable and generous always. If I had not known that the head of our government was in these sentiments, and that his national and private ethics were the same, I would never have been where I am. I am sorry to tell you his health is less firm than it used to be. However, there is nothing in it to give alarm. The opposition to our new Constitution has almost totally disappeared. Some few indeed had gone such lengths in their declarations of hostility, that they feel it awkward perhaps to come over; but the amendments proposed by Congress, have brought over almost all their followers. If the President can be preserved a few years till habits of authority and obedience can be established generally, we have nothing to fear. The little vautrien, Rhode Island, will come over with a little more time. Our last news from Paris is of the 8th of January. So far it seemed that your revolution had got along with a steady peace; meeting indeed occasional difficulties and dangers, but we are not to expect to be translated from despotism to liberty in a feather-bed. I have never feared for the ultimate result, though I have feared for you personally. Indeed, I hope you will never see such another 5th or 6th of October.

# Weather Report

## TO MR. THOMAS MANN RANDOLPH.

NEW YORK, *May 30, 1790.*

Thank you for your attention to the Paccan, Gloucester and European walnuts, which will be great acquisitions at Monticello. I will still ask your attention to Mr. Foster's boring machines, lest he should go away suddenly, and the opportunity of getting it be lost. I enquired of Mr. Hamilton the quantity of coal imported; but he tells me there are not returns as yet sufficient to ascertain it; but as soon as there shall be I shall be informed. I am told there is a considerable prejudice against our coal in these Northern States. I do not know whence it proceeds; perhaps from the want of attention to the different species, and an ignorant application of them to cross purposes. I have not begun my meteorological diary, because I have not yet removed to the house I have taken. I remove to-morrow; but as far as I can judge from its aspects, there will not be one position to be had for the thermometer free from the influence of the sun both morning and evening. However, as I go into it only till I can get a better, I shall hope ere long to find a less objectionable situation.

You know that during my short stay at Monticello I kept a diary of the weather. Mr. Madison has just received one comprehending the same period, kept at his father's at Orange. The hours of observation were the same, and he has the fullest confidence in the accuracy of the observer. All the morning observations in Orange are lower than those of Monticello, from one to, I believe, fifteen or sixteen degrees; the afternoon observations are near as much higher as those of Monticello. Nor will the variations permit us to ascribe them to any supposed irregularities in either tube; because, in that case, at the same point the variation would always be the same, which it is not. You have often been sensible that in the afternoon, or rather evening, the air has become warmer in ascending the mountain. The same is true in the morning. This might account for a higher station of the mercury in the morning observations at Monticello. Again, when the air is equally dry in the lower and higher situations, which may be supposed the case in the warmest part of the day, the mercury should be lower on the latter, because, all other circumstances the same, the nearer the common surface the warmer the air. So that on a mountain it ought really to be warmer in the morning and cooler in the heat of the day than on the common plain, but not in so great a degree as these observations indicate. As soon as I am well enough I intend to examine them more accurately. Your resolution to apply to the study of the law, is wise in my opinion, and at the same time to mix with it a good degree of attention to the farm. The one will relieve the other. The study of the law is useful in a variety of points of view. It qualifies a man to be useful to himself, to his neighbors, and to the public. It is the most certain stepping-stone to preferment in the political line. In political economy, I think Smith's Wealth of Nations the best book extant . . . Locke's little book on Government is perfect as far as it goes. Descending from theory to practice there is no better book than the Federalist. Burgh's Political Disquisitions are good also, especially after reading De Lome. Several of Hume's Political Essays are good. There are some excellent books of theory written by Turgot and the economists of France. For parliamentary knowledge, the Lex Parliamentaria is the best book. On my return to Virginia in the fall, I cannot help hoping some practicable plan may be devised for your settling in Albemarle, should your inclination lead you to it. Nothing could contribute so much to my happiness were it at the same time consistent with yours. You might get into the Assembly for that county as soon as you should please.

A motion has been made in the Senate to remove the Federal Government to Philadelphia. There was a trial of strength on a question for a week's postponement. On that it was found there would be eleven for the removal, and thirteen against it. The motion was therefore withdrawn and made in the other house, where it is still depending, and of very uncertain event. . . .

The French revolution still goes on well, though the danger of a suspension of payments is very imminent. Their appeal to the inhabitants of their colonies to say on what footing they wish to be placed, will end, I hope, in our free admissions into their islands with our produce. This precedent must have consequences. It is impossible the world should continue long insensible to so evident a truth as that the right to have commerce and intercourse with our neighbors, is a natural right. To suppress this neighborly intercourse is an exercise of force, which we shall have a just right to remove when the superior force. Dear Sir, your affectionate friend.

## Trade Quarantines

### TO EDWARD RUTLEDGE, ESQ.

NEW YORK, *July 4, 1790.*

In yours of April 28 you mention Dr. Turnbull's opinion that force alone can do our business with the Algerines. I am glad to have the concurrence of so good an authority on that point. I am clear myself that nothing but a perpetual cruise against them, or at least for eight months of the year, and for several years, can put an end to their piracies; and I believe that a confederacy of the nations not in treaty with them can be effected, so as to make that perpetual cruise, or our share of it, a very light thing, as soon as we shall have money to answer even a light thing; and I am in hopes this may shortly be the case.

I participate fully of your indignation at the trammels imposed on our commerce with Great Britain. Some attempts have been made in Congress, and others are still making to meet their restrictions by effectual restriction on our part. It was proposed to double the foreign tonnage for a certain time, and after that to prohibit the exportation of our commodities in the vessels of nations not in treaty with us. This has been rejected. It is now proposed to prohibit any nation from bringing or carrying in their vessels what may not be brought or carried in ours from or to the same ports; also to prohibit those from bringing to us anything not of their own produce, who prohibit us from carrying to them anything but our own produce. It is thought, however, that this cannot be carried. The fear is that it would irritate Great Britain were we to feel any irritation ourselves. You will see by the debates of Congress that there are good men and bold men, and sensible men, who publicly avow these sentiments.

# Importance of New Orleans

## TO WILLIAM SHORT.

New York, *August 10, 1790.*

Dear Sir,—This letter, with the very confidential papers it encloses, will be delivered to you by Mr. Barrett with his own hands. If there be no war between Spain and England, they need be known to yourself alone. But if that war be begun, or whenever it shall begin, we wish you to communicate them to the Marquis de La Fayette, on whose assistance we know we can count in matters which interest both our countries. He and you will consider how far the contents of these papers may be communicated to the Count de Montmorin, and his influence be asked with the court of Madrid. France will be called into the war, as an ally, and not on any pretence of the quarrel being in any degree her own. She may reasonably require then, that Spain should do everything which depends on her, to lessen the number of her enemies. She cannot doubt that we shall be of that number, if she does not yield our right to the common use of the Mississippi, and the means of using and securing it. You will observe, we state in general the necessity, not only of our having a port near the mouth of the river, (without which we could make no use of the navigation at all) but of its being so well separated from the territories of Spain and her jurisdiction, as not to engender daily disputes and broils between us. It is certain, that if Spain were to retain any jurisdiction over our entrepôt, her officers would abuse that jurisdiction, and our people would abuse their privileges in it. Both parties must foresee this, and that it will end in war. Hence the necessity of a well-defined separation. Nature has decided what shall be the geography of that in the end, whatever it might be in the beginning, by cutting off from the adjacent countries of Florida and Louisiana, and enclosing between two of its channels, a long and narrow slip of land, called the Island of New Orleans. The idea of ceding this, could not be hazarded to Spain, in the first step; it would be too disagreeable at first view; because this island, with its town, constitutes, at present, their principal settlement in that part of their dominions, containing about ten thousand white inhabitants of every age and sex. Reason and events, however, may, by little and little, familiarize them to it. That we have a right to some spot as an entrepôt for our commerce, may be at once affirmed. The expediency, too, may be expressed, of so locating it as to cut off the source of future quarrels and wars. A disinterested eye, looking on a map, will remark how conveniently this tongue of land is formed for the purpose; the Iberville and Amit channel offering a good boundary and convenient outlet, on the one side, for Florida, and the main channel an equally good boundary and outlet, on the other side, for Louisiana; while the slip of land between, is almost entirely morass or sandbank; the whole of it lower than the water of the river, in its highest floods, and only its western margin (which is the highest ground) secured by banks and inhabited. I suppose this idea too much even for the Count de Montmorin at first, and that, therefore, you will find it prudent to urge, and get him to recommend to the Spanish court, only in general terms, "a port near the mouth of the river, with a circumjacent territory sufficient for its support, well defined, and extra-territorial to Spain," leaving the idea to future growth.

## "Congress Separated"

### TO MR. RANDOLPH.

NEW YORK, *August 14, 1790.*

DEAR SIR,—I am setting out on a trip to Rhode Island with the President to-morrow, by water. We shall be absent five or six days, and of course his departure hence to the southward will be that much later than he intended; and my departure, which must be after his, a little delayed. Still I hope to reach Monticello by the 15th of September, or from that to the 20th. We have just concluded a treaty with the Creeks, which is important, as drawing a line between them and Georgia, and enabling the government to do, as it will do, justice against either party offending. Congress separated the day before yesterday, having in the latter part of their session re-acquired the harmony which had always distinguished their proceedings, till the two disagreeable subjects of the assumption and residence were introduced. These really threatened, at one time, a separation of the legislature *sine die.* They saw the necessity of suspending almost all business for some time; and, when they resumed it, of some mutual sacrifices of opinion. It is not foreseen that anything so generative of dissension can arise again, and therefore the friends of the government hope that, this difficulty once surmounted in the States, everything will work well. I am principally afraid that commerce will be overloaded by the assumption, believing that it would be better that property should be duly taxed. Present me affectionately to my dear daughters, and believe me to be sincerely yours.

# On Altering a Constitution

## TO MR. NOAH WEBSTER, AT HARTFORD.

PHILADELPHIA, *December 4, 1790.*

In mentioning me in your Essays, and canvassing my opinions, you have done what every man has a right to do, and it is for the good of society that that right should be freely exercised. No republic has more zeal than that of letters, and I am the last in principles, as I am the least in pretensions, to any dictatorship in it. Had I other dispositions, the philosophical and dispassionate spirit with which you have expressed your own opinions in opposition to mine, would still have commanded my approbation. A desire of being set right in your opinion, which I respect too much not to entertain that desire, induces me to hazard to you the following observations. It had become an universal and almost uncontroverted position in the several States, that the purposes of society do not require a surrender of all our rights to our ordinary governors; that there are certain portions of right not necessary to enable them to carry on an effective government, and which experience has nevertheless proved they will be constantly encroaching on, if submitted to them; that there are also certain fences which experience has proved peculiarly efficacious against wrong, and rarely obstructive of right, which yet the governing powers have ever shown a disposition to weaken and remove. Of the first kind, for instance, is freedom of religion; of the second, trial by jury, habeas corpus laws, free presses. These were the settled opinions of all the States,—of that of Virginia, of which I was writing, as well as of the others. The others had, in consequence, delineated these unceded portions of right, and these fences against wrong, which they meant to exempt from the power of their governors, in instruments called declarations of rights and constitutions; and as they did this by conventions, which they appointed for the express purpose of reserving these rights, and of delegating others to their ordinary legislative, executive and judiciary bodies, none of the reserved rights can be touched without resorting to the people to appoint another convention for the express purpose of permitting it. Where the constitutions then have been so formed by conventions named for this express purpose, they are fixed and unalterable but by a convention or other body to be specially authorized; and they have been so formed by, I believe, all the States, except Virginia. That State concurs in all these opinions, but has run into the wonderful error that her constitution, though made by the ordinary legislature, cannot yet be altered by the ordinary legislature. I had, therefore, no occasion to prove to them the expediency of a constitution alterable only by a special convention. Accordingly, I have not in my notes advocated that opinion, though it was and is mine, as it was and is theirs. I take that position as admitted by them, and only proceed to adduce arguments to prove that they were mistaken in supposing their constitution could not be altered by the common legislature. Among other arguments I urge that the convention which formed the constitution had been chosen merely for ordinary legislation; that they had no higher power than every subsequent legislature was to have; that all their acts are consequently repealable by subsequent legislatures; that their own practice at a subsequent session proved they were of this opinion themselves; that the opinion and practice of several subsequent legislatures had been the same, and so conclude "that their constitution is alterable by the common legislature." Yet these arguments urged to prove that their constitution *is* alterable, you cite as if urged to prove that it *ought not to be* alterable, and you combat them on that ground. An argument which is good to prove one thing, may become ridiculous when exhibited as intended to prove another thing. I will beg the favor of you to look over again the passage in my notes, and am persuaded you will be sensible that you have misapprehended the object of my arguments, and therefore have combated them on a ground for which they were not intended.

# News from France

### TO COLONEL MASON.

PHILADELPHIA, *February 4, 1791.*

DEAR SIR,—I am to make you my acknowledgments for your favor of January 10th, and the information from France which it contained. It confirmed what I had heard more loosely before, and accounts still more recent are to the same effect. I look with great anxiety for the firm establishment of the new government in France, being perfectly convinced that if it takes place there, it will spread sooner or later all over Europe. On the contrary, a check there would retard the revival of liberty in other countries. I consider the establishment and success of their government as necessary to stay up our own, and to prevent it from falling back to that kind of a half-way house, the English constitution. It cannot be denied that we have among us a sect who believe that to contain whatever is perfect in human institutions; that the members of this sect have, many of them, names and offices which stand high in the estimation of our countrymen. I still rely that the great mass of our community is untainted with these heresies, as is its head. On this I build my hope that we have not labored in vain, and that our experiment will still prove that men can be governed by reason. You have excited my curiosity in saying "there is a particular circumstance, little attended to, which is continually sapping the republicanism of the United States." What

is it? What is said in our country of the fiscal arrangements now going on?
I really fear their effect when I consider the present temper of the southern
States. Whether these measures be right or wrong abstractedly, more atten-
tion should be paid to the general opinion.

## Memories of Franklin

TO ————.[1]

PHILADELPHIA, *February 19, 1791.*

DEAR SIR,—I feel both the wish and the duty to communicate, in compliance with your request, whatever, within my knowledge, might render
justice to the memory of our great countryman, Dr. Franklin, in which
Philosophy has to deplore one of its principal luminaries extinguished. But
my opportunities of knowing the interesting facts of his life, have not been
equal to my desire of making them known. I could indeed relate a number
of those bon mots, with which he used to charm every society, as having
heard many of them. But these are not your object. Particulars of greater
dignity happened not to occur during his stay of nine months, after my
arrival in France.

A little before that, Argand had invented his celebrated lamp, in which the
flame is spread into a hollow cylinder, and thus brought into contact with
the air within as well as without. Doctor Franklin had been on the point
of the same discovery. The idea had occurred to him; but he had tried a
bull-rush as a wick, which did not succeed. His occupations did not permit
him to repeat and extend his trials to the introduction of a larger column
of air than could pass through the stem of a bull-rush.

The animal magnetism too of the maniac Mesmer, had just received its
death wound from his hand in conjunction with his brethren of the learned
committee appointed to unveil that compound of fraud and folly. But after
this, nothing very interesting was before the public, either in philosophy or
politics, during his stay; and he was principally occupied in winding up his
affairs there.

I can only therefore testify in general, that there appeared to me more
respect and veneration attached to the character of Doctor Franklin in
France, than to that of any other person in the same country, foreign or
native. I had opportunities of knowing particularly how far these sentiments
were felt by the foreign ambassadors and ministers at the court of Versailles.
The fable of his capture by the Algerines, propagated by the English newspapers, excited no uneasiness; as it was seen at once to be a dish cooked up
to the palate of their readers. But nothing could exceed the anxiety of his
diplomatic brethren, on a subsequent report of his death, which, though
premature, bore some marks of authenticity.

[1]Address illegible.

I found the ministers of France equally impressed with the talents and integrity of Dr. Franklin. The Count de Vergennes particularly gave me repeated and unequivocal demonstrations of his entire confidence in him.

When he left Passy, it seemed as if the village had lost its patriarch. On
taking leave of the court, which he did by letter, the King ordered him to be
handsomely complimented, and furnished him with a litter and mules of his
own, the only kind of conveyance the state of his health could bear. . . .

The succession to Dr. Franklin, at the court of France, was an excellent
school of humility. On being presented to any one as the minister of America, the commonplace question used in such cases was *"c'est vous, Monsieur,
qui remplace le Docteur Franklin?"* "it is you, Sir, who replace Doctor
Franklin?" I generally answered, "no one can replace him, Sir: I am only his
successor."

## Capital Plans

### TO MAJOR L'ENFANT.

*March —, 1791.*

SIR,—You are desired to proceed to Georgetown, where you will find Mr.
Ellicot employed in making a survey and map of the federal territory. The
special object of asking your aid is to have drawings of the particular grounds
most likely to be approved for the site of the federal town and buildings.
You will therefore be pleased to begin on the eastern branch, and proceed
from thence upwards, laying down the hills, valleys, morasses, and waters between that, the Potomac, the Tyber, and the road leading from Georgetown
to the eastern branch, and connecting the whole with certain fixed points of
the map Mr. Ellicot is preparing. Some idea of the height of the hills above
the base on which they stand, would be desirable. For necessary assistance
and expenses, be pleased to apply to the Mayor of Georgetown, who is
written to on this subject. I will beg the favor of you to mark to me your
progress about twice a week, by letter, say every Wednesday and Saturday
evening, that I may be able in proper time to draw your attention to some
other objects, which I have not at this moment sufficient information to de-
fine. I am, with great esteem, Sir, your most obedient humble servant.

## Town Planning

### TO MAJOR L'ENFANT.

PHILADELPHIA, *April 10, 1791.*

I am happy that the President has left the planning of the town in such
good hands, and have no doubt it will be done to general satisfaction. Con-

sidering that the grounds to be reserved for the public are to be paid for by the acre, I think very liberal reservations should be made for them; and if this be about the Tyber and on the back of the town, it will be of no injury to the commerce of the place, which will undoubtedly establish itself on the deep waters towards the eastern branch and mouth of Rock Creek; the water about the mouth of the Tyber not being of any depth. Those connected with the government will prefer fixing themselves near the public grounds in the centre, which will also be convenient to be resorted to as walks from the lower and upper town. Having communicated to the President, before he went away, such general ideas on the subject of the town as occurred to me, I make no doubt that, in explaining himself to you on the subject, he has interwoven with his own ideas, such of mine as he approved. For fear of repeating therefore what he did not approve, and having more confidence in the unbiassed state of his mind, than in my own, I avoided interfering with what he may have expressed to you. Whenever it is proposed to prepare plans for the Capitol, I should prefer the adoption of some one of the models of antiquity, which have had the approbation of thousands of years; and for the President's house, I should prefer the celebrated fronts of modern buildings, which have already received the approbation of all good judges. Such are the Galerie du Louire, the Gardes meubles, and two fronts of the Hotel de Salm.

# On Public Taste

## TO THE PRESIDENT OF THE UNITED STATES.

PHILADELPHIA, *April 10, 1791.*

The bill for the federal buildings passed the Representatives here by 42 to 10, but it was rejected yesterday by 9 to 6 in the Senate, or to speak more exactly, it was postponed till the next session. In the meantime, spirited proceedings at Georgetown will probably, under the continuance of your patronage, prevent the revival of the bill. I received last night from Major L'Enfant a request to furnish him any plans of towns I could, for his examination. I accordingly send him, by this post, plans of Frankfort-on-the-Mayne, Carlsruhe, Amsterdam, Strasburg, Paris, Orleans, Bordeaux, Lyons, Montpelier, Marseilles, Turin, and Milan, on large and accurate scales, which I procured while in those towns respectively. They are none of them, however, comparable to the old Babylon, revived in Philadelphia, and exemplified. While in Europe, I selected about a dozen or two of the handsomest fronts of private buildings, of which I have the plates. Perhaps it might decide the taste of the new town, were these to be engraved here, and distributed gratis among the inhabitants of Georgetown. The expense would be trifling.

## Indian Trouble

TO CHARLES CARROLL OF CARROLLTON.

PHILADELPHIA, *April 15, 1791.*

Our news from the westward is disagreeable. Constant murders committing by the Indians, and their combination threatens to be more and more extensive. I hope we shall give them a thorough drubbing this summer, and then change our tomahawk into a golden chain of friendship. The most economical as well as most humane conduct towards them is to bribe them into peace, and to retain them in peace by eternal bribes. The expedition this year would have served for presents on the most liberal scale for one hundred years; nor shall we otherwise ever get rid of an army, or of our debt. The least rag of Indian depredation will be an excuse to raise troops for those who love to have troops, and for those who think that a public debt is a good thing.

## Maple Sugar

TO THE PRESIDENT OF THE UNITED STATES.

PHILADELPHIA, *May 1, 1791.*

A Mr. Noble has been here, from the country where they are busied with the sugar-maple tree. He thinks Mr. Cooper will bring three thousand pounds worth to market this season, and gives the most flattering calculations of what may be done in that way. He informs me of another most satisfactory fact, that less profit is made by converting the juice into spirit than into sugar. He gave me specimens of the spirit, which is exactly whiskey.

I have arrived at Baltimore from Marseilles forty olive trees of the best kind from Marseilles, and a box of seed, the latter to raise stocks, and the former, cuttings to engraft on the stocks. I am ordering them on instantly to Charleston, where, if they arrive in the course of this month, they will be in time. Another cargo is on its way from Bordeaux, so that I hope to secure the commencement of this culture, and from the best species. Sugar and oil will be no mean addition to the articles of our culture.

## Prosperity

TO MR. DUMAS.

PHILADELPHIA, *May 13, 1791.*

In general, our affairs are proceeding in a train of unparalleled prosperity. This arises from the real improvements of our government, from the unbounded confidence reposed in it by the people, their zeal to support it, and their conviction that a solid Union is the best rock of their safety, from the favorable seasons which for some years past have co-operated with a fertile soil and a genial climate to increase the productions of agriculture, and from the growth of industry, economy and domestic manufactures; so that I believe I may say with truth, that there is not a nation under the sun enjoying more present prosperity, nor with more in prospect. The Indians on our frontier, indeed, still continue to cut off straggling individuals or families falling in their way. An expedition against them the last summer was less successful than there was reason to expect. We lost in it about one hundred men. The operations of the present summer will more probably bring them to peace, which is all we desire of them, it having been a leading object of our present Government to guaranty them in their present possessions, and to protect their persons with the same fidelity which is extended to its own citizens. We ask nothing of them but that they will accept our peace, friendship and services; and we hope soon to make them sensible of this, in spite of the incitements against us, which they have been so much the dupes of.

## Sunday Letter

### TO THOMAS MANN RÁNDOLPH.

BENNINGTON, in Vermont, *June 5, 1791.*

DEAR SIR,—Mr. Madison and myself are so far on the tour we had projected. We have visited, in the course of it, the principal scenes of General Burgoyne's misfortunes, to wit, the grounds at Stillwater, where the action of that name was fought, and particularly the breastworks, which cost so much blood to both parties, the encampments at Saratoga and ground where the British piled their arms, and the field of the battle of Bennington, about nine miles from this place. We have also visited Forts William, Henry and George, Ticonderoga, Crown Point, etc., which have been scenes of blood from a very early part of our history. We were more pleased, however, with the botanical objects which continually presented themselves. Those either unknown or rare in Virginia, were the sugar maple in vast abundance. The silver fir, white pine, pitch pine, spruce pine, a shrub with decumbent stems, which they call juniper, an aralea, very different from the nudiflora, with very large clusters of flowers, more thickly set on the branches, of a deeper red, and high pink-fragrance. It is the richest shrub I have seen. The honey-suckle of the gardens growing wild on the banks of Lake George, the paper-birch, an aspen with a velvet leaf, a shrub-willow with downy catkins, a wild gooseberry, the wild cherry with single fruit, (not the bunch cherry,) strawberries in abundance. From the highlands to the lakes it is a limestone country. It is in vast quantities on the eastern sides of the lakes, but none on the western sides. The Sandy Hill Falls and Wing's Falls, two very remarkable cataracts of the Hudson, of about thirty-five feet or forty feet each,

between Fort Edward and Fort George, are of limestone, in horizontal
strata. Those of the Cohoes, on the west side of the Hudson, and of seventy
feet height, we thought not of limestone. We have met with a small red
squirrel, of the color of our fox-squirrel, with a black stripe on each side,
weighing about six ounces generally, and in such abundance on Lake Champlain particularly, as that twenty odd were killed at the house we lodged in,
opposite Crown Point, the morning we arrived there, without going ten
yards from the door. We killed three crossing the lakes, one of them just as
he was getting ashore, where it was three miles wide, and where, with the
high wind then blowing, he must have made it five or six miles.

I think I asked the favor of you to send for Anthony in the season for
inoculation, as well as to do what is necessary in the orchard, as to pursue
the object of inoculating all the spontaneous cherry trees in the fields with
good fruit.

We have now got over about four hundred miles of our tour, and have
still about four hundred and fifty more to go over. Arriving here on the
Saturday evening, and the laws of the State not permitting us to travel on the
Sunday, has given me time to write to you from hence.

# The Rights of Man

## TO T. M. RANDOLPH.

PHILADELPHIA, *July 3, 1791.*

The President is not yet arrived, but we expect him the day after to-
morrow. He has probably protracted his journey so as to avoid the ceremonies of to-morrow. We expect daily to hear the events of the expedition
under General Scott into the Indian country. Perhaps you will hear it sooner
than we shall. Having nothing to communicate in the line of public news
I will state something personal. You will observe by the enclosed and preceding papers that I am mentioned on the subject of Paine's pamphlet on the
Rights of Man; and you will have seen a note of mine prefixed to that
pamphlet whence it has been inferred that I furnished the pamphlet to the
printer and procured its publication. This is not true. The fact was this:
Mr. Beckley had the only copy of that pamphlet in town. He lent it to Mr.
Madison, who lent it to me under the injunction to return it to Mr. Beckley
within the day. Beckley came for it before I had finished reading it and desired as soon as I had done I would send it to a Mr. Jonathan B. Smith whose
brother was to reprint it. Being an utter stranger to Mr. J. B. Smith I explained to him in a note that I sent the pamphlet to him by order of Mr.
Beckley, and to take off somewhat of the dryness of the note I added that I
was glad to find it was to be reprinted here, etc., as you have seen in the
printed note. I thought so little of this note that I did not even retain a copy
of it; and without the least information or suspicion that it would be published, out it comes the next week at the head of the pamphlet. I knew im-

mediately that it would give displeasure to some gentlemen just by the chair of government who were in sentiment with Burke and as much opposed to the sentiments of Paine.

I could not disavow my note, because I had written it. I could not disavow my approbation of the pamphlet, because I was fully in sentiment with it, and it would have been trifling to have disavowed merely the publication of the note approving at the same time of the pamphlet. I determined, therefore, to be utterly silent except so far as verbal explanations could be made.

## The Rebel Paine

### TO COLONEL MONROE.

PHILADELPHIA, *July 10, 1791.*

The papers which I send Mr. Randolph weekly, and which I presume you see, will have shown you what a dust Paine's pamphlet has kicked up here. My last to Mr. Randolph will have given an explanation as to myself, which I had not time to give when I sent you the pamphlet. A writer, under the name of Publicola, in attacking all Paine's principles, is very desirous of involving me in the same censure with the author. I certainly merit the same, for I profess the same principles; but it is equally certain I never meant to have entered as a volunteer into the cause. My occupations do not permit it.

## Indian Rights

### TO GENERAL KNOX.

PHILADELPHIA, *August 10, 1791.*

DEAR SIR,—I have now the honor to return you the petition of Mr. Moultrie on behalf of the South Carolina Yazoo company. Without noticing that some of the highest functions of sovereignty are assumed in the very papers which he annexes as his justification, I am of opinion that government should firmly maintain this ground; that the Indians have a right to the occupation of their lands, independent of the States within whose chartered lines they happen to be; that until they cede them by treaty or other transaction equivalent to a treaty, no act of a State can give a right to such lands; that neither under the present constitution, nor the ancient confederation, had any State or person a right to treat with the Indians, without the consent of the General Government; that that consent has never been given to any treaty for the cession of the lands in question; that the government is determined to exert all its energy for the patronage and protection of the rights of the Indians, and the preservation of peace between the United States and them; and that if any settlements are made on lands not ceded by them, *without the previous consent of the United States,* the government will think itself bound, not only to declare to the Indians that such settlements are without the authority or protection of the United States, but to remove them also by the public force.

## Hope for the World

### TO SIR JOHN SINCLAIR.

PHILADELPHIA, *August 24, 1791.*

We are now under the first impression of the news of the King's flight from Paris, and his re-capture. It would be unfortunate were it in the power of any one man to defeat the issue of so beautiful a revolution. I hope and trust it is not, and that, for the good of suffering humanity all over the earth, that revolution will be established and spread through the whole world.

## First Four Million

### TO ADMIRAL PAUL JONES.

PHILADELPHIA, *August 31, 1791.*

Our new Constitution works well, and gives general satisfaction. Public credit is high. We have made a successful expedition against the Indians this summer, and another is gone against them, and we hope will induce them to peace. A census of our numbers, taken this summer, gives us reason to believe we are about four millions of all ages and sexes. A state of tranquil prosperity furnishing no particular and interesting events to communicate to you, I have only to add assurances of the constant esteem and attachment of, dear Sir, your most obedient humble servant.

## Rapid Transit

### TO COLONEL PICKERING.

PHILADELPHIA, *March 28, 1792.*

SIR,—The President has desired me to confer with you on the proposition I made the other day, of endeavoring to move the posts at the rate of one hundred miles a day. It is believed to be practicable here, because it is prac-tised in every other country. The difference of expense alone appeared to produce doubts with you on the subject. If you have no engagement for dinner to-day, and will do me the favor to come and dine with me, we will be entirely alone, and it will give us time to go over the matter and weigh it thoroughly.

## Scarlet Beans

### TO BENJAMIN HAWKINS.

PHILADELPHIA, *April 1, 1792.*

DEAR SIR,—At Mrs. Trist's desire I forward to you about a dozen beans of three different kinds, having first taken toll of them as she had done before. They are of the scarlet flowering kind. This is all I know of them. The most beautiful bean in the world is the Caracalla bean which, though in England a green-house plant, will grow in the open air in Virginia and Carolina. I never could get one of these in my life. They are worth your enquiry.

Some friendly Indians have been killed near Fort Pitt lately, on a trading visit, by a party of Virginians. This will not only defeat the measures set on foot for peace, but spread the war order. There has been also a small fracas on our disputed territory to the eastward, by our sheriffs levying taxes on the inhabitants of Moose Island, who as to that article wished to be neutrals. A sale of 1,200,000 acres of land by Mr. R. M. in Europe and the purchase of five millions more is the report of the day. Things are going on well in France by the last authentic accounts. The English papers have since killed the Duke of Orleans. It seems to be thought that the affairs of Europe are by no means settled, and that the late pacification has only covered a fire which will burst out again immediately. Adieu. Yours affectionately.

## Plea for Unity

### TO THE PRESIDENT OF THE UNITED STATES.

PHILADELPHIA, *May 23, 1792.*

I can scarcely contemplate a more incalculable evil than the breaking of the Union into two or more parts. Yet when we consider the mass which opposed the original coalescence; when we consider that it lay chiefly in the Southern quarter; that the Legislature have availed themselves of no occasion of allaying it, but on the contrary, whenever Northern and Southern prejudices have come into conflict, the latter have been sacrificed and the former soothed; that the owners of the debt are in the Southern, and the holders of it in the Northern division; that the anti-federal champions are now strengthened in argument by the fulfillment of their predictions; that this has been brought about by the monarchical federalists themselves, who, having been for the new government merely as a stepping stone to monarchy, have themselves adopted the very constructions of the Constitution, of which, when advocating its acceptance before the tribunal of the people, they declared it unsusceptible; that the republican federalists who espoused the same government for its intrinsic merits, are disarmed of their weapons; that which they denied as prophecy, having now become true history, who can be sure that these things may not proselyte the small number which was wanting to place the majority on the other side? And this is the event at which I tremble, and to prevent which I consider your continuing at the head of affairs as of the last importance. The confidence of the whole Union is centred in you. Your being at the helm will be more than an answer to every argument which can be used to alarm and lead the people in any quarter, into violence and secession. North and South will hang together if they have you to hang on; and if the first correction of a numerous representation should fail in its effect, your presence will give time for trying others, not inconsistent with the union and peace of the States.

## Answering Hamilton

### TO THE PRESIDENT OF THE UNITED STATES.

MONTICELLO, *September 9, 1792.*

No man in the United States, I suppose, approved of every tittle in the Constitution: no one, I believe, approved more of it than I did, and more of it was certainly disapproved by my accuser than by me, and of its parts most vitally republican. Of this the few letters I wrote on the subject (not half a dozen I believe) will be a proof; and for my own satisfaction and justification, I must tax you with the reading of them when I return to where they are. You will there see that my objection to the Constitution was, that it wanted a bill of rights securing freedom of religion, freedom of the press, freedom from standing armies, trial by jury, and a constant habeas corpus act. Colonel Hamilton's was, that it wanted a king and house of lords. The sense of America has approved my objection and added the bill of rights, not the king and lords.

. . . No government ought to be without censors; and where the press is free, no one ever will. If virtuous, it need not fear the fair operation of attack and defence. Nature has given to man no other means of sifting out the truth, either in religion, law, or politics.

## French Government De Facto

### TO GOUVERNEUR MORRIS.

PHILADELPHIA, *November 7, 1792.*

With what kind of government you may do business, is another question. It accords with our principles to acknowledge any government to be rightful, which is formed by the will of the nation substantially declared. The late government was of this kind, and was accordingly acknowledged by all the branches of ours. So, any alteration of it which shall be made by the will of the nation substantially declared, will doubtless be acknowledged in like manner. With such a government *every kind* of business may be done. But there are *some matters* which, I conceive, might be transacted with a government *de facto;* such, for instance, as the reforming the unfriendly restrictions on our commerce and navigation. Such cases you will readily distinguish as they occur.

## Relief Administration

### TO MONSIEUR DE TERNANT.

PHILADELPHIA, *November 20, 1792.*

SIR,—Your letter on the subject of further supplies to the colony of St. Domingo, has been duly received and considered. When the distresses of that colony first broke forth, we thought we could not better evidence our friendship to that and to the mother country also, than to step in to its relief, on your application, without waiting a formal authorization from the National Assembly. As the case was unforeseen, so it was unprovided for on their part, and we did what we doubted not they would have desired us to do, had there been time to make the application, and what we presumed they would sanction as soon as known to them. We have now been going on more than a twelvemonth, in making advances for the relief of the colony, without having, as yet, received any such sanction; for the decree of four millions of livres in aid of the colony, besides the circuitous and informal manner by which we became acquainted with it, describes and applies to operations very different from those which have actually taken place. The wants of the colony appear likely to continue, and their reliance on our supplies to become habitual. We feel every disposition to continue our efforts for administering to those wants; but that cautious attention to forms which would have been unfriendly in the first moment becomes a duty to ourselves, when the business assumes the appearance of long continuance . . . but the want of express approbation from the national Legislature, must ere long produce a presumption that they contemplate perhaps other modes of relieving the colony, and dictate to us the propriety of doing only what they shall have regularly and previously sanctioned. Their decree before mentioned, contemplates purchases made *in the United States only*. In this they might probably have in view, as well to keep the business of providing supplies under a single direction, as that these supplies should be bought where they can be had cheapest, and where the same sum will consequently effect the greatest measure of relief to the colony.

## Olive Trees

### TO STEPHEN CATHALAN.

PHILADELPHIA, *December 2, 1792.*

DEAR SIR,—The small essay which has been commenced under your kind assistance for colonizing the olive tree to South Carolina has induced some patriotic gentlemen of that country to turn their attention further toward its importance, and to give to their efforts a more steady and permanent form. I gave it as my opinion to them that the best plan which could be pursued at a moderate expense, would be to rent, near Marseilles, an acre of ground, or say your quarterelle, which is something less than an acre, to employ by the year a laboring man who understands engrafting, to make it his business to sow olives in this ground, to engraft on them cuttings from the best kinds, and to send to Carolina in the winter of every year all the plants he could have in readiness, together with a quantity of the olive berries to be sown in Carolina in order to be engrafted on them.

If before a given day in winter, say the first of January, any ship should be sailing from Marseilles to Charleston, it should be his business to pack properly his olive berries and young plants and put them on board; if no vessel should occur before that, or any more convenient day, it should be his business to proceed himself with his olive berries and plants, through the canal of Languedoc to Bordeaux, there to remain (under the patronage of Fenwick) till a vessel should sail from thence to Charleston, on board of which he should put his cargo and then return to Marseilles to recommence for the next year the same operation of sowing, engrafting, packing and dispatching in the same way to Charleston, the olive berries and plants which he could prepare for that year, and so to continue for a number of years.

It may not be amiss to add annually a few plants of the best figs for drying as also of the best grapes for making what we call "dried raisins," and you, I believe, "des panses." . . .

## Tenant Farming

### TO SAMUEL BIDDLE.

PHILADELPHIA, *December 12, 1792.*

SIR,—Having asked the favor of Mr. Hollingsworth to look out for a person in his neighborhood who would be willing to go to Virginia and overlook a farm for me, he informs me that you will undertake it for a hundred and twenty dollars a year. He seems to have mistaken me in the circumstance of time, as he mentions that you would expect to go about the new year. I had observed to him that I should not want a person till after the next harvest. The person who now takes care of the place is engaged for the ensuing year, which finishes with us about November; but I should wish you to be there by seed time in order to prepare the crop of the following year. The wages are a good deal higher than I expected, as Mr. Hollingsworth mentioned that the usual wages in your neighborhood were from £25 to £30 Maryland currency. However, I consent to give them, and the rather as there will be some matters under your care beyond the lines of the farm. I have a smith and some sawyers who will require to be seen once a day, and the first year of your being there I shall have some people employed in finishing a canal, who will also be to be attended to.

The place you are to overlook is that on which I live, and to which I shall return in March next. It is 70 miles above Richmond, on the North branch of James River, exactly where it breaks through the first ridge of little mountains, near the village of Charlottesville, in Albemarle county. It is 225 miles from Elkton, a southwest course. From this description you may find it in any map of the country. The climate is very temperate both summer and winter, and as healthy as any part of America, without a single exception.

The farm is of about five or six hundred acres of cleared land, very hilly, originally as rich as any highlands in the world, but much worried by Indian corn and tobacco. It is still however very strong, and remarkably friendly to wheat and rye. These will be my first object. Next will be grasses, cattle, sheep, and the introduction of potatoes for the use of the farm, instead of Indian corn, in as great a degree as possible. You will have from 12 to 15 laborers under you. They will be well clothed, and as well fed as your management of the farm will enable us, for it is chiefly with a view to place them on the comfortable footing of the laborers of other countries that I come into another country to seek an overlooker for them, as also to have my lands a little more taken care. For these purposes I have long banished tobacco, and wish to do the same by Indian corn in a great degree. The house wherein you will live will be about half a mile from my own. You will, of course, keep bachelor's house. It is usual with us to give a fixed allowance of pork; I shall much rather substitute beef and mutton, as I consider pork to be as destructive an article in a farm as Indian corn. On this head we shall not disagree, and as I shall pass Elkton in March, I will contrive to give you notice to meet me there, when we may descend to other details. But for the present I shall wish to receive your answer in writing, that I may know whether you consider yourself as engaged, so that I need not look out for another. I leave you free as to the time of going, from harvest till Christmas. If you will get yourself conveyed as far as Fredericksburg, which is as far as the stages go on that road, I will find means of conveying you from thence, which will be 70 miles. So far respects the farm over which I wish to place you.

Besides this I have on the opposite side of the little river running through my lands, 2000 acres of lands of the same quality, and which has been cultivated in the same way, which I wish to tenant out at a quarter of a dollar an acre, in farms of such sizes as the tenants would choose. I would hire the laborers now employed on them from year to year to the same tenants, at about 50 dollars for a man and his wife, the tenant feeding and clothing them and paying their taxes and those of the land, which are very trifling. The lands to be leased for seven years or more, the laborers only from year to year, to begin next November. I would like the farms to be not less than 200 acres, because such a farmer would probably like to hire a man and his wife as laborers. I have mentioned these circumstances to you, because I have understood that tenants might probably be got from Maryland, and perhaps it would be agreeable to you to engage some of your acquaintances to go and settle so near where you will be. Perhaps you could inform me in what other part of Maryland or the neighboring States tenants might be more probably found, and I should willingly incur the expense of having them sought for. Your assistance in this would particularly oblige me. I would ease the rent of the first year, that the tenant might get himself under way with as few difficulties as possible, but I should propose restrictions against cultivating too great a quantity of Indian corn.

In expectation of hearing from you immediately I am, Sir, your humble servant.

P. S. There is a market for wheat, rye, etc., in two little towns on each side of my lands, neither more than two miles and a half distant.

## Family Letter

### TO MARTHA JEFFERSON RANDOLPH.

PHILADELPHIA, *December 31, 1792.*

MY DEAR MARTHA,—I received three days ago Mr. Randolph's letter of the 14th from Richmond, and received it with great joy, as it informed me of the re-establishment of dear Anne's health. I apprehend from an expression in his letter that some of mine may have miscarried. I have never failed to write every Thursday or Friday. Perceiving by the Richmond paper that the Western post now leaves that place on Monday, I change my day of writing also to Sunday or Monday. One of the Indian chiefs now here, whom you may remember to have seen at Monticello a day or two before Tarleton drove us off, remembers you and enquired after you. He is of the Pioria nation; perhaps you may recollect that he gave our name to an infant son he then had with him, and who, he now tells me, is a fine lad. Blanchard is arrived here and is to ascend in his balloon within a few days. The affairs of France are going on well. Tell Mr. Randolph that I write him a letter by this post in answer to the application to rent Elkhall, but under the possibility that the sale of it may be completed, I inclose his letter to Mr. Hylton with a desire that he will return it to me if the place is sold, otherwise to forward it to Mr. Randolph. My best esteem to him and our friends with you. Adieu, my dear. Yours affectionately.

# On Public Opinion

### TO WILLIAM SHORT.

PHILADELPHIA, *January 3, 1793.*

. . . The tone of your letters had for some time given me pain, on account of the extreme warmth with which they censured the proceedings of the Jacobins of France. I considered that sect as the same with the Republican patriots, and the Feuillants as the Monarchical patriots, well known in the early part of the Revolution, and but little distant in their views, both having in object the establishment of a free constitution, differing only on the question whether their chief Executive should be hereditary or not. The Jacobins (as since called) yielded to the Feuillants, and tried the experiment of retaining their hereditary Executive. The experiment failed completely, and would have brought on the re-establishment of despotism had it been pursued. The Jacobins knew this, and that the expunging that office was of absolute necessity. And the nation was with them in opinion, for however they might have been formerly for the constitution framed by the first assembly, they were come over from their hope in it, and were now generally Jacobins. In the struggle which was necessary, many guilty persons fell without the forms of trial, and with them some innocent. These I deplore as much as any body, and shall deplore some of them to the day of my death. But I deplore them as I should have done had they fallen in battle. It was necessary to use the arm of the people, a machine not quite so blind as balls and bombs, but blind to a certain degree. A few of their cordial friends met at their hands the fate of enemies. But time and truth will rescue and embalm their memories, while their posterity will be enjoying that very liberty for which they would never have hesitated to offer up their lives. The liberty of the whole earth was depending on the issue of the contest, and was ever such a prize won with so little innocent blood? My own affections have been deeply wounded by some of the martyrs to this cause, but rather than it should have failed I would have seen half the earth desolated; were there but an Adam and an Eve left in every country, and left free, it would be better than as it now is. I have expressed to you my sentiments, because they are really those of ninety-nine in an hundred of our citizens. The universal feasts, and rejoicings which have lately been, had on account of the successes of the French, showed the genuine effusions of their hearts. You have been wounded by the sufferings of your friends, and have by this circumstance been hurried into a temper of mind which would be extremely disrelished if known to your countrymen.

There are in the United States some characters of opposite principles; some of them are high in office, others possessing great wealth, and all of them hostile to France, and fondly looking to England as the staff of their hope. These I named to you on a former occasion. Their prospects have certainly not brightened. Excepting them, this country is entirely republican, friends to the Constitution, anxious to preserve it, and to have it administered according to its own republican principles. The little party above mentioned have espoused it only as a stepping-stone to monarchy, and have endeavored to approximate it to that in its administration in order to render its final transition more easy. The successes of republicanism in France have given the coup de grace to their prospects, and I hope to their projects. I have developed to you faithfully the sentiments of your country, that you may govern yourself accordingly. I know your republicanism to be pure, and that it is no decay of that which has embittered you against its votaries in France, but too great a sensibility at the partial evil which its object has been accomplished there.

## Friendship with France

### TO GOUVERNEUR MORRIS.

PHILADELPHIA, *March 12, 1793.*

DEAR SIR,—Your Nos. 8 to 13, inclusive, have been duly received. I am sensible that your situation must have been difficult during the transition from the late form of government to the re-establishment of some other legitimate authority, and that you may have been at a loss to determine with whom business might be done. Nevertheless, when principles are well understood, their application is less embarrassing. We surely cannot deny to any nation that right whereon our own government is founded, that every one may govern itself according to whatever form it pleases, and change these forms at its own will; and that it may transact its business with foreign nations through whatever organ it thinks proper, whether King, Convention, Assembly, Committee, President, or anything else it may choose. The will of the nation is the only thing essential to be regarded.

Mutual good offices, mutual affection, and similar principles of government, seem to destine the two nations for the most intimate communion; and I cannot too much press it on you, to improve every opportunity which may occur in the changeable scenes which are passing, and to seize them as they occur, for placing our commerce with that nation and its dependencies, on the freest and most encouraging footing possible.

## British Attitude

### TO THOMAS PINCKNEY.

PHILADELPHIA, *March 16, 1793.*

I am in hopes you will have been able to enter into proper arrangements with the British minister for the protection of our seamen from impress-

ment, before the preparations for war shall have produced inconvenience
to them. While he regards so minutely the inconveniences to themselves
which may result from a due regulation of this practice, it is just he should
regard our inconveniences also, from the want of it. His observations in
your letter imply merely, that if they should abstain from injuring us, it
might be attended with inconvenience to themselves.

## On Private Business

### TO ————.[1]

PHILADELPHIA, *March 18, 1793.*

When I first entered on the stage of public life (now twenty-four years
ago), I came to a resolution never to engage while in public office in any
kind of enterprise for the improvement of my fortune, nor to wear any
other character than that of a farmer. I have never departed from it in a
single instance; and I have in multiplied instances found myself happy in
being able to decide and to act as a public servant, clear of all interest, in
the multiform questions that have arisen, wherein I have seen others embarrassed and biased by having got themselves into a more interested situation.

We have just received here the news of the decapitation of the King of
France. Should the present foment in Europe not produce republics everywhere, it will at least soften the monarchical governments by rendering
monarchs amenable to punishment like other criminals, and doing away that
rages of insolence and oppression, the inviolability of the King's person. We
I hope shall adhere to our republican government, and keep it to its original
principles by narrowly watching it.

## Classic Reading

### TO JOHN GARLAND JEFFERSON.

PHILADELPHIA, *April 14, 1793.*

With respect to the Roman history, if you have read Suetonius and
Tacitus, Gibbon's will be sufficient to conduct you down to the time when
that empire broke to pieces and the modern states of Europe arose out of
them. As I do not suppose you can get a copy of Gibbon you may leave him
for the next winter when I shall have mine in Virginia. In the meanwhile
study well Blair, Mason, Quintilian, and endeavor to catch the oratorical
style of Bolingbroke. I should imagine that at the courts of the next fall
you might venture to take your stand at the bar of such of them as you conclude to enter into, and argue some cause, judiciously selected for you by

[1]No address.

some friendly gentleman of the bar. This will present you to the view of clients and bring in something perhaps during the winter to begin on in the spring. In the meantime the winter may be employed in finishing your course of reading and studying the forms of pleading.

## Spirit of '76

### TO COLONEL JAMES MONROE.

PHILADELPHIA, *May 5, 1793.*

The war between France and England seems to be producing an effect not contemplated. All the old spirit of 1776, rekindling the newspapers from Boston to Charleston, proves this; and even the monocrat papers are obliged to publish the most furious philippics against England. A French frigate took a British prize off the capes of Delaware the other day, and sent her up here. Upon her coming into sight, thousands and thousands of the *yeomanry* of the city crowded and covered the wharves. Never before was such a crowd seen there; and when the British colors were seen *reversed*, and the French flying above them, they burst into peals of exultation. I wish we may be able to repress the spirit of the people within the limits of a fair neutrality. In the meantime, H. is panic-struck, if we refuse our breech to every kick which Great Britain may choose to give it. He is for proclaiming at once the most abject principles, such as would invite and merit habitual insults; and indeed every inch of ground must be fought in our councils to desperation, in order to hold up the face of even a sneaking neutrality, for our votes are generally two and a half against one and a half. Some propositions have come from him which would astonish Mr. Pitt himself with their boldness. If we preserve even a sneaking neutrality, we shall be indebted for it to the President, and not to his counsellors.

## "The line is drawn"

### TO JAMES MADISON.

PHILADELPHIA, *May 13, 1793.*

We are going on here in the same spirit still. The Anglophobia has seized violently on three members of our council. This sets almost every day on questions of neutrality.

Everything, my dear Sir, hangs upon the opinion of a single person, and that the most indecisive one I ever had to do business with. He always contrives to agree in principle with one, but in conclusion with the other. Anglophobia, secret anti-gallomany, a *federalisme outrée*, and a present ease in his circumstances not usual, have decided the complexion of our dispositions, and our proceedings towards the conspirators against human liberty, and the asserters of it, which is unjustifiable in principle, in interest, and in respect to the wishes of our constituents. A manly neutrality, claiming the liberal rights ascribed to that condition by the very persons at war, was the part we should have taken, and would I believe have given satisfaction to our allies. If anything prevents its being a mere English neutrality, it will be that the penchant of the President is not that way, and above all, the ardent spirit of our constituents. The line is now drawn so clearly as to show on one side, 1. The fashionable circles of Philadelphia, New York, Boston and Charleston, (natural aristocrats). 2. Merchants trading on British capital. 3. Paper men, (all the old tories are found in some one of the three descriptions). On the other side are, 1. Merchants trading on their own capital. 2. Irish merchants. 3. Tradesmen, mechanics, farmers, and every other possible description of our citizens. Genet is not yet arrived though hourly expected.

## Presidential Character

### TO JAMES MADISON.

PHILADELPHIA, *June 9, 1793.*

The President is not well. Little lingering fevers have been hanging about him for a week or ten days, and affected his looks most remarkably. He is also extremely affected by the attacks made and kept up on him in the public papers. I think he feels those things more than any person I ever yet met with. I am sincerely sorry to see them. I remember an observation of yours, made when I first went to New York, that the satellites and sycophants which surrounded him had wound up the ceremonials of the government to a pitch of stateliness which nothing but his personal character could have supported, and which no character after him could ever maintain.

## A Free Press

### TO MESSRS. DE VIAR AND JAUDENES.[1]

PHILADELPHIA, *July 14, 1793.*

GENTLEMEN,—I have laid before the President your letters of the 11th and 13th instant. Your residence in the United States has given you an opportunity of becoming acquainted with the extreme freedom of the press in these States. Considering its great importance to the public liberty, and the difficulty of subjecting it to very precise rules, the laws have thought it less mischievous to give greater scope to its freedom, than to the restraint of it. The President has therefore no authority to prevent publications of the

[1]Representatives of Spain.

nature of those you complain of in your favor of the 11th. I can only assure you that the government of the United States has no part in them, and that all its expressions of respect towards his Catholic Majesty, public and private, have been as uniform as their desire to cultivate his friendship has been sincere.

# Appeal for Advice

## TO THE CHIEF JUSTICE AND JUDGES OF THE SUPREME COURT OF THE UNITED STATES.

PHILADELPHIA, *July 18, 1793.*

GENTLEMEN,—The war which has taken place among the powers of Europe, produces frequent transactions within our ports and limits, on which questions arise of considerable difficulty, and of greater importance to the peace of the United States. These questions depend for their solution on the construction of our treaties, on the laws of nature and nations, and on the laws of the land; and are often presented under circumstances which do not give a cognizance of them to the tribunals of the country. Yet their decision is so little analogous to the ordinary functions of the executive, as to occasion much embarrassment and difficulty to them. The President would, therefore, be much relieved, if he found himself free to refer questions of this description to the opinions of the judges of the Supreme Court of the United States, whose knowledge of the subject would secure us against errors dangerous to the peace of the United States, and their authority insure the respect of all parties. He has therefore asked the attendance of such judges as could be collected in time for the occasion, to know, in the first place, their opinion, whether the public may with propriety be availed of their advice on these questions? And if they may, to present, for their advice, the abstract questions which have already occurred, or may soon occur, from which they will themselves strike out such as any circumstances might, in their opinion, forbid them to pronounce on.

I have the honor to be, with sentiments of great esteem and respect, Gentlemen, your most obedient humble servant.

# Threshing Machine

## TO JAMES MADISON.

PHILADELPHIA, *September 1, 1793.*

Nothing further has passed with Mr. Genet, but one of his consuls has committed a pretty serious deed at Boston, by going with an armed force taken from a French frigate in the harbor, and rescuing a vessel out of the hands of the marshal who had arrested her by process from a court of justice; in another instance he kept off the marshal by an armed force from serving a process on a vessel. He is ordered, consequently, to be arrested himself, prosecuted and punished for the rescue, and his exequatur will be revoked. You will see in the newspapers the attack made on our commerce by the British king in his *additional instructions* of June 8. Though we have only newspaper information of it, *provisional* instructions are going to Mr. Pinckney to require a revocation of them, and indemnification for all losses which individuals may sustain by them in the meantime. Of the revocation I have not the least expectation. I shall therefore be for laying the whole business (respecting both nations) before Congress.

A malignant fever has been generated in the filth of Water street, which gives great alarm. About 70 people had died of it two days ago, and as many more were ill of it. It has now got into most parts of the city, and is considerably infectious. . . . I have withdrawn my daughter from the city, but am obliged to go to it every day myself.

My threshing machine has arrived at New York. Mr. Pinckney writes me word that the original from which this model is copied, threshes 150 bushels of wheat in 8 hours, with 6 horses and 5 men. It may be moved either by water or horses. Fortunately the workman who made it (a millwright) is come in the same vessel to settle in America. I have written to persuade him to go on immediately to Richmond, offering him the use of my model to exhibit, and to give him letters to get him into immediate employ in making them. I expect an answer before I write to you again. I understand that the model is made mostly in brass, and in the simple form in which it was first ordered, to be worked by horses. It was to have cost 5 guineas, but Mr. Pinckney having afterwards directed it to be accommodated to water movement also, it has made it more complicated, and costs 13 guineas. It will thresh any grain from the Windsor bean down to the smallest. Adieu.

## Southern Viewpoint

### TO JAMES MADISON.

PHILADELPHIA, *September 8, 1793.*

I went through Franklin with enchantment; and what peculiarly pleased me was, that there was not a sentence from which it could be conjectured whether it came from north, south, east or west. At last a whole page of Virginia flashed on me. It was in the section on the state of parties, and was an apology for the continuance of slavery among us. However, this circumstance may be justly palliated, it . . . encumbered a good cause with a questionable argument. Many readers who would have gone heart and hand with the author so far, would have flown off in a tangent from that paragraph. I struck it out. Justify this if you please to those concerned, and if it cannot be done, say so, and it may still be re-established.

. . . The yellow fever increases. The week before last about three a day died. This last week about eleven a day have died; consequently, from known data about thirty-three a day are taken, and there are about three hundred and thirty patients under it. They are much scattered through the town, and it is the opinion of the physicians that there is no possibility of stopping it. They agree it is a nondescript disease, and no two agree in any one part of their process of cure. The President goes off the day after to-morrow, as he had always intended. Knox then takes flight. Hamilton is ill of the fever, as is said.

## Housing Problem

### TO JAMES MADISON.

GERMANTOWN, *November 2, 1793.*

I overtook the President at Baltimore, and we arrived here yesterday, myself fleeced of seventy odd dollars to get from Fredericksburg here, the stages running no further than Baltimore. I mention this to put yourself and Monroe on your guard. The fever in Philadelphia has so much abated as to have almost disappeared. The inhabitants are about returning. It has been determined that the President shall not interfere with the meeting of Congress. R. H. and K. were of opinion he had a right to call them to any place, but that the occasion did not call for it. I think the President inclined to the opinion. I proposed a proclamation notifying that the Executive business would be done here till further notice, which I believe will be agreed. H. R. Lewis, Rawle, etc., all concur in the necessity that Congress should meet in Philadelphia, and vote there their own adjournment. If it shall then be necessary to change the place, the question will be between New York and Lancaster. The Pennsylvania members are very anxious for the latter, and will attend punctually to support it, as well as to support much for Muhlenberg, and oppose the appointment of Smith (S. C.) speaker, which is intended by the Northern members. According to present appearances this place cannot lodge a single person more. As a great favor, I have got a bed in the corner of the public room of a tavern; and must continue till some of the Philadelphians make a vacancy by removing into the city. Then we must give him from four to six or eight dollars a week for cuddies without a bed, and sometimes without a chair or table. There is not a single lodging house in the place. Ross and Willing are alive. Hancock is dead. Johnson of Maryland has *refused* Rec. L. and McE. in contemplation; the last least. You will have seen Genet's letters to Moultree and to myself. Of the last I know nothing but from the public papers; and he published Moultree's letter and his answer the moment he wrote it. You will see that his inveteracy against the President leads him to meditate the embroiling him with Congress. They say he is going to be married to a daughter of Clinton's. If so, he is afraid to return to France. Hamilton is ill, and suspicious he has taken the fever again by returning to his house. He, of course, could not attend here to-day; but the President had showed me his letter on the right of calling Congress to another place. Adieu.

## Bed and Breakfast

### TO JAMES MADISON.

GERMANTOWN, *November 17, 1793.*

DEAR SIR,—I have got good lodgings for Monroe and yourself, that is to say, a good room with a fireplace and two beds, in a pleasant and convenient position, with a quiet family. They will breakfast you, but you must mess in a tavern; there is a good one across the street. This is the way in which all must do, and all I think will not be able to get even half beds.

## Fatherly Counsel

### TO MARIA JEFFERSON.

GERMANTOWN, *November 17, 1793.*

No letter yet from my dear Marie, who is so fond of writing, so punctual in her correspondence! I enjoin as a penalty that the next be written in French. Now for news. The fever is entirely vanished from Philadelphia. Not a single person has taken infection since the great rains about the first of the month, and those who had it before are either dead or recovered. All the inhabitants who had fled are returning into the city, probably will all be returned in the course of the ensuing week. The President has been into the city, but will probably remain here till the meeting of Congress to form a point of union for them before they will have had time to gather knowledge and courage. Follow closely your music, reading, sewing, housekeeping, and love me as I do you. Most affectionately.

P. S. Tell Mr. Randolph that General Wayne has had a convoy of twenty-two wagons of provisions and seventy men cut off in his rear by Indians.

## Open Diplomacy

### TO THE PRESIDENT OF THE UNITED STATES.

PHILADELPHIA, *December 2, 1793.*

Thomas Jefferson, with his respects to the President, has the honor to send him the letters and orders referred to in Mr. Morris' letter . . .

He encloses the message respecting France and Great Britain. He first wrote it fair as it was agreed the other evening at the President's. He then drew a line with a pen through the passages he proposes to alter, in consequence of subsequent information, (but so lightly as to leave the passages still legible for the President,) and interlined the alterations he proposes . . .

On a severe review of the question, whether the British communication should carry any such mark of being confidential, as to prevent the Legislature from publishing them, he is clearly of opinion they ought not. Will they be kept secret if secrecy is enjoined? certainly not, and all the offence will be given (if it be possible any should be given) which would follow their complete publication. If they would be kept secret, from whom would it be? from our own constituents only, for Great Britain is possessed of every tittle. Why, then, keep it secret from them? no ground of support for the Executive will ever be so sure as a complete knowledge of their proceedings by the people; and it is only in cases where the public good would be injured, and *because* it would be injured, that proceedings should be secret. In such cases it is the duty of the Executive to sacrifice their personal interests (which would be promoted by publicity) to the public interest. If the negotiations with England are at an end, if not given to the public now, when are they to be given? and what moment can be so interesting? If anything amiss should happen from the concealment, where will the blame *originate* at last? It may be said, indeed, that the President *puts it in the power* of the Legislature to communicate these proceedings to *their constituents;* but is it more their duty to communicate them to their constituents, than it is the President's to communicate them to *his constituents?* And if they were desirous of communicating them, ought the President to restrain them by making the communication confidential? I think no harm can be done by the publication, because it is impossible England, after doing us an injury, should *declare war* against us, merely because we tell our constituents of it; and I think good may be done, because while it puts it in the power of the Legislature to adopt peaceable measures of doing ourselves justice, it prepares the minds of our constituents to go cheerfully into an acquiescence under the measures, by impressing them with a thorough and enlightened conviction that they are founded in right. The motive, too, of proving to the people the impartiality of the Executive between the two nations of France and England, urges strongly that while they are to see the disagreeable things which have been going on as to France, we should not conceal from them what has been passing with England, and induce a belief that nothing has been doing.

## Resignation

### TO THE PRESIDENT OF THE UNITED STATES.

PHILADELPHIA, *December 31, 1793.*

DEAR SIR,—Having had the honor of communicating to you in my letter of the last of July, my purpose of returning from the office of Secretary of

State, at the end of the month of September, you were pleased, for particular reasons, to wish its postponement to the close of the year. That term being now arrived, and my propensities to retirement becoming daily more and more irresistible, I now take the liberty of resigning the office into your hands. Be pleased to accept with it my sincere thanks for all the indulgences which you have been so good as to exercise towards me in the discharge of its duties. Conscious that my need of them has been great, I have still ever found them greater, without any other claim on my part, than a firm pursuit of what has appeared to me to be right, and a thorough disdain of all means which were not as open and honorable, as their object was pure. I carry into my retirement a lively sense of your goodness, and shall continue gratefully to remember it. With very sincere prayers for your life, health and tranquillity, I pray you to accept the homage of the great and constant respect and attachment with which I have the honor to be, dear Sir, your most obedient, and most humble servant.

## Cover Crops

### TO JOHN TAYLOR.

MONTICELLO, *December 29, 1794.*

DEAR SIR,—I have long owed you a letter, for which my conscience would not have let me rest in quiet but on the consideration that the payment would not be worth your acceptance. The debt is not merely for a letter the common traffic of every day, but for valuable ideas, which instructed me, which I have adopted, and am acting on them. I am sensible of the truth of your observations that the atmosphere is the great storehouse of matter for recruiting our lands, that though efficacious, it is slow in its operation, and we must therefore give them time instead of the loads of quicker manure given in other countries, that for this purpose we must avail ourselves of the great quantities of land we possess in proportion to our labor, and that while putting them to nurse with the atmosphere, we must protect them from the bite and tread of animals, which are nearly a counterpoise for the benefits of the atmosphere. As good things, as well as evil, go in a train, this relieves us from the labor and expense of cross fences, now very sensibly felt on account of the scarcity and distance of timber. I am accordingly now engaged in applying my cross fences to the repair of the outer ones and substituting rows of peach trees to preserve the boundaries of the fields. And though I observe your strictures on rotations of crops, yet it appears that in this I differ from you only in words. You keep half your lands in culture, the other half at nurse; so I propose to do. Your scheme indeed requires only four years and mine six; but the proportion of labor and rest is the same. My years of rest, however, are employed, two of them in producing clover, yours in volunteer herbage. But I still understand it to be your opinion that clover is best where lands will produce them. In -

deed I think that the important improvement for which the world is indebted to Young is the substitution of clover crops instead of unproductive fallows; and the demonstration that lands are more enriched by clover than by volunteer herbage or fallows; and the clover crops are highly valuable. That our red lands which are still in tolerable heart will produce fine clover I know from the experience of the last year; and indeed that of my neighbors had established the fact. And from observations on accidental plants in the fields which have been considerably harassed with corn, I believe that even these will produce clover fit for soiling of animals green. I think, therefore, I can count on the success of that improver. My third year of rest will be devoted to cowpenning, and to a trial of the buckwheat dressing. A further progress in surveying my open arable lands has shewn me that I can have seven fields in each of my farms where I expected only six; consequently that I can add more to the portion of rest and ameliorating crops. I have doubted on a question on which I am sure you can advise me well, whether I had better give this newly acquired year as an addition to the continuance of my clover, or throw it with some improving crop between two of my crops of grain, as for instance between my corn and rye. I strongly incline to the latter, because I am not satisfied that one cleansing crop in seven years will be sufficient; and indeed I think it important to separate my exhausting crops by alternations of amelioraters. With this view I think to try an experiment of what Judge Parker informs me he practises. That is, to turn in my wheat stubble the instant the grain is off, and sow turnips to be fed out by the sheep. But whether this will answer in our fields which are harassed, I do not know. We have been in the habit of sowing only our freshest lands in turnips, hence a presumption that wearied lands will not bring them. But Young's making turnips to be fed on by sheep the basis of his improvement of poor lands, affords evidence that though they may not bring great crops, they will bring them in a sufficient degree to improve the lands. I will try that experiment, however, this year, as well as the one of buckwheat. I have also attended to another improver mentioned by you, the winter vetch, and have taken measures to get the seed of it from England, as also of the Siberian vetch which Millar greatly commends, and being a biennial might perhaps take the place of clover in lands which do not suit that. The winter vetch I suspect may be advantageously thrown in between crops, as it gives a choice to use it as green feed in the spring if fodder be run short, or to turn it in as a green-dressing. My rotation, with these amendments, is as follows:—

1. Wheat, followed the same year by turnips, to be fed on by the sheep.

2. Corn and potatoes mixed, and in autumn the vetch to be used as fodder in the spring if wanted, or to be turned in as a dressing.

3. Peas or potatoes, or both according to the quality of the field.

4. Rye and clover sown on it in the spring. Wheat may be substituted here for rye, when it shall be found that the second, third, fifth, and sixth fields will subsist the farm.

5. Clover.

6. Clover, and in autumn turn it in and sow the vetch.

7. Turn in the vetch in the spring, then sow buckwheat and turn that in, having hurdled off the poorest spots for cowpenning. In autumn sow wheat to begin the circle again.

I am for throwing the whole force of my husbandry on the wheat-field, because it is the only one which is to go to market to produce money. Perhaps the clover may bring in something in the form of stock. The other fields are merely for the consumption of the farm. Melilot, mentioned by you, I never heard of. The horse bean I tried this last year. It turned out nothing. The President has tried it without success. An old English farmer of the name of Spuryear, settled in Delaware, has tried it there with good success; but he told me it would not do without being well shaded, and I think he planted it among his corn for that reason. But he acknowledged our pea was as good an ameliorater and a more valuable pulse, as being food for man as well as horse. The succory is what Young calls Chicoria Intudbus. He sent some seed to the President, who gave me some, and I gave it to my neighbors to keep up till I should come home. One of them has cultivated it with great success, is very fond of it, and gave me some seed which I sowed last spring. Though the summer was favorable it came on slowly at first, but by autumn became large and strong. It did not seed that year, but will the next, and you shall be furnished with seed. I suspect it requires rich ground, and then produces a heavy crop for green feed for horses and cattle. I had poor success with my potatoes last year, not having made more than 60 or 70 bushels to the acre. But my neighbors having made good crops, I am not disheartened. The first step towards the recovery of our lands is to find substitutes for corn and bacon. I count on potatoes, clover, and sheep. The two former to feed every animal on the farm except my negroes, and the latter to feed them, diversified with rations of salted fish and molasses, both of them wholesome, agreeable, and cheap articles of food.

For pasture I rely on the forests by day, and soiling the evening. Why could we not have a moveable airy cow house, to be set up in the middle of the field which is to be dunged, and soil our cattle in that through the summer as well as winter, keeping them constantly up and well littered? This with me, would be in the clover field of the first year, because during the second year it would be rotting, and would be spread on it in fallow the beginning of the third, but such an effort would be far above the present tyro state of my farming. The grosser barbarisms in culture which I have to encounter are more than enough for all my attentions at present. The dung-yard must be my last effort but one. The last would be irrigation. It might be thought at first view, that the interposition of these ameliorations or dressings between my crops will be too laborious, but observe that the turnips and two dressings of vetch do not cost a single ploughing. The turning the wheat-stubble for the turnips is the fallow for the corn of the succeeding year. The first sowing of vetches is on the corn (as is now practised for wheat), and the turning it in is the flush-ploughing for the crop of potatoes and peas. The second sowing of the vetch is on the wheat fallow, and the turning it in is the ploughing necessary for sowing the buck-wheat. These three ameliorations, then, will cost but a harrowing each. On the subject of the drilled husbandry, I think experience has established its preference for some plants, as the turnip, pea, bean, cabbage, corn, etc., and that of the broadcast for other plants as all the bread grains and grasses, except perhaps lucerne and Saint foin in soils and climates very productive of weeds. In dry soils and climates the broadcast is better for lucerne and Saint foin, as all the south of France can testify.

I have imagined and executed a mould-board which may be mathe-matically demonstrated to be perfect, as far as perfection depends on mathematical principles, and one great circumstance in its favor is that it may be made by the most bungling carpenter, and cannot possibly vary a hair's breadth in its form, by but gross negligence. You have seen the musical instrument called a sticcado. Suppose all its sticks of equal length, hold the fore-end horizontally on the floor to receive the turf which pre-sents itself horizontally, and with the right hand twist the hind-end to the perpendicular, or rather as much beyond the perpendicular as will be neces-sary to cast over the turf completely. This gives an idea (though not abso-lutely exact) of my mould-board. It is on the principle of two wedges com-bined at right angles, the first in the direct line of the furrow to raise the turf gradually, the other across the furrow to turn it over gradually. For both these purposes the wedge is the instrument of the least resistance. I will make a model of the mould-board and lodge it with Colonel Harvie in Richmond for you. This brings me to my thanks for the drill plough lodged with him for me, which I now expect every hour to receive, and the price of which I have deposited in his hands to be called for when you please. A good instrument of this kind is almost the greatest desideratum in hus-bandry. I am anxious to conjecture beforehand what may be expected from the sowing turnips in jaded ground, how much from the acre, and how large they will be? Will your experience enable you to give me a probable con-jecture? Also what is the produce of potatoes and what of peas in the same kind of ground?

# Soft Pillow

## TO EDMUND RANDOLPH.

MONTICELLO, *February 3, 1794.*

I think it is Montaigne who has said, that ignorance is the softest pillow on which a man can rest his head. I am sure it is true as to everything political, and shall endeavor to estrange myself to everything of that char-acter. I indulge myself on one political topic only, that is, in declaring to my countrymen the shameless corruption of a portion of the Representatives to the first and second Congresses, and their implicit devotion to the treasury.

I think I do good in this, because it may produce exertions to reform the evil, on the success of which the form of the government is to depend.

## From Retirement

### TO JAMES MADISON.

MONTICELLO, *April 3, 1794.*

As to the naval armament, the land armament, and the marine fortifications which are in question with you, I have no doubt they will all be carried. Not that the monocrats and paper men in Congress want war; but they want armies and debts; and though we may hope that the sound part of Congress is now so augmented as to insure a majority in cases of general interest merely, yet I have always observed that in questions of expense, where members may hope either for offices or jobs for themselves or their friends, some few will be debauched, and that is sufficient to turn the decision where a majority is, at most, but small.

I have never seen a Philadelphia paper since I left it, till those you enclosed me; and I feel myself so thoroughly weaned from the interest I took in the proceedings there, while there, that I have never had a wish to see one, and believe that I never shall take another newspaper of any sort. I find my mind totally absorbed in my rural occupations.

## Enough of War

### TO GEORGE WASHINGTON.

MONTICELLO, *April 25, 1794.*

DEAR SIR,—I am to thank you for the book you were so good as to transmit me, as well as the letter covering it, and your felicitations on my present quiet. The difference of my present and past situation is such as to leave me nothing to regret, but that my retirement has been postponed four years too long. The principles on which I calculated the value of life, are entirely in favor of my present course. I return to farming with an ardor which I scarcely knew in my youth, and which has got the better entirely of my love of study. Instead of writing ten or twelve letters a day, which I have been in the habit of doing as a thing of course, I put off answering my letters now, farmer-like, till a rainy day, and then find them sometimes postponed by other necessary occupations. The case of the Pays de Vaud is new to me. The claims of both parties are on grounds which, I fancy, we have taught the world to set little store by. The rights of one generation will scarcely be considered hereafter as depending on the paper transactions of another. My countrymen are groaning under the insults of Great Britain.

I hope some means will turn up of reconciling our faith and honor with peace. I confess to you I have seen enough of one war never to wish to see another. With wishes of every degree of happiness to you, both public and private, and with my best respects to Mrs. Adams,[1] I am, your affectionate and humble servant.

## No Newspapers

### TO TENCH COXE.

MONTICELLO, *May 1, 1794.*

Your letters give a comfortable view of French affairs, and later events seem to confirm it. Over the foreign powers I am convinced they will triumph completely, and I cannot but hope that that triumph, and the consequent disgrace of the invading tyrants, is destined, in order of events, to kindle the wrath of the people of Europe against those who have dared to embroil them in such wickedness, and to bring at length, kings, nobles and priests to the scaffolds which they have been so long deluging with human blood. I am still warm whenever I think of these scoundrels, though I do it as seldom as I can, preferring infinitely to contemplate the tranquil growth of my lucerne and potatoes. I have so completely withdrawn myself from these spectacles of usurpation and misrule, that I do not take a single newspaper, nor read one a month; and I feel myself infinitely the happier for it.

We are alarmed here with the apprehensions of war; and sincerely anxious that it may be avoided; but not at the expense either of our faith or honor. It seems much the general opinion here, the latter has been too much wounded not to require reparation, and to seek it even in war, if that be necessary. As to myself, I love peace, and I am anxious that we should give the world still another useful lesson, by showing to them other modes of punishing injuries than by war, which is as much a punishment to the punisher as to the sufferer. I love, therefore, Mr. Clarke's proposition of cutting off all communication with the nation which has conducted itself so atrociously. This, you will say, may bring on war. If it does, we will meet it like men; but it may not bring on war, and then the experiment will have been a happy one.

## Rotation of Crops

### TO GEORGE WASHINGTON.

MONTICELLO, *May 14, 1794.*

DEAR SIR.—I am honored with your favor of April the 24th, and received, at the same time, Mr. Bertrand's agricultural prospectus. . . .

[1] A classic error; for Mrs. Washington.

I find on a more minute examination of my lands than the short visits heretofore made to them permitted, that a ten years' abandonment of them to the ravages of overseers, has brought on them a degree of degradation far beyond what I had expected. As this obliges me to adopt a milder course of cropping, so I find that they have enabled me to do it, by having opened a great deal of lands during my absence. I have therefore determined on a division of my farm into six fields, to be put under this rotation: first year, wheat; second, corn, potatoes, peas; third, rye or wheat, according to circumstances; fourth and fifth, clover where the fields will bring it, and buckwheat dressings where they will not; sixth, folding, and buckwheat dressings. But it will take me from three to six years to get this plan under way. I am not yet satisfied that my acquisition of overseers from the head of Elk has been a happy one, or that much will be done this year towards rescuing my plantations from their wretched condition. Time, patience and perseverance must be the remedy; and the maxim of your letter, "slow and sure," is not less a good one in agriculture than in politics. I sincerely wish it may extricate us from the event of a war, if this can be done saving our faith and our rights. My opinion of the British government is, that nothing will force them to do justice but the loud voice of their people, and that this can never be excited but by distressing their commerce. But I cherish tranquillity too much, to suffer political things to enter my mind at all. I do not forget that I owe you a letter for Mr. Young; but I am waiting to get full information. With every wish for your health and happiness, and my most friendly respects for Mrs. Washington, I have the honor to be, dear Sir, your most obedient, and most humble servant.

# Refugee Professor

## TO WILSON NICHOLAS, ESQ.

MONTICELLO, *November 22, 1794.*

SIR,—I take the liberty of enclosing for your perusal and consideration a proposal from a Mr. D'Ivernois, a Genevan, of considerable distinction for science and patriotism, and that, too, of the republican kind, though you will see that he does not carry it so far as our friends of the National Assembly of France. While I was at Paris, I knew him as an exile from his democratic principles, the aristocracy having then the upper hand in Geneva. He is now obnoxious to the democratic party. The sum of his proposition is to translate the academy of Geneva in a body to this country. You know well that the colleges of Edinburgh and Geneva, as seminaries of science, are considered as the two eyes of Europe; while Great Britain and America give the preference to the former, and all other countries give it to the latter. I am fully sensible that two powerful obstacles are in the way of this proposition. 1st. The expense: 2d. The communication of science in foreign languages; that is to say, in French and Latin; but I have been so long absent from my own country as to be an incompetent judge either of the force of the objections, or of the dispositions of those who are to decide on them. The respectability of Mr. D'Ivernois' character, and that, too, of the proposition, require an answer from me, and that it should be given on due inquiry. He desires secrecy to a certain degree for the reasons which he explains. What I have to request of you, my dear Sir, is, that you will be so good as to consider his proposition, to consult on its expediency and practicability with such gentlemen of the Assembly as you think best, and take such other measures as you shall think best to ascertain what would be the sense of that body, were the proposition to be hazarded to them. If yourself and friends approve of it, and there is hope that the Assembly would do so, your zeal for the good of our country in general, and the promotion of science, as an instrument towards that, will, of course, induce you to aid them to bring it forward in such a way as you shall judge best. If, on the contrary, you disapprove of it yourselves, or think it would be desperate with the Assembly, be so good as to return it to me with such information as I may hand forward to Mr. D'Ivernois, to put him out of suspense. Keep the matter by all means out of the public papers, and particularly, if you please, do not couple my name with the proposition if brought forward, because it is much my wish to be in nowise implicated in public affairs. It is necessary for me to appeal to all my titles for giving you this trouble, whether founded in representation, patriotism or friendship. The latter, however, as the broadest, is that on which I wish to rely, being with sentiments of very cordial esteem, dear Sir, your sincere friend and humble servant.

## Constitutional Liberties

### TO JAMES MADISON.

MONTICELLO, *December 28, 1794.*

The denunciation of the democratic societies is one of the extraordinary acts of boldness of which we have seen so many from the faction of monocrats. It is wonderful indeed, that the President should have permitted himself to be the organ of such an attack on the freedom of discussion, the freedom of writing, printing and publishing. It must be a matter of rare curiosity to get at the modifications of these rights proposed by them, and to see what line their ingenuity would draw between democratical societies, whose avowed object is the nourishment of the republican principles of our Constitution, and the society of the Cincinnati, *a self-created* one, carving out for itself hereditary distinctions, lowering over our Constitution eternally, meeting together in all parts of the Union, periodically, with closed doors, accumulating a capital in their separate treasury, corresponding secretly and regularly, and of which society the very persons denouncing the democrats are themselves the fathers, founders and high officers. Their sight must be perfectly dazzled by the glittering of crowns and coronets, not to see the extravagance of the proposition to suppress the friends of general freedom, while those who wish to confine that freedom to the few, are permitted to go on in their principles and practices. I here put out of sight the persons whose misbehavior has been taken advantage of to slander the friends of popular rights; and I am happy to observe, that as far as the circle of my observation and information extends, everybody has lost sight of them, and views the abstract attempt on their natural and constitutional rights in all its nakedness. I have never heard, or heard of, a single expression or opinion which did not condemn it as an inexcusable aggression. And with respect to the transactions against the excise law, it appears to me that you are all swept away in the torrent of governmental opinions, or that we do not know what these transactions have been. We know of none which, according to the definitions of the law, have been anything more than riotous. There was indeed a meeting to consult about a separation. But to consult on a question does not amount to a determination of that question in the affirmative, still less to the acting on such a determination; but we shall see, I suppose, what the court lawyers, and courtly judges, and would-be ambassadors will make of it.

The excise law is an infernal one. The first error was to admit it by the Constitution; the second, to act on that admission; the third and last will be, to make it the instrument of dismembering the Union, and setting us all afloat to choose what part of it we will adhere to. The information of our militia, returned from the westward, is uniform, that though the people there let them pass quietly, they were objects of their laughter, not of their fear; that one thousand men could have cut off their whole force in a thousand places of the Alleghany; that their detestation of the excise law is universal, and has now associated to it a detestation of the government; and that a separation which perhaps was a very distant and problematical event, is now near, and certain, and determined in the mind of every man. I expected to have seen some justification of arming one part of the society against another; of declaring a civil war the moment before the meeting of that body which has the sole right of declaring war; of being so patient of the kicks and scoffs of our enemies, and rising at a feather against our friends . . .

## On Clover

### TO JAMES MADISON.

MONTICELLO, *April 27, 1795.*

My little essay in red clover, the last year, has had the most encouraging success. I sowed then about forty acres. I have sowed this year about one hundred and twenty, which the rain now falling comes very opportunely on. From one hundred and sixty to two hundred acres, will be my yearly sowing. The seed-box described in the agricultural transactions of New York, reduces the expense of seeding from six shillings to two shillings and three pence the acre, and does the business better than is possible to be done by the human hand.

## Estimate of an Enemy

### TO JAMES MADISON.

MONTICELLO, *September 21, 1795.*

. . . Hamilton is really a colossus to the anti-republican party. Without numbers, he is an host within himself. They have got themselves into a defile, where they might be finished; but too much security on the republican part will give time to his talents and indefatigableness to extricate them. We have had only middling performances to oppose to him. In truth, when he comes forward, there is nobody but yourself who can meet him.

## Threat to Freedom

### TO WILLIAM B. GILES.

MONTICELLO, *March 19, 1796.*

We are in suspense here to see the fate and effect of Mr. Pitt's bill against democratic societies. I wish extremely to get at the true history of this effort to suppress freedom of meeting, speaking, writing and printing. Your acquaintance with Sedgwick will enable you to do it. Pray get the outlines of the bill he intended to have brought in for this purpose. This will enable us to judge whether we have the merit of the invention; whether we were really beforehand with the British minister on this subject; whether he took his hint from our proposition, or whether the concurrence in the sentiment is merely the result of the general truth that great men will think alike and act alike, though without intercommunication. I am serious in desiring extremely the outlines of the bill intended for us.

We have had a fine winter. Wheat looks well. Corn is scarce and dear. Twenty-two shillings here, thirty shillings in Amherst. Our blossoms are, but just opening. I have begun the demolition of my house, and hope to get through its re-edification in the course of the summer. We shall have the eye of a brick-kiln to poke you into, or an octagon to air you in. Adieu affectionately.

# Green Pastures

## TO GEORGE WASHINGTON.

MONTICELLO, *June 19, 1796.*

I think I have had, both the last and present year, as good clover from common grounds, which had brought several crops of wheat and corn without ever having been manured, as I ever saw on the lots around Philadelphia. I verily believe that a yield of thirty-four acres, sowed on wheat April was twelvemonth, has given me a ton to the acre at its first cutting this spring. The stalks extended, measured three and a half feet long very commonly. Another field, a year older, and which yielded as well the last year, has sensibly fallen off this year. My exhausted fields bring a clover not high enough for hay, but I hope to make seed from it. Such as these, however, I shall hereafter put into peas in the broadcast, proposing that one of my sowings of wheat shall be after two years of clover, and the other after two years of peas. I am trying the white boiling pea of Europe (the Albany pea) this year, till I can get the hog pea of England, which is the most productive of all. But the true winter vetch is what we want extremely. I have tried this year the Carolina drill. It is absolutely perfect. Nothing can be more simple, nor perform its office more perfectly for a single row. I shall try to make one to sow four rows at a time of wheat or peas, at twelve inches distance. I have one of the Scotch threshing machines nearly finished. It is copied exactly from a model Mr. Pinckney sent me, only that I have put the whole works (except the horse wheel) into a single frame, movable from one field to another on the two axles of a wagon. It will be ready in time for the harvest which is coming on, which will give it a full trial. Our wheat and rye are generally fine, and the prices talked of bid fair to indemnify us for the poor crops of the two last years.

# Measure of Mountains

## TO JONATHAN WILLIAMS.

MONTICELLO, *July 3, 1796.*

DEAR SIR,—I take shame to myself for having so long left unanswered your valuable favor on the subject of the mountains. But in truth, I am become lazy as to everything except agriculture. The preparations for harvest, and the length of the harvest itself, which is not yet finished, would have excused the delay, however, at all times and under all dispositions. I examined, with great satisfaction, your barometrical estimate of the heights of our mountains; and with the more, as they corroborated conjectures on this subject which I had made before. My estimates had made them a little higher than yours (I speak of the Blue Ridge). Measuring with a very nice instrument the angle subtended vertically by the highest mountain of the Blue Ridge opposite to my own house, a distance of about eighteen miles south-westward, I made the highest about two thousand feet, as well as I remember, for I can no longer find the notes I made. You make the south side of the mountain near Rockfish Gap, one thousand seven hundred and twenty-two feet above Woods'. You make the other side of the mountain seven hundred and sixty-seven feet. Mr. Thomas Lewis, deceased, an accurate man, with a good quadrant, made the north side of the highest mountain opposite my house something more (I think) than one thousand feet; but the mountain estimated by him and myself is probably higher than that next Rockfish Gap. I do not remember from what principles I estimated the Peaks of Otter at four thousand feet; but some late observations of Judge Tucker's coincided very nearly with my estimate. Your measures confirm another opinion of mine, that the Blue Ridge, on its south side, is the highest ridge in our country compared with its base.

## Old Bones

### TO COLONEL JOHN STUART.

MONTICELLO, *November 10, 1796.*

DEAR SIR,—I have to acknowledge the receipt of your last favor, together with the bones of the great claw, which accompanied it. My anxiety to obtain a thigh bone is such, that I defer communicating what we have to the Philosophical Society, in the hope of adding that bone to the collection. We should then be able to fix the stature of the animal, without going into conjecture and calculation, as we should possess a whole limb, from the haunch bone to the claw inclusive. However, as you announce to me that the recovery of a thigh bone is desperate, I shall make the communication to the Philosophical Society.

## Campaign Talk

### TO EDWARD RUTLEDGE.

MONTICELLO, *December 27, 1796.*

You have seen my name lately tacked to so much of eulogy and of abuse, that I dare say you hardly thought it meant your old acquaintance of '76. In truth, I did not know myself under the pens either of my friends or foes. It is unfortunate for our peace, that unmerited abuse wounds, while unmerited praise has not the power to heal. These are hard wages for the services of all the active and healthy years of one's life. I had retired after five and twenty years of constant occupation in public affairs, and total abandonment of my own. I retired much poorer than when I entered the public service, and desired nothing but rest and oblivion. My name, however, was again brought forward, without concert or expectation on my part; (on my salvation I declare it). I do not as yet know the result, as a matter of fact; for in my retired canton we have nothing later from Philadelphia than of the second week of this month. Yet I have never one moment doubted the result. I knew it was impossible Mr. Adams should lose a vote north of the Delaware, and that the free and moral agency of the South would furnish him an abundant supplement. On principles of public respect I should not have refused; but I protest before my God, that I shall, from the bottom of my heart, rejoice at escaping. I know well that no man will ever bring out of that office the reputation which carries him into it. The honeymoon would be as short in that case as in any other, and its moments of ecstasy would be ransomed by years of torment and hatred. I shall highly value, indeed, the share which I may have had in the late vote, as an evidence of the share I hold in the esteem of my countrymen. But in this point of view, a few votes more or less will be little sensible, and in every other, the minor will be preferred by me to the major vote. I have no ambition to govern men; no passion which would lead me to delight to ride in a storm. *Flumina amo, sylvasque, inglorius.* My attachment to my home has enabled me to make the calculation with rigor, perhaps with partiality, to the issue which keeps me there. The newspapers will permit me to plant my corn, peas, etc., in hills or drills as I please (and my oranges, by-the-bye, when you send them), while our eastern friend will be struggling with the storm which is gathering over us; perhaps be shipwrecked in it. This is certainly not a moment to covet the helm.

## Election Returns

### TO JAMES MADISON.

MONTICELLO, *Jan. 1, '97.*

Yours of Dec. 19 has come safely. The event of the election has never been a matter of doubt in my mind. I knew that the Eastern States were disciplined in the schools of their town meetings to sacrifice differences of opinion to the great object of operating in phalanx, and that the more free and moral agency practiced in the other States would always make up the supplement of their weight. Indeed the vote comes much nearer an equality than I had expected.

## Prevailing Winds

### TO MR. VOLNEY.

MONTICELLO, *January 8, 1797.*

It seems possible, from what we hear of the votes at the election, that you may see me in Philadelphia about the beginning of March, exactly in that character which, if I were to reappear at Philadelphia, I would prefer to all others; for I change the sentiment of Clorinda to "L'Alte temo, l'humile non sdegno." I have no inclination to govern men. I should have no views of my own in doing it; and as to those of the governed, I had rather that their disappointment (which must always happen) should be pointed to any other cause, real or supposed, than to myself. I value the late vote highly; but it is only as the index of the place I hold in the esteem of my fellow-citizens. In this point of view, the difference between sixty-eight and seventy-one votes is little sensible, and still less that between the real vote, which was sixty-nine and seventy; because one real elector in Pennsylvania was excluded from voting by the miscarriage of the votes, and one who was not an elector was admitted to vote. My farm, my family, my books and my building, give me much more pleasure than any public office would, and, especially, one which would keep me constantly from them. I had hoped, when you were here, to have finished the walls of my house in the autumn, and to have covered it early in winter. But we did not finish them at all. I have to resume the work, therefore, in the spring, and to take off the roof of the old part during the summer, to cover the whole. This will render it necessary for me to make a very short stay in Philadelphia, should the late vote have given me any public duty there. My visit there will be merely out of respect to the public, and to the new President.

I am sorry you have received so little information on the subject of our winds. I had once (before our revolution war) a project on the same subject. As I had then an extensive acquaintance over this State, I meant to have engaged some person in every county of it, giving them each a thermometer, to observe that and the winds twice a day, for one year, to wit, at sun-rise and at four P. M., (the coldest and the warmest point of the twenty-four hours,) and to communicate their observations to me at the end of the year. I should then have selected the days in which it appeared that the winds blew to a centre within the State, and have made a map of them, and seen how far they had analogy with the temperature of the air. I meant this to be merely a specimen to be communicated to the Philosophical Society at Philadelphia, in order to engage them, by means of their correspondents, to have the same thing done in every State, and through a series of years. By seizing the days when the winds centred in any part of the United States, we might, in time, have come to some of the causes which determine the direction of the winds, which I suspect to be very various. But this long-winded project was prevented by the war which came upon us, and since that I have been far otherwise engaged.

## Notice of Election

### TO HENRY TAZEWELL.

MONTICELLO, *January 16, 1797.*

DEAR SIR,—As far as the public papers are to be credited, I may suppose that the choice of Vice-President has fallen on me. On this hypothesis I trouble you, and only pray, if it be wrong, that you will consider this letter as not written. I believe it belongs to the Senate to notify the Vice-President of his election. I recollect to have heard, that on the first election of President and Vice-President, gentlemen of considerable office were sent to notify the parties chosen. But this was the inauguration of our new government, and ought not to be drawn into example. At the second election, both gentlemen were on the spot and needed no messengers. On the present occasion, the President will be on the spot, so that what is now to be done respects myself alone; and considering that the season of notification will always present one difficulty, that the distance in the present case adds a second, not inconsiderable, and which may in future happen to be sometimes much more considerable, I hope the Senate will adopt that method of notification, which will always be least troublesome and most certain. The channel of the post is certainly the least troublesome, is the most rapid, and, considering also that it may be sent by duplicates and triplicates, is unquestionably the most certain. Indorsed to the postmaster at Charlottesville, with an order to send it by express, no hazard can endanger the notification. Apprehending, that should there be a difference of opinion on this subject in the Senate, my ideas of self-respect might be supposed by some to require something more formal and inconvenient, I beg leave to avail myself of your friendship to declare, if a different proposition should make it necessary, that I consider the channel of the post-office as the most eligible in every respect, and that it is to me the most desirable; which I take the liberty of expressing, not with a view of encroaching on the respect due to that discretion which the Senate have a right to exercise on the occasion, but to render them the more free in the exercise of it, by taking off whatsoever weight the supposition of a contrary desire in me might have on the mind of any member.

# Rules of Order

### TO GEORGE WYTHE.

MONTICELLO, *January 22, 1797.*

It seems probable that I will be called on to preside in a legislative chamber. It is now so long since I have acted in the legislative line, that I am entirely rusty in the Parliamentary rules of procedure. I know they have been more studied and are better known by you than by any man in America, perhaps by any man living. I am in hopes that while inquiring into the subject you made notes on it. If any such remain in your hands, however informal, in books or in scraps of paper, and you will be so good as to trust me with them a little while, they shall be most faithfully returned.

## Natural History

TO DOCTOR BENJAMIN RUSH.

MONTICELLO, *January 22, 1797.*

I am indebted to the Philosophical Society a communication of some bones of an animal of the lion kind, but of most exaggerated size. What are we to think of a creature whose claws were eight inches long, when those of the lion are not 1½ inches; whose thigh-bone was 6¼ diameter; when that of the lion is not 1½ inches? Were not the things within the jurisdiction of the rule and compass, and of ocular inspection, credit to them could not be obtained. I have been disappointed in getting the femur as yet, but shall bring on the bones I have, if I can, for the Society, and have the pleasure of seeing you for a few days in the first week of March.

## No Ceremony

TO JAMES MADISON.

MONTICELLO, *January 30, 1797.*

I have turned to the Constitution and laws, and find nothing to warrant the opinion that I might not have been qualified here, or wherever else could meet with a Senator; any member of that body being authorized to administer the oath, without being confined to time or place, and consequently to make a record of it, and to deposit it with the records of the Senate. However, I shall come on, on the principle which had first determined me,—respect to the public. I hope I shall be made a part of no ceremony whatever. If Governor Mifflin should show any symptoms of ceremony, pray contrive to parry them. We have now fine mild weather here. The thermometer is above the point which renders fires necessary. Adieu affectionately.

## Breadfruit for Georgia

TO MR. GIROUD.

PHILADELPHIA, *May 22, 1797.*

SIR,—I received at this place, from Mr. Bache, the letter of 20th Germinal, with the seeds of the bread-tree which you were so kind as to send me. I am happy that the casual circumstances respecting Oglethorpe's affairs, has led to this valuable present, and I shall take immediate measures to improve the opportunity it gives us of introducing so precious a plant into our Southern

States. The successive supplies of the same seeds which you are kind enough to give me expectations of receiving from you, will, in like manner, be thankfully received, and distributed to those persons and places most likely to render the experiment successful. One service of this kind rendered to a nation, is worth more to them than all the victories of the most splendid pages of their history, and becomes a source of exalted pleasure to those who have been instrumental to it.

## Foreign Policy

### TO GENERAL GATES.

PHILADELPHIA, *May 30, 1797.*

DEAR GENERAL,—I thank you for the pamphlet of Erskine enclosed in your favor of the 9th instant, and still more for the evidence which your letter affords me of the health of your mind, and I hope of your body also. Erskine has been reprinted here, and has done good. It has refreshed the memory of those who had been willing to forget how the war between France and England had been produced; and who, aping St. James', called it a defensive war on the part of England. I wish any events could induce us to cease to copy such a model, and to assume the dignity of being original. They had their paper system, stockjobbing, speculations, public debt, moneyed interest, etc., and all this was contrived for us. They raised their cry against jacobinism and revolutionists, we against democratic societies and anti-federalists; their alarmists sounded insurrection, ours marched an army to look for one, but they could not find it. I wish the parallel may stop here, and that we may avoid, instead of imitating, a general bankruptcy and disastrous war.

## On Emancipation

### TO ST. GEORGE TUCKER.

MONTICELLO, *August 28, 1797.*

DEAR SIR,—I have to acknowledge the receipt of your two favors of the 2d and 22d instant, and to thank you for the pamphlet covered by the former. You know my subscription to its doctrines; and as to the mode of emancipation, I am satisfied that that must be a matter of compromise between the passions, the prejudices, and the real difficulties which will each have their weight in that operation. Perhaps the first chapter of this history, which has begun in St. Domingo, and the next succeeding ones, which will recount how all the whites were driven from all the other islands, may prepare our minds for a peaceable accommodation between justice, policy and necessity; and furnish an answer to the difficult question, whither shall the colored emigrants go? and the sooner we put some plan under way, the greater hope there is that it may be permitted to proceed peaceably to its ultimate effect. But if something is not done, and soon done, we shall be the murderers of our own children. The "murmura venturos nautis prudentia ventos" has already reached us; the revolutionary storm, now sweeping the globe, will be upon us, and happy if we make timely provision to give it an easy passage over our land. From the present state of things in Europe and America, the day which begins our combustion must be near at hand; and only a single spark is wanting to make that day to-morrow. If we had begun sooner, we might probably have been allowed a lengthier operation to clear ourselves, but every day's delay lessens the time we may take for emancipation.

## Son of Liberty

### TO GENERAL GATES.

PHILADELPHIA, *February 21, 1798.*

DEAR GENERAL,—I received duly your welcome favor of the 15th, and had an opportunity of immediately delivering the one it enclosed to General Kosciusko. I see him often, and with great pleasure mixed with commiseration. He is as pure a son of liberty as I have ever known, and of that liberty which is to go to all, and not to the few or the rich alone.

Kosciusko has been disappointed by the sudden peace between France and Austria. A ray of hope seemed to gleam on his mind for a moment, that the extension of the revolutionary spirit through Italy and Germany, might so have occupied the remnants of monarchy there, as that his country might have risen again.

## Farm Problem

### TO ————.¹

PHILADELPHIA, *March 23, 1798.*

DEAR SIR,—I have to acknowledge the receipt of your favors of August 16th and 18th, together with the box of seed accompanying the former, which has just come to hand. The letter of the 4th of June, which you mention to have committed to Mr. King, has never been received. It has most likely been intercepted on the sea, now become a field of lawless and indiscriminate rapine and violence. The first box which came through Mr. Donald, arrived safely the last year, but being a little too late for that season, its contents have been divided between Mr. Randolph and myself, and will be committed to the earth now immediately. The peas and the vetch are most acceptable indeed. Since you were here, I have tried that species of your field pea which is cultivated in New York, and begin to fear that that

¹Address lost.

plant will scarcely bear our sun and soil. A late acquisition too of a species of our country pea, called the cow pea, has pretty well supplied the place in my husbandry which I had destined for the European field pea. It is very productive, excellent food for man and beast, awaits without loss our leisure for gathering, and shades the ground very closely through the hottest months of the year. This with the loosening of the soil, I take to be the chief means by which the pea improves the soil. . . . My experience leaves me no fear as to the success of clover. I have never seen finer than in some of my fields which have never been manured. My rotation is triennial; to wit, one year of wheat and two of clover in the stronger fields, or two of peas in the weaker, with a crop of Indian corn and potatoes between every other rotation, that is to say once in seven years. Under this easy course of culture, aided with some manure, I hope my fields will recover their pristine fertility, which had in some of them been completely exhausted by perpetual crops of Indian corn and wheat alternately. The atmosphere is certainly the great workshop of nature for elaborating the fertilizing principles and insinuating them into the soil. It has been relied on as the sole means of regenerating our soil by most of the land-holders in the canton I inhabit, and where rest has been resorted to before a total exhaustion, the soil has never failed to recover. If, indeed, it be so run down as to be incapable of throwing weeds or herbage of any kind, to shade the soil from the sun, it either goes off in gullies, and is entirely lost, or remains exhausted till a growth springs up of such trees as will rise in the poorest soils. Under the shade of these and the cover soon formed of their deciduous leaves, and a commencing herbage, such fields sometimes recover in a long course of years; but this is too long to be taken into a course of husbandry. Not so, however, is the term within which the atmosphere alone will reintegrate a soil rested in due season. A year of wheat will be balanced by one, two, or three years of rest and atmospheric influence, according to the quality of the soil. It has been said that no rotation of crops will keep the earth in the same degree of fertility without the aid of manure. But it is well known here that a space of rest greater or less in spontaneous herbage, will restore the exhaustion of a single crop. This then is a rotation; and as it is not to be believed that spontaneous herbage is the only or best covering during rest, so may we expect that a substitute for it may be found which will yield profitable crops. Such perhaps are clover, peas, vetches, etc.

# House on Fire

## TO JAMES LEWIS, JUNIOR.

PHILADELPHIA, *May 9, 1798.*

It is our duty still to endeavor to avoid war; but if it shall actually take place, no matter by whom brought on, we must defend ourselves. If our house be on fire, without inquiring whether it was fired from within or without, we must try to extinguish it. In that, I have no doubt, we shall act as one man. But if we can ward off actual war till the crisis of England is over, I shall hope we may escape it altogether.

## On Secession

### TO JOHN TAYLOR.

PHILADELPHIA, *June 1, 1798.*

Mr. New showed me your letter on the subject of the patent, which gave me an opportunity of observing what you said as to the effect, with you, of public proceedings, and that it was not unwise now to estimate the separate mass of Virginia and North Carolina, with a view to their separate existence. It is true that we are completely under the saddle of Massachusetts and Connecticut, and that they ride us very hard, cruelly insulting our feelings, as well as exhausting our strength and subsistence. Their natural friends, the three other Eastern States join them from a sort of family pride, and they have the art to divide certain other parts of the Union, so as to make use of them to govern the whole. This is not new, it is the old practice of despots; to use a part of the people to keep the rest in order. And those who have once got an ascendancy, and possessed themselves of all the resources of the nation, their revenues and offices, have immense means for retaining their advantage. But our present situation is not a natural one. The republicans, through every part of the Union, say, that it was the irresistible influence and popularity of General Washington played off by the cunning of Hamilton, which turned the government over to anti-republican hands, or turned the republicans chosen by the people into anti-republicans. He delivered it over to his successor in this state, and very untoward events since, improved with great artifice, have produced on the public mind the impressions we see. But still I repeat it, this is not the natural state. Time alone would bring round an order of things more correspondent to the sentiments of our constituents. But are there no events impending, which will do it within a few months? The crisis with England, the public and authentic avowal of sentiments hostile to the leading principles of our Constitution, the prospect of a war, in which we shall stand alone, land tax, stamp tax, increase of public debt, etc. Be this as it may, in every free and deliberating society, there must, from the nature of man, be opposite parties, and violent dissensions and discords; and one of these, for the most part, must prevail over the other for a longer or shorter time. Perhaps this party division is necessary to induce each to watch and delate to the people the proceedings of the other. But if on a temporary superiority of the one party, the other is to resort to a scission of the Union, no federal government can ever exist. If to rid ourselves of the present rule of Massachusetts and Connecticut, we break the Union, will the evil stop there? Suppose the New England States alone cut off, will our nature be changed? Are we not men still to the south of that, and with all the passions of men? Immediately, we shall see a Pennsylvania and a Virginia party arise in the residuary confederacy, and the public mind will be distracted with the same party spirit. What a game too will the one party have in their hands, by eternally threatening the other that unless they do so and so, they will join their northern neighbors. If we reduce our Union to Virginia and North Carolina, immediately the conflict will be established between the representatives of these two States, and they will end by breaking into their simple units. Seeing, therefore, that an association of men who will not quarrel with one another is a thing which never yet existed, from the greatest confederacy of nations down to a town meeting or a vestry; seeing that we must have somebody to quarrel with, I had rather keep our New England associates for that purpose, than to see our bickerings transferred to others. . . . If the game runs sometimes against us at home, we must have patience till luck turns, and then we shall have an opportunity of winning back the *principles* we have lost. For this is a game where principles are the stake.

## To "Thomas Kanberg"

### TO GENERAL THADDEUS KOSCIUSKO.

PHILADELPHIA, *June 1, 1798.*

DEAR SIR,—Mr. Volney's departure for France gives me an opportunity of writing to you. I was happy in observing, for many days after your departure, that our winds were favorable for you. I hope, therefore, you quickly passed the cruising grounds on our coast, and have safely arrived at the term of your journey. Your departure is not yet known, or even suspected.[1] Niemsevioz was much affected. He is now at the federal city. He desired me to have some things taken care of for you. There were some kitchen furniture, backgammon table and chess men, and a pelise of fine fur. The latter I have taken to my own apartment and had packed in hops, and sewed up; the former are put into a warehouse of Mr. Barnes; all subject to your future orders. . . .

The times do not permit an indulgence in political disquisitions. But they forbid not the effusion of friendship, and not my warmest toward you, which no time will alter. Your principles and dispositions were made to be honored, revered and loved. True to a single object, the freedom and happiness of man, they have not veered about with the changelings and apostates

'On March 27, Mr. Jefferson had obtained passports for General Kosciusko under an assumed name. The application read:
"Thomas Jefferson . . . asks the favor of the passport for his friend Thomas Kanberg. . . . He is a native of the north of Europe, (perhaps of Germany,) has been known to Thomas Jefferson these twenty years in America, is of a most excellent character."

of our acquaintance. May health and happiness ever attend you. Accept sincere assurances of my affectionate esteem and respect. Adieu.

## Fear of the Jacobins

TO JAMES MADISON.

PHILADELPHIA, *June 21, 1798.*

Doctor Logan, about a fortnight ago, sailed for Hamburg. Though for a twelvemonth past he had been intending to go to Europe as soon as he could get money enough to carry him there, yet when he had accomplished this, and fixed a time for going, he very unwisely made a mystery of it: so that his disappearance without notice excited conversation. This was seized by the war hawks, and given out as a secret mission from the Jacobins here to solicit an army from France, instruct them as to their landing, etc. This extravagance produced a real panic among the citizens; and happening just when Bache published Talleyrand's letter, Harper, on the 18th, gravely announced to the House of Representatives, that there existed a traitorous correspondence between the Jacobins here and the French Directory; that he had got hold of some threads and clues of it, and would soon be able to develop the whole. This increased the alarm; their libelists immediately set to work, directly and indirectly to implicate whom they pleased. Porcupine gave me a principal share in it, as I am told, for I never read his papers. This state of things added to my reasons for not departing at the time I intended. These follies seem to have died away in some degree already. Perhaps I may renew my purpose by the 25th. Their system is, professedly, to keep up an alarm. Tracy, at the meeting of the joint committee for adjournment, declared it necessary for Congress to stay together to keep up the inflammation of the public mind.

## Wild Horses

TO PHILIP NOLAN.

PHILADELPHIA, *June 24, 1798.*

SIR,—It is sometime since I have understood that there are large herds of horses in a wild state, in the country west of the Mississippi, and have been desirous of obtaining details of their history in that State. Mr. Brown, Senator from Kentucky, informs me it would be in your power to give interesting information on this subject, and encourages me to ask it. The circumstances of the old world have, beyond the records of history, been such as admitted not that animal to exist in a state of nature. The condition of America is rapidly advancing to the same. The present then is probably the only moment in the age of the world, and the herds above mentioned the only subjects, of which we can avail ourselves to obtain what has never yet been recorded, and never can be again in all probability. I will add that your information is the sole reliance, as far as I can at present see, for obtaining this desideratum. You will render to natural history a very acceptable service, therefore, if you will enable our Philosophical Society to add so interesting a chapter to the history of this animal.

## Exaggeration

### TO SAMUEL SMITH.

MONTICELLO, *August 22, 1798.*

DEAR SIR,—Your favor of August the 4th came to hand by our last post, together with the "extract of a letter from a gentleman of Philadelphia, dated July the 10th," cut from a newspaper stating some facts which respect me. I shall notice these facts. The writer says that "the day after the last despatches were communicated to Congress, Bache, Leib, etc., and a Dr. Reynolds, were *closeted* with me." If the receipt of visits in my public room, the door continuing free to every one who should call at the same time, may be called *closeting*, then it is true that I was *closeted* with every person who visited me; in no other sense is it true as to any person. I sometimes received visits from Mr. Bache and Dr. Leib. I received them always with pleasure, because they are men of abilities, and of principles the most friendly to liberty and our present form of government. Mr. Bache has another claim on my respect, as being the grandson of Dr. Franklin, the greatest man and ornament of the age and country in which he lived. Whether I was visited by Mr. Bache or Dr. Leib the day after the communication referred to, I do not remember. I know that all my motions in Philadelphia, here, and everywhere, are watched and recorded. Some of these spies, therefore, may remember better than I do, the dates of these visits.

## Confidential

### TO ELBRIDGE GERRY.

PHILADELPHIA, *January 26, 1799.*

I do then, with sincere zeal, wish an inviolable preservation of our present federal Constitution, according to the true sense in which it was adopted by the States, that in which it was advocated by its friends, and not that which its enemies apprehended, who therefore became its enemies. . . . I am for freedom of religion, and against all manœuvres to bring about a legal ascendancy of one sect over another: for freedom of the press, and against all violations of the Constitution to silence by force and not by reason the complaints or criticisms, just or unjust, of our citizens against the conduct of their agents. And I am for encouraging the progress of science in all its branches; and not for raising a hue and cry against the sacred name of philosophy; for awing the human mind by stories of raw-head and bloody bones to a distrust of its own vision, and to repose implicitly on that of others; to go backwards instead of forwards to look for improvement; to believe that government, religion, morality, and every other science were in the highest perfection in ages of the darkest ignorance, and that nothing can ever be devised more perfect than what was established by our forefathers. To these I will add, that I was a sincere well-wisher to the success of the French revolution, and still wish it may end in the establishment of a free and well-ordered republic; but I have not been insensible under the atrocious depredations they have committed on our commerce. The first object of my heart is my own country. In that is embarked my family, my fortune, and my own existence. I have not one farthing of interest, nor one fibre of attachment out of it, nor a single motive of preference of any one nation to another, but in proportion as they are more or less friendly to us. But though deeply feeling the injuries of France, I did not think war the surest means of redressing them. I did believe, that a mission sincerely disposed to preserve peace, would obtain for us a peaceable and honorable settlement and retribution; and I appeal to you to say, whether this might not have been obtained, if either of your colleagues had been of the same sentiment with yourself.

These, my friend, are my principles; they are unquestionably the principles of the great body of our fellow-citizens, and I know there is not one of them which is not yours also. . . . And did we ever expect to see the day, when, breathing nothing but sentiments of love to our country and its freedom and happiness, our correspondence must be as secret as if we were hatching its destruction! Adieu, my friend, and accept my sincere and affectionate salutations. I need not add my signature.

## Revolt in Haiti

TO JAMES MADISON.

PHILADELPHIA, *February 5, 1799.*

The bill for continuing the suspension of intercourse with France and her dependencies, is still before the Senate, but will pass by a very great vote. An attack is made on what is called the Toussaint's clause, the object of which, as is charged by the one party and *admitted* by the other, is to facilitate the separation of the island from France. The clause will pass, however, by about nineteen to eight, or perhaps eighteen to nine. Rigaud, at the head of the people of color, maintains his allegiance. But they are only twenty-five thousand souls, against five hundred thousand, the number of the blacks. The treaty made with them by Maitland is (if they are to be separated from France) the best thing for us. They must get their provisions from us. It will indeed be in English bottoms, so that we shall lose the carriage. But the

English will probably forbid them the ocean, confine them to their island, and thus prevent their becoming an American Algiers. It must be admitted too, that they may play them off on us when they please. Against this there is no remedy but timely measures on our part, to clear ourselves, by degrees, of the matter on which that lever can work.

# The Public Mind

## TO ARCHIBALD STUART.

PHILADELPHIA, *February 13, 1799.*

DEAR SIR,—I avoid writing to my friends because the fidelity of the post office is very much doubted. I will give you briefly a statement of what we have done and are doing . . . The President has appointed Rufus King to make a commercial treaty with the Russians in London, and William Smith, of South Carolina, to go to Constantinople to make one with the Turks. Both appointments are confirmed by the Senate. A little dissatisfaction was expressed by some that we should never have treated with them till the moment when they had formed a coalition with the English against the French. You have seen that the Directory had published an arret declaring they would treat as pirates any neutrals they should take in the ships of their enemies. The President communicated this to Congress as soon as he received it. A bill was brought into Senate reciting that arret, and authorizing retaliation. The President received information almost in the same instant that the Directory had suspended the arret (which fact was privately declared by the Secretary of State to two of the Senate), and, though it was known we were passing an act founded on that arret, yet the President has never communicated the suspension. However, the Senate, informed indirectly of the fact, still passed the act yesterday, an hour after we had heard of the return of our vessel and crew before mentioned. It is acknowledged on all hands, and declared by the insurance companies that the British depredations during the last six months have greatly exceeded the French, yet not a word is said about it officially. However, all these things are working on the public mind. They are getting back to the point where they were when the X. Y. Z. story was passed off on them. A wonderful and rapid change is taking place in Pennsylvania, Jersey, and New York. Congress is daily plied with petitions against the alien and sedition laws and standing armies. Several parts of this State are so violent that we fear an insurrection. This will be brought about by some if they can. It is the only thing we have to fear. The appearance of an attack of force against the government would check the present current of the middle States, and rally them around the government; whereas, if suffered to go on, it will pass on to a reformation of abuses. The materials now bearing on the public mind will infallibly restore it to its republican soundness in the course of the present summer, if the knowledge of facts can only be disseminated among the people. Under separate cover you will receive some pamphlets written by George Nichols on the acts of the last session. These I would wish you to distribute, not to sound men who have no occasion for them, but to such as have been misled, are candid and will be open to the conviction of truth, and are of influence among their neighbors. It is the sick who need medicine, and not the well. Do not let my name appear in the matter. Perhaps I shall forward you some other things to be distributed in the same way.

## War vs. Freedom

### TO GENERAL THADDEUS KOSCIUSKO.

PHILADELPHIA, *February 21, 1799.*

DEAR FRIEND,—On politics I must write sparingly, lest it should fall into the hands of persons who do not love either you or me. . . . If we are forced into war, we must give up political differences of opinion, and unite as one man to defend our country. But whether at the close of such a war, we should be as free as we are now, God knows. In fine, if war takes place, republicanism has everything to fear; if peace, be assured that your forebodings and my alarms will prove vain; and that the spirit of our citizens now rising as rapidly as it was then running crazy, and rising with a strength and majesty which show the loveliness of freedom, will make this government in practice, what it is in principle, a model for the protection of man in a state of *freedom* and *order.* May heaven have in store for your country a restoration of these blessings, and you be destined as the instrument it will use for that purpose. But if this be forbidden by Fate, I hope we shall be able to preserve here an asylum where your love of liberty and disinterested patriotism will be forever protected and honored.

## Home Problems

### TO CHANCELLOR ROBERT R. LIVINGSTON.

PHILADELPHIA, *February 28, 1799.*

DEAR SIR,—I have received with great pleasure your favor on the subject of the steam engine. Though deterred by the complexity of that hitherto known, from making myself minutely acquainted with it, yet I am sufficiently acquainted with it to be sensible of the superior simplicity of yours, and its superior economy.

There is one object to which I have often wished a steam engine could be adapted. You know how desirable it is both in town and country to be able to have large reservoirs of water on the top of our houses, not only for use (by pipes) in the apartments, but as a resource against fire. This last is most especially a desideratum in the country. We might indeed have water carried from time to time in buckets to cisterns on the top of the house, but this is troublesome, and therefore we never do it,—consequently are without resource when a fire happens. Could any agent be employed which would be little or no additional expense or trouble except the first purchase, it would be done. Every family has such an agent, its kitchen fire. It is small indeed, but if its small but constant action could be accumulated so as to give a stroke from time to time which might throw ever so small a quantity of water from the bottom of a well to the top of the house (say one hundred feet), it would furnish more than would waste by evaporation, or be used by the family. I know nobody who must better know the value of such a machine than yourself, nor more equal to the invention of it, and especially with your familiarity with the subject. I have imagined that the iron back of the chimney might be a cistern for holding the water, which should supply steam and would be constantly kept in a boiling state by the ordinary fire. I wish the subject may appear as interesting to you as it does to me, it would then engage your attention, and we might hope this desideratum would be supplied.

A want of confidence in the post office deters me from writing to my friends on subjects of politics. Indeed I am tired of writing Jeremiades on that subject. What person, who remembers the times and tempers we have seen, would have believed that within so short a period, not only the jealous spirit of liberty which shaped every operation of our revolution, but even the common principles of English whigism would be scouted, and the tory principle of passive obedience under the new-fangled names of *confidence* and *responsibility*, become entirely triumphant? That the tories, whom in mercy we did not crumble to dust and ashes, could so have entwined us in their scorpion tails, that we cannot now move hand or foot. But the spell is dissolving. The public mind is recovering from the delirium into which it had been thrown, and we may still believe with security that the great body of the American people must for ages yet be substantially republican.

## Confusion Ended

### TO THOMAS LOMAX.

MONTICELLO, *March 12, 1799.*

You ask for any communication I may be able to make, which may administer comfort to you. I can give that which is solid. The spirit of 1776 is not dead. It has only been slumbering. The body of the American people is substantially republican. But their virtuous feelings have been played on by some fact with more fiction; they have been the dupes of artful manœuvres, and made for a moment to be willing instruments in forging chains for themselves. But time and truth have dissipated the delusion, and opened their eyes. They see now that France has sincerely wished peace, and their seducers have wished war, as well for the loaves and fishes which arise out of war expenses, as for the chance of changing the Constitution, while the people should have time to contemplate nothing but the levies of men and money.

The Anglomen and monocrats had so artfully confounded the cause of France with that of Freedom, that both went down in the same scale. I sincerely join you in abjuring all political connection with every foreign power; and though I cordially wish well to the progress of liberty in all nations, and would forever give it the weight of our countenance, yet they are not to be touched without contamination from their other bad principles. Commerce with all nations, alliance with none, should be our motto.

## College in Virginia

### TO DR. JOSEPH PRIESTLEY.

PHILADELPHIA, *January 18, 1800.*

We wish to establish in the upper country, and more centrally for the State, an University on a plan so broad and liberal and *modern,* as to be worth patronizing with the public support, and be a temptation to the youth of other States to come and drink of the cup of knowledge and fraternize with us. The first step is to obtain a good plan; that is, a judicious selection of the sciences, and a practicable grouping of some of them together, and ramifying of others, so as to adopt the professorships to our uses and our means. In an institution meant chiefly for use, some branches of science, formerly esteemed, may be now omitted; so may others now valued in Europe, but useless to us for ages to come. As an example of the former, the Oriental learning, and of the latter, almost the whole of the institution proposed to Congress by the Secretary of War's report of the 5th instant. . . . I will venture even to sketch the sciences which seem useful and practicable for us, as they occur to me while holding my pen. Botany, chemistry, zoology, anatomy, surgery, medicine, natural philosophy, agriculture, mathematics, astronomy, geography, politics, commerce, history, ethics, law, arts, fine arts. This list is imperfect because I make it hastily, and because I am unequal to the subject. It is evident that some of these articles are too much for one professor and must therefore be ramified; others may be ascribed in groups to a single professor. This is the difficult part of the work, and requires a head perfectly knowing the extent of each branch, and the limits within which it may be circumscribed, so as to bring the whole within the powers of the fewest professors possible, and consequently within the degree of expense practicable for us. We should propose that the professors follow no other calling, so that their whole time may be given to their academical functions; and we should propose to draw from Europe the first characters in science, by considerable temptations, which would not need to be repeated after the first set should have prepared fit successors and given reputation to the institution. From some splendid characters I have received offers most perfectly reasonable and practicable.

I do not propose to give you all this trouble merely of my own head, that would be arrogance. It has been the subject of consultation among the ablest and highest characters of our State, who only wait for a plan to make a joint and I hope a successful effort to get the thing carried into effect.

## School Plans

### TO DR. JOSEPH PRIESTLEY.

PHILADELPHIA, *January 27, 1800.*

DEAR SIR,—In my last letter of the 18th, I omitted to say any thing of the languages as part of our proposed University. It was not that I think, as some do, that they are useless. I am of a very different opinion. I do not think them very essential to the obtaining eminent degrees of science; but I think them very useful towards it. I suppose there is a portion of life during which our faculties are ripe enough for this, and for nothing more useful. I think the Greeks and Romans have left us the present models which exist of fine composition, whether we examine them as works of reason, or of style and fancy; and to them we probably owe these characteristics of modern composition. I know of no composition of any other ancient people, which merits the least regard as a model for its matter or style. To all this I add, that to read the Latin and Greek authors in their original, is a sublime luxury; and I deem luxury in science to be at least as justifiable as in architecture, painting, gardening, or the other arts. I enjoy Homer in his own language infinitely beyond Pope's translation of him, and both beyond the dull narrative of the same events by Dares Phrygius; and it is an innocent enjoyment. I thank on my knees, Him who directed my early education, for having put into my possession this rich source of delight; and I would not exchange it for anything which I could then have acquired, and have not since acquired. With this regard for those languages, you will acquit me of meaning to omit them.

About twenty years ago, I drew a bill for our legislature, which proposed to lay off every county into hundreds or townships of five or six miles square, in the centre of each of them was to be a free English school; the whole State was further laid off into ten districts, in each of which was to be a college for teaching the languages, geography, surveying, and other useful things of that grade; and then a single University for the sciences. It was received with enthusiasm; but as I had proposed that William and Mary, under an improved form, should be the University, and that was at that time pretty highly Episcopal, the dissenters after awhile began to apprehend some secret design of a preference to that sect. About three years ago they enacted that part of my bill which related to English schools, except that instead of obliging, they left it optional in the court of every county to carry it into execution or not. I think it probable the part of the plan for the middle grade of education, may also be brought forward in due time. In the meanwhile, we are not without a sufficient number of good country schools, where the languages, geography, and the first elements of mathematics, are taught. Having omitted this information in my former letter, I thought it necessary now to supply it, that you might know on what base your superstructure was to be reared. . . . The Gothic idea that we are to look backwards instead of forwards for the improvement of the human mind, and to recur to the annals of our ancestors for what is most perfect in government, in religion and in learning, is worthy of those bigots in religion and government, by whom it has been recommended, and whose purposes it would answer. But it is not an idea which this country will endure; and the moment of their showing it is fast ripening; and the signs of it will be their respect for you, and growing detestation of those who have dishonored our country by endeavors to disturb our tranquillity in it. No one has felt this with more sensibility than, my dear Sir, your respectful and affectionate friend and servant.

## On Napoleon

### TO T. M. RANDOLPH.

PHILADELPHIA, *February 2, 1800.*

Should it be really true that Bonaparte has usurped the government with an intention of making it a free one, whatever his talents may be for war, we have no proof that he is skilled in forming governments friendly to the people. Wherever he has meddled we have seen nothing but fragments of the old Roman government stuck into materials with which they can form no cohesion: we see the bigotry of an Italian to the ancient splendor of his country, but nothing which bespeaks a luminous view of the organization of rational government.

## Indian Languages

### TO COLONEL BENJAMIN HAWKINS.

PHILADELPHIA, *March 14, 1800.*

I particularly take great interest in whatever respects the Indians, and the present state of the Creeks, mentioned in your letter is very interesting. But you must not suppose that your official communications will ever be seen or known out of the offices. Reserve as to all their proceedings is the fundamental maxim of the Executive department. I must, therefore, ask from you one communication to be made to me separately, and I am encouraged to it by that part of your letter which promises me something on the Creek language. I have long believed we can never get any information of the ancient history of the Indians, of their descent and filiation, but from a knowledge and comparative view of their languages. I have, therefore, never failed to avail myself of any opportunity which offered of getting their vocabularies. I have now made up a large collection, and afraid to risk it any longer, lest by some accident it might be lost, I am about to print it. But I still want the great southern languages, Cherokee, Creeks, Choctaw, Chickasaw. For the Cherokee, I have written to another, but for the three others, I have no chance but through yourself. I have indeed an imperfect vocabulary of the Choctaw, but it wants all the words marked in the enclosed vocabulary with either this mark (*) or this (†). I therefore throw myself on you to procure me the Creek, Choctaw, and Chickasaw; and I enclose you a vocabulary of the particular words I want. You need not take the trouble of having any others taken, because all my other vocabularies are confined to these words, and my object is only a comparative view.

## Property and Votes

### TO JEREMIAH MOOR.

MONTICELLO, *August 14, 1800.*

. . . Notes on Virginia . . . shows what I think on the question of the right of electing and being elected . . . on a year's residence in the country; or the possession of property in it, or a year's enrollment in its militia. When the constitution of Virginia was framed I was in attendance at Congress. Had I been here I should probably have proposed a general suffrage: because my opinion has always been in favor of it. Still I find very honest men who, thinking the possession of some property necessary to give independence of mind, are for restraining the elective franchise to property. I believe we may lessen the danger of buying and selling votes, by making the number of voters too great for any means of purchase: I may further say that I have not observed men's honesty to increase with their riches.

## Freedom of Religion

### TO DR. BENJAMIN RUSH.

MONTICELLO, *September 23, 1800.*

I promised you a letter on Christianity, which I have not forgotten. On the contrary, it is because I have reflected on it, that I find much more time necessary for it than I can at present dispose of. I have a view of the subject which ought to displease neither the rational Christian nor Deists, and would reconcile many to a character they have too hastily rejected. I do not know that it would reconcile the *genus irritabile vatum* who are all in arms against me. Their hostility is on too interesting ground to be softened. The delusion into which the X. Y. Z. plot showed it possible to push the people; the successful experiment made under the prevalence of that delusion on the clause of the Constitution, which, while it secured the freedom of the press, covered also the freedom of religion, had given to the clergy a very favorite hope of obtaining an establishment of a particular form of Christianity through the United States; and as every sect believes its own form the true one, every one perhaps hoped for his own, but especially the Episcopalians and Congregationalists. The returning good sense of our country threatens abortion to their hopes, and they believe that any portion of power confided to me, will be exerted in opposition to their schemes. And they believe rightly: for I have sworn upon the altar of God, eternal hostility against every form of tyranny over the mind of man. But this is all they have to fear from me: and enough too in their opinion.

## Mammoth Bones

### TO ROBERT R. LIVINGSTON.

WASHINGTON, *December 14, 1800.*

DEAR SIR,—Your former communications on the subject of the steam engine, I took the liberty of laying before the American Philosophical Society, by whom they will be printed in their volume of the present year. I have heard of the discovery of some large bones, supposed to be of the mammoth, at about thirty or forty miles distance from you; and among the bones found, are said to be some of which we have never been able to procure. The first interesting question is, whether they are the bones of the mammoth? The second, what are the particular bones, and could I possibly procure them? The bones I am most anxious to obtain, are those of the head and feet, which are said to be among those found in your State, as also the ossa innominata, and the scapula. Others would also be interesting, though similar ones may be possessed, because they would show by their similarity that the set belong to the mammoth. Could I so far venture to trouble you on this subject, as to engage some of your friends near the place, to procure for me the bones above mentioned? If they are to be bought I will gladly pay for them whatever you shall agree to as reasonable.

## American Bird

### TO DR. HUGH WILLIAMSON.

WASHINGTON, *January 10, 1801.*

I suppose the opinion to be universal that the turkey is a native of America. Nobody, as far as I know, has ever contradicted it but Daines Barrington; and the arguments he produces are such as none but a head, entangled and kinked as his is, would ever have urged. Before the discovery of America, no such bird is mentioned in a single author, all those quoted by Barrington, by description referring to the crane, hen, pheasant or peacock; but the book of every traveller, who came to America soon after its discovery, is full of accounts of the turkey and its abundance; and immediately after that discovery we find the turkey served up at the feasts of Europe, as their most extraordinary rarity. Mr. William Strickland, the eldest son of St. George Strickland, of York, in England, told me the anecdote. Some ancestor of his commanded a vessel in the navigations of Cabot. Having occasion to consult the Herald's office concerning his family, he found a petition from that ancestor to the crown, stating that Cabot's circumstances being slender, he had been rewarded by the bounties he needed from the crown; that as to himself, he asked nothing in that way, but that as a consideration for his services in the same way, he might be permitted to assume for the crest of his family arms, the turkey, an American bird; and Mr. Strickland observed that their crest is actually a turkey.

## On Climate

### TO WILLIAM DUNBAR, ESQ.

WASHINGTON, *January 12, 1801.*

The papers addressed to me, I took the liberty of communicating to the Philosophical Society. That on the language by signs is quite new. Soon after receiving your meteorological diary, I received one of Quebec; and was struck with the comparison between—32 and 19¾ the lowest depression of the thermometer at Quebec and the Natchez. I have often wondered that any human being should live in a cold country who can find room in a warm one. I have no doubt but that cold is the source of more sufferance to all animal nature than hunger, thirst, sickness, and all the other pains of life and of death itself put together. I live in a temperate climate, and under circumstances which do not expose me often to cold. Yet when I recollect on one hand all the sufferings I have had from cold, and on the other all my other pains, the former preponderate greatly. What then must be the sum of that evil if we take in the vast proportion of men who are obliged to be out in all weather, by land and by sea, all the families of beasts, birds, reptiles, and even the vegetable kingdom! for that too has life, and where there is life there may be sensation.

I remark a rainbow of a great portion of the circle observed by you when on the line of demarcation. I live in a situation which has given me an opportunity of seeing more than the semicircle often. I am on a hill five hundred feet perpendicularly high. On the west side it breaks down abruptly to the base, where a river passes through. A rainbow, therefore, about sunset, plunges one of its legs down to the river, five hundred feet below the level of the eye on the top of the hill. I have twice seen bows formed by the moon. They were of the color of the common circle round the moon, and were very near, being within a few paces of me in both instances.

I thank you for the little vocabularies of Bedais, Tankawis and Teghas. I have it much at heart to make as extensive a collection as possible of the Indian tongues.

## On Forgery

### TO COLONEL AARON BURR.

WASHINGTON, *February 1, 1801.*

DEAR SIR,—It was to be expected that the enemy would endeavor to sow tares between us, that they might divide us and our friends. Every consideration satisfies me you will be on your guard against this, as I assure you I am strongly. I hear of one stratagem so imposing and so base that it is proper I should notice it to you. Mr. Munford, who is here, says he saw at New York before he left it, an original letter of mine to Judge Breckenridge, in which are sentiments highly injurious to you. He knows my handwriting, and did not doubt that to be genuine. I enclose you a copy taken from the press copy of the only letter I ever wrote to Judge Breckenridge in my life: the press copy itself has been shown to several of our mutual friends here. Of consequence, the letter seen by Mr. Munford must be a forgery, and if it contains a sentiment unfriendly or disrespectful to you, I affirm it solemnly to be a forgery; as also if it varies from the copy enclosed. With the common trash of slander I should not think of troubling you; but the forgery of one's handwriting is too imposing to be neglected. A mutual knowledge of each other furnishes us with the best test of the contrivances which will be practised by the enemies of both.

Accept assurances of my high respect and esteem.

## Inauguration

### TO THE HONORABLE JOHN MARSHALL.

WASHINGTON, *March 2, 1801.*

I propose to take the oath or oaths of office as President of the United States, on Wednesday the 4th inst., at twelve o'clock, in the Senate chamber. May I hope the favor of your attendance to administer the oath?

## Good Hope

### TO JOHN DICKINSON.

WASHINGTON, *March 6, 1801.*

A just and solid republican government maintained here, will be a standing monument and example for the aim and imitation of the people of other countries; and I join with you in the hope and belief that they will see, from our example, that a free government is of all others the most energetic; that the inquiry which has been excited among the mass of mankind by our revolution and its consequences, will ameliorate the condition of man over a great portion of the globe. What a satisfaction have we in the contemplation of the benevolent effects of our efforts, compared with those of the leaders on the other side, who have discountenanced all advances in science as dangerous innovations, have endeavored to render philosophy and republicanism terms of reproach, to persuade us that man cannot be governed but by the rod, etc. I shall have the happiness of living and dying in the contrary hope.

## Danger Averted

### TO GOVERNOR THOMAS M'KEAN.

WASHINGTON, *March 9, 1801.*

DEAR SIR,—I have to acknowledge the receipt of your favor of February the 20th, and to thank you for your congratulations on the event of the election. Had it terminated in the elevation of Mr. Burr, every republican would, I am sure, have acquiesced in a moment; because, however it might have been variant from the intentions of the voters, yet it would have been agreeable to the Constitution. No man would more cheerfully have submitted than myself, because I am sure the administration would have been republican, and the chair of the Senate permitting me to be at home eight months in the year, would, on that account, have been much more consonant to my real satisfaction. But in the event of an usurpation, I was decidedly with those who were determined not to permit it. Because that precedent once set, would be artificially reproduced, and end soon in a dictator. Virginia was bristling up I believe.

## Panic Ended

### TO JOEL BARLOW.

WASHINGTON, *March 14, 1801.*

You have understood that the revolutionary movements in Europe had, by industry and artifice, been wrought into objects of terror even to this country, and had really involved a great portion of our well-meaning citizens in a panic which was perfectly unaccountable, and during the prevalence of which they were led to support measures the most insane. They are now pretty thoroughly recovered from it, and sensible of the mischief which was done, and preparing to be done, had their minds continued a little longer under that derangement. The recovery bids fair to be complete, and to obliterate entirely the line of party division which had been so strongly drawn. Not that their late leaders have come over, or ever can come over. But they stand, at present, almost without followers. The principal of them have retreated into the judiciary as a stronghold, the tenure of which renders it difficult to dislodge them.

# Return of a Friend

### TO THOMAS PAINE.

WASHINGTON, *March 18, 1801.*

DEAR SIR,—Your letters of October the 1st, 4th, 6th, and 16th, came duly to hand, and the papers which they covered were, according to your permission, published in the newspapers and in a pamphlet, and under your own name. These papers contain precisely our principles, and I hope they will be generally recognized here. Determined as we are to avoid, if possible, wasting the energies of our people in war and destruction, we shall avoid implicating ourselves with the powers of Europe, even in support of principles which we mean to pursue. They have so many other interests different from ours, that we must avoid being entangled in them. We believe we can enforce those principles, as to ourselves, by peaceable means, now that we are likely to have our public councils detached from foreign views. The return of our citizens from the phrenzy into which they had been wrought, partly by ill conduct in France, partly by artifices practised on them, is almost entire, and will, I believe, become quite so. . . . I am in hopes you will find us returned generally to sentiments worthy of former times. In these it will be your glory to have steadily labored, and with as much effect as any man living.

# After the Storm

### TO DR. JOSEPH PRIESTLEY.

WASHINGTON, *March 21, 1801.*

What an effort, my dear Sir, of bigotry in politics and religion have we gone through! The barbarians really flattered themselves they should be able to bring back the times of Vandalism, when ignorance put everything into the hands of power and priestcraft. All advances in science were proscribed as innovations. They pretended to praise and encourage education, but it was to be education of our ancestors. We were to look backwards, not forwards, for improvements; the President himself declaring, in one of his answers to addresses, that we were never to expect to go beyond them in real science. This was the real ground of all the attacks on you. . . . It is with heartfelt satisfaction that, in the first moments of my public action, I can hail you with welcome in our land, tender to you the homage of its respect and esteem, cover you under the protection of those laws which were made for the wise and good like you, and disdain the legitimacy of that libel on legislation, which, under the form of a law, was for some time placed among them.[1]

As the storm is now subsiding, and the horizon becoming serene, it is pleasant to consider the phenomenon with attention. We can no longer say there is nothing new under the sun. For this whole chapter in the history of man is new. The great extent of our republic is new. Its sparse habitation is new. The mighty wave of public opinion which has rolled over it is new. But the most pleasing novelty is, its so quietly subsiding over such an extent of surface to its true level again. The order and good sense displayed in this recovery from delusion, and in the momentous crisis which lately arose, really bespeak a strength of character in our nation which augurs well for the duration of our republic; and I am much better satisfied now of its stability than I was before it was tried. I have been, above all things, solaced by the prospect which opened on us, in the event of a non-election of a President; in which case, the federal government would have been in the situation of a clock or watch run down. There was no idea of force, nor of any occasion for it. A convention, invited by the republican members of Congress, with the virtual President and Vice-President, would have been on the ground in eight weeks, would have repaired the Constitution where it was defective, and wound it up again.

## Safety in Size

### TO NATHANIEL NILES, ESQ.

WASHINGTON, *March 22, 1801.*

The late chapter of our history furnishes a lesson to man perfectly new. The times have been awful, but they have proved an useful truth, that the good citizen must never despair of the commonwealth. How many good men abandoned the deck, and gave up the vessel as lost! It furnishes a new proof of the falsehood of Montesquieu's doctrine, that a republic can be preserved only in a small territory. The reverse is the truth. Had our territory been even a third only of what it is, we were gone. But while frenzy and delusion like an epidemic, gained certain parts, the residue remained sound and untouched, and held on till their brethren could recover from the temporary delusion; and that circumstance has given me great comfort. There was general alarm during the pending of the election in Congress, lest no President should be chosen, the government be dissolved and anarchy

[1]In the margin is written by the author, "Alien law."

ensue. But the cool determination of the really patriotic to call a convention in that case, which might be on the ground in eight weeks, and wind up the machine again which had only run down, pointed out to my mind a perpetual and peaceable resource. . . .

## No Nepotism

### TO GEORGE JEFFERSON.

WASHINGTON, *March 27, 1801.*

The resolution you so properly approved had long been formed in my mind. The public will never be made to believe that an appointment of a relative is made on the ground of merit alone, uninfluenced by family views; nor can they ever see with approbation offices, the disposal of which they entrust to their Presidents for public purposes, divided out as family property. Mr. Adams degraded himself infinitely by his conduct on this subject, as General Washington had done himself the greatest honor. With two such examples to proceed by, I should be doubly inexcusable to err. It is true that this places the relations of the President in a worse situation than if he were a stranger, but the public good, which cannot be affected if its confidence be lost, requires this sacrifice.

## On Reforms

### TO DR. WALTER JONES.

WASHINGTON, *March 31, 1801.*

DEAR SIR,—I was already almost in the act of mounting my horse for a short excursion home, when your favor of the 14th was put into my hands. I stop barely to acknowledge it, and to thank you for your kind congratulations, and still more for your interesting observations on the course of things. I am sensible how far I should fall short of effecting all the reformation which reason would suggest, and experience approve, were I free to do whatever I thought best; but when we reflect how difficult it is to move or inflect the great machine of society, how impossible to advance the notions of a whole people suddenly to ideal right, we see the wisdom of Solon's remark, that no more good must be attempted than the nation can bear, and that all will be chiefly to reform the waste of public money, and thus drive away the vultures who prey upon it, and improve some little on old routines. Some new fences for securing constitutional rights may, with the aid of a good legislature, perhaps be attainable.

# Contraband

## TO ROBERT R. LIVINGSTON.

MONTICELLO, *September 9, 1801.*

We believe the practice of seizing what is called contraband of war, is an abusive practice, not founded in natural right. War between two nations cannot diminish the rights of the rest of the world remaining at peace. The doctrine that the rights of nations remaining quietly in the exercise of moral and social duties, are to give way to the convenience of those who prefer plundering and murdering one another, is a monstrous doctrine; and ought to yield to the more rational law, that "the wrong which two nations endeavor to inflict on each other, must not infringe on the rights or conveniences of those remaining at peace." And what is *contraband*, by the law of nature? Either everything which may aid or comfort an enemy, or nothing. Either all commerce which would accommodate him is unlawful, or none is. The difference between articles of one or another description, is a difference in degree only. No line between them can be drawn. Either all intercourse must cease between neutrals and belligerents, or all be permitted. Can the world hesitate to say which shall be the rule? Shall two nations turning tigers, break up in one instant the peaceable relations of the whole world? Reason and nature clearly pronounce that the neutral is to go on in the enjoyment of all its rights, that its commerce remains free, not subject to the jurisdiction of another, nor consequently its vessels to search, or to enquiries whether their contents are the property of an enemy, or are of those which have been called contraband of war.

Although I consider the observance of these principles as of great importance to the interests of peaceable nations, among whom I hope the United States will ever place themselves, yet in the present state of things they are not worth a war. Nor do I believe war the most certain means of enforcing them. Those peaceable coercions which are in the power of every nation, if undertaken in concert and in time of peace, are more likely to produce the desired effect.

# Simplified Finance

## TO THE SECRETARY OF THE TREASURY.
## (ALBERT GALLATIN.)

WASHINGTON, *April 1, 1802.*

DEAR SIR,—I have read and considered your report on the operations of the sinking fund, and entirely approve of it, as the best plan on which we can set out. I think it an object of great importance, to be kept in view and to be undertaken at a fit season, to simplify our system of finance, and bring it within the comprehension of every member of Congress. Hamilton set out on a different plan. In order that he might have the entire government of his machine, he determined so to complicate it as that neither the President nor Congress should be able to understand it, or to control him. He succeeded in doing this, not only beyond their reach, but so that he at length could not unravel it himself. He gave to the debt, in the first instance, in funding it, the most artificial and mysterious form he could devise. He then moulded up his appropriations of a number of scraps and remnants, many of which were nothing at all, and applied them to different objects in reversion and remainder, until the whole system was involved in impenetrable fog; and while he was giving himself the airs of providing for the payment of the debt, he left himself free to add to it continually, as he did in fact, instead of paying it. I like your idea of kneading all his little scraps and fragments into one batch, and adding to it a complementary sum, which, while it forms it into a single mass from which everything is to be paid, will enable us, should a breach of appropriation ever be charged on us, to prove that the sum appropriated, and more, has been applied to its specific object.

But there is a point beyond this on which I should wish to keep my eye, and to which I should aim to approach by every tack which previous arrangements force on us. That is, to form into one consolidated mass all the moneys received into the treasury, and to the several expenditures, giving them a preference of payment according to the order in which they should be arranged. As for example. 1. The interest of the public debt. 2. Such portions of principal as are exigible. 3. The expenses of government. 4. Such other portions of principal as, though not exigible, we are still free to pay when we please. The last object might be made to take up the residuum of money remaining in the treasury at the end of every year, after the three first objects were complied with, and would be the barometer whereby to test the economy of the administration. It would furnish a simple measure by which every one could mete their merit, and by which every one could decide when taxes were deficient or superabundant. If to this can be added a simplification of the form of accounts in the treasury department, and in the organization of its officers, so as to bring everything to a single centre, we might hope to see the finances of the Union as clear and intelligible as a merchant's books, so that every member of Congress, and every man of any mind in the Union, should be able to comprehend them to investigate abuses, and consequently to control them.

# Foreign Relations

TO THE UNITED STATES MINISTER TO FRANCE.
(ROBERT E. LIVINGSTON.)

WASHINGTON, *April 18, 1802.*

The cession of Louisiana and the Floridas by Spain to France, works most sorely on the United States. . . .

There is on the globe one single spot, the possessor of which is our natural and habitual enemy. It is New Orleans, through which the produce of three-eighths of our territory must pass to market, and from its fertility it will ere long yield more than half of our whole produce, and contain more than half of our inhabitants. . . . The day that France takes possession of New Orleans, fixes the sentence which is to restrain her forever within her low-water mark. It seals the union of two nations, who, in conjunction, can maintain exclusive possession of the ocean. From that moment, we must marry ourselves to the British fleet and nation. We must turn all our attention to a maritime force, for which our resources place us on very high ground; and having formed and connected together a power which may render reinforcement of her settlements here impossible to France, make the first cannon which shall be fired in Europe the signal for the tearing up any settlement she may have made, and for holding the two continents of America in sequestration for the common purposes of the United British and American nations.

This is not a state of things we seek or desire. It is one which this measure, if adopted by France, forces on us as necessarily, as any other cause, by the laws of nature, brings on its necessary effect. It is not from a fear of France that we deprecate this measure proposed by her. For however greater her force is than ours, compared in the abstract, it is nothing in comparison of ours, when to be exerted on our soil. But it is from a sincere love of peace, and a firm persuasion, that bound to France by the interests and the strong sympathies still existing in the minds of our citizens, and holding relative positions which insure their continuance, we are secure of a long course of peace. Whereas, the change of friends, which will be rendered necessary if France changes that position, embarks us necessarily as a belligerent power in the first war of Europe. In that case, France will have held possession of New Orleans during the interval of a peace, long or short, at the end of which it will be wrested from her. Will this short-lived possession have been an equivalent to her for the transfer of such a weight into the scale of her enemy? Will not the amalgamation of a young, thriving nation, continue to that enemy the health and force which are at present so evidently on the decline? And will a few years' possession of New Orleans add equally to the strength of France? She may say she needs Louisiana for the supply of her West Indies. She does not need it in time of peace, and in war she could not depend on them, because they would be so easily intercepted. I should suppose that all these considerations might, in some proper form, be brought into view of the government of France. Though stated by us, it ought not to give offence; because we do not bring them forward as a menace, but as consequences not controllable by us, but inevitable from the course of things. We mention them, not as things which we desire by any means, but as things we deprecate; and we beseech a friend to look forward and to prevent them for our common interest.

If France considers Louisiana, however, as indispensable for her views, she might perhaps be willing to look about for arrangements which might reconcile it to our interests. If anything could do this, it would be the ceding to us the island of New Orleans and the Floridas. This would certainly, in a great degree, remove the causes of jarring and irritation between us, and perhaps for such a length of time, as might produce other means of making the measure permanently conciliatory to our interests and friendships. It would, at any rate, relieve us from the necessity of taking immediate measures for countervailing such an operation by arrangements in another quarter. But still we should consider New Orleans and the Floridas as no equivalent for the risk of a quarrel with France, produced by her vicinage.

## Use of a Minority

### TO JOEL BARLOW.

WASHINGTON, *May 3, 1802.*

Our majority in the House of Representatives has been about two to one, in the Senate, eighteen to fifteen. After another election it will be of two to one in the Senate, and it would not be for the public good to have it greater. A respectable minority is useful as censors. The present one is not respectable, being the bitterest remains of the cup of federalism, rendered desperate and furious by despair. We shall now be so strong that we shall certainly split again; for freemen, thinking differently and speaking and acting as they think, will form into classes of sentiment. But it must be under another name. That of federalism is become so odious that no party can rise under it. As the division into whig and tory is founded in the nature of man; the weakly and nerveless, the rich and the corrupt, seeing more safety and accessibility in a strong executive; the healthy, firm, and virtuous, feeling a confidence in their physical and moral resources, and willing to part with only so much power as is necessary for their good government; and, therefore, to retain the rest in the hands of the many, the division will substantially be into whig and tory, as in England formerly.

## On Personal Responsibility

### TO DR. JOSEPH PRIESTLEY.

WASHINGTON, *June 19, 1802.*

In the great work which has been effected in America, no individual has a right to take any great share to himself. Our people in a body are wise, because they are under the unrestrained and unperverted operation of their own understanding. Those whom they have assigned to the direction of their affairs, have stood with a pretty even front. If any one of them was withdrawn, many others entirely equal, have been ready to fill his place with as good abilities. A nation, composed of such materials, and free in all its members from distressing wants, furnishes hopeful implements for the interesting experiment of self-government; and we feel that we are acting under obligations not confined to the limits of our own society. It is impossible not to be sensible that we are acting for all mankind; that circumstances denied to others, but indulged to us, have imposed on us the duty of proving what is the degree of freedom and self-government in which a society may venture to leave its individual members. One passage, in the paper you enclosed me, must be corrected. It is the following, "and all say it was yourself more than any other individual, that planned and established it," *i.e.*, the Constitution. I was in Europe when the Constitution was planned, and never saw it till after it was established. On receiving it I wrote strongly to Mr. Madison, urging the want of provision for the freedom of religion, freedom of the press, trial by jury, habeas corpus, the substitution of militia for a standing army, and an express reservation to the States of all rights not specifically granted to the Union. He accordingly moved in the first session of Congress for these amendments, which were agreed to and ratified by the States as they now stand. This is all the hand I had in what related to the Constitution. Our predecessors made it doubtful how far even these were of any value; for the very law which endangered your personal safety, as well as that which restrained the freedom of the press, were gross violations of them. However, it is still certain that though written constitutions may be violated in moments of passion or delusion, yet they furnish a text to which those who are watchful may again rally and recall the people; they fix too for the people the principles of their political creed.

## On Public Works

### TO ALBERT GALLATIN.

*October 13, 1802.*

Although the power to regulate commerce does not give a power to build piers, wharves, open ports, clear the beds of rivers, dig canals, build warehouses, build manufacturing machines, set up manufactories, cultivate the earth, to all of which the power would go if it went to the first, yet a power to provide and maintain a navy, is a power to provide receptacles for it, and places to cover and preserve it. In choosing the places where this money should be laid out, I should be much disposed, as far as contracts will permit, to confine it to such place or places as the ships of war may lie at, and be protected from ice; and I should be for stating this in a message to Congress, in order to prevent the effect of the present example. This act has been built on the exercise of the power of building light houses, as a regulation of commerce. But I well remember the opposition, on this very ground, to the first act for building a light house. The utility of the thing has sanctioned the infraction. But if on that infraction we build a second, on that second a third, etc., any one of the powers in the Constitution may be made to comprehend every power of government. Will you read the enclosed letters on the subject of New Orleans, and think what we can do or propose in the case?

## Hope for France

TO THOMAS COOPER, ESQ.

WASHINGTON, *November 29, 1802.*

It delights me to find that there are persons who still think that all is not lost in France: that their retrogradation from a limited to an unlimited despotism, is but to give themselves a new impulse. But I see not how or when. The press, the only tocsin of a nation, is completely silenced there, and all means of a general effort taken away. However, I am willing to hope, and as long as anybody will hope with me; and I am entirely persuaded that the agitations of the public mind advance its powers, and that at every vibration between the points of liberty and despotism, something will be gained for the former. As men become better informed, their rulers must respect them the more.

## River Traffic

TO MONSIEUR DUPONT DE NEMOURS.

WASHINGTON, *February 1, 1803.*

While we were preparing such modifications of the propositions of your letter of October the 4th as we could assent to, an event happened which obliged us to adopt measures of urgency. The suspension of the right of deposit at New Orleans, ceded to us by our treaty with Spain . . . showed the necessity of making effectual arrangements to secure the peace of the two countries against the indiscreet acts of subordinate agents. For the

occlusion of the Mississippi is a state of things in which we cannot exist . . .
Our circumstances are so imperious as to admit of no delay as to our course;
and the use of the Mississippi so indispensable, that we cannot hesitate one
moment to hazard our existence for its maintenance. If we fail in this effort
to put it beyond the reach of accident, we see the destinies we have to run,
and prepare at once for them. Not but that we shall still endeavor to go on
in peace and friendship with our neighbors as long as we can, *if our rights
of navigation and deposit are respected;* but as we foresee that the caprices
of the local officers, and the abuse of those rights by our boatmen and navi-
gators, which neither government can prevent, will keep up a state of irritation which cannot long be kept inactive, we should be criminally im-
provident not to take at once eventual measures for strengthening ourselves
for the contest. It may be said, if this object be so all-important to us, why
do we not offer such a sum so as to insure its purchase? The answer is simple.
We are an agricultural people, poor in money, and owing great debts. These
will be falling due by instalments for fifteen years to come, and require
from us the practice of a rigorous economy to accomplish their payment;
and it is our principle to pay to a moment whatever we have engaged, and
never to engage what we cannot, and mean not faithfully to pay. We have
calculated our resources, and find the sum to be moderate which they would
enable us to pay, and we know from late trials that little can be added to it
by borrowing. The country, too, which we wish to purchase, except the
portion already granted, and which must be confirmed to the private holders, is a barren sand, six hundred miles from east to west, and from thirty to
forty and fifty miles from north to south, formed by deposition of the sands
by the Gulf Stream in its circular course round the Mexican Gulf, and which
being spent after performing a semicircle, has made from its last depositions
the sand bank of East Florida. In West Florida, indeed, there are on the
borders of the rivers some rich bottoms, formed by the mud brought from
the upper country. These bottoms are all possessed by individuals. But the
spaces between river and river are mere banks of sand; and in East Florida
there are neither rivers, nor consequently any bottoms. We cannot then
make anything by a sale of the lands to individuals. So that it is peace alone
which makes it an object with us, and which ought to make the cession of
it desirable to France.

# On Public Judgment

## TO MR. PICTET.

WASHINGTON, *February 5, 1803.*

In the line of science we have little new here. Our citizens almost all follow
some industrious occupation, and, therefore, have little time to devote to
abstract science. In the arts, and especially in the mechanical arts, many
ingenious improvements are made in consequence of the patent-right giving

exclusive use of them for fourteen years. But the great mass of our people are agricultural; and the commercial cities, though, by the command of newspapers, they make a great deal of noise, have little effect in the direction of the government. They are as different in sentiment and character from the country people as any two distinct nations, and are clamorous against the order of things established by the agricultural interest. Under this order, our citizens generally are enjoying a very great degree of liberty and security in the most temperate manner. Every man being at his ease, feels an interest in the preservation of order, and comes forth to preserve it at the first call of the magistrate. We are endeavoring, too, to reduce the government to the practice of a rigorous economy, to avoid burdening the people, and arming the magistrate with a patronage of money, which might be used to corrupt and undermine the principles of our government. I state these general outlines to you, because I believe you take some interest in our fortune, and because our newspapers, for the most part, present only the caricatures of disaffected minds. Indeed, the abuses of the freedom of the press here have been carried to a length never before known or borne by any civilized nation. But it is so difficult to draw a clear line of separation between the abuse and the wholesome use of the press, that as yet we have found it better to trust the public judgment, rather than the magistrate, with the discrimination between truth and falsehood. And hitherto the public judgment has performed that office with wonderful correctness.

## Indian Future

### TO COLONEL BENJAMIN HAWKINS.

WASHINGTON, *February 18, 1803.*

I consider the business of hunting as already become insufficient to furnish clothing and subsistence to the Indians. The promotion of agriculture, therefore, and household manufacture, are essential in their preservation, and I am disposed to aid and encourage it liberally. In truth, the ultimate point of rest and happiness for them is to let our settlements and theirs meet and blend together, to intermix, and become one people. Incorporating themselves with us as citizens of the United States, this is what the natural progress of things will, of course, bring on, and it will be better to promote than to retard it. Surely it will be better for them to be identified with us, and preserved in the occupation of their lands, than be exposed to the many casualties which may endanger them while a separate people. I have little doubt but that your reflections must have led you to view the various ways in which their history may terminate, and to see that this is the one most for their happiness. And we have already had an application from a settlement of Indians to become citizens of the United States. It is possible, perhaps probable, that this idea may be so novel as that it might shock the Indians, were it even hinted to them. Of course, you will keep it for your own reflection; but, convinced of its soundness, I feel it consistent with pure morality to lead them towards it, to familiarize them to the idea . . .

# On Christian Morals

## TO EDWARD DOWSE, ESQ.

WASHINGTON, *April 19, 1803.*

DEAR SIR,—I now return the sermon you were so kind as to enclose me, having perused it with attention. . . . I must also add that though I concur with the author in considering the moral precepts of Jesus as more pure, correct, and sublime than those of the ancient philosophers, yet I do not concur with him in the mode of proving it. He thinks it necessary to libel and decry the doctrines of the philosophers; but a man must be blinded, indeed, by prejudice, who can deny them a great degree of merit. I give them their just due, and yet maintain that the morality of Jesus, as taught by himself, and freed from the corruptions of latter times, is far superior. Their philosophy went chiefly to the government of our passions, so far as respected ourselves, and the procuring our own tranquillity. In our duties to others they were short and deficient. They extended their cares scarcely beyond our kindred and friends individually, and our country in the abstract. Jesus embraced with charity and philanthropy our neighbors, our countrymen, and the whole family of mankind. They confined themselves to actions; he pressed his sentiments into the region of our thoughts, and called for purity at the fountain head.

# Natchez Trace

## TO GOVERNOR W. C. C. CLAIBORNE.

WASHINGTON, *May 24, 1803.*

We have an idea of running a path in a direct line from Knoxville to Natchez, believing it would save 200 miles in the carriage of our mail. The consent of the Indians will be necessary, and it will be very important to get individuals among them to take each a white man into partnership, and to establish at every nineteen miles a house of entertainment, and a farm for its support. The profits of this would soon reconcile the Indians to the practice, and extend it, and render the public use of the road as much an object of desire as it is now of fear; and such a horse-path would soon, with their consent, become a wagon-road. Your country is so abundant in everything which is good, that one does not know what there is here of that description which you have not, and which could be offered in exchange for a barrel of fresh peccans every autumn. Yet I will venture to propose such an exchange. . . .

# Land Use; Sea Power

## TO SIR JOHN SINCLAIR.

WASHINGTON, *June 30, 1803.*

DEAR SIR,—It is so long since I have had the pleasure of writing to you, that it would be vain to look back to dates to connect the old and the new. Yet I ought not to pass over my acknowledgments to you for various publications received from time to time, and with great satisfaction and thankfulness. I send you a small one in return, the work of a very unlettered farmer, yet valuable, as it relates plain facts of importance to farmers. You will discover that Mr. Binns is an enthusiast for the use of gypsum. But there are two facts which prove he has a right to be so: 1. He began poor, and has made himself tolerably rich by his farming alone. 2. The county of Loudon, in which he lives, had been so exhausted and wasted by bad husbandry, that it began to depopulate, the inhabitants going southwardly in quest of better lands. Binns' success has stopped that emigration. It is now becoming one of the most productive counties of the State of Virginia, and the price given for the lands is multiplied manifold.

We are still uninformed here whether you are again at war. Bonaparte has produced such a state of things in Europe as it would seem difficult for him to relinquish in any sensible degree, and equally dangerous for Great Britain to suffer to go on, especially if accompanied by maritime preparations on his part. The events which have taken place in France have lessened in the American mind the motives of interest which it felt in that revolution, and its amity towards that country now rests on its love of peace and commerce. We see, at the same time, with great concern, the position in which Great Britain is placed, and should be sincerely afflicted were any disaster to deprive mankind of the benefit of such a bulwark against the torrent which has for some time been bearing down all before it. But her power and powers at sea seem to render everything safe in the end. Peace is our passion, and the wrongs might drive us from it. We prefer trying *ever* other just principles, right and safety, before we would recur to war.

# Letter of Credit

## TO CAPTAIN MERIWETHER LEWIS.

WASHINGTON, U. S. of A., *July 4, 1803.*

DEAR SIR,—In the journey which you are about to undertake, for the discovery of the course and source of the Missouri, and of the most convenient water communication from thence to the Pacific Ocean, your party being small, it is to be expected that you will encounter considerable dangers from the Indian inhabitants. Should you escape those dangers, and reach the Pacific Ocean, you may find it imprudent to hazard a return the same way, and be forced to seek a passage round by sea, in such vessels as you may find on the Western coast; but you will be without money, without clothes, and other necessaries, as a sufficient supply cannot be carried from hence. Your resource, in that case, can only be in the credit of the United States; for which purpose I hereby authorize you to draw on the Secretaries of State, of the Treasury, of War, and of the Navy of the United States, according as you may find your draughts will be most negotiable, for the purpose of obtaining money or necessaries for yourself and men; and I solemnly pledge the faith of the United States, that these draughts shall be paid punctually at the date at which they are made payable. I also ask of the consuls, agents, merchants, and citizens of any nation with which we have intercourse or amity, to furnish you with those supplies which your necessities may call for, assuring them of honorable and prompt retribution; and our own consuls in foreign parts, where you may happen to be, are hereby instructed and required to be aiding and assisting to you in whatsoever may be necessary for procuring your return back to the United States. And to give more entire satisfaction and confidence to those who may be disposed to aid you, I, Thomas Jefferson, President of the United States of America, have written this letter of general credit for you with my own hand, and signed it with my name.

## Louisiana Purchase

### TO GENERAL HORATIO GATES.

WASHINGTON, *July 11, 1803.*

DEAR GENERAL,—I accept with pleasure, and with pleasure reciprocate your congratulations on the acquisition of Louisiana; for it is a subject of mutual congratulation, as it interests every man of the nation. The territory acquired, as it includes all the waters of the Missouri and Mississippi, has more than doubled the area of the United States, and the new part is not inferior to the old in soil, climate, productions and important communications. If our Legislature dispose of it with the wisdom we have a right to expect, they may make it the means of tempting all our Indians on the east side of the Mississippi to remove to the west, and of condensing instead of scattering our population.

## On Birthdays

### TO LEVI LINCOLN.

MONTICELLO, *August 30, 1803.*

DEAR SIR,—The enclosed letter came to hand by yesterday's post. You will be sensible of the circumstances which make it improper that I should

hazard a formal answer, . . . With respect to the day on which they wish to
fix their anniversary, they may be told, that disapproving myself of trans-
ferring the honors and veneration for the great birthday of our republic
to any individual, or of dividing them with individuals, I have declined let-
ting my own birthday be known, and have engaged my family not to communicate it. This has been the uniform answer to every application of the
kind.

## Lions and Tigers

### TO DOCTOR BENJAMIN RUSH.

WASHINGTON, *October 4, 1803.*

Tremendous times in Europe! How mighty this battle of lions and tigers!
With what sensations should the common herd of cattle look on it? With
no partialities, certainly. If they can so far worry one another as to destroy
their power of tyrannizing, the one over the earth, the other the waters, the
world may perhaps enjoy peace, till they recruit again.

## On Employment

### TO DAVID WILLIAMS.

WASHINGTON, *November 14, 1803.*

The greatest evils of populous society have ever appeared to me to spring
from the vicious distribution of its members among the occupations called
for. I have no doubt that those nations are essentially right, which leave
this to individual choice, as a better guide to an advantageous distribution
than any other which could be devised. But when, by a blind concourse,
particular occupations are ruinously overcharged, and others left in want of
hands, the national authorities can do much towards restoring the equilibrium. On the revival of letters, learning became the universal favorite.
And with reason, because there was not enough of it existing to manage the
affairs of a nation to the best advantage, nor to advance its individuals to
the happiness of which they were susceptible, by improvements in their
minds, their morals, their health, and in those conveniences which contribute
to the comfort and embellishment of life. All the efforts of the society, therefore, were directed to the increase of learning, and the inducements of respect, ease, and profit were held up for its encouragement. Even the charities
of the nation forgot that misery was their object, and spent themselves in
founding schools to transfer to science the hardy sons of the plough. To
these incitements were added the powerful fascinations of great cities. These
circumstances have long since produced an overcharge in the class of competitors for learned occupation, and great distress among the supernumerary

candidates; and the more, as their habits of life have disqualified them for re-entering into the laborious class. The evil cannot be suddenly, nor perhaps ever entirely cured: nor should I presume to say by what means it may be cured. Doubtless there are many engines which the nation might bring to bear on this object. Public opinion, and public encouragement are among these.

The class principally defective is that of agriculture. It is the first in utility, and ought to be the first in respect. The same artificial means which have been used to produce a competition in learning, may be equally successful in restoring agriculture to its primary dignity in the eyes of men. It is a science of the very first order. It counts among its handmaids the most respectable sciences, such as Chemistry, Natural Philosophy, Mechanics, Mathematics generally, Natural History, Botany. In every College and University, a professorship of agriculture, and the class of its students, might be honored as the first. Young men closing their academical education with this, as the crown of all other sciences, fascinated with its solid charms, and at a time when they are to choose an occupation, instead of crowding the other classes, would return to the farms of their fathers, their own, or those of others, and replenish and invigorate a calling, now languishing under contempt and oppression. The charitable schools, instead of storing their pupils with a lore which the present state of society does not call for, converted into schools of agriculture, might restore them to that branch qualified to enrich and honor themselves, and to increase the productions of the nation instead of consuming them. A gradual abolition of the useless offices, so much accumulated in all governments, might close this drain also from the labors of the field, and lessen the burdens imposed on them. By these, and the better means which will occur to others, the surcharge of the learned, might in time be drawn off to recruit the laboring class of citizens, the sum of industry be increased, and that of misery diminished.

Among the ancients, the redundance of population was sometimes checked by exposing infants. To the moderns, America has offered a more humane resource. Many, who cannot find employment in Europe, accordingly come here. Those who can labor do well, for the most part. Of the learned class of emigrants, a small portion find employments analogous to their talents. But many fail, and return to complete their course of misery in the scenes where it began. Even here we find too strong a current from the country to the towns; and instances beginning to appear of that species of misery, which you are so humanely endeavoring to relieve with you. Although we have in the old countries of Europe the lesson of their experience to warn us, yet I am not satisfied we shall have the firmness and wisdom to profit by it. The general desire of men to live by their heads rather than their hands, and the strong allurements of great cities to those who have any turn for dissipation, threaten to make them here, as in Europe, the sinks of voluntary misery.

# On Human Differences

### TO JOHN RANDOLPH.

WASHINGTON, *December 1, 1803.*

DEAR SIR,—The explanations in your letter of yesterday were quite unnecessary to me. I have had too satisfactory proofs of your friendly regard, to be disposed to suspect anything of a contrary aspect. I understood perfectly the expressions stated in the newspaper to which you allude, to mean, that "though the proposition came from the *republican quarter* of the House, yet you should not concur with it." . . . I see too many proofs of the imperfection of human reason, to entertain wonder or intolerance at any difference of opinion on any subject; and acquiesce in that difference as easily as on a difference of feature or form; experience having long taught me the reasonableness of mutual sacrifices of opinion among those who are to act together for any common object, and the expediency of doing what good we can, when we cannot do all we would wish.

# Books, Old and New

### TO DOCTOR JOSEPH PRIESTLEY.

WASHINGTON, *January 29, 1804.*

I rejoice that you have undertaken the task of comparing the moral doctrines of Jesus with those of the ancient Philosophers. You are so much in possession of the whole subject, that you will do it easier and better than any other person living. I think you cannot avoid giving, as preliminary to the comparison, a digest of his moral doctrines, extracted in his own words from the Evangelists, and leaving out everything relative to his personal history and character. It would be short and precious. With a view to do this for my own satisfaction, I had sent to Philadelphia to get two testaments (Greek) of the same edition, and two English, with a design to cut out the morsels of morality, and paste them on the leaves of a book, in the manner you describe as having been pursued in forming your Harmony. But I shall now get the thing done by better hands.

I very early saw that Louisiana was indeed a speck in our horizon which was to burst in a tornado . . . The *dénouement* has been happy; and I confess I look to this duplication of area for the extending a government so free and economical as ours, as a great achievement to the mass of happiness which is to ensue. Whether we remain in one confederacy, or form into Atlantic and Mississippi confederacies, I believe not very important to the happiness of either part. Those of the western confederacy will be as much our children and descendants as those of the eastern, and I feel myself as much identified with that country, in future time, as with this; and did I now foresee a separation at some future day, yet I should feel the duty and the desire to promote the western interests as zealously as the eastern, doing all the good for both portions of our future family which should fall within my power.

Have you seen the new work of Malthus on population? It is one of the ablest I have ever seen. Although his main object is to delineate the effects of redundancy of population, and to test the poor laws of England, and other palliations for that evil, several important questions in political economy, allied to his subject incidentally, are treated with a masterly hand. It is a single octavo volume, and I have been only able to read a borrowed copy, the only one I have yet heard of. Probably our friends in England will think of you, and give you an opportunity of reading it.

## On Economic Man

### TO JEAN BAPTISTE SAY.

WASHINGTON, *February 1, 1804.*

DEAR SIR,—I have to acknowledge the receipt of your obliging letter, and with it, of two very interesting volumes on Political Economy. These found me engaged in giving the leisure moments I rarely find, to the perusal of Malthus' work on population, a work of sound logic, in which some of the opinions of Adam Smith, as well as of the economists, are ably examined. . . .

The differences of circumstance between this and the old countries of Europe, furnish differences of fact whereon to reason, in questions of political economy, and will consequently produce sometimes a difference of result. There, for instance, the quantity of food is fixed, or increasing in a slow and only arithmetical ratio, and the proportion is limited by the same ratio. Supernumerary births consequently add only to your mortality. Here the immense extent of uncultivated and fertile lands enables every one who will labor, to marry young, and to raise a family of any size. Our food, then, may increase geometrically with our laborers, and our births, however multiplied, become effective. Again, there the best distribution of labor is supposed to be that which places the manufacturing hands alongside the agricultural; so that the one part shall feed both, and the other part furnish both with clothes and other comforts. Would that be best here? Egoism and first appearances say yes. Or would it be better that all our laborers should be employed in agriculture? In this case a double or treble portion of fertile lands would be brought into culture; a double or treble creation of food be produced, and its surplus go to nourish the now perishing births of Europe, who in return would manufacture and send us in exchange our clothes and other comforts. Morality listens to this, and so invariably do the laws of nature create our duties and interests, that when they seem to be at variance, we ought to suspect some fallacy in our reasonings. In solving this question, too, we should allow its just weight to the moral and physical preference of the agricultural, over the manufacturing, man. My occupations permit me only to ask questions. They deny me the time, if I had the information, to answer them. Perhaps, as worthy the attention of the author of the *Traité d'Economie Politique*, I shall find them answered in that work. If they are not, the reason will have been that you wrote for Europe; while I shall have asked them because I think for America.

## On Party Groups

### TO GIDEON GRANGER.

MONTICELLO, *April 16, 1804.*

In our last conversation you mentioned a federal scheme afloat, of forming a coalition between the federalists and republicans, of what they called the seven eastern States. The idea was new to me, and after time for reflection I had no opportunity of conversing with you again. The federalists know, that, *eo nomine*, they are gone forever. Their object, therefore, is, how to return into power under some other form. Undoubtedly they have but one means, which is to divide the republicans, join the minority, and barter with them for the cloak of their name. I say, *join the minority;* because the majority of the republicans not needing them, will not buy them. The minority, having no other means of ruling the majority, will give a price for auxiliaries, and that price must be principle. It is true that the federalists, needing their numbers also, must also give a price, and principle is the coin they must pay in. Thus a bastard system of federo-republicanism will rise on the ruins of the true principles of our revolution. And when this party is formed, who will constitute the majority of it, which majority is then to dictate? Certainly the federalists. Thus their proposition of putting themselves into gear with the republican minority, is exactly like Roger Sherman's proposition to add Connecticut to Rhode Island. I cannot believe any portion of real republicans will enter into this trap; and if they do, I do not believe they can carry with them the mass of their States, advancing so steadily as we see them, to an union of principle with their brethren. It will be found in this, as in all other similar cases, that crooked schemes will end by overwhelming their authors and coadjutors in disgrace, and that he alone who walks strict and upright, and who, in matters of opinion, will be contented that others should be as free as himself, and acquiesce when his opinion is fairly overruled, will attain his object in the end.

## College Friends

TO GOVERNOR JOHN PAGE.

WASHINGTON, *June 25, 1804.*

When you and I look back on the country over which we have passed, what a field of slaughter does it exhibit! Where are all the friends who entered it with us, under all the inspiring energies of health and hope? As if pursued by the havoc of war, they are strewed by the way, some earlier, some later, and scarce a few stragglers remain to count the numbers fallen, and to mark yet, by their own fall, the last footsteps of their part. . . . Of our college friends (and they are the dearest) how few have stood with us in the great political questions which have agitated our country; and these were of a nature to justify agitation. I did not believe the Lilliputian fetters of that day strong enough to have bound so many.

Present me respectfully to Mrs. Page, and accept yourself my friendly salutations, and assurances of constant affection.

## People and Press

TO JUDGE JOHN TYLER.

WASHINGTON, *June 28, 1804.*

No experiment can be more interesting than that we are now trying, and which we trust will end in establishing the fact, that man may be governed by reason and truth. Our first object should therefore be, to leave open to him all the avenues to truth. The most effectual hitherto found, is the freedom of the press. It is, therefore, the first shut up by those who fear the investigation of their actions. The firmness with which the people have withstood the late abuses of the press, the discernment they have manifested between truth and falsehood, show that they may safely be trusted to hear everything true and false, and to form a correct judgment between them. As little is it necessary to impose on their senses, or dazzle their minds by pomp, splendor, or forms. Instead of this artificial, how much surer is that real respect, which results from the use of their reason, and the habit of bringing everything to the test of common sense.

I hold it, therefore, certain, that to open the doors of truth, and to fortify the habit of testing everything by reason, are the most effectual manacles we can rivet on the hands of our successors to prevent their manacling the people with their own consent.

## Presidential Term

TO JOHN TAYLOR, ESQ.

WASHINGTON, *January 6, 1805.*

My opinion originally was that the President of the United States should have been elected for seven years, and forever ineligible afterwards. I have since become sensible that seven years is too long to be irremovable, and that there should be a peaceable way of withdrawing a man in midway who is doing wrong. The service for eight years, with a power to remove at the end of the first four, comes nearly to my principle as corrected by experience; and it is in adherence to that, that I determine to withdraw at the end of my second term. The danger is that the indulgence and attachments of the people will keep a man in the chair after he becomes a dotard, that re-election through life shall become habitual, and election for life follow that. General Washington set the example of voluntary retirement after eight years. I shall follow it. And a few more precedents will oppose the obstacle of habit to any one after awhile who shall endeavor to extend his term. Perhaps it may beget a disposition to establish it by an amendment of the Constitution. I believe I am doing right therefore in pursuing my principle. I had determined to declare my intention, but I have consented to be silent on the opinion of friends, who think it best not to put a continuance out of my power in defiance of all circumstances. There is, however, but one circumstance which could engage my acquiescence in another election; to wit, such a division about a successor, as might bring in a monarchist. But that circumstance is impossible.

## Our Cloudless Skies

TO C. F. C. DE VOLNEY.

WASHINGTON, *February 8, 1805.*

In no case, perhaps, does habit attach our choice or judgment more than in climate. The Canadian glows with delight in his sleigh and snow; the very idea of which gives me the shivers. The comparison of climate between Europe and North America, taking together its corresponding parts, hangs chiefly on three great points. 1. The changes between heat and cold in America are greater and more frequent, and the extremes comprehend a greater scale on the thermometer in America than in Europe. Habit, however, prevents these from affecting us more than the smaller changes of Europe affect the European. But he is greatly affected by ours. 2. Our sky is always clear; that of Europe always cloudy. Hence a greater accumulation of heat here than there, in the same parallel. 3. The changes between wet and dry are much more frequent and sudden in Europe than in America. Though we have double the rain, it falls in half the time. Taking all these together, I prefer much the climate of the United States to that of Europe. I think it a more cheerful one. It is our cloudless sky which has eradicated from our constitutions all disposition to hang ourselves, which we might otherwise have inherited from our English ancestors.

## Indian Brothers

### TO THE BROTHERS OF THE CHOCTAW NATION.

WASHINGTON, *March 13, 1805.*

MY CHILDREN,—I learn with great satisfaction that you have leased to us three stations of one mile square each on the road from Chickesaws to Natchez, and one on the Pearl river; and you desire me to send you a paper under my own hand to show to your warriors that these lands are not sold but lent. I now accordingly declare that the property in those lands remains in your nation, that they are lent to us for a rent of four hundred pounds weight of powder annually, and that your nation has a right to take them back at their pleasure; and this paper now signed by my own hand will be evidence of these things to future generations. We will, according to your desire, settle but one white family on each section, and take care that they conduct themselves peaceably and friendly toward you; or being made known to me that they do otherwise they shall be removed. They will be placed there merely for the accommodation of our paper carriers and travellers.

My children, you have asked whether I did not promise to send you ploughs to enable you to improve in husbandry? I did promise it and immediately sent the ploughs; but by a mistake in forwarding them, they were delayed some time before we knew of it. You must, however, have received them before this time.

You ask if I did not promise to send your deputation ten rifles for yourselves and other deserving warriors? I did not promise it. You said they would be acceptable, but I said nothing in reply. But although I did not promise, yet to show my good will to you, I will send you the rifles.

You ask if we will allow commissions to you according to your rank and medals and commissions to such chiefs as you may appoint to assist in the government of your country? It has not been a custom with us to give commissions to our friends among the red men; and it is a new thing. We will take it into consideration. We wish to do what is agreeable to you, if we find we can do it with prudence.

We shall be willing to give medals to a certain number of distinguished chiefs who aid you in the government of your country, and who manifest dispositions to preserve peace and friendship between your nation and ours. We wish you, therefore, to recommend such to us.

My children, persevere in your friendship to the United States. We will never injure you nor permit you to be injured by any white people, and we trust you will take care that none of our people are injured by yours. Encourage among you the cultivation of the earth, raising of cattle, spinning and weaving, and we will assist you in it. With plenty of food and clothing you will raise many children, multiply, be strong and happy. May the Great Spirit protect and prosper you in all your just pursuits. Farewell.

### TO THE CHIEFS OF THE CHEROKEE NATION.

WASHINGTON, *January 10, 1806.*

MY FRIENDS AND CHILDREN, CHIEFLY OF THE CHEROKEE NATION,—Having now finished our business and finished it I hope to mutual satisfaction, I cannot take leave of you without expressing the satisfaction I have received from your visit. I see with my own eyes that the endeavors we have been making to encourage and lead you in the way of improving your situation have not been unsuccessful; it has been like grain sown in good ground, producing abundantly. You are becoming farmers, learning the use of the plough and the hoe, enclosing your grounds and employing that labor in their cultivation which you formerly employed in hunting and in war; and I see handsome specimens of cotton cloth raised, spun and wove by yourselves. You are also raising cattle and hogs for your food, and horses to assist your labors. Go on, my children, in the same way and be assured the further you advance in it the happier and more respectable you will be.

Our brethren, whom you have happened to meet here from the West and Northwest, have enabled you to compare your situation now with what it was formerly. They also make the comparison, and they see how far you are ahead of them, and seeing what you are they are encouraged to do as you have done. You will find your next wants to be mills to grind your corn, which by relieving your women from the loss of time in beating it into meal, will enable them to spin and weave more. When a man has enclosed and improved his farm, builds a good house on it and raised plentiful stocks of animals, he will wish when he dies that these things shall go to his wife and children, whom he loves more than he does his other relations, and for whom he will work with pleasure during his life. You will, therefore, find it necessary to establish laws for this. When a man has property, earned by his own labor, he will not like to see another come and take it from him because he happens to be stronger, or else to defend it by spilling blood. You will find it necessary then to appoint good men, as judges, to decide contests between man and man, according to reason and to the rules you shall establish. If you wish to be aided by our counsel and experience in these things we shall always be ready to assist you with our advice.

My children, it is unnecessary for me to advise you against spending all your time and labor in warring with and destroying your fellow-men, and wasting your own members. You already see the folly and iniquity of it. Your young men, however, are not yet sufficiently sensible of it. Some of them cross the Mississippi to go and destroy people who have never done them an injury. My children, this is wrong and must not be; if we permit them to cross the Mississippi to war with the Indians on the other side of that river, we must let those Indians cross the river to take revenge on you. I say again, this must not be. The Mississippi now belongs to us. It must not be a river of blood. It is now the water-path along which all our people of Natchez, St. Louis, Indiana, Ohio, Tennessee, Kentucky and the western parts of Pennsylvania and Virginia are constantly passing with their property, to and from New Orleans. Young men going to war are not easily restrained. Finding our people on the river they will rob them, perhaps kill them. This would bring on a war between us and you. It is better to stop this in time by forbidding your young men to go across the river to make war. If they go to visit or to live with the Cherokees on the other side of the river we shall not object to that. That country is ours. We will permit them to live in it.

My children, this is what I wished to say to you. To go on in learning to cultivate the earth and to avoid war. If any of your neighbors injure you, our beloved men whom we place with you will endeavor to obtain justice for you and we will support them in it. If any of your bad people injure your neighbors, be ready to acknowledge it and to do them justice. It is more honorable to repair a wrong than to persist in it. Tell all your chiefs, your men, women and children, that I take them by the hand and hold it fast. That I am their father, wish their happiness and well-being, and am always ready to promote their good.

My children, I thank you for your visit and pray to the Great Spirit who made us all and planted us all in this land to live together like brothers that He will conduct you safely to your homes, and grant you to find your families and your friends in good health.

# The Link of Language

## TO DOCTOR JOHN SIBLEY.

WASHINGTON, *May 27, 1805.*

The question whether the Indians of America have emigrated from another continent, is still undecided. Their vague and imperfect traditions can satisfy no mind on that subject. I have long considered their languages as the only remaining monument of connection with other nations, or the want of it, to which we can now have access. They will likewise show their connections with one another. Very early in life, therefore, I formed a vocabulary of such objects as, being present everywhere, would probably have a name in every language . . . A similar work, but on a much greater scale, has been executed under the auspices of the late empress of Russia, as to the red nations of Asia, which, however, I have never seen. A comparison of our collection with that will probably decide the question of the sameness or difference of origin, although it will not decide which is the mother country, and which the colony.

# Rebel in Retirement

### TO THOMAS PAINE.

WASHINGTON, *June 5, 1805.*

I congratulate you on your retirement to your farm, and still more that it is of a character so worthy of your attention. I much doubt whether the open room on your second story will answer your expectations. There will be a few days in the year in which it will be delightful, but not many. Nothing but trees, or Venetian blinds, can protect it from the sun. The semi-cylindrical roof you propose will have advantages. You know it has been practised on the cloth market at Paris. De Lorme, the inventor, shows many forms of roofs in his book to which it is applicable. I have used it at home for a dome, being one hundred and twenty degrees of an oblong octagon, and in the capitol we unite two quadrants of a sphere by a semi-cylinder; all framed in De Lorme's manner. How has your planing machine answered? Has it been tried and persevered in by any workmen?

. . . It seems very difficult to find out what turns things are to take in Europe. I suppose it depends on Austria, which, knowing it is to stand in the way of receiving the first hard blows, is cautious of entering into a coalition. As to France and England we can have but one wish, that they may disable one another from injuring others.

Accept my friendly salutations, and assurances of esteem and respect.

# On Foreign Missions

### TO DOCTORS ROGERS AND SLAUGHTER.

WASHINGTON, *March 2, 1806.*

I deem it the duty of every man to devote a certain portion of his income for charitable purposes; and that it is his further duty to see it so applied as to do the most good of which it is capable. This I believe to be best insured, by keeping within the circle of his own inquiry and information the subjects of distress to whose relief his contributions shall be applied. If this rule be reasonable in private life, it becomes so necessary in my situation, that to relinquish it would leave me without rule or compass. The applications of this kind from different parts of our own, and from foreign countries, are far beyond any resources within my command. The mission of Serampore, in the East Indies, the object of the present application, is but one of many items. However disposed the mind may feel to unlimited good, our means having limits, we are necessarily circumscribed by them. They are too narrow to relieve even the distresses under my own eye; and to desert these for others which we neither see nor know, is to omit doing a certain good for one which is uncertain. I know, indeed, there have been splendid associations for effecting benevolent purposes in remote regions of the earth. But no experience of their effect has proved that more good would not have been done by the same means employed nearer home. In explaining, however, my own motives of action, I must not be understood as impeaching those of others. Their views are those of an expanded liberality. Mine may be too much restrained by the law of usefulness. But it is a law to me, and with minds like yours, will be felt as a justification. With this apology, I pray you to accept my salutations, and assurances of high esteem and respect.

## President's Problem

### TO WILLIAM DUANE.

WASHINGTON, *March 22, 1806*.

Our situation is difficult; and whatever we do is liable to the criticisms of those who wish to represent it awry. If we recommend measures in a public message, it may be said that members are not sent here to obey the mandates of the President, or to register the edicts of a sovereign. If we express opinions in conversation, we have then our Charles Jenkinsons, and back-door counsellors. If we say nothing, "we have no opinions, no plans, no Cabinet." In truth it is the fable of the old man, his son and ass, over again.

## The Senate and Treaties

### TO WILSON C. NICHOLAS.

WASHINGTON, *April 13, 1806*.

A majority of the Senate means well. But Tracy and Bayard are too dexterous for them, and have very much influenced their proceedings. Tracy has been of nearly every committee during the session, and for the most part the chairman, and of course drawer of the reports. Seven federalists voting always in phalanx, and joined by some discontented republicans, some oblique ones, some capricious, have so often made a majority, as to produce very serious embarrassment to the public operations; and very much do I dread the submitting to them, at the next session, any treaty which can be made with either England or Spain, when I consider that five joining the federalists, can defeat a friendly settlement of our affairs.

## Intercourse of Nations

### TO THE EMPEROR OF RUSSIA.

WASHINGTON, *April 19, 1806.*

I owe an acknowledgment to your Imperial Majesty for the great satisfaction I have received from your letter of August the 20th, 1805, and embrace the opportunity it affords of giving expression to the sincere respect and veneration I entertain for your character. It will be among the latest and most soothing comforts of my life, to have seen advanced to the government of so extensive a portion of the earth, and at so early a period of his life, a sovereign whose ruling passion is the advancement of the happiness and prosperity of his people; and not of his own people only, but who can extend his eye and his good will to a distant and infant nation, unoffending in its course, unambitious in its views.

The events of Europe come to us so late, and so suspiciously, that observations on them would certainly be stale, and possibly wide of their actual state. From their general aspect, however, I collect that your Majesty's interposition in them has been disinterested and generous, and having in view only the general good of the great European family. When you shall proceed to the pacification which is to re-establish peace and commerce, the same dispositions of mind will lead you to think of the general intercourse of nations, and to make that provision for its future maintenance which, in times past, it has so much needed.

## English Friendship

### TO COLONEL JAMES MONROE.

WASHINGTON, *May 4, 1806.*

The late change in the ministry I consider as insuring us a just settlement of our differences, and we ask no more. . . . No two countries upon earth have so many points of common interest and friendship; and their rulers must be great bunglers indeed, if, with such dispositions, they break them asunder. The only rivalry that can arise is on the ocean. England may, by petty larceny thwartings, check us on that element a little, but nothing she can do will retard us there one year's growth.

## On Congress

TO BARNABAS BIDWELL.

WASHINGTON, *July 5, 1806.*

I will not say that this time, more than all others, calls for the service of every man; but I will say, there never was a time when the services of those who possess talents, integrity, firmness, and sound judgment, were more wanted in Congress. Some one of that description is particularly wanted to take the lead in the House of Representatives, to consider the business of the nation as his own business, to take it up as if he were singly charged with it, and carry it through.

## Burr's Expedition

TO CHARLES CLAY.

WASHINGTON, *January 11, 1807.*

Burr's enterprise is the most extraordinary since the days of Don Quixote. It is so extravagant that those who know his understanding, would not believe it if the proofs admitted doubt. He has meant to place himself on the throne of Montezuma, and extend his empire to the Alleghany, seizing on New Orleans as the instrument of compulsion for our western States. I think his undertaking effectually crippled by the activity of Ohio. Whether Kentucky will give him the *coup de grace* is doubtful; but if he is able to descend the river with any means, we are sufficiently prepared at New Orleans.

## On Falsehood in Print

TO THOMAS SEYMOUR, ESQ.

WASHINGTON, *February 11, 1807.*

Conscious that there was not a *truth* on earth which I feared should be known, I have lent myself willingly as the subject of a great experiment, which was to prove that an administration, conducting itself with integrity and common understanding, cannot be battered down, even by the falsehoods of a licentious press, and consequently still less by the press, as restrained within the legal and wholesome limits of truth. This experiment was wanting for the world to demonstrate the falsehood of the pretext that freedom of the press is incompatible with orderly government. I have never therefore even contradicted the thousands of calumnies so industriously propagated against myself. But the fact being once established, that the press is impotent when it abandons itself to falsehood, I leave to others to restore it to its strength, by recalling it within the pale of truth. Within that it is a noble institution, equally the friend of science and of civil liberty. . . . It would seem impossible that an intelligent people, with the faculty of reading and right of thinking, should continue much longer to slumber under the pupilage of an interested aristocracy of priests and lawyers, persuading them to distrust themselves, and to let them think for them.

## For the Indian Trade

### TO GENERAL HENRY DEARBORN.

*February 14, 1807.*

Thomas Jefferson salutes General Dearborn with friendship, and communicates the following information from Captain Lewis, which may be useful to Colonel Freeman, and our future explorers; and indeed may enable us understandingly to do acceptable things to our Louisiana neighbors when we wish to gratify them.

He says the following are the articles in highest value with them:

1. *Blue* beads. This is a coarse cheap bead imported from China, and costing in England 13*d.* the pound, in strands. It is far more valued by the Indians than the *white* beads of the same manufacture, and answers all the purposes of money, being counted by the fathom. He says that were his journey to be performed again, one-half or two-thirds of his stores *in value* should be of these.

2. Common brass buttons, more valued than anything except beads.

3. Knives.

4. Battleaxes and tomahawks.

5. Saddlers' seat awls, which answer for moccasin awls.

6. Some glovers' needles.

7. Some iron combs.

8. Some nests of camp kettles; brass is much preferred to iron, though both are very useful to the Indians.

Arrow-points should have been added.

## More about the Mammoth

### TO DR. CASPAR WISTAR.

WASHINGTON, *February 25, 1807.*

DEAR SIR,—I enclose you a letter from Dr. Goforth on the subject of the bones of the mammoth. Immediately on the receipt of this, as I found it was in my power to accomplish the wishes of the society for the completion of this skeleton with more certainty than through the channel proposed in the letter, I set the thing into motion, so that it will be effected without any expense to the society, or other trouble than to indicate the particular bones wanting. Being acquainted with Mr. Ross, proprietor of the big bone lick, I wrote to him for permission to search for such particular bones as the society might desire, and I expect to receive it in a few days. Captain Clarke (companion of Captain Lewis) who is now here, agrees, as he passes through that country, to stop at the Lick, employ laborers, and superintend the search at my expense, not that of the society . . .

## Money Matters

### TO ROBERT PATTERSON.

WASHINGTON, *March 29, 1807.*

I should approve of your employing the Mint on small silver coins, rather than on dollars and gold coins, as far as the consent of those who employ it can be obtained. It would be much more valuable to the public to be supplied with abundance of dimes and half dimes, which would stay among us, than with dollars and eagles which leave us immediately.

## On Newspapers

### TO JOHN NORVELL.

WASHINGTON, *June 11, 1807.*

To your request of my opinion of the manner in which a newspaper should be conducted, so as to be most useful, I should answer, "by restraining it to true facts and sound principles only." Yet I fear such a paper would find few subscribers. It is a melancholy truth, that a suppression of the press could not more completely deprive the nation of its benefits, than is done by its abandoned prostitution to falsehood. Nothing can now be believed which is seen in a newspaper. Truth itself becomes suspicious by being put into that polluted vehicle. The real extent of this state of misinformation is known only to those who are in situations to confront facts within their knowledge with the lies of the day. I really look with commiseration over the great body of my fellow citizens, who, reading newspapers, live and die in the belief, that they have known something of what has been passing in the world in their time; whereas the accounts they have read in newspapers are just as true a history of any other period of the world as of the present, except that the real names of the day are affixed to their fables. General facts may indeed be collected from them, such as that Europe is now at war, that Bonaparte has been a successful warrior, that he has subjected a great portion of Europe to his will, etc., etc.; but

no details can be relied on. I will add, that the man who never looks into
a newspaper is better informed than he who reads them; inasmuch as he
who knows nothing is nearer to truth than he whose mind is filled with
falsehoods and errors. He who reads nothing will still learn the great facts,
and the details are all false.

Perhaps an editor might begin a reformation in some such way as this.
Divide his paper into four chapters, heading the 1st, Truths. 2d, Probabilities.
3d, Possibilities. 4th, Lies. The first chapter would be very short, as it
would contain little more than authentic papers, and information from
such sources, as the editor would be willing to risk his own reputation for
their truth. The second would contain what, from a mature consideration
of all circumstances, his judgment should conclude to be probably true.
This, however, should rather contain too little than too much. The third
and fourth should be professedly for those readers who would rather have
lies for their money than the blank paper they would occupy.

## On Physicians

### TO DOCTOR CASPAR WISTAR.

WASHINGTON, *June 21, 1807.*

To an unknown disease, there cannot be a known remedy. Here then,
the judicious, the moral, the humane physician should stop. Having been
so often a witness to the salutary efforts which nature makes to re-establish the disordered functions, he should rather trust to their action, than
hazard the interruption of that, and a greater derangement of the system,
by conjectural experiments on a machine so complicated and so unknown
as the human body, and a subject so sacred as human life. Or, if the appearance of doing something be necessary to keep alive the hope and spirits
of the patient, it should be of the most innocent character. One of the most
successful physicians I have ever known, has assured me, that he used more
bread pills, drops of colored water, and powders of hickory ashes, than of
all other medicines put together. It was certainly a pious fraud. But the
adventurous physician goes on, and substitutes presumption for knowledge.
From the scanty field of what is known, he launches into the boundless
region of what is unknown. He establishes for his guide some fanciful
theory of corpuscular attraction, of chemical agency, of mechanical powers,
of stimuli, of irritability accumulated or exhausted, of depletion by the
lancet and repletion by mercury, or some other ingenious dream, which
lets him into all nature's secrets at short hand. On the principle which he
thus assumes, he forms his table of nosology, arrays his diseases into families,
and extends his curative treatment, by analogy, to all the cases he has thus
arbitrarily marshalled together. I have lived myself to see the disciples of
Hoffman, Boerhaave, Stahl, Cullen, Brown, succeed one another like the
shifting figures of a magic lantern, and their fancies, like the dresses of the

annual doll-babies from Paris, becoming, from their novelty, the vogue of the day, and yielding to the next novelty their ephemeral favor. The patient, treated on the fashionable theory, sometimes gets well in spite of the medicine. The medicine, therefore, restored him, and the young doctor receives new courage to proceed in his bold experiments on the lives of his fellow-creatures.

I believe we may safely affirm, that the inexperienced and presumptuous band of medical tyros let loose upon the world, destroys more of human life in one year, than all the Robinhoods, Cartouches, and Macheaths do in a century. It is in this part of medicine that I wish to see a reform, an abandonment of hypothesis for sober facts, the first degree of value set on clinical observation, and the lowest of visionary theories. I would wish the young practitioner, especially, to have deeply impressed on his mind, the real limits of his art, and that when the state of his patient gets beyond these, his office is to be a watchful, but quiet spectator of the operations of nature, giving them fair play by a well-regulated regimen, and by all the aid they can derive from the excitement of good spirits and hope in the patient. . . .

## Threshold of War

### TO THE SECRETARY OF WAR (HENRY DEARBORN).

WASHINGTON, *July* 7, *1807.*

DEAR SIR,—I enclose you copies of two letters sent by express from Captain Decatur. By these you will perceive that the British commanders have their foot on the threshold of war. They have begun the blockade of Norfolk; have sounded the passage to the town, which appears practicable for three of their vessels, and menace an attack on the Chesapeake and Cybele. These, with four gun-boats, form the present defence, and there are four more gun-boats in Norfolk nearly ready. The four gun-boats at Hampton are hauled up, and in danger, four in Mopjack bay are on the stocks. Blows may be hourly possible.

## On Munitions

### TO MONSIEUR DUPONT DE NEMOURS.

WASHINGTON, *July 14, 1807.*

Your exhortation to make a provision of arms is undoubtedly wise, and we have not been inattentive to it. Our internal resources for cannon are great, and those for small arms considerable, and in full employment. We shall not suffer from that want, should we have war; and of the possibility of that you will judge by the enclosed proclamation, and by what you know of the character of the English government. Never since the battle of Lexington have I seen this country in such a state of exasperation as at present, and even that did not produce such unanimity. The federalists themselves coalesce with us as to the object, though they will return to their trade of censuring every measure taken to obtain it.

## Policy of Russia

### TO WILLIAM DUANE.

WASHINGTON, *July 20, 1807.*

I have often wished for an occasion of saying a word to you on the subject of the Emperor of Russia, of whose character and value to us, I suspect you are not apprised correctly. A more virtuous man, I believe, does not exist, nor one who is more enthusiastically devoted to better the condition of mankind. He will probably, one day, fall a victim to it, as a monarch of that principle does not suit a Russian noblesse. He is not of the very first order of understanding, but he is of a high one. He has taken a peculiar affection to this country and its government, of which he has given me public as well as personal proofs. Our nation being, like his, habitually neutral, our interests as to neutral rights, and our sentiments agree. And whenever conferences for peace shall take place, we are assured of a friend in him. In fact, although in questions of restitution he will be with England, in those of neutral rights he will be with Bonaparte and with every other power in the world, except England; and I do presume that England will never have peace until she subscribes to a just code of marine law. I have gone into this subject, because I am confident that Russia (while her present monarch lives) is the most cordially friendly to us of any power on earth, will go furthest to serve us, and is most worthy of conciliation. And although the source of this information must be a matter of confidence with you, yet it is desirable that the sentiments should become those of the nation. I salute you with esteem and respect.

## On Submarines

### TO COLONEL ROBERT FULTON.

MONTICELLO, *August 16, 1807.*

I consider your torpedoes as very valuable means of the defence of harbors, and have no doubt that we should adopt them to a considerable degree. Not that I go the whole length (as I believe you do) of considering them as solely to be relied on. Neither a nation nor those entrusted with its affairs, could be justifiable, however sanguine its expectations, in trusting solely to an engine not yet sufficiently tried, under all the circumstances which may occur, and against which we know not as yet what means of parrying may be devised. If, indeed, the mode of attaching them to the cable of a ship be the only one proposed, modes of prevention cannot be difficult. But I have ever looked to the submarine boat as most to be depended on for attaching them, and though I see no mention of it in your letter, or your publications, I am in hopes it is not abandoned as impracticable. I should wish to see a corps of young men trained to this service.

## Germ Theory

### TO JOHN CRAWFORD.

MONTICELLO, *September 8, 1807.*

Thomas Jefferson presents his compliments to Mr. Crawford, and his thanks for his Observations on Quarantines, which he has read with great pleasure. Not himself a friend to quarantines, nor having confidence in their efficacy, even if they are necessary, he sees with pleasure every effort to lessen their credit. But the theory which derives all infection, and ascribes to unseen animals the effects hitherto believed to be produced by it, is as yet too new and unreceived to justify the public servants in resting thereon the public health, until time and further investigation shall have sanctioned it by a more general confidence. He salutes Mr. Crawford with great respect.

## Naval Disarmament

### TO TENCH COXE.

MONTICELLO, *September 21, 1807.*

SIR,—I have read with great satisfaction your observations on the principles for equalizing the power of the different nations on the sea, and think them perfectly sound. Certainly it will be better to produce a balance on that element, by reducing the means of its great monopolizer, than by endeavoring to raise our own to an equality with theirs.

## On Quaker Methods

### TO JAMES PEMBERTON.

WASHINGTON, *November 16, 1807.*

SIR,—Your favor of October 31st has been duly received, and I thank you for the communication of the report of the Committee of Friends. It gives me great satisfaction to see that we are likely to render our Indian neighbors happier in themselves and well affected to us; that the measures we are pursuing are prescribed equally by our duty to them, and by the good of our own country. It is a proof the more of the indissoluble alliance between our duties and interest, which if ever they appear to lead in opposite directions, we may be assured it is from our own defective views. It is evident that your society has begun at the right end for civilizing these people. Habits of industry, easy subsistence, attachment to property, are necessary to prepare their minds for the first elements of science, and afterwards for moral and religious instruction. To begin with the last has ever ended either in effecting nothing, or ingrafting bigotry on ignorance, and setting them to tomahawking and burning old women and others as witches, of which we have seen a commencement among them.

## State of the Nation

### TO JAMES MAURY.

WASHINGTON, *November 21, 1807.*

The world, as you justly observe, is truly in an awful state. Two nations of overgrown power are endeavoring to establish, the one an universal dominion by sea, the other by land. We naturally fear that which comes into immediate contact with us, leaving remoter dangers to the chapter of accidents. We are now in hourly expectation of hearing from our ministers in London, by the return of the Revenge. Whether she will bring us war or peace, or the middle state of non-intercourse, seems suspended in equal balance. With every wish for peace, permitted by the circumstances forced upon us, we look to war as equally probable. The crops of the present year have been great beyond example. The wheat sown for the ensuing year is in a great measure destroyed by the drought and the fly. A favorable winter and spring sometimes do wonders towards recovering unpromising grain; but nothing can make the next crop of wheat a good one.

The present aspect of our foreign relations has encouraged here a general spirit of encouragement to domestic manufacture. The Merino breed of sheep is well established with us, and fine samples of cloth are sent on from the north. Considerable manufactures of cotton are also commencing. Philadelphia, particularly, is becoming more manufacturing than commercial.

## Homesickness

### TO MARTHA JEFFERSON RANDOLPH.

WASHINGTON, *November 23, 1807.*

. . . Davy will set out on his return to-morrow. He will carry an earthen box of monthly strawberries, which I must put under Anne's care till spring, when we will plant them at Monticello. I have stuck several sprigs of geranium in a pot which contained a plant supposed to be orange, but not known to be so.

We have little company of strangers in town this winter. The only ladies are the wives of Messrs. Newton, Thurston, W. Alston, Marion, Mumford, Blount, Adams, Cutts, and Mrs. McCreary expected. Congress are all expectation and anxiety for the news expected by the Revenge or by Colonel Monroe, whose immediate return, however, may be doubted. The war-fever is past, and the probability against its return rather prevalent. A caucus of malcontent members has been held and an organized opposition to the government arranged, J. R. and J. C. at its head;[1] about 20 members composed it. Their object is to embarrass, avoiding *votes of opposition* beyond what they think the nation will bear. Their chief mischief will be done by letters of misrepresentations to their constituents, for in neither house, even with the assured aid of the Federalists, can they shake the good sense and honest intentions of the mass of real Republicans. But I am tired of a life of contention and of being the personal object for the hatred of every man who hates the present state of things. I long to be among you, where I know nothing but love and delight, and where instead of being chained to a writing table I could be indulged as others are with the blessings of domestic society and pursuits of my own choice. Adieu, my ever dear Martha; present me affectionately to Mr. Randolph and the family.

## On Education

### TO JOEL BARLOW.

WASHINGTON, *December 10, 1807.*

There is a snail-paced gait for the advance of new ideas on the general mind, under which we must acquiesce. A forty years' experience of popular assemblies has taught me, that you must give them time for every step you take. If too hard pushed, they balk, and the machine retrogrades. I doubt whether precedence will be given to your part of the plan before Mr. Fulton's. People generally have more feeling for canals and roads than education. However, I hope we can advance them with equal pace.

## The "Fleecy Goat"

### TO DOCTOR CASPAR WISTAR.

WASHINGTON, *December 19, 1807.*

DEAR SIR,—I have never known to what family you ascribed the Wild Sheep, or Fleecy Goat, as Governor Lewis called it, or the *Potio-trajos*, if its name must be Greek. He gave me a skin, but I know he carried a more perfect one, with the horns on, to Mr. Peale; and if I recollect well those horns, they, with the fleece, would induce one to suspect it to be the Lama,

[1] John Randolph of Roanoke, and Joseph Clay of Pennsylvania.

or at least a *Lamæ affinis*. I will thank you to inform me what you determine it to be.

I have lately received a letter from General Clarke. He has employed ten laborers several weeks, at the Big-bone Lick, and has shipped the result, in three large boxes, down the Ohio, via New Orleans, for this place, where they are daily expected. He has sent, 1st, of the Mammoth, as he calls it, frontals, jaw-bones, tusks, teeth, ribs, a thigh, and a leg, and some bones of the paw; 2d, of what he calls the Elephant, a jaw-bone, tusks, teeth, ribs; 3d, of something of the Buffalo species, a head and some other bones unknown.

## Gift for France

### TO GENERAL WILLIAM CLARKE.

WASHINGTON, *December 19, 1807.*

DEAR SIR,—I have duly received your two favors of September 20th, and November 10th, and am greatly obliged, indeed, by the trouble you have been so good as to take in procuring for me as thorough a supplement to the bones of the Mammoth as can now be had. I expect daily to receive your bill for all the expenses, which shall be honored with thanks.

The collection you have made is so considerable that it has suggested an idea I had not before. I see that after taking out for the Philosophical Society everything they shall desire, there will remain such a collection of duplicates as will be a grateful offering from me to the National Institute of France, for whom I am bound to do something.

## On Land Settlement

### TO ALBERT GALLATIN.

*December 24, 1807.*

I am glad to find we have 4,000,000 acres west of Chafalaya. How much better to have every 160 acres settled by an able-bodied militia man, than by purchasers with their hordes of negroes, to add weakness instead of strength. Affectionate salutations.

## Instead of Olive Oil

### TO ROBERT R. LIVINGSTON, ESQ.

WASHINGTON, *January 3, 1808.*

It is now among my most fervent longings to be on my farm, which, with a garden and fruitery, will constitute my principal occupation in retirement.

I have lately received the proceedings of the Agricultural Society of Paris. They are proceeding with enthusiasm and understanding. I have been surprised to find that the rotation of crops and substitution of some profitable growth preparatory for grain, instead of the useless and expensive fallow, is yet only dawning among them. I lately received from Colonel Few in New York, a bottle of the oil of Beni, believed to be a sesamum. I did not believe there existed so perfect a substitute for olive oil. Like that of Florence, it has no taste, and is perhaps rather more limpid. A bushel of seed yields three gallons of oil; and Governor Milledge, of Georgia, says the plant will grow wherever the Palmi Christi will. It is worth your attention.

## On Good Humor

### TO DOCTOR BENJAMIN RUSH.

WASHINGTON, *January 3, 1808.*

In the ensuing autumn, I shall be sending on to Philadelphia a grandson of about fifteen years of age, to whom I shall ask your friendly attentions. Without that bright fancy which captivates, I am in hopes he possesses sound judgment and much observation; and, what I value more than all things, good humor. For thus I estimate the qualities of the mind: 1, good humor; 2, integrity; 3, industry; 4, science. The preference of the first to the second quality may not at first be acquiesced in; but certainly we had all rather associate with a good-humored, light-principled man, than with an ill-tempered rigorist in morality.

## Embargo

### TO JOHN TAYLOR, ESQ.

WASHINGTON, *January 6, 1808.*

I see by the agricultural transactions of the Paris Society, they are cultivating the Jerusalem artichoke for feeding their animals. They make 10,000 lb. to the acre, which they say is three times as much as they generally make of the potato. The African Negroes brought over to Georgia a seed which they called beni, and the botanists sesamum. I lately received a bottle of the oil, which was eaten with salad by various companies. All agree it is equal to the olive oil. A bushel of seed yields three gallons of oil. I propose to cultivate it for my own use at least.

The embargo keeping at home our vessels, cargoes and seamen, saves us the necessity of making their capture the cause of immediate war; for, if going to England, France had determined to take them, if to any other place, England was to take them. Till they return to some sense of moral duty, therefore, we keep within ourselves. This gives time. Time may produce peace in Europe; peace in Europe removes all causes of difference, till another European war; and by that time our debt may be paid, our revenues clear, and our strength increased.

## Sailors Must Eat

### TO ROBERT SMITH.

*January 14, 1808.*

I am sorry to see the seamen working for rations only, and that we cannot allow even them. And further, indeed, that we shall be under the necessity of discharging a number of those we have. This is so serious a question that I propose to call a consultation on it a day or two hence.

## Cotton and Weights

### TO MR. J. DORSEY.

WASHINGTON, *January 21, 1808.*

SIR,—I have to acknowledge the receipt of your favor of December 20th, and am much pleased to find our progress in manufactures to be so great. That of cotton is peculiarly interesting, because we raise the raw material in such abundance, and because it may, to a great degree, supply our deficiencies both in wool and linen.

It will give me real pleasure to see some good system of measures and weights introduced and combined with the decimal arithmetic. It is a great and difficult question whether to venture only on a half reformation, which by presenting fewer innovations, may be more easily adopted, or, as the French have tried with success, make a radical reform.

## Religious Freedom

### TO THE REV. SAMUEL MILLER.

WASHINGTON, *January 23, 1808.*

Certainly, no power to prescribe any religious exercise, or to assume authority in religious discipline, has been delegated to the General Government. It must then rest with the States, as far as it can be in any human authority. But it is only proposed that I should *recommend*, not prescribe a day of fasting and prayer. That is, that I should *indirectly* assume to the United States an authority over religious exercises, which the Constitution has directly precluded them from. It must be meant, too, that this recommendation is to carry some authority, and to be sanctioned by some penalty on those who disregard it; not indeed of fine and imprisonment, but of some degree of proscription, perhaps in public opinion. And does the change in the nature of the penalty make the recommendation less a *law* of conduct for those to whom it is directed? I do not believe it is for the interest of religion to invite the civil magistrate to direct its exercises, its discipline, or its doctrines; nor of the religious societies, that the General Government should be invested with the power of effecting any uniformity of time or matter among them. Fasting and prayer are religious exercises; the enjoining them an act of discipline. Every religious society has a right to determine for itself the times for these exercises, and the objects proper for them, according to their own particular tenets; and this right can never be safer than in their own hands, where the Constitution has deposited it.

## Meteorite

### TO DANIEL SALMON.

WASHINGTON, *February 15, 1808.*

SIR,—I have duly received your letter of the 8th instant, on the subject of the stone in your possession, supposed meteoric. Its descent from the atmosphere presents so much difficulty as to require careful examination. But I do not know that the most effectual examination could be made by the members of the National Legislature, to whom you have thought of exhibiting it. Some fragments of these stones have been already handed about among them. But those most highly qualified for acting in *their* stations, are not necessarily supposed most familiar with subjects of natural history; and such of them as have that familiarity, are not in situations here to make the investigation. I should think that an inquiry by some one of our scientific societies, as the Philosophical Society of Philadelphia for example, would be most likely to be directed with such caution and knowledge of the subject, as would inspire a general confidence.

We certainly are not to deny whatever we cannot account for. A thousand phenomena present themselves daily which we cannot explain, but where facts are suggested, bearing no analogy with the laws of nature as yet known to us, their verity needs proofs proportioned to their difficulty. A cautious mind will weigh well the opposition of the phenomenon to everything hitherto observed, the strength of the testimony by which it is supported, and the errors and misconceptions to which even our senses are liable. It may be very difficult to explain how the stone you possess came into the position in which it was found. But is it easier to explain how it got into the clouds from whence it is supposed to have fallen? The actual fact however is the thing to be established, and this I hope will be done by those whose situations and qualifications enable them to do it. I salute you with respect.

# Man in the White House

## TO RICHARD M. JOHNSON.

WASHINGTON, *March 10, 1808.*

It has been a source of great pain to me, to have met with so many among our opponents, who had not the liberality to distinguish between political and social opposition; who transferred at once to the person, the hatred they bore to his political opinions. I suppose, indeed, that in public life, a man whose political principles have any decided character, and who has energy enough to give them effect, must always expect to encounter political hostility from those of adverse principles. But I came to the government under circumstances calculated to generate peculiar acrimony. . . . I became of course the butt of everything which reason, ridicule, malice and falsehood could supply. They have concentrated all their hatred on me, till they have really persuaded themselves, that I am the sole source of all their imaginary evils. I hope, therefore, that my retirement will abate some of their disaffection to the government of their country.

# Fur Trade

## TO JOHN JACOB ASTOR.

WASHINGTON, *April 13, 1808.*

I learn with great satisfaction the disposition of our merchants to form into companies for undertaking the Indian trade within our own territories. I have been taught to believe it an advantageous one for the individual adventurers, and I consider it as highly desirable to have that trade centered in the hands of our own citizens. The field is immense, and would occupy a vast extent of capital by different companies engaging in different districts. All beyond the Mississippi is ours exclusively, and it will be in our power to give our own traders great advantages over their foreign competitors on this side the Mississippi. You may be assured that in order to get the whole of this business passed into the hands of our own citizens, and to oust foreign traders, who so much abuse their privilege by endeavoring to excite the Indians to war on us, every reasonable patronage and facility in the power of the Executive will be afforded. I salute you with respect.

## On Cotton Culture

### TO MONSIEUR LASTEYRIE.

WASHINGTON, *July 15, 1808.*

I have no doubt the cotton plant will succeed in some of the southern parts of France. Whether its culture will be as advantageous as those they are now engaged in, remains to be tried. We could, in the United States, make as great a variety of wines as are made in Europe, not exactly of the same kinds, but doubtless as good. Yet I have ever observed to my countrymen, who think its introduction important, that a laborer cultivating wheat, rice, tobacco, or cotton here, will be able with the proceeds, to purchase double the quantity of the wine he could make. Possibly the same quantity of land and labor in France employed on the rich produce of your Southern counties, would purchase double the quantity of the cotton they would yield there. This however may prove otherwise on trial, and therefore it is worthy the trial. In general, it is a truth that if every nation will employ itself in what it is fittest to produce, a greater quantity will be raised of the things contributing to human happiness, than if every nation attempts to raise everything it wants within itself. . . .

When retired to rural occupations, as I shall be ere long, I shall . . . devote myself to occupations much more congenial with my inclinations than those to which I have been called by the character of the times into which my lot was cast. . . .

## Embargo Enforcement

### TO THE SECRETARY OF THE NAVY
### (JACOB CROWNINSHIELD).

WASHINGTON, *July 16, 1808.*

DEAR SIR,—Complaints multiply upon us of evasions of the embargo laws, by fraud and force. These come from Newport, Portland, Machias, Nantucket, Martha's Vineyard, etc., etc. As I do consider the severe enforcement of the embargo to be of an importance, not to be measured by money, for our future government as well as present objects, I think it will be advisable that during this summer all the gunboats, actually manned and in commission, should be distributed through as many ports and bays as may be necessary to assist the embargo.

## Indian Policy

TO THE SECRETARY OF WAR (HENRY DEARBORN).

MONTICELLO, *August 20, 1808.*

I hope the Governor will be able to settle with the Sacs and Foxes without war, to which, however, he seems too much committed. If we had gone to war for every hunter or trader killed, and murderer refused, we should have had general and constant war. The process to be followed, in my opinion, when a murder has been committed, is first to demand the murderer, and not regarding a first refusal to deliver, give time and press it. If perseveringly refused, recall all traders, and interdict commerce with them, until he be delivered. I believe this would rarely fail in producing the effect desired; and we have seen that, by steadily following this line, the tribes become satisfied of our moderation, justice, and friendship to them, and become firmly attached to us. The want of time to produce these dispositions in the Indians west of the Mississippi, has been the cause of the Kanzas, the Republican, the Great and the Wolf Panis, the Matas, and Poncaras, adhering to the Spanish interest against us. But if we use forbearance, and open commerce for them, they will come to, and give us time to attach them to us. The factories proposed on the Missouri and Mississippi, as soon as they can be in activity, will have more effect than as many armies. It is on their interests we must rely for their friendship, and not on their fears.

## Frontier Justice

TO GOVERNOR MERIWETHER LEWIS.

MONTICELLO, *August 24, 1808.*

Isham Lewis arrived here last night and tells me . . . that four Iowas had been delivered up to you as guilty of the murder which had been charged to the Sacs and Foxes, and that you supposed three of them would be hung. As there was but one white murdered by them, I should be averse to the execution of more than one of them, selecting the most guilty and worst character. Nothing but extreme criminality should induce the execution of a second, and nothing beyond that. Besides their idea that justice allows only man for man, that all beyond that is new aggression, which must be expiated by a new sacrifice of an equivalent number of our people, it is our great object to impress them with a firm persuasion that all our dispositions towards them are fatherly . . . There is the more reason for this moderation, as we know we cannot punish any murder which shall be committed by us on them. Even if the murderer can be taken, our juries have never yet convicted the murderer of an Indian.

# Natural Bridge

## TO ARCHIBALD STUART.

WASHINGTON, *October 22, 1808.*

DEAR SIR,—A Mr. William Jenkings, who lives four or five miles from the Natural Bridge, and whom I suppose to be a merchant, called on me two days ago to propose to purchase my lands at the bridge. I asked him some questions about the adjacent land in order to get his ideas of the value. He said the adjacent tract had been sold two or three times at about ten dollars and some of it as high as four pounds the acre. I enquired if the land on mine was as good. I think he said it was, but that it was all thin land, would not make a good farm, but that his object was to erect a public house there, as the curiosity of the bridge drew great numbers to see it. I told him the idea of selling it had never before presented itself to my mind, and he concluded to call on me at Monticello in March next.

# Decimal System

## TO THOMAS COOPER, ESQ.

WASHINGTON, *October 27, 1808.*

DEAR SIR,—When I received your letter of the 16th, I thought I had not a copy of my report on measures, weights, and coins, except one bound up in a volume with other reports; but on carefully searching a bundle of duplicates, I found the one I now enclose you, being the only detached one I possess. It is defective in one article. The report was composed under a severe attack of periodical headache, which came on every day at sunrise, and never left me till sunset. What had been ruminated in the day under a paroxysm of the most excruciating pain, was committed to paper by candlelight, and then the calculations were made. After delivering in the report, it was discovered that in calculating the money unit § 5 page 49, there was a small error in the third or fourth column of decimals, the correction of which however brought the proposed unit still nearer to the established one. I reported the correction in a single leaf to Congress. The copy I send you has not that leaf.

The first question to be decided is between those who are for units of measures, weights, and coins, having a known relation to something in nature of fixed dimension, and those who are for an arbitrary standard. On this *"dice vexata quaestio"* it is useless to say a word, every one having made up his mind on a view of all that can be said. Mr. Dorsey was so kind as to send me his pamphlet, by which I found he was for the arbitrary standard of one-third of the standard yard of H. G. of England, supposed to be in the Exchequer of that nation, a fac simile of which was to be procured and lodged in Philadelphia. I confess myself to be of the other sect, and to prefer an unit bearing a given relation to some fixed subject of nature, and of preference to the pendulum, because it may be in the possession of every man, so that he may verify his measures for himself. You will observe that I proposed alternative plans to Congress, that they might take the one or the other, according to the degree of courage they felt. The first is from page 18 to 38; the second from page 39 to 44. Were I now to decide, it would be in favor of the first, with this single addition, that each of the denominations there adopted, should be devisible decimally at the will of every individual. The iron-founder deals in tons; let him take the ton for his unit, and divide it into 10ths, 100ths, and 1000ths. The dry-goods merchant deals in pounds and yards; let him divide them decimally. The land-measurer deals in miles and poles; divide them decimally, only noting over his figures what the unit

Tons.    Lbs.    Yds.    Miles.

is, thus: 18.943, 18.943, 1.8943, 189.43, etc. I have lately had a proof how familiar this division into dimes, cents, and mills, is to the people when transferred from their money to anything else. I have an adometer fixed to my carriage, which gives the distances in miles, dimes, and cents. The people on the road inquire with curiosity what exact distance I have found from such a place to such a place; I answer, so many miles, so many cents. I find they universally and at once form a perfect idea of the relation of the cent to the mile as an unit. They would do the same as to yards of cloth, pounds of shot, ounces of silver, or of medicine. I believe, therefore, they are susceptible of this degree of approximation to a standard rigorously philosophical; beyond this I might doubt. However, on this too, every one has an opinion, and I am open to compromise, as I am also to other plans of reformation, of which multitudes have been published. I can conclude, therefore, candidly with the "*si quid novisti rectius*," etc., and sincerely with assurances of my constant esteem and respect.

## Peace at Any Price

TO HIS EXCELLENCY GOVERNOR CHARLES PINCKNEY.

WASHINGTON, *November 8, 1808.*

I seize the first moment it is in my power to answer your question as to our foreign relations, which I do by enclosing you a copy of my message this moment delivered to the two houses of Congress, in which they are fully stated. It is evident we have before us three only alternatives; 1, embargo; 2, war; 3, submission and tribute. This last will at once be put out of question by every American, and the two first only considered.

## Standards for the Young

TO THOMAS JEFFERSON RANDOLPH.

WASHINGTON, *November 24, 1808.*

When I recollect that at fourteen years of age, the whole care and direction of myself was thrown on myself entirely, without a relation or friend qualified to advise or guide me, and recollect the various sorts of bad company with which I associated from time to time, I am astonished I did not turn off with some of them, and become as worthless to society as they were. I had the good fortune to become acquainted very early with some characters of very high standing, and to feel the incessant wish that I could ever become what they were. Under temptations and difficulties, I would ask myself what would Dr. Small, Mr. Wythe, Peyton Randolph do in this situation? What course in it will insure me their approbation? I am certain that this mode of deciding on my conduct, tended more to correctness than any reasoning powers I possessed. Knowing the even and dignified line they pursued, I could never doubt for a moment which of two courses would be in character for them. Whereas, seeking the same object through a process of moral reasoning, and with the jaundiced eye of youth, I should often have erred. From the circumstances of my position, I was often thrown into the society of horse racers, card players, fox hunters, scientific and professional men, and of dignified men; and many a time have I asked myself, in the enthusiastic moment of the death of a fox, the victory of a favorite horse, the issue of a question eloquently argued at the bar, or in the great council of the nation, well, which of these kinds of reputation should I prefer? That of a horse jockey? a fox hunter? an orator? or the honest advocate of my country's rights? Be assured, my dear Jefferson, that these little returns into ourselves, this self-catechising habit, is not trifling nor useless, but leads to the prudent selection and steady pursuit of what is right.

I have mentioned good humor as one of the preservatives of our peace and tranquillity. It is among the most effectual, and its effect is so well imitated and aided, artificially, by politeness, that this also becomes an acquisition of first rate value. In truth, politeness is artificial good humor, it covers the natural want of it, and ends by rendering habitual a substitute nearly equivalent to the real virtue. It is the practice of sacrificing to those whom we meet in society, all the little conveniences and preferences which will gratify them, and deprive us of nothing worth a moment's consideration; it is the giving a pleasing and flattering turn to our expressions, which will conciliate others, and make them pleased with us as well as themselves. How cheap a price for the good will of another! When this is in return for a rude thing said by another, it brings him to his senses, it mortifies and corrects him in the most salutary way, and places him at the feet of your good nature, in the eyes of the company. But in stating prudential rules for our government in society, I must not omit the important one of never entering into dispute or argument with another. I never saw an instance of one of two disputants convincing the other by argument. I have seen many, on their getting warm, becoming rude, and shooting one another. Conviction is the effect of our own dispassionate reasoning, either in solitude, or weighing within ourselves, dispassionately, what we hear from others, standing uncommitted in argument ourselves. It was one of the rules which, above all others, made Doctor Franklin the most amiable of men in society, "never to contradict anybody." If he was urged to announce an opinion, he did it rather by asking questions, as if for information, or by suggesting doubts. When I hear another express an opinion which is not mine, I say to myself, he has a right to his opinion, as I to mine; why should I question it? His error does me no injury, and shall I become a Don Quixote, to bring all men by force of argument to one opinion? If a fact be misstated, it is probable he is gratified by a belief of it, and I have no right to deprive him of the gratification. If he wants information, he will ask it, and then I will give it in measured terms; but if he still believes his own story, and shows a desire to dispute the fact with me, I hear him and say nothing. It is his affair, not mine, if he prefers error.

## Mimosa Flowers

### TO ANNE CARY BANKHEAD.

WASHINGTON, *Dec. 8, 1808.*

MY DEAR ANNE,—Your letter of Nov. 26 came safely to hand, and in it the delicious flower of the Acacia, or rather the Mimosa Nilotica, from Mr. Lomax. The mother tree of full growth which I had when I gave him the small one, perished from neglect the first winter I was from home. Does his produce seed? If it does I will thank him for some, and you to take care of them; although he will think it a vain thing at my time of life to be planting a tree of as slow a growth. In fact the Mimosa Nilotica and Orange are the only things I have ever proposed to have in my green house. I like much your choice of books for your winter's reading. Middleton's Life of Cicero is among the most valuable accounts we have of the period of which he writes; and Tacitus I consider as the first writer in the world without a single exception. His book is a compound of history and morality of which we have no other example. In your arithmetic, if you keep yourself familiar with the four elementary operations of addition, subtraction, multiplication, and division, or rather of addition and division, because this last includes subtraction and multiplication, it is as much as you will need. The rule of three, of universal utility, is a thing of mere common-sense; for if one yard of cloth costs three dollars, common-sense will tell you that twenty yards will cost twenty multiplied by three.

## End of an Administration

### TO DOCTOR GEORGE LOGAN.

WASHINGTON, *December 27, 1808.*

I have within a few days had visits from the Pottawattamies, Miamis, Chippewas, Delawares, and Cherokees, and there arrived some yesterday, of, I believe, the Ottoways, Wyandots, and others of that neighborhood. Our endeavors are to impress on them all profoundly, temperance, peace, and agriculture; and I am persuaded they begin to feel profoundly the soundness of the advice.

Congress seems as yet to have been able to make up no opinion. Some are for taking off the embargo before they separate; others not till their meeting next autumn; but both with a view to substitute war, if no change takes place with the powers of Europe. A middle opinion is to have an extra session in May, to come then to a final decision. I have thought it right to take no part myself in proposing measures, the execution of which will devolve on my successor. I am therefore chiefly an unmeddling listener to what others say. On the same ground, I shall make no new appointments which can be deferred till the 4th of March, thinking it fair to leave to my successor to select the agents for his own administration. As the moment of my retirement approaches, I become more anxious for its arrival, and to begin at length to pass what yet remains to me of life and health in the bosom of my family and neighbors, and in communication with my friends, undisturbed by political concerns or passions.

## Due Balance

### TO THOMAS LEIPER.

WASHINGTON, *January 21, 1809.*

I have lately inculcated the encouragement of manufactures to the extent of our own consumption at least, in all articles of which we raise the raw material. On this the federal papers and meetings have sounded the alarm of Chinese policy, destruction of commerce, etc.; that is to say, the iron which we make must not be wrought here into ploughs, axes, hoes, etc., in order that the ship-owner may have the profit of carrying it to Europe, and bringing it back in a manufactured form, as if after manufacturing our own raw materials for our own use, there would not be a surplus produce sufficient to employ a due proportion of navigation in carrying it to market and exchanging it for those articles of which we have not the raw material. Yet this absurd hue and cry has contributed much to federalize New England, their doctrine goes to the sacrificing agriculture and manufactures to commerce; to the calling all our people from the interior country to the sea-shore to turn merchants, and to convert this great agricultural country into a city of Amsterdam. But I trust the good sense of our country will see that its greatest prosperity depends on a due balance between agriculture, manufactures and commerce, and not in this protuberant navigation which has kept us in hot water from the commencement of our government, and is now engaging us in war. That this may be avoided, if it can be done without a surrender of rights, is my sincere prayer. Accept the assurances of my constant esteem and respect.

## Civilized Correspondence

### TO JOHN HOLLINS.

WASHINGTON, *February 19, 1809.*

DEAR SIR,—A little transaction of mine, as innocent a one as I ever entered into, and where an improper construction was never less expected, is making some noise, I observe, in your city. I beg leave to explain it to you, because I mean to ask your agency in it. The last year, the Agricultural Society of Paris, of which I am a member, having had a plough presented to them, which, on trial with a graduated instrument, did equal work with half the force of their best ploughs, they thought it would be a benefit to mankind to communicate it. They accordingly sent one to me, with a view to its being made known here, and they sent one to the Duke of Bedford also, who is one of their members, to be made use of for England, although the two nations were then at war. By the Mentor, now going to France, I have given permission to two individuals in Delaware and New York, to import two parcels of Merino sheep from France, which they have procured there, and to some gentlemen in Boston, to import a very valuable machine which spins cotton, wool, and flax equally. The last spring, the Society informed me they were cultivating the cotton of the Levant and other parts of the Mediterranean, and wished to try also that of our southern States. I immediately got a friend to have two tierces of seed forwarded to me.

I had, on a like request, some time ago, (but before the embargo,) from the President of the Board of Agriculture of London, of which I am also a member, to send them some of the genuine May wheat of Virginia, forwarded to them two or three barrels of it. General Washington, in his time, received from the same Society the seed of the perennial succory, which Arthur Young had carried over from France to England, and I have since received from a member of it the seed of the famous turnip of Sweden, now so well known here. I mention these things, to show the nature of the correspondence which is carried on between societies instituted for the benevolent purpose of communicating to all parts of the world whatever useful is discovered in any one of them. These societies are always in peace, however their nations may be at war. Like the republic of letters, they form a great fraternity spreading over the whole earth, and their correspondence is never interrupted by any civilized nation.

## Prejudice Past

TO M. HENRI GREGOIRE, BISHOP AND SENATOR, PARIS.

WASHINGTON, *February 25, 1809.*

SIR,—I have received the favor of your letter of August 17th, and with it the volume you were so kind as to send me on the "Literature of Negroes." Be assured that no person living wishes more sincerely than I do, to see a complete refutation of the doubts I have myself entertained and expressed on the grade of understanding allotted to them by nature, and to find that in this respect they are on a par with ourselves. My doubts were the result of personal observation on the limited sphere of my own State, where the opportunities for the development of their genius were not favorable, and those of exercising it still less so. I expressed them therefore with great hesitation; but whatever be their degree of talent it is no measure of their rights. Because Sir Isaac Newton was superior to others in understanding, he was not therefore lord of the person or property of others. On this subject they are gaining daily in the opinions of nations, and hopeful advances are making towards their re-establishment on an equal footing with the other colors of the human family. I pray you therefore to accept my thanks for the many instances you have enabled me to observe of respectable intelligence in that race of men, which cannot fail to have effect in hastening the day of their relief.

## Mexican Independence

TO GENERAL JOHN ARMSTRONG.

WASHINGTON, *March 5, 1809.*

I suppose Napoleon will get possession of Spain; but her colonies will deliver themselves to any member of the Bourbon family. Perhaps Mexico will choose its sovereign within itself. He will find them much more difficult to subdue than Austria or Prussia; because an enemy (even in peace an enemy) possesses the element over which he is to pass to get at them; and a more powerful enemy (climate) will soon mow down his armies after arrival. This will be, without any doubt, the most difficult enterprise the emperor has ever undertaken. He may subdue the small colonies; he never can the old and strong; and the former will break off from him the first war he has again with a naval power.

I thank you for having procured for me the dynamometer which I have safely received, as well as the plough. Within two or three days I retire from scenes of difficulty, anxiety, and of contending passions, to the elysium of domestic affections, and the irresponsible direction of my own affairs. Safe in port myself, I shall look anxiously at my friends still buffeting the storm, and wish you all safe in port also.

## Back to the Land

### TO THE PRESIDENT OF THE UNITED STATES (JAMES MADISON).

MONTICELLO, *March 17, 1809.*

The spring is remarkably backward. No oats sown, not much tobacco seed, and little done in the gardens. Wheat has suffered considerably. No vegetation visible yet but the red maple, weeping willow and lilac. Flour is said to be at eight dollars at Richmond, and all produce is hurrying down.

I feel great anxiety for the occurrences of the ensuing four or five months. If peace can be preserved, I hope and trust you will have a smooth administration. I know no government which would be so embarrassing in war as ours. This would proceed very much from the lying and licentious character of our papers; but much, also, from the wonderful credulity of the members of Congress in the floating lies of the day. And in this no experience seems to correct them. I have never seen a Congress during the last eight years, a great majority of which I would not implicitly have relied on in any question, could their minds have been purged of all errors of fact. The evil, too, increases greatly with the protraction of the session, and I apprehend, in case of war, their session would have a tendency to become permanent.

## Commercial Limits

### TO GOVERNOR JAMES JAY.

MONTICELLO, *April 7, 1809.*

An equilibrium of agriculture, manufactures, and commerce, is certainly become essential to our independence. Manufactures, sufficient for our own consumption, of what we raise the raw material (and no more). Commerce sufficient to carry the surplus produce of agriculture, beyond our own consumption, to a market for exchanging it for articles we cannot raise (and no more). These are the true limits of manufactures and commerce. To go beyond them is to increase our dependence on foreign nations, and our liability to war.

These three important branches of human industry will then grow to-gether, and be really handmaids to each other.

## Skeptical Comment

### TO THE PRESIDENT OF THE UNITED STATES (JAMES MADISON).

MONTICELLO, *April 19, 1809.*

I have to acknowledge your favor of the 9th, and to thank you for the political information it contained. Reading the newspapers but little and that little but as the romance of the day, a word of truth now and then comes like the drop of water on the tongue of Dives. If the British ministry are changing their policy towards us, it is because their nation, or rather the city of London, which is the nation to them, is shaken as usual, by the late reverses in Spain. . . .

## Liberty and Libraries

### TO JOHN WYCHE.

MONTICELLO, *May 19, 1809.*

SIR,—Your favor of March 19th came to hand but a few days ago, and in-forms me of the establishment of the Westward Mill Library Society, of its general views and progress. I always hear with pleasure of institutions for the promotion of knowledge among my countrymen. The people of every country are the only safe guardians of their own rights, and are the only instruments which can be used for their destruction. And certainly they would never consent to be so used were they not deceived. To avoid this, they should be instructed to a certain degree. I have often thought that nothing would do more extensive good at small expense than the establish-ment of a small circulating library in every county, to consist of a few well-chosen books, to be lent to the people of the country, under such regulations as would secure their safe return in due time. These should be such as would give them a general view of other history, and particular view of that of their own country, a tolerable knowledge of Geography, the elements of Natural Philosophy, of Agriculture and Mechanics. Should your example lead to this, it will do great good.

# Rocky Mountain Sheep

## TO GENERAL WILLIAM CLARKE.

MONTICELLO, *September 10, 1809.*

DEAR GENERAL,—Your favor of June 2d came duly to hand in July, and brought me a repetition of the proofs of your kindness to me. Mr. Fitzhugh delivered the skin of the sheep of the Rocky Mountains to the President, from whom I expect to receive it in a few days at his own house. For this, as well as the blanket of Indian manufacture of the same material, which you are so kind as to offer me, accept my friendly thanks. Your donations, and Governor Lewis', have given to my collection of Indian curiosities an importance much beyond what I had ever counted on. The three boxes of bones which you had been so kind as to send to New Orleans for me, as mentioned in your letter of June 2d, arrived there safely, and were carefully shipped by the collector, and the bill of lading sent to me. But the vessel put into the Havana, under embargo distress, was there condemned as unseaworthy, and her enrollment surrendered at St. Mary's. What was done with my three boxes I have not learned, but have written to Mr. Brown, the collector, to have inquiry made after them. The bones of this animal are now in such a state of evanescence as to render it important to save what we can of them. Of those you had formerly sent me, I reserved a very few for myself; I got Dr. Wistar to select from the rest every piece which could be interesting to the Philosophical Society, and sent the residue to the National Institute of France. These have enabled them to decide that the animal was neither a mammoth nor an elephant, but of a distinct kind, to which they have given the name of Mastodont, from the protuberance of its teeth. These, from their forms, and the immense mass of their jaws, satisfy me this animal must have been arboriverous. Nature seems not to have provided other food sufficient for him, and the limb of a tree would be no more to him than a bough of a cotton tree to a horse.

# Diplomacy

## TO THE PRESIDENT OF THE UNITED STATES (JAMES MADISON).

MONTICELLO, *September 12, 1809.*

Canning's equivocations degrade his government as well as himself. I despair of accommodation with them, because I believe they are weak enough to intend seriously to claim the ocean as their conquest, and think to amuse us with embassies and negotiations, until the claim shall have been strengthened by time and exercise, and the moment arrive when they may boldly avow what hitherto they have only squinted at.

# Collector's Loss

## TO DOCTOR B. S. BARTON.

MONTICELLO, *September 21, 1809.*

DEAR SIR,—I received last night your favor of the 14th, and would with all possible pleasure have communicated to you any part or the whole of the Indian vocabularies which I had collected, but an irreparable misfortune has deprived me of them. I have now been thirty years availing myself of every possible opportunity of procuring Indian vocabularies to the same set of words; my opportunities were probably better than will ever occur again to any person having the same desire. I had collected about fifty, and had digested most of them in collateral columns, and meant to have printed them the last of my stay in Washington. But not having yet digested Captain Lewis' collection, nor having leisure then to do it, I put it off till I should return home. The whole, as well digest as originals, were packed in a trunk of stationery, and sent round by water with about thirty other packages of my effects from Washington, and while ascending James river, this package on account of its weight and presumed precious contents, was singled out and stolen. The thief being disappointed on opening it, threw into the river all its contents, of which he thought he could make no use. Among them were the whole of the vocabularies. Some leaves floated ashore and were found in the mud; but these were very few, and so defaced by the mud and water that no general use can be made of them. On the receipt of your letter I turned to them, and was very happy to find, that the only morsel of an original vocabulary among them, was Captain Lewis' of the Pani language, of which you say you have not one word. I therefore enclose it to you as it is, and a little fragment of some other, which I see is in his handwriting, but no indication remains on it of what language it is. It is a specimen of the condition of the little which was recovered. I am the more concerned at this accident, as of the two hundred and fifty words of my vocabularies, and the one hundred and thirty words of the great Russian vocabularies of the languages of the other quarters of the globe, seventy-three were common to both, and would have furnished materials for a comparison from which something might have resulted. Although I believe no general use can ever be made of the wrecks of my loss, yet I will ask the return of the Pani vocabulary when you are done with it. Perhaps I may make another attempt to collect, although I am too old to expect to make much progress in it.

I learn with pleasure your acquisition of the pamphlet on the astronomy of the ancient Mexicans. If it be ancient and genuine, or modern and rational, it will be of real value. It is one of the most interesting countries of our hemisphere, and merits every attention.

I am thankful for your kind offer of sending the original Spanish for my perusal. But I think it a pity to trust it to the accidents of the post, and whenever you publish the translation, I shall be satisfied to read that which shall be given by your translator, who is, I am sure, a greater adept in the language than I am.

## Moral Principles

### TO JAMES FISHBACK.

MONTICELLO, *September 27, 1809.*

Reading, reflection and time have convinced me that the interests of society require the observation of those moral precepts only in which all religions agree, (for all forbid us to murder, steal, plunder, or bear false witness,) and that we should not intermeddle with the particular dogmas in which all religions differ, and which are totally unconnected with morality. In all of them we see good men, and as many in one as another. The varieties in the structure and action of the human mind as in those of the body, are the work of our Creator, against which it cannot be a religious duty to erect the standard of uniformity. The practice of morality being necessary for the well-being of society, he has taken care to impress its precepts so indelibly on our hearts that they shall not be effaced by the subtleties of our brain. We all agree in the obligation of the moral precepts of Jesus, and nowhere will they be found delivered in greater purity than in his discourses. It is, then, a matter of principle with me to avoid disturbing the tranquillity of others by the expression of any opinion on the innocent questions on which we schismatize.

## Sheep from Spain

### TO GEORGE WASHINGTON IRVING, ESQ.

MONTICELLO, *November 23, 1809.*

SIR,—An American vessel, the property of a respectable merchant of Georgetown, on a voyage to some part of Europe for general purposes of commerce, proposes to touch at some part of Spain with the view of obtaining Merino sheep to be brought to our country. The necessity we are under, and the determination we have formed of emancipating ourselves from a dependence on foreign countries for manufactures which may be advantageously established among ourselves, has produced a very general desire to improve the quality of our wool by the introduction of the Merino race of sheep. Your sense of the duties you owe to your station will not permit me to ask, nor yourself to do any act which might compromit you with the government with which you reside, or forfeit that confidence on their part which can alone enable you to be useful to your country. But as far as that will permit you to give aid to the procuring and bringing away some of the valuable race, I take the liberty of soliciting you to do so—it will be an important service rendered to your country; to which you will be further encouraged by the assurance that the enterprise is solely on the behalf of agricultural gentlemen of distinguished character in Washington and its neighborhood, with a view of disseminating the benefits of their success as widely as they can.

## Bulldog Breed

TO THE PRESIDENT OF THE UNITED STATES (JAMES MADISON).

MONTICELLO, *November 26, 1809.*

The infatuation of the British government and nation is beyond everything imaginable. A thousand circumstances announce that they are on the point of being blown up, and they still proceed with the same madness and increased wickedness.

## Snows of Yesteryear

TO DR. N. CHAPMAN.

MONTICELLO, *December 11, 1809.*

The change which has taken place in our climate, is one of those facts which all men of years are sensible of, and yet none can prove by regular evidence; they can only appeal to each other's general observation for the fact. I remember that when I was a small boy, (say 60 years ago,) snows were frequent and deep in every winter—to my knee very often, to my waist sometimes—and that they covered the earth long. And I remember while yet young, to have heard from very old men, that in their youth, the winters had been still colder, with deeper and longer snows. In the year 1772, (37 years ago,) we had a snow two feet deep in the champaign parts of this State, and three feet in the counties next below the mountains. That year is still marked in conversation by the designation of "the year of the deep snow." But I know of no regular diaries of the weather very far back. In latter times, they might perhaps be found. While I lived at Washington, I kept a diary, and by recurring to that, I observe that from the winter of 1802–3, to that of 1808–9, inclusive, the average fall of snow of the seven winters was only fourteen and a half inches, and that the ground was covered but sixteen days in each winter on an average of the whole. The maximum in any one winter, during that period, was twenty-one inches fall, and thirty-four days on the ground. The change in our climate is very shortly noticed in the Notes on Virginia, because I had few facts to state but from my own recollections, then only of thirty or thirty-five years. Since that my whole time has been so completely occupied in public vocations, that I have been able to pay but little attention to this subject.

## Congressional Record

### TO JOHN WAYLES EPPES.

MONTICELLO, *January 17, 1810.*

I observe that the H. of R. are sensible of the ill effects of the long speeches in their house on their proceedings. But they have a worse effect in the disgust they excite among the people, and the disposition they are producing to transfer their confidence from the legislature to the executive branch, which would soon sap our Constitution. These speeches, therefore, are less and less read, and if continued will cease to be read at all.

## On Clericalism

### TO SAMUEL KERCHEVAL.

MONTICELLO, *January 19, 1810.*

SIR,—Yours of the 7th instant has been duly received, with the pamphlet enclosed, for which I return you my thanks. Nothing can be more exactly and seriously true than what is there stated: that but a short time elapsed after the death of the great reformer of the Jewish religion, before his principles were departed from by those who professed to be his special servants, and perverted into an engine for enslaving mankind, and aggrandizing their oppressors in Church and State: that the purest system of morals ever before preached to man has been adulterated and sophisticated by artificial constructions, into a mere contrivance to filch wealth and power to themselves: that rational men, not being able to swallow their impious heresies, in order to force them down their throats, they raise the hue and cry of infidelity, while themselves are the greatest obstacles to the advancement of the real doctrines of Jesus, and do, in fact, constitute the real Anti-Christ.

# Honorable Opposition

## TO JOEL BARLOW.

MONTICELLO, *January 24, 1810.*

I am sorry to learn that your rural occupations impede so much the progress of your much to be desired work. You owe to republicanism, and indeed to the future hopes of man, a faithful record of the *march* of this government, which may encourage the oppressed to go and do so likewise. Your talents, your principles, and your means of access to public and private sources of information, with the leisure which is at your command, point you out as the person who is to do this act of justice to those who believe in the improvability of the condition of man, and who have acted on that behalf, in opposition to those who consider man as a beast of burden made to be rode by him who has genius enough to get a bridle into his mouth.

The dissensions between two members of the Cabinet are to be lamented. But why should these force Mr. Gallatin to withdraw? They cannot be greater than between Hamilton and myself, and yet we served together four years in that way. We had indeed no personal dissensions. Each of us, perhaps, thought well of the other as a man, but as politicians it was impossible for two men to be of more opposite principles.

# World Hurricane

## TO CÆSAR A. RODNEY.

MONTICELLO, *February 10, 1810.*

It has been peculiarly unfortunate for us, personally, that the portion in the history of mankind, at which we were called to take a share in the direction of their affairs, was such an one as history has never before presented. At any other period, the even-handed justice we have observed towards all nations, the efforts we have made to merit their esteem by every act which candor or liberality could exercise, would have preserved our peace, and secured the unqualified confidence of all other nations in our faith and probity. But the hurricane which is now blasting the world, physical and moral, has prostrated all the mounds of reason as well as right.

It is a blessing, however, that our people are reasonable; that they are kept so well informed of the state of things as to judge for themselves, to see the true sources of their difficulties, and to maintain their confidence undiminished in the wisdom and integrity of their functionaries. *Macte virtute* therefore. Continue to go straight forward, pursuing always that which is right, as the only clue which can lead us out of the labyrinth. Let nothing be spared of either reason or passion, to preserve the public confidence entire, as the only rock of our safety. In times of peace the people look most to their representatives; but in war, to the executive solely. It is visible that their confidence is even now veering in that direction; that they are looking to the executive to give the proper direction to their affairs, with a confidence as auspicious as it is well founded.

## Proper Ploughing

### TO WILLIAM A. BURWELL.

MONTICELLO, *February 25, 1810.*

We have had the most devastating rain which has ever fallen within my knowledge. Three inches of water fell in the space of about an hour. Every hollow of every hill presented a torrent which swept everything before it. I have never seen the fields so much injured. Mr. Randolph's farm is the only one which has not suffered; his horizontal furrows arrested the water at every step till it was absorbed, or at least had deposited the soil it had taken up. Everybody in this neighborhood is adopting his method of ploughing, except tenants who have no interest in the preservation of the soil.

## Friendly Report

### TO GENERAL THADDEUS KOSCIUSKO.

MONTICELLO, *February 26, 1810.*

MY DEAR GENERAL AND FRIEND,—I have rarely written to you; never but by safe conveyances; and avoiding everything political, lest coming from one in the station I then held, it might be imputed injuriously to our country, or perhaps even excite jealousy of you. Hence my letters were necessarily dry. Retired now from public concerns, totally unconnected with them, and avoiding all curiosity about what is done or intended, what I say is from myself only, the workings of my own mind, imputable to nobody else.

Now a word as to myself. I am retired to Monticello, where, in the bosom of my family, and surrounded by my books, I enjoy a repose to which I have been long a stranger. My mornings are devoted to correspondence. From breakfast to dinner, I am in my shops, my garden, or on horseback among my farms; from dinner to dark, I give to society and recreation with my neighbors and friends; and from candle light to early bed-time, I read. My health is perfect; and my strength considerably reinforced by the activity of the course I pursue; perhaps it is as great as usually falls to the lot of near sixty-seven years of age. I talk of ploughs and harrows, of seeding and harvesting, with my neighbors, and of politics too, if they choose, with as little reserve as the rest of my fellow citizens, and feel, at length, the blessings of being free to say and do what I please, without being responsible for it to any mortal. A part of my occupation, and by no means the least pleasing, is the direction of the studies of such young men as ask it. They place themselves in the neighboring village, and have the use of my library and counsel, and make a part of my society. In advising the course of their reading, I endeavor to keep their attention fixed on the main objects of all science, the freedom and happiness of man. So that coming to bear a share in the councils and government of their country, they will keep ever in view the sole objects of all legitimate government.

## Bed of Roses

### TO DOCTOR WALTER JONES.

MONTICELLO, *March 5, 1810.*

Our difficulties are indeed great, if we consider ourselves alone. But when viewed in comparison to those of Europe, they are the joys of Paradise. In the eternal revolution of ages, the destinies have placed our portion of existence amidst such scenes of tumult and outrage, as no other period, within our knowledge, had presented. Every government but one on the continent of Europe, demolished, a conqueror roaming over the earth with havoc and destruction, a pirate spreading misery and ruin over the face of the ocean. Indeed, my friend, ours is a bed of roses. And the system of government which shall keep us afloat amidst the wreck of the world, will be immortalized in history. We have, to be sure, our petty squabbles and heart burnings, and we have something of the blue devils at times, as to these rawheads and bloodybones who are eating up other nations. But happily for us, the Mammoth cannot swim, nor the Leviathan move on dry land; and if we will keep out of their way, they cannot get at us.

## On Royalty

### TO GOVERNOR JOHN LANGDON.[1]

MONTICELLO, *March 5, 1810.*

For five and thirty years we have walked together through a land of tribulations. Yet these have passed away, and so, I trust, will those of the present day. The toryism with which we struggled in '77, differed but in name from the federalism of '99, with which we struggled also; and the Anglicism of 1808, against which we are now struggling, is but the same thing still in another form. It is a longing for a King, and an English King rather than any other. . . . It may be asked, what, in the nature of her

[1]Of New Hampshire.

government, unfits England for the observation of moral duties? In the first place, her King is a cypher; his only function being to name the oligarchy which is to govern her. The parliament is, by corruption, the mere instrument of the will of the administration. The real power and property in the government is in the great aristocratical families of the nation. The nest of office being too small for all of them to cuddle into at once, the contest is eternal, which shall crowd the other out. For this purpose, they are divided into two parties, the Ins and the Outs, so equal in weight that a small matter turns the balance. To keep themselves in, when they are in, every stratagem must be practiced, every artifice used which may flatter the pride, the passions or power of the nation. Justice, honor, faith must yield to the necessity of keeping themselves in place. The question whether a measure is moral, is never asked; but whether it will nourish the avarice of their merchants, or the piratical spirit of their navy, or produce any other effect which may strengthen them in their places. As to engagements, however positive, entered into by the predecessors of the Ins, why, they were their enemies; they did everything which was wrong; and to reverse everything which they did, must, therefore, be right. This is the true character of the English government in practice, however different its theory; and it presents the singular phenomenon of a nation, the individuals of which are as faithful to their private engagements and duties, as honorable, as worthy, as those of any nation on earth, and whose government is yet the most unprincipled at this day known. In an absolute government there can be no such equiponderant parties. The despot is the government. His power suppressing all opposition, maintains his ministers firm in their places. What he has contracted, therefore, through them, he has the power to observe with good faith; and he identifies his own honor and faith with that of his nation.

When I observed, however, that the King of England was a cypher, I did not mean to confine the observation to the mere individual now on that throne. The practice of Kings marrying only in the families of Kings, has been that of Europe for some centuries. Now, take any race of animals, confine them in idleness and inaction, whether in a stye, a stable or a state-room, pamper them with high diet, gratify all their sexual appetites, immerse them in sensualities, nourish their passions, let everything bend before them, and banish whatever might lead them to think, and in a few generations they become all body and no mind; and this, too, by a law of nature, by that very law by which we are in the constant practice of changing the characters and propensities of the animals we raise for our own purposes. Such is the regimen in raising Kings, and in this way they have gone on for centuries. While in Europe, I often amused myself with contemplating the characters of the then reigning sovereigns of Europe. Louis the XVI. was a fool, of my own knowledge, and in despite of the answers made for him at his trial. The King of Spain was a fool, and of Naples the same. They passed their lives in hunting, and despatched two couriers a week, one thousand miles, to let each other know what game they had killed the preceding days. The King of Sardinia was a fool. All these were Bourbons. The Queen of Portugal, a Braganza, was an idiot by nature. And so was the King of Denmark. Their sons, as regents, exercised the powers of government. The King of Prussia, successor to the great Frederick, was a mere hog in body as well as in mind. Gustavus of Sweden, and Joseph of Austria, were really crazy, and George of England, you know, was in a straight waistcoat. There remained, then, none but old Catharine, who had been too lately picked up to have lost her common sense. In this state Bonaparte found Europe; and it was this state of its rulers which lost it with scarce a struggle. These animals had become without mind and powerless; and so will every hereditary monarch be after a few generations. Alexander, the grandson of Catharine, is as yet an exception. He is able to hold his own. But he is only of the third generation. His race is not yet worn out. And so endeth the book of Kings, from all of whom the Lord deliver us, and have you, my friend, and all such good men and true, in His holy keeping.

## "The Finest Plough"

### TO ROBERT FULTON.

MONTICELLO, *April 16, 1810.*

DEAR SIR,—I received yesterday, on my return from a journey, your letter of March 28th and have to thank you for the drawing of your self-moving belier hydraulique, which a first reading shows to be simple and ingenious, and I have no doubt will answer. It shall have my early attention. The object of this prompt reply to your letter, is the offer you so kindly made of lending me your dynamometer. It will be the greatest favor you can do me.

The Agricultural Society of the Seine sent me one of Guillaume's famous ploughs, famous for taking but half the moving power of their best ploughs before used. They, at the same time, requested me to send them one of our best, with my mould board to it. I promised I would, as soon as I retired home and could see to its construction myself. In the meantime I wrote to a friend at Paris to send me a dynamometer, which he did. Unfortunately this, with some other valued articles of mine, was lost on its passage from Washington to Monticello. I have made the plough and am greatly deceived if it is not found to give less resistance than theirs. In fact I think it is the finest plough which has ever been constructed in America. But it is the actual experiment alone which can decide this, and I was with great reluctance about to send off the plough untried when I received your kind offer. I will pray you to send the instrument to Mr. Jefferson of Richmond by some careful passenger in the stage, who will see that it does not miscarry by the way; or by some vessel bound from New York direct to Richmond, which is the safest though slowest conveyance. I suppose there can never be a week that some vessel is not coming. I sincerely wish the torpedo may go the whole length you expect of putting down navies. I wish it too much not to become an easy convert and to give it all my prayers and interest.

## Letter of the Law

### TO J. B. COLVIN.

MONTICELLO, *September 20, 1810.*

The question you propose, whether circumstances do not sometimes occur, which make it a duty in officers of high trust, to assume authorities beyond the law, is easy of solution in principle, but sometimes embarrassing in practice. A strict observance of the written laws is doubtless *one* of the high duties of a good citizen, but it is not *the highest*. The laws of necessity, of self-preservation, of saving our country when in danger, are of higher obligation. To lose our country by a scrupulous adherence to written law, would be to lose the law itself, with life, liberty, property and all those who are enjoying them with us; thus absurdly sacrificing the end to the means. When, in the battle of Germantown, General Washington's army was annoyed from Chew's house, he did not hesitate to plant his cannon against it, although the property of a citizen. When he besieged York-town, he leveled the suburbs, feeling that the laws of property must be postponed to the safety of the nation. While the army was before York, the Governor of Virginia took horses, carriages, provisions and even men by force, to enable that army to stay together till it could master the public enemy; and he was justified. A ship at sea in distress for provisions, meets another having abundance, yet refusing a supply; the law of self-preservation authorizes the distressed to take a supply by force. In all these cases, the unwritten laws of necessity, of self-preservation, and of the public safety, control the written laws of *meum* and *tuum*. Further to exemplify the principle, I will state an hypothetical case. Suppose it had been made known to the Executive of the Union in the autumn of 1805, that we might have the Floridas for a reasonable sum, that that sum had not indeed been so appropriated by law, but that Congress were to meet within three weeks, and might appropriate it on the first or second day of their session. Ought he, for so great an advantage to his country, to have risked himself by transcending the law and making the purchase? The public advantage offered, in this supposed case, was indeed immense; but a reverence for law, and the probability that the advantage might still be *legally* accomplished by a delay of only three weeks, were powerful reasons against hazarding the act. But suppose it foreseen that a John Randolph would find means to protract the proceeding on it by Congress, until the ensuing spring, by which time new circumstances would change the mind of the other party. Ought the Executive, in that case, and with that foreknowledge, to have secured the good to his country, and to have trusted to their justice for the transgression of the law? I think he ought, and that the act would have been approved. After the affair of the Chesapeake, we thought war a very possible result. Our magazines were illy provided with some necessary articles, nor had any appropriations been made for their purchase. We ventured, however, to provide them, and to place our country in safety; and stating the case to Congress, they sanctioned the act.

It is incumbent on those only who accept of great charges, to risk themselves on great occasions, when the safety of the nation, or some of its very high interests are at stake. An officer is bound to obey orders; yet he would be a bad one who should do it in cases for which they were not intended, and which involved the most important consequences. The line of discrimination between cases may be difficult; but the good officer is bound to draw it at his own peril, and throw himself on the justice of his country and the rectitude of his motives.

## Supreme Court Vacancy

### TO ALBERT GALLATIN.

MONTICELLO, *September 27, 1810.*

At length, then, we have a chance of getting a republican majority in the supreme judiciary. For ten years has that branch braved the spirit and will of the nation, after the nation had manifested its will by a complete reform in every branch depending on them. The event is a fortunate one, and so timed as to be a God-send to me. I am sure its importance to the nation will be felt, and the occasion employed to complete the great operation they have so long been executing, by the appointment of a decided republican, with nothing equivocal about him. But who will it be? Was there ever a profound common lawyer known in any of the Eastern States? There never was, nor never can be one from those States. The basis of their law is neither common nor civil; it is an original, if any compound can so be called. Its foundation seems to have been laid in the spirit and principles of Jewish law, incorporated with some words and phrases of common law, and an abundance of notions of their own.

## On the Emperor of Russia

### TO COLONEL WILLIAM DUANE.

MONTICELLO, *November 13, 1810.*

Alexander is unquestionably a man of an excellent heart, and of very respectable strength of mind; and he is the only sovereign who cordially loves us. Bonaparte hates our government because it is a living libel on his. The English hate us because they think our prosperity filched from theirs. Of Alexander's sense of the merits of our form of government, of its wholesome operation on the condition of the people, and of the interest he takes in the success of our experiment, we possess the most unquestionable proofs; and to him we shall be indebted if the rights of neutrals, to be settled whenever peace is made, shall be extended beyond the present belligerents; that is to say, European neutrals, as George and Napoleon, of mutual consent and common hatred against us, would concur in excluding us. I thought it a salutary measure to engage the powerful patronage of Alexander at conferences for peace, at a time when Bonaparte was courting him; and although circumstances have lessened its weight, yet it is prudent for us to cherish his good dispositions, as those alone which will be exerted in our favor when that occasion shall occur. He, like ourselves, sees and feels the atrociousness of both the belligerents. I salute you with great esteem and respect.

## An Honest People

### TO JAMES RONALDSON.

MONTICELLO, *December 3, 1810.*

The hint to the two belligerents of disarming each other of their auxiliaries, by opening asylums to them and giving them passages to this country, is certainly a good one. Bonaparte has mind enough to adopt it, but not the means. England, again, has the means but not mind enough; she would prefer losing an advantage over her enemy to giving one to us. It is an unhappy state of mind for her, but I am afraid it is the true one. She presents a singular phenomenon of an honest people whose constitution, from its nature, must render their government forever dishonest; and accordingly, from the time that Sir Robert Walpole gave the constitution that direction which its defects permitted, morality has been expunged from their political code.

## Old Acquaintance

### TO DOCTOR BENJAMIN RUSH.

MONTICELLO, *January 16, 1811.*

I receive with sensibility your observations on the discontinuance of friendly correspondence between Mr. Adams and myself, and the concern you take in its restoration. This discontinuance has not proceeded from me, nor from the want of sincere desire and of effort on my part, to renew our intercourse. You know the perfect coincidence of principle and of

action, in the early part of the Revolution, which produced a high degree
of mutual respect and esteem between Mr. Adams and myself. Certainly
no man was ever truer than he was, in that day, to those principles of rational republicanism which, after the necessity of throwing off our monarchy, dictated all our efforts in the establishment of a new government.
And although he swerved, afterwards, towards the principles of the English constitution, our friendship did not abate on that account. While he
was Vice-President, and I Secretary of State, I received a letter from President Washington, then at Mount Vernon, desiring me to call together the
Heads of departments, and to invite Mr. Adams to join us (which, by-the-
bye, was the only instance of that being done) in order to determine on
some measure which required despatch; and he desired me to act on it,
as decided, without again recurring to him. I invited them to dine with me,
and after dinner, sitting at our wine, having settled our question, other
conversation came on, in which a collision of opinion arose between Mr.
Adams and Colonel Hamilton, on the merits of the British constitution,
Mr. Adams giving it as his opinion, that, if some of its defects and abuses
were corrected, it would be the most perfect constitution of government
ever devised by man. Hamilton, on the contrary, asserted, that with its
existing vices, it was the most perfect model of government that could be
formed; and that the correction of its vices would render it an impracticable
government. And this you may be assured was the real line of difference
between the political principles of these two gentlemen. Another incident
took place on the same occasion, which will further delineate Mr. Hamilton's political principles. The room being hung around with a collection
of the portraits of remarkable men, among them were those of Bacon,
Newton and Locke, Hamilton asked me who they were. I told him they
were my trinity of the three greatest men the world had ever produced,
naming them. He paused for some time: "the greatest man," said he, "that
ever lived, was Julius Cæsar." Mr. Adams was honest as a politician, as well
as a man; Hamilton honest as a man, but, as a politician, believing in the
necessity of either force or corruption to govern men.

You remember the machinery which the federalists played off, about
that time, to beat down the friends to the real principles of our Constitution, to silence by terror every expression in their favor, to bring us into
war with France and alliance with England, and finally to homologize our
Constitution with that of England. Mr. Adams, you know, was overwhelmed with feverish addresses, dictated by the fear, and often by the
pen, of the *bloody buoy*, and was seduced by them into some open indica-
tions of his new principles of government, and in fact, was so elated as to
mix with his kindness a little superciliousness towards me. Even Mrs.
Adams, with all her good sense and prudence, was sensibly flushed. And
you recollect the short suspension of our intercourse, and the circumstance
which gave rise to it, which you were so good as to bring to an early explanation, and have set to rights, to the cordial satisfaction of us all. The
nation at length passed condemnation on the political principles of the

federalists, by refusing to continue Mr. Adams in the Presidency. On the day on which we learned in Philadelphia the vote of the city of New York, which it was well known would decide the vote of the State, and that, again, the vote of the Union, I called on Mr. Adams on some official business. He was very sensibly affected, and accosted me with these words: "Well, I understand that you are to beat me in this contest, and I will only say that I will be as faithful a subject as any you will have." "Mr. Adams," said I, "this is no personal contest between you and me. Two systems of principles on the subject of government divide our fellow citizens into two parties. With one of these you concur, and I with the other. As we have been longer on the public stage than most of those now living, our names happen to be more generally known. One of these parties, therefore, has put your name at its head, the other mine. Were we both to die to-day, to-morrow two other names would be in the place of ours, without any change in the motion of the machinery. Its motion is from its principle, not from you or myself." "I believe you are right," said he, "that we are but passive instruments, and should not suffer this matter to affect our personal dispositions." But he did not long retain this just view of the subject. I have always believed that the thousand calumnies which the federalists, in bitterness of heart, and mortification at their ejection, daily invented against me, were carried to him by their busy intriguers, and made some impression. When the election between Burr and myself was kept in suspense by the federalists, and they were meditating to place the President of the Senate at the head of the government, I called on Mr. Adams with a view to have this desperate measure prevented by his negative. He grew warm in an instant, and said with a vehemence he had not used towards me before, "Sir, the event of the election is within your own power. You have only to say you will do justice to the public creditors, maintain the navy, and not disturb those holding offices, and the government will instantly be put into your hands. We know it is the wish of the people it should be so." "Mr. Adams," said I, "I know not what part of my conduct, in either public or private life, can have authorized a doubt of my fidelity to the public engagements. I say, however, I will not come into the government by capitulation. I will not enter on it, but in perfect freedom to follow the dictates of my own judgment." I had before given the same answer to the same intimation from Gouverneur Morris. "Then," said he, "things must take their course." I turned the conversation to something else, and soon took my leave. It was the first time in our lives we had ever parted with anything like dissatisfaction. And then followed those scenes of midnight appointment, which have been condemned by all men. The last day of his political power, the last hours, and even beyond the midnight, were employed in filling all offices, and especially permanent ones, with the bitterest federalists, and providing for me the alternative, either to execute the government by my enemies, whose study it would be to thwart and defeat all my measures, or to incur the odium of such numerous removals from office, as might bear me down. A little time and reflection effaced in my mind this temporary dissatisfaction with Mr. Adams, and restored me to that just estimate of his virtues and passions, which a long acquaintance had enabled me to fix.

## Last Hope

### TO COLONEL WILLIAM DUANE.

MONTICELLO, *March 28, 1811.*

I do not know whether I am able at present to form a just idea of the situation of our country. If I am, it is such as, during the *bellum omnium in omnia* of Europe, will require the union of all its friends to resist its enemies within and without. . . .

The last hope of human liberty in this world rests on us. We ought, for so dear a state, to sacrifice every attachment and every enmity. Leave the President free to choose his own coadjutors, to pursue his own measures, and support him and them, even if we think we are wiser than they, honester than they are, or possessing more enlarged information of the state of things. If we move in mass, be it ever so circuitously, we shall attain our object; but if we break into squads, every one pursuing the path he thinks most direct, we become an easy conquest to those who can now barely hold us in check. I repeat again, that we ought not to schismatize on either men or measures. Principles alone can justify that. If we find our government in all its branches rushing headlong, like our predecessors, into the arms of monarchy, if we find them violating our dearest rights, the trial by jury, the freedom of the press, the freedom of opinion, civil or religious, or opening on our peace of mind or personal safety the sluices of terrorism, if we see them raising standing armies, when the absence of all other danger points to these as the sole objects on which they are to be employed, then indeed let us withdraw and call the nation to its tents. But while our functionaries are wise, and honest, and vigilant, let us move compactly under their guidance, and we have nothing to fear. Things may here and there go a little wrong. It is not in their power to prevent it. But all will be right in the end, though not perhaps by the shortest means.

## Of Latin America

### TO BARON ALEXANDER VON HUMBOLDT.

MONTICELLO, *April 14, 1811.*

. . . Those countries are beginning to be interesting to the whole world. They are now becoming the scenes of political revolution, to take their stations as integral members of the great family of nations. All are now in insurrection. In several, the Independents are already triumphant, and they will undoubtedly be so in all. What kind of government will they establish? How much liberty can they bear without intoxication? Are their chiefs sufficiently enlightened to form a well-guarded government, and their people to watch their chiefs? Have they mind enough to place their domesticated Indians on a footing with the whites? All these questions you can answer better than any other. I imagine they will copy our outlines of confederation and elective government, abolish distinction of ranks, bow the neck to their priests, and persevere in intolerantism. Their greatest difficulty will be in the construction of their executive. I suspect that, regardless of the experiment of France, and of that of the United States in 1784, they will begin with a directory, and when the unavoidable schisms in that kind of executive shall drive them to something else, their great question will come on whether to substitute an executive elective for years, for life, or an hereditary one. But unless instruction can be spread among them more rapidly than experience promises, despotism may come upon them before they are qualified to save the ground they will have gained.

## Suppressed Book

TO MONSIEUR PAGANEL.

MONTICELLO, *April 15, 1811.*

SIR,—I received, through Mr. Warden, the copy of your valuable work on the French Revolution, for which I pray you to accept my thanks. That its sale should have been suppressed is no matter of wonder with me. The friend of liberty is too feelingly manifested, not to give umbrage to its enemies. We read in it, and weep over, the fatal errors which have lost to nations the present hope of liberty, and to reason for fairest prospect of its final triumph over all imposture, civil and religious. The testimony of one who himself was an actor in the scenes he notes, and who knew the true mean between rational liberty and the frenzies of demagogy, are a tribute to truth of inestimable value. The perusal of this work has given me new views of the causes of failure in a revolution of which I was a witness in its early part, and then augured well of it. I had no means, afterwards, of observing its progress but the public papers, and their information came through channels too hostile to claim confidence. An acquaintance with many of the principal characters, and with their fate, furnished me grounds for conjectures, some of which you have confirmed, and some corrected. Shall we ever see as free and faithful a tableau of subsequent acts of this deplorable tragedy? Is reason to be forever amused with the *hochets* of physical sciences, in which she is indulged merely to divert her from solid speculations on the rights of man, and wrongs of his oppressors? It is impossible. The day of deliverance will come, although I shall not live to see it. The art of printing secures us against the retrogradation of reason and information, the examples of its safe and wholesome guidance in government, which will be exhibited through the wide-spread regions of the American continent, will obliterate, in time, the impressions left by the abortive experiment of France. With my prayers for the hastening of that auspicious day, and for the due effect of the lessons of your work to those who ought to profit by them, accept the assurances of my great esteem and respect.

## On Taxing the Rich

### TO GENERAL THADDEUS KOSCIUSKO.

MONTICELLO, *April 13, 1811.*

Knowing your affections to this country, and the interest you take in whatever concerns it, I therein gave you a tableau of its state when I retired from the administration. Peace . . . has been our principle, peace is our interest, and peace has saved to the world this only plant of free and rational government now existing in it. If it can still be preserved, we shall soon see the final extinction of our national debt, and liberation of our revenues for the defence and improvement of our country.

These revenues will be levied entirely on the rich, the business of household manufacture being now so established that the farmer and laborer clothe themselves entirely. The rich alone use imported articles, and on these alone the whole taxes of the General Government are levied. The poor man who uses nothing but what is made in his own farm or family, or within his own country, pays not a farthing of tax to the general government, but on his salt; and should we go into that manufacture also, as is probable, he will pay nothing. Our revenues liberated by the discharge of the public debt, and its surplus applied to canals, roads, schools, etc., the farmer will see his government supported, his children educated, and the face of his country made a paradise by the contributions of the rich alone, without his being called on to spend a cent from his earnings. However, therefore, we may have been reproached for pursuing our Quaker system, time will affix the stamp of wisdom on it, and the happiness and prosperity of our citizens will attest its merit. And this, I believe, is the only legitimate object of government, and the first duty of governors . . .

And behold! another example of man rising in his might and bursting the chains of his oppressor, and in the same hemisphere. Spanish America is all in revolt. The insurgents are triumphant in many of the States, and will be so in all. But there the danger is that the cruel arts of their oppressors have enchained their minds, have kept them in the ignorance of children, and as incapable of self-government as children. If the obstacles of bigotry and priest-craft can be surmounted, we may hope that common sense will suffice to do everything else. God send them a safe deliverance.

# Lecture Subject

## TO JAMES OGILVIE.

MONTICELLO, *August 4, 1811.*

What would you think of a discourse on the benefit of the union, and miseries which would follow a separation of the States, to be exemplified in the eternal and wasting wars of Europe, in the pillage and profligacy to which these lead, and the abject oppression and degradation to which they reduce its inhabitants?

# On Gardening

## TO CHARLES W. PEALE.

POPLAR FOREST, *August 20, 1811.*

Here, as you know, we are all farmers, but not in a pleasing style. We have so little labor in proportion to our land that, although perhaps we make more profit from the same labor, we cannot give to our grounds that style of beauty which satisfies the eye of the amateur. Our rotations are corn, wheat, and clover, or corn, wheat, clover and clover, or wheat, corn, wheat, clover and clover; preceding the clover by a plastering. But some, instead of clover, substitute mere rest, and all are slovenly enough. We are adding the care of Merino sheep. I have often thought that if heaven had given me choice of my position and calling, it should have been on a rich spot of earth,. well watered, and near a good market for the productions of the garden. No occupation is so delightful to me as the culture of the earth, and no culture comparable to that of the garden. Such a variety of subjects, some one always coming to perfection, the failure of one thing repaired by the success of another, and instead of one harvest a continued one through the year. Under a total want of demand except for our family table, I am still devoted to the garden. But though an old man, I am but a young gardener.

# Astronomical Observations

## TO H. A. S. DEARBORN.

MONTICELLO, *November 15, 1811.*

SIR,—Your favor of October 14 was duly received, and with it Mr. Bowditch's observations on the comet, for which I pray you to accept my thanks, and be so good as to present them to Mr. Bowditch also. I am much pleased to find that we have so able a person engaged in observing the path of this great phenomenon.

With respect to the eclipse of September 17. I know of no observations made in this State but my own, although I had no doubt that others had observed it. I used myself an equatorial telescope, and was aided by a friend who happened to be with me, and observed through an achromatic telescope of Dollard's. Two others attended the time-pieces. I had a perfect observation of the passage of the sun over the meridian, and the eclipse commencing but a few minutes after, left little room for error in our time. This little was corrected by the known rate of going of the clock. But we as good as lost the first appulse by a want of sufficiently early attention to be at our places, and composed.

## Friendship Renewed

### TO JOHN ADAMS.

MONTICELLO, *January 21, 1812.*

DEAR SIR,—I thank you beforehand (for they are not yet arrived) for the specimens of homespun you have been so kind as to forward me by post. I doubt not their excellence, knowing how far you are advanced in these things in your quarter. Here we do little in the fine way, but in coarse and middling goods a great deal. Every family in the country is a manufactory within itself, and is very generally able to make within itself all the stouter and middling stuffs for its own clothing and household use. We consider a sheep for every person in the family as sufficient to clothe it, in addition to the cotton, hemp and flax which we raise ourselves. For fine stuff we shall depend on your northern manufactories. Of these, that is to say, of company establishments, we have none. We use little machinery. The spinning jenny, and loom with the flying shuttle, can be managed in a family; but nothing more complicated. The economy and thriftiness resulting from our household manufactures are such that they will never again be laid aside; and nothing more salutary for us has ever happened than the British obstructions to our demands for their manufactures. Restore free intercourse when they will, their commerce with us will have totally changed its form, and the articles we shall in future want from them will not exceed their own consumption of our produce.

A letter from you calls up recollections very dear to my mind. It carries me back to the times when, beset with difficulties and dangers, we were fellow laborers in the same cause, struggling for what is most valuable to man, his right of self-government. Laboring always at the same oar, with some wave ever ahead, threatening to overwhelm us . . . In your day, French depredations; in mine, English, and the Berlin and Milan decrees; now, the English orders of council, and the piracies they authorize. When these shall be over, it will be the impressment of our seamen or something else; and so we have gone on, and so we shall go on, puzzled and prospering beyond example in the history of man. And I do believe we shall continue to growl, to multiply and prosper until we exhibit an association, powerful, wise and happy, beyond what has yet been seen by men. As for France and England, with all their preëminence in science, the one is a den of robbers, and the other of pirates. And if science produces no better fruits than tyranny, murder, rapine and destitution of national morality, I would rather wish our country to be ignorant, honest and estimable, as our neighboring savages are. But whither is senile garrulity leading me? Into politics, of which I have taken final leave. I think little of them and say less. I have given up newspapers in exchange for Tacitus and Thucydides, for Newton and Euclid, and I find myself much the happier. Sometimes, indeed, I look back to former occurrences, in remembrance of our old friends and fellow laborers, who have fallen before us. Of the signers of the Declaration of Independence, I see now living not more than half a dozen on your side of the Potomac, and on this side, myself alone. You and I have been wonderfully spared, and myself with remarkable health, and a considerable activity of body and mind. I am on horseback three or four hours of every day; visit three or four times a year a possession I have ninety miles distant, performing the winter journey on horseback.

## Spark Once Kindled

### TO BENJAMIN GALLOWAY.

MONTICELLO, *February 2, 1812.*

I hope and firmly believe that the whole world will, sooner or later, feel benefit from the issue of our assertion of the rights of man. Although the horrors of the French Revolution have damped for awhile the ardor of the patriots in every country, yet it is not extinguished—it will never die. The sense of right has been excited in every breast, and the spark will be rekindled by the very oppressions of that detestable tyranny employed to quench it. The errors of the honest patriots of France, and the crimes of her Dantons and Robespierres, will be forgotten in the more encouraging contemplation of our sober example, and steady march to our object. Hope will strengthen the presumption that what has been done once may be done again.

## Object of Government

### TO F. A. VAN DER KEMP.

MONTICELLO, *March 22, 1812.*

The only orthodox object of the institution of government is to secure the greatest degree of happiness possible to the general mass of those associated under it. The events which this work proposes to embrace will establish the fact that unless the mass retains sufficient control over those intrusted with the powers of their government, these will be perverted to their own oppression, and to the perpetuation of wealth and power in the individuals and their families selected for the trust. Whether our Constitution has hit on the exact degree of control necessary, is yet under experiment; and it is a most encouraging reflection that distance and other difficulties securing us against the brigand governments of Europe, in the safe enjoyment of our farms and firesides, the experiment stands a better chance of being satisfactorily made here than on any occasion yet presented by history.

## Friendly Enemies

### TO JAMES MAURY.

MONTICELLO, *April 25, 1812.*

MY DEAR AND ANCIENT FRIEND AND CLASSMATE,—Our two countries are to be at war, but not you and I. And why should our two countries be at war, when by peace we can be so much more useful to one another? Surely the world will acquit our government from having sought it. . . .
The English newspapers suppose me the personal enemy of their nation. I am not so. I am an enemy to its injuries, as I am to those of France. . . . Had I been personally hostile to England, and biased in favor of either the character or views of her great antagonist, the affair of the Chesapeake put war into my hand. I had only to open it and let havoc loose. But if ever I was gratified with the possession of power, and of the confidence of those who had entrusted me with it, it was on that occasion when I was enabled to use both for the prevention of war, towards which the torrent of passion here was directed almost irresistibly, and when not another person in the United States, less supported by authority and favor, could have resisted it.

## Indian Farewell

### TO JOHN ADAMS.

MONTICELLO, *June 11, 1812.*

. . . So much in answer to your inquiries concerning Indians, a people with whom, in the early part of my life, I was very familiar, and acquired impressions of attachment and commiseration for them which have never been obliterated. Before the Revolution, they were in the habit of coming often and in great numbers to the seat of government, where I was very much with them. I knew much the great Ontasseté, the warrior and orator of the Cherokees; he was always the guest of my father, on his journeys to and from Williamsburg. I was in his camp when he made his great fare-well oration to his people the evening before his departure for England. The moon was in full splendor, and to her he seemed to address himself in his prayers for his own safety on the voyage, and that of his people during his absence; his sounding voice, distinct articulation, animated action, and the solemn silence of his people at their several fires, filled me with awe and veneration, although I did not understand a word he uttered. That nation, consisting now of about 2,000 warriors, and the Creeks of about 3,000 are far advanced in civilization. They have good cabins, enclosed fields, large herds of cattle and hogs, spin and weave their own clothes of cotton, have smiths and other of the most necessary tradesmen, write and read, are on the increase in numbers, and a branch of Cherokees is now instituting a regular representative government. Some other tribes are advancing in the same line. On those who have made any progress, English seductions will have no effect. But the backward will yield, and be thrown further back. Those will relapse into barbarism and misery, lose numbers by war and want, and we shall be obliged to drive them with the beasts of the forest into the stony mountains.

## On Dangerous Praise

### TO ELBRIDGE GERRY.

MONTICELLO, *June 11, 1812.*

I do not condole with you on your release from your government. The vote of your opponents is the most honorable mark by which the sound-ness of your conduct could be stamped. I claim the same honorable testi-monial. There was but a single act of my whole administration of which that party approved. That was the proclamation on the attack of the Chesa-peake. And when I found they approved of it, I confess I began strongly to apprehend I had done wrong, and to exclaim with the Psalmist, "Lord, what have I done that the wicked should praise me!"

## Travellers' Tales

### TO NATHANIEL GREENE.

MONTICELLO, *July 5, 1812.*

SIR,—Your favor of May 19th, from New Orleans is just now received. I have no doubt that the information you will present to your countrymen on the subject of the Asiatic countries into which you have travelled, will be acceptable as sources both of amusement and instruction; and the more so, as the observations of an American will be more likely to present what are peculiarities to us, than those of any foreigner on the same countries.

In reading the travels of a Frenchman through the United States what he remarks as peculiarities in us, prove to us the contrary peculiarities of the French. We have the accounts of Barbary from European and American travellers. It would be more amusing if Melli Melli would give us his observations on the United States. If, with the foibles and follies of the Hindoos, so justly pointed out to us by yourselves and other travellers, we could compare the contrast of those which an Hindoo traveller would imagine he found among us, it might enlarge our instruction. It would be curious to see what parallel among us he would select for his Veeshni. What you will have seen in your western tour will also instruct many who often know least of things nearest home.

## Building the Capitol

### TO B. H. LATROBE.

MONTICELLO, *July 12, 1812.*

I am sorry to learn that Congress has relinquished the benefit of the engagements of Andrei & Franzoni, on the sculpture of the Capitol. They are artists of a grade far above what we can expect to get again. With respect to yourself, the little disquietudes from individuals not chosen for their taste in works of art, will be sunk into oblivion, while the Representatives' chamber will remain a durable monument of your talents as an architect. I say nothing of the Senate room, because I have never seen it. I shall live in the hope that the day will come when an opportunity will be given you of finishing the middle building in a style worthy of the two wings, and worthy of the first temple dedicated to the sovereignty of the people, embellishing with Athenian taste the course of a nation looking far beyond the range of Athenian destinies.

## Privateers' War

### TO GENERAL THADDEUS KOSCIUSKO.

MONTICELLO, *August 5, 1812.*

I have little to add to my letter of June. We have entered Upper Canada, and I think there can be no doubt of our soon having in our possession the whole of the St. Lawrence except Quebec. We have at this moment about two hundred privateers on the ocean, and numbers more going out daily. It is believed we shall fit out about a thousand in the whole. Their success has been already great, and I have no doubt they will cut up more of the commerce of England than all the navies of Europe could do, could those navies venture to sea at all. You will find that every sea on the globe where England has any commerce, and where any port can be found to sell prizes, will be filled with our privateers. God bless you and give you a long and happy life.

## Perpetual Motion

TO DR. ROBERT PATTERSON.

MONTICELLO, *December 27, 1812.*

I am very thankful to you for the description of Redhefer's machine. I had never before been able to form an idea of what his principle of deception was. He is the first of the inventors of perpetual motion within my knowledge, who has had the cunning to put his visitors on a false pursuit, by amusing them with a sham machinery whose loose and vibratory motion might impose on them the belief that it is the real source of the motion they see. To this device he is indebted for a more extensive delusion than I have before witnessed on this point. We are full of it as far as this State, and I know not how much farther. In Richmond they have done me the honor to quote me as having said that it was a possible thing. A poor Frenchman who called on me the other day, with another invention of perpetual motion, assured me that Dr. Franklin, many years ago, expressed his opinion to him that it was not impossible. Without entering into contest on this abuse of the Doctor's name, I gave him the answer I had given to others before, that the Almighty himself could not construct a machine of perpetual motion while the laws exist which He has prescribed for the government of matter in our system; that the equilibrium established by Him between cause and effect must be suspended to effect that purpose. But Redhefer seems to be reaping a rich harvest from the public deception. The office of science is to instruct the ignorant.

## Cotton Is King

TO JAMES RONALDSON.

MONTICELLO, *January 12, 1813.*

I have been long endeavoring to procure the Cork tree from Europe, but without success. A plant which I brought with me from Paris died after languishing some time, and of several parcels of acorns received from a correspondent at Marseilles, not one has ever vegetated. I shall continue my endeavors, although disheartened by the nonchalance of our Southern fellow citizens, with whom alone they can thrive. It is now twenty-five years since I sent them two shipments (about 500 plants) of the Olive tree of Aix, the finest Olives in the world. If any of them still exist, it is merely as a curiosity in their gardens; not a single orchard of them has been planted. I sent them also the celebrated species of Sainfoin,[1] from Malta, which yields good crops without a drop of rain through the season. It was lost. The upland rice which I procured fresh from Africa and sent them, has been preserved and spread in the upper parts of Georgia, and I believe in Kentucky. But we must acknowledge their services in furnishing us an abundance of cotton, a substitute for silk, flax and hemp. The ease with which it is spun will occasion it to supplant the two last, and its cleanliness the first. Household manufacture is taking deep root with us. I have a carding machine, two spinning machines, and looms with the flying shuttle in full operation for clothing my own family; and I verily believe that by the next winter this State will not need a yard of imported coarse or middling clothing. I think we have already a sheep for every inhabitant, which will suffice for clothing, and one-third more, which a single year will add, will furnish blanketing.

## On Men and Principles

### TO JOHN MELISH.

MONTICELLO, *January 13, 1813.*

DEAR SIR,—I received duly your favor of December the 15th, and with it the copies of your map and travels, for which be pleased to accept my thanks. The book I have read with extreme satisfaction and information. As to the Western States, particularly, it has greatly edified me; for of the actual condition of that interesting portion of our country, I had not an adequate idea. I feel myself now as familiar with it as with the condition of the maritime States. I had no conception that manufactures had made such progress there, and particularly of the number of carding and spinning machines dispersed through the whole country. . . . I have not formerly been an advocate for great manufactories. I doubted whether our labor, employed in agriculture, and aided by the spontaneous energies of the earth, would not procure us more than we could make ourselves of other necessaries. But other considerations entering into the question, have settled my doubts.

Amidst this mass of approbation which is given to every other part of the work, there is a single sentiment which I cannot help wishing to bring to what I think the correct one. . . . Stating in volume one, page sixty-three, the principle of difference between the two great political parties here, you conclude it to be, "whether the controlling power shall be vested in this or that set of men." That each party endeavors to get into the administration of the government, and exclude the other from power, is true, and may be stated as a motive of action: but this is only secondary; the

[1]Called Sulia.

primary motive being a real and radical difference of political principle. . . . An honest man can feel no pleasure in the exercise of power over his fellow citizens.

Power is not alluring to pure minds, and is not, with them, the primary principle of contest. This is my belief of it; it is that on which I have acted; and had it been a mere contest who should be permitted to administer the government according to its genuine republican principles, there has never been a moment of my life in which I should have relinquished for it the enjoyments of my family, my farm, my friends and books.

You expected to discover the difference of our party principles in General Washington's valedictory, and my inaugural address. Not at all. General Washington did not harbor one principle of federalism. He was neither an Angloman, a monarchist, nor a separatist. He sincerely wished the people to have as much self-government as they were competent to exercise themselves. The only point on which he and I ever differed in opinion, was, that I had more confidence than he had in the natural integrity and discretion of the people, and in the safety and extent to which they might trust themselves with a control over their government.

## Many Inventions

### TO ROBERT FULTON.

MONTICELLO, *March 8, 1813.*

DEAR SIR,—It has been some time since I have tried the experiments for which you were so kind as to lend me your dynamometer and the reconveyance by sea and under the care of some passenger. This to New York never happens from our quarter, to Philadelphia once or twice a year only, if I knew with whom to lodge it there for you. To Washington I could more frequently send it. I must, therefore, ask your instructions on this subject.

A Mr. Abraham Howard Quincy, number 108 Chatham street, New York, informs me he has made an improvement in fireplaces, such as that with one-tenth of the fuel ordinarily laid on a fire and that kept up but one hour in five, maintains summer temperature in the room, and he has requested me to ask some friend in whom I have confidence to call on him and receive his demonstrations of it. I have no acquaintance there whose turn is mechanical, of whom I could ask this; but it occurs to me that you may possibly be there occasionally, and that your affection to improvements in the arts might induce you to take the trouble to examine this one, my confidence in your judgment as to the reality of the improvement would settle my opinion. I would therefore ask you to give a leisure moment to this examination.

I rejoice at your success in your steamboats and have no doubt they will be the source of great wealth to yourself and permanent blessing to your country. I hope your torpedoes will equally triumph over doubting friends and presumptuous enemies.

# Ideology

## TO COLONEL WILLIAM DUANE.

MONTICELLO, *April 4, 1813.*

DEAR SIR,—Your favor of February 14th has been duly received, and the MS. of the commentary on Montesquieu is also safe at hand. I now forward to you the work of Tracy, which you will find a valuable supplement and corrective to those we already possess on political economy. It is a little unlucky that its outset is of a metaphysical character, which may damp the ardor of perusal in some readers. He has been led to this by a desire to embody this work, as well as a future one he is preparing on morals, with his former treatise on Ideology. By-the-bye, it is merely to this work that Bonaparte alludes in his answer to his Council of State, published not long since, in which he scouts "the dark and metaphysical doctrine of Ideology, which, diving into first causes, founds on this basis a legislation of the people, etc." If, indeed, this answer be not a forgery, for everything is now forged, even to the fat of our beef and mutton: yet the speech is not unlike him, and affords scope for an excellent parody . . . made known. But the book will make its way, and will become a standard work. A copy which I sent to France was under translation by one of the ablest men of that country.

It is true that I am tired of practical politics, and happier while reading the history of ancient than of modern times. The total banishment of all moral principle from the code which governs the intercourse of nations, the melancholy reflection that after the mean, wicked and cowardly cunning of the cabinets of the age of Machiavelli had given place to the integrity and good faith which dignified the succeeding one of a Chatham and Turgot, that this is to be swept away again by the daring profligacy and avowed destitution of all moral principle of a Cartouche and a Blackbeard, sickens my soul unto death. I turn from the contemplation with loathing, and take refuge in the histories of other times, where, if they also furnish their Tarquins, their Catilines and Caligulas, their stories are handed to us under the brand of a Livy, a Sallust and a Tacitus, and we are comforted with the reflection that the condemnation of all succeeding generations has confirmed the censures of the historian, and consigned their memories to everlasting infamy, a solace we cannot have with the Georges and Napoleons but by anticipation.

In surveying the scenes of which we make a part, I confess that three frigates taken by our gallant little navy, do not balance in my mind three armies lost by the treachery, cowardice, or incapacity of those to whom they were intrusted. I see that our men are good, and only want generals.

We may yet hope, however, that the talents which always exist among men will show themselves with opportunity, and that it will be found that this age also can produce able and honest defenders of their country, at what further expense, however, of blood and treasure, is yet to be seen. Perhaps this Russian mediation may cut short the history of the present war, and leave to us the laurels of the sea, while our enemies are bedecked with those of the land. This would be the reverse of what has been expected, and perhaps of what was to be wished.

## Contour Ploughing

### TO CHARLES W. PEALE.

MONTICELLO, *April 17, 1813.*

Your position that a small farm well worked and well manned will produce more than a larger one ill-tended, is undoubtedly true in a certain degree. There are extremes in this as in all other cases. The true medium may really be considered and stated as a mathematical problem: "Given the quantum of labor within our command, and land ad libitum offering its spontaneous contributions: required the proportion in which these two elements should be employed to produce a maximum." It is a difficult problem, varying probably in every country according to the relative value of land and labor. The spontaneous energies of the earth are a gift of nature, but they require the labor of man to direct their operation. And the question is so to husband his labor as to turn the greatest quantity of this useful action of the earth to his benefit. Ploughing deep, your recipe for killing weeds, is also the recipe for almost everything good in farming. The plough is to the farmer what the wand is to the sorcerer. Its effect is really like sorcery. In the country wherein I live we have discovered a new use for it, equal in value almost to its services before known. Our country is hilly and we have been in the habit of ploughing in straight rows whether up and down hill, in oblique lines, or however they lead; and our soil was all rapidly running into the rivers. We now plough horizontally, following the curvatures of the hills and hollows, on the dead level, however crooked the lines may be. Every furrow thus acts as a reservoir to receive and retain the waters, all of which go to the benefit of the growing plant, instead of running off into the streams. In a farm horizontally and deeply ploughed, scarcely an ounce of soil is now carried off from it. In point of beauty nothing can exceed that of the waving lines and rows winding along the face of the hills and valleys. The horses draw much easier on the dead level, and it is in fact a conversion of hilly grounds into a plain. The improvement of our soil from this cause the last half dozen years strikes every one with wonder. For this improvement we are indebted to my son-in-law, Mr. Randolph, the best farmer, I believe, in the United States, and who has taught us to make more than two blades of corn to grow where only one grew before. If your farm is hilly, let me beseech you to make a trial of this method. To direct the plough horizontally we take a rafter level of this form ⟨/A⟩. A boy of thirteen or fourteen is able to work it round the hill, a still smaller one with a little hough marking the points traced by the feet of the level. The plough follows running through these marks. The leveller having completed one level line through the field, moves with his level 30 or 40 yards up or down the hill, and runs another which is marked in like manner and traced by the plough, and having thus run what may be called guide furrows every 30 or 40 yards through the field, the ploughman runs the furrows of the intervals parallel to these. In proportion, however, as the declevity of the hill varies in different parts of the line, the guide furrows will approach or recede from each other in different parts, and the parallel furrows will at length touch in one part when far asunder in others, leaving unploughed gores between them. These gores we plough separately. They occasion short rows and turnings which are a little inconvenient, but not materially so. I pray you to try this recipe for hilly grounds. You will say with me, "Probatum est," and I shall have the happiness of being of some use to you, and through your example to your neighbors, and of adding something solid to the assurances of my great esteem and respect.

# Letter to a Lady

## TO MADAME LA BARONNE DE STAËL-HOLSTEIN.

### UNITED STATES OF AMERICA, *May 24, 1813.*

I received with great pleasure, my dear Madam and friend, your letter of November the 10th, from Stockholm, and am sincerely gratified by the occasion it gives me of expressing to you the sentiments of high respect and esteem which I entertain for you. It recalls to my remembrance a happy portion of my life, passed in your native city; then the seat of the most amiable and polished society of the world, and of which yourself and your venerable father were such distinguished members. But of what scenes has it since been the theatre, and with what havoc has it overspread the earth! Robespierre met the fate, and his memory the execration, he so justly merited. The rich were his victims, and perished by thousands. It is by millions that Bonaparte destroys the poor, and he is eulogized and deified by the syncophants even of science. These merit more than the mere oblivion to which they will be consigned; and the day will come when a just posterity will give to their hero the only preëminence he has earned, that of having been the greatest of the destroyers of the human race. What year of his military life has not consigned a million of human beings to death, to poverty and wretchedness! What field in Europe may not raise a monument of the murders, the burnings, the desolations, the famines and miseries it has witnessed from him! And all this to acquire a reputation, which Cartouche attained with less injury to mankind, of being fearless of God or man. . . .

Shall I apologize to you my dear Madam, for this long political letter? But yours justifies the subject, and my feelings must plead for the unreserved expression of them; and they have been the less reserved, as being from a private citizen, retired from all connection with the government of his country, and whose ideas, expressed without communication with any one, are neither known, nor imputable to them.

The dangers of the sea are now so great, and the possibilities of interception by sea and land such, that I shall subscribe no name to this letter. You will know from whom it comes, by its reference to the date of time and place of yours, as well as by its subject in answer to that.

## The Indian Mystery

### TO JOHN ADAMS.

MONTICELLO, *May 27, 1813.*

Another of our friends of seventy-six is gone, my dear Sir, another of the co-signers of the Independence of our country. And a better man than Rush could not have left us, more benevolent, more learned, of finer genius, or more honest. We too must go; and that ere long. I believe we are under half a dozen at present; I mean the signers of the Declaration. Yourself, Gerry, Carroll, and myself, are all I know to be living. I am the only one south of the Potomac. Is Robert Treat Payne, or Floyd living? It is long since I heard of them, and yet I do not recollect to have heard of their deaths.

Moreton's deduction of the origin of our Indians from the fugitive Trojans, stated in your letter of January the 26th, and his manner of accounting for the sprinkling of their Latin with Greek, is really amusing. Adair makes them talk Hebrew. Reinold Foster derives them from the soldiers sent by Kouli Khan to conquer Japan. Brerewood, from the Tartars, as well as our bears, wolves, foxes, etc., which, he says, "must of necessity fetch their beginning from Noah's ark, which rested, after the deluge in Asia, seeing they could not proceed by the course of nature, as the imperfect sort of living creatures do, from putrefaction." Bernard Romans is of opinion that God created an original man and woman in this part of the globe. Doctor Barton thinks they are not specifically different from the Persians; but, taking afterwards a broader range, he thinks, "that in all the vast countries of America, there is but one language, nay, that it may be proven, or rendered highly probable, that all the languages of the earth bear some affinity together." This reduces it to a question of definition, in which every one is free to use his own: to wit, what constitutes identity, or difference in two things, in the common acceptation of *sameness?* All languages may be called the same, as being all made up of the same primitive sounds, expressed by the letters of the different alphabets. But, in this sense, all things on earth are the same as consisting of matter. This gives up the useful distribution into genera and species, which we form, arbitrarily indeed, for the relief of our imperfect memories. To aid the question, from whence our Indian tribes descended, some have gone into their religion, their morals, their manners, customs, habits, and physical forms. By such helps it may be learnedly proved, that our trees and plants of every kind are descended from those of Europe; because, like them, they have no locomotion, they draw nourishment from the earth, they clothe themselves with leaves in spring, of which they divest themselves in autumn for the sleep of winter, etc. Our animals too must be descended from those of Europe, because our wolves eat lambs, our deer are gregarious, our ants hoard, etc.

## On Human Progress

### TO JOHN ADAMS.

MONTICELLO, *June 15, 1813.*

By your kind quotation of the dates of my two letters, I have been enabled to turn to them. They had completely vanished from my memory. The last is on the subject of religion, and by its publication will gratify the priesthood with new occasion of repeating their comminations against me. They wish it to be believed that he can have no religion who advocates its freedom. The first letter is political. . . . One of the questions, you know, on which our parties took different sides, was on the improvability of the human mind in science, in ethics, in government, etc. Those who advocated reformation of institutions, *pari passu* with the progress of science, maintained that no definite limits could be assigned to that progress. The enemies of reform, on the other hand, denied improvement, and advocated steady adherence to the principles, practices and institutions of our fathers, which they represented as the consummation of wisdom, and acme of excellence, beyond which the human mind could never advance. Although in the passage of your answer alluded to, you expressly disclaim the wish to influence the freedom of inquiry, you predict that that will produce nothing more worthy of transmission to posterity than the principles, institutions and systems of education received from their ancestors. I do not consider this as your deliberate opinion. You possess, yourself, too much science, not to see how much is still ahead of you, unexplained and unexplored. Your own consciousness must place you as far before our ancestors as in the rear of our posterity.

About facts you and I cannot differ; because truth is our mutual guide. And if any opinions you may express should be different from mine, I shall receive them with the liberality and indulgence which I ask for my own, and still cherish with warmth the sentiments of affectionate respect, of which I can with so much truth tender you the assurance.

# Duration of Debt

TO JOHN W. EPPES.

MONTICELLO, *June 24, 1813.*

It is a wise rule, and should be fundamental in a government disposed to cherish its credit, and at the same time to restrain the use of it within the limits of its faculties, "never to borrow a dollar without laying a tax in the same instant for paying the interest annually, and the principal within a given term; and to consider that tax as pledged to the creditors on the public faith." On such a pledge as this, sacredly observed, a government may always command, on a *reasonable interest,* all the lendable money of their citizens, while the necessity of an equivalent tax is a salutary warning to them and their constituents against oppressions, bankruptcy, and its inevitable consequence, revolution. But the term of redemption must be moderate, and at any rate within the limits of their rightful powers. But what limits, it will be asked, does this prescribe to their powers? What is to hinder them from creating a perpetual debt? The laws of nature, I answer. The earth belongs to the living, not to the dead. . . . We may consider each generation as a distinct nation, with a right, by the will of its majority, to bind themselves, but none to bind the succeeding generation, more than the inhabitants of another country. . . . Suppose the annual births of the State of New York to be twenty-three thousand nine hundred and ninety-four, the whole number of its inhabitants, according to Buffon, will be six hundred and seventeen thousand seven hundred and three, of all ages. Of these there would constantly be two hundred and sixty-nine thousand two hundred and eighty-six minors, and three hundred and forty-eight thousand four hundred and seventeen adults, of which last, one hundred and seventy-four thousand two hundred and nine will be a majority. Suppose that majority, on the first day of the year 1794, had borrowed a sum of money equal to the fee-simple value of the State, and to have consumed it in eating, drinking and making merry in their day; or, if you please, in quarrelling and fighting with their unoffending neighbors. Within eighteen years and eight months, one-half of the adult citizens were dead. Till then, being the majority, they might rightfully levy the interest of their debt annually on themselves and their fellow revelers, or fellow champions. But at that period, say at this moment, a new majority have come into place, in their own right, and not under the rights, the conditions, or laws of their predecessors. Are they bound to acknowledge the debt, to consider the preceding generation as having had a right to eat up the whole soil of their country, in the course of a life, to alienate it from them, (for it would be an alienation to the creditors,) and would they think themselves either legally or morally bound to give up their country and emigrate to another for subsistence? Every one will say no; that the soil is the gift of God to the living, as much as it had been to the deceased generation; and that the laws of nature impose no obligation on them to pay this debt. And although, like some other natural rights, this has not yet entered into any declaration of rights, it is no less a law, and ought to be acted on by honest governments. It is, at the same time, a salutary curb on the spirit of war and indebtment, which, since the modern theory of the perpetuation of debt, has drenched the earth with blood, and crushed its inhabitants under burdens ever accumulating.

## Conflict Remembered

### TO JOHN ADAMS.

MONTICELLO, *June 27, 1813.*

The *summum bonum* with me is now truly epicurian, ease of body and tranquillity of mind; and to these I wish to consign my remaining days. Men have differed in opinion, and been divided into parties by these opinions, from the first origin of societies, and in all governments where they have been permitted freely to think and to speak. The same political parties which now agitate the United States, have existed through all time. Whether the power of the people or that of the αριστοι should prevail, were questions which kept the States of Greece and Rome in eternal convulsions, as they now schismatize every people whose minds and mouths are not shut up by the gag of a despot. And in fact, the terms of whig and tory belong to natural as well as to civil history. They denote the temper and constitution of mind of different individuals. To come to our own country, and to the times when you and I became first acquainted, we well remember the violent parties which agitated the old Congress, and their bitter contests. There you and I were together, and the Jays, and the Dickinsons, and other anti-independents, were arrayed against us. They cherished the monarchy of England, and we the rights of our countrymen. When our present government was in the mew, passing from Confederation to Union, how bitter was the schism between the Feds and Antis! Here you and I were together again. For although, for a moment, separated by the Atlantic from the scene of action, I favored the opinion that nine States should confirm the constitution, in order to secure it, and the others hold off until certain amendments, deemed favorable to freedom, should be made. I rallied in the first instant to the wiser proposition of Massachusetts, that all should confirm, and then all instruct their delegates to urge those amendments. The amendments were made, and all were reconciled to the government. But as soon as it was put into motion, the line of division was again drawn. We broke into two parties, each wishing to give the government a different direction; the one to strengthen the most popular branch, the other the more permanent branches, and to extend their permanence. Here you and I separated for the first time, and as we had been longer than most others on the public theatre, and our names therefore were more familiar to our countrymen, the party which considered you as thinking with them, placed your name at their head; the other, for the same reason, selected mine. But neither decency nor inclination permitted us to become the advocates of ourselves, or to take part personally in the violent contests which followed. We suffered ourselves, as you so well expressed it, to be passive subjects of public discussion. And these discussions, whether relating to men, measures or opinions, were conducted by the parties with an animosity, a bitterness and an indecency which had never been exceeded. All the resources of reason and of wrath were exhausted by each party in support of its own, and to prostrate the adversary opinions; one was upbraided with receiving the anti-federalists, the other the old tories and refugees, into their bosom. Of this acrimony, the public papers of the day exhibit ample testimony, in the debates of Congress, of State Legislatures, of stump-orators, in addresses, answers, and newspaper essays; and to these, without question, may be added the private correspondences of individuals; and the less guarded in these, because not meant for the public eye, not restrained by the respect due to that, but poured forth from the overflowings of the heart into the bosom of a friend, as a momentary easement of our feelings. In this way, and in answers to addresses, you and I could indulge ourselves. We have probably done it, sometimes with warmth, often with prejudice, but always, as we believed, adhering to truth.

## National Interest

### TO JAMES MADISON.

MONTICELLO, *July 13, 1813.*

Mr. Fulton's ingenuity is inexhaustible and his disinterested devotion of it to his country very laudable. If his present device depended on me, I should try it on the judgment of an officer so well skilled as Decatur. It is one of those experiments which neither the personal interest nor the faculties of a private individual can ever bring into use, while it is highly interesting to the nation. Intersected as we are by many and deep waters, and unable to meet the enemy on them with an equal force, our only hope is in the discovery of the means which ingenuity may devise whereby the weak may defend themselves against the strong. This is done at land by fortifications, and not being against any law of nature, we may hope that something equivalent may be discovered for the water.

## Diving Boats

### TO ROBERT FULTON.

MONTICELLO, *July 21, 1813.*

DEAR SIR,—Immediately on the receipt of your favor of July 8th I forwarded it to the President, and had no hesitation in expressing my own wish that it should be tried. In fact as we cannot meet the British with an equality of physical force, we must supply it by other devices, in which I know nobody equal to yourself and so likely to point out to us a mode of salvation.

Accordingly I hope this honor is reserved for you, and that either by subaqueous guns, torpedoes, or diving boats you will accomplish it by the aid of government. . . . I confess I have more hopes of the mode of destruction by the submarine boat than any other. No law of nature opposes it, and in that case nothing is to be despaired of by human invention, nor particularly by yours.

Accept the just tribute of an American citizen, and of a friend in the assurances of my great esteem and respect.

## Patents and Monopolies

### TO ISAAC MCPHERSON.

MONTICELLO, *August 13, 1813.*

It has been pretended by some, (and in England especially,) that inventors have a natural and exclusive right to their inventions, and not merely for their own lives, but inheritable to their heirs. But while it is a moot question whether the origin of any kind of property is derived from nature at all, it would be singular to admit a natural and even an hereditary right to inventors. It is agreed by those who have seriously considered the subject, that no individual has, of natural right, a separate property in an acre of land, for instance. By an universal law, indeed, whatever, whether fixed or movable, belongs to all men equally and in common, is the property for the moment of him who occupies it, but when he relinquishes the occupation, the property goes with it. Stable ownership is the gift of social law, and is given late in the progress of society. It would be curious then, if an idea, the fugitive fermentation of an individual brain, could, of natural right, be claimed in exclusive and stable property. If nature has made any one thing less susceptible than all others of exclusive property, it is the action of the thinking power called an idea, which an individual may exclusively possess as long as he keeps it to himself; but the moment it is divulged, it forces itself into the possession of every one, and the receiver cannot dispossess himself of it. Its peculiar character, too, is that no one possesses the less, because every other possesses the whole of it. He who receives an idea from me, receives instruction himself without lessening mine; as he who lights his taper at mine, receives light without darkening me. That ideas should freely spread from one to another over the globe, for the moral and mutual instruction of man, and improvement of his condition, seems to have been peculiarly and benevolently designed by nature, when she made them, like fire, expansible over all space, without lessening their density in any point, and like the air in which we breathe, move, and have our physical being, incapable of confinement or exclusive appropriation. Inventions then cannot, in nature, be a subject of property. Society may give an exclusive right to the profits arising from them, as an encouragement to men to pursue ideas which may produce utility, but this may or may not be done, according to the will and convenience of the society, without claim or complaint from anybody. Accordingly, it is a fact, as far as I am informed, that England was, until we copied her, the only country on earth which ever, by a general law, gave a legal right to the exclusive use of an idea. In some other countries it is sometimes done, in a great case, and by a special and personal act, but, generally speaking, other nations have thought that these monopolies produce more embarrassment than advantage to society; and it may be observed that the nations which refuse monopolies of invention, are as fruitful as England in new and useful devices.

## The American Language

### TO JOHN WALDO.

MONTICELLO, *August 16, 1813.*

I have been pleased to see that in all cases you appeal to usage, as the arbiter of language; and justly consider that as giving law to grammar, and not grammar to usage. I concur entirely with you in opposition to Purists, who would destroy all strength and beauty of style, by subjecting it to a rigorous compliance with their rules.

. . . I have been not a little disappointed, and made suspicious of my own judgment, on seeing the Edinburgh Reviewers, the ablest critics of the age, set their faces against the introduction of new words into the English language; they are particularly apprehensive that the writers of the United States will adulterate it. Certainly so great growing a population, spread over such an extent of country, with such a variety of climates, of productions, of arts, must enlarge their language, to make it answer its purpose of expressing all ideas, the new as well as the old. The new circumstances under which we are placed, call for new words, new phrases, and for the transfer of old words to new objects. An American dialect will therefore be formed; so will a West-Indian and Asiatic, as a Scotch and an Irish are already formed. But whether will these adulterate, or enrich the English language? Has the beautiful poetry of Burns, or his Scottish dialect, disfigured it? Did the Athenians consider the Doric, the Ionian, the Æolic, and other dialects, as disfiguring or as beautifying their language? Did they fastidiously disavow Herodotus, Pindar, Theocritus, Sappho, Alcæus, or Grecian writers? On the contrary, they were sensible that the variety of dialects, still infinitely varied by poetical license, constituted the riches of their language, and made the Grecian Homer the first of poets.

# Time for Reading

## TO ABIGAIL ADAMS (MRS. JOHN ADAMS).

MONTICELLO, *August 22, 1813.*

DEAR MADAM,—A kind note at the foot of Mr. Adams' letter of July 15 reminds me of the duty of saluting you with friendship and respect, a duty long suspended by the unremitting labors of public engagement and which ought to have been sooner revived, since I am the proprietor of my own time. And yet so it is, that in no course of life have I been ever more closely pressed by business than in the present. Much of this proceeds from my own affairs, much from the calls of others; leaving little time for indulgence in my greatest of all amusements, reading. Dr. Franklin used to say that when he was young and had time to read he had not books; and now when he has become old and had books, he had no time. Perhaps it is that when habit has strengthened our sense of duties, they leave us no time for other things; but when young we neglect them and this gives us time for anything.

However, I will now take time to ask you how you do, how you have done? and to express the interest I take in whatever affects your happiness. . . .

I have compared notes with Mr. Adams on the score of progeny and find I am ahead of him and think I am in a fair way to keep so. I have ten and one-half grandchildren, and two and three-fourths great-grandchildren, and these fractions will ere long become units.

I was glad to learn from Mr. Adams that you have a grandson far enough advanced in age and acquirements to be reading Greek. These young scions give us comfortable cares, when we cease to care about ourselves. Under all circumstances of health or sickness, of blessing or affliction, I tender you assurances of my sincere affection and respect.

# On Public Works

## TO JOHN W. EPPES.

POPLAR FOREST, *September 11, 1813.*

The objects of finance in the United States have hitherto been very simple; merely to provide for the support of the government on its peace establishment, and to pay the debt contracted in the Revolutionary war, a war which will be sanctioned by the approbation of posterity through all future ages. The means provided for these objects were ample, and resting on a consumption which little affected the poor, may be said to have been sensibly felt by none. The fondest wish of my heart ever was that the surplus portion of these taxes, destined for the payment of that debt, should, when that object was accomplished, be continued by annual or biennial re-enactments, and applied, in time of peace, to the improvement of our country by canals, roads and useful institutions, literary or others. . . .

## Heretics in Heaven

TO WILLIAM CANBY.

MONTICELLO, *September 18, 1813.*

An eloquent preacher of your religious society, Richard Motte, in a discourse of much emotion and pathos, is said to have exclaimed aloud to his congregation, that he did not believe there was a Quaker, Presbyterian, Methodist or Baptist in heaven, having paused to give his hearers time to stare and to wonder. He added, that in heaven, God knew no distinctions, but considered all good men as his children, and as brethren of the same family. I believe, with the Quaker preacher, that he who steadily observes those moral precepts in which all religions concur, will never be questioned at the gates of heaven, as to the dogmas in which they all differ. That on entering there, all these are left behind us, and the Aristides and Catos, the Penns and Tillotsons, Presbyterians and Baptists, will find themselves united in all principles which are in concert with the reason of the supreme mind. Of all the systems of morality, ancient or modern, which have come under my observation, none appear to me so pure as that of Jesus. He who follows this steadily need not, I think, be uneasy, although he cannot comprehend the subtleties and mysteries erected on his doctrines by those who, calling themselves his special followers and favorites, would make him come into the world to lay snares for all understandings but theirs. These metaphysical heads, usurping the judgment seat of God, denounce as his enemies all who cannot perceive the Geometrical logic of Euclid in the demonstrations of St. Athanasius, that three are one, and one is three; and yet that the one is not three nor the three one. In all essential points you and I are of the same religion; and I am too old to go into inquiries and changes as to the unessential.

## On Aristocrats

TO JOHN ADAMS.

MONTICELLO, *October 28, 1813.*

I agree with you that there is a natural aristocracy among men. The grounds of this are virtue and talents. Formerly, bodily powers gave place among the aristoi. But since the invention of gunpowder has armed the weak as well as the strong with missile death, bodily strength, like beauty, good humor, politeness and other accomplishments, has become but an auxiliary ground of distinction. There is also an artificial aristocracy, founded on wealth and birth, without either virtue or talents; for with these it would belong to the first class. The natural aristocracy I consider as the most precious gift of nature, for the instruction, the trusts, and government of society. And indeed, it would have been inconsistent in creation to have formed man for the social state, and not to have provided virtue and wisdom enough to manage the concerns of the society. May we not even say, that that form of government is the best, which provides the most effectually for a pure selection of these natural aristoi into the offices of government?

The artificial aristocracy is a mischievous ingredient in government, and provision should be made to prevent its ascendency. On the question, what is the best provision, you and I differ; but we differ as rational friends, using the free exercise of our own reason, and mutually indulging its errors. You think it best to put the pseudo-aristoi into a separate chamber of legislation, where they may be hindered from doing mischief by their co-ordinate branches, and where, also, they may be a protection to wealth against the agrarian and plundering enterprises of the majority of the people. I think that to give them power in order to prevent them from doing mischief, is arming them for it, and increasing instead of remedying the evil. For if the co-ordinate branches can arrest their action, so may they that of the co-ordinates. Mischief may be done negatively as well as positively. Of this, a cabal in the Senate of the United States has furnished many proofs. Nor do I believe them necessary to protect the wealthy; because enough of these will find their way into every branch of the legislation, to protect themselves. From fifteen to twenty legislatures of our own, in action for thirty years past, have proved that no fears of an equalization of property are to be apprehended from them. I think the best remedy is exactly that provided by all our constitutions, to leave to the citizens the free election and separation of the aristoi from the pseudo-aristoi, of the wheat from the chaff. In general they will elect the really good and wise. In some instances, wealth may corrupt, and birth blind them; but not in sufficient degree to endanger the society.

It is probable that our difference of opinion may, in some measure, be produced by a difference of character in those among whom we live. From what I have seen of Massachusetts and Connecticut myself, and still more from what I have heard, and the character given of the former by yourself, who know them so much better, there seems to be in those two States a traditionary reverence for certain families, which has rendered the offices of the government nearly hereditary in those families. I presume that from an early period of your history, members of those families happening to possess virtue and talents, have honestly exercised them for the good of the people, and by their services have endeared their names to them.

In Virginia . . . laws, drawn by myself, laid the axe to the foot of pseudo-aristocracy. And had another which I prepared been adopted by the legislature, our work would have been complete. It was a bill for the more general diffusion of learning. This proposed to divide every county into wards of five or six miles square, like your townships; to establish in each ward a free school for reading, writing and common arithmetic; to provide for the annual selection of the best subjects from these schools, who might receive, at the public expense, a higher degree of education at a district school; and from these district schools to select a certain number of the most promising subjects, to be completed at an university, where all the useful sciences should be taught. Worth and genius would thus have been sought out from every condition of life, and completely prepared by education for defeating the competition of wealth and birth for public trusts.

With respect to aristocracy, we should further consider, that before the establishment of the American States, nothing was known to history but the man of the old world, crowded within limits either small or overcharged, and steeped in the vices which that situation generates. A government adapted to such men would be one thing; but a very different one, that for the man of these States. . . .

But even in Europe a change has sensibly taken place in the mind of man. Science had liberated the ideas of those who read and reflect, and the American example had kindled feelings of right in the people. An insurrection has consequently begun, of science, talents, and courage, against rank and birth, which have fallen into contempt. It has failed in its first effort, because the mobs of the cities, the instrument used for its accomplishment, debased by ignorance, poverty, and vice, could not be restrained to rational action. But the world will recover from the panic of this first catastrophe. Science is progressive, and talents and enterprise on the alert. Resort may be had to the people of the country, a more governable power from their principles and subordination; and rank, and birth, and tinsel-aristocracy will finally shrink into insignificance, even there. . . .

I have thus stated my opinion on a point on which we differ, not with a view to controversy, for we are both too old to change opinions which are the result of a long life of inquiry and reflection; but on the suggestions of a former letter of yours, that we ought not to die before we have explained ourselves to each other.

## National University

### TO DUPONT DE NEMOURS.

MONTICELLO, *November 29, 1813.*

I am indebted to you . . . for your letter by Mr. Correa, and the benefit it procured me of his acquaintance. He was so kind as to pay me a visit at Monticello, which enabled me to see for myself that he was still beyond all the eulogies with which yourself and other friends had preconized him. Learned beyond any one I had before met with, good, modest and of the simplest manners, the idea of losing him again filled me with regret, and how much did I lament that we could not place him at the head of that great institution which I have so long nourished the hope of seeing established in my country, and towards which you had so kindly contributed your luminous views. But, my friend, that institution is still in embryo as you left it, and from the complexion of our popular legislature and the narrow and niggardly views of ignorance courting the suffrage of ignorance to obtain a seat in it, I see little prospect of such an establishment until the national government shall be authorized to take it up and form it on the comprehensive basis of all the useful sciences.

## Hemisphere Solidarity

### TO BARON ALEXANDER VON HUMBOLDT.

MONTPELIER, *December 6, 1813.*

Mexico, where we learn from you that men of science are not wanting, may revolutionize itself under better auspices than the Southern provinces. These last, I fear, must end in military despotisms. The different castes of their inhabitants, their mutual hatreds and jealousies, their profound ignorance and bigotry, will be played off by cunning leaders, and each be made the instrument of enslaving the others. But of all this you can best judge, for in truth we have little knowledge of them to be depended on, but through you. But in whatever governments they end they will be *American* governments, no longer to be involved in the never-ceasing broils of Europe. The European nations constitute a separate division of the globe; their localities make them part of a distinct system; they have a set of interests of their own in which it is our business never to engage ourselves. America has a hemisphere to itself. It must have its separate system of interests, which must not be subordinated to those of Europe. The insulated state in which nature has placed the American continent, should so far avail it that no spark of war kindled in the other quarters of the globe should be wafted across the wide oceans which separate us from them.

## Gardener's Gift

### TO MADAME DE TESSE.

MONTICELLO, *December 8, 1813.*

Lewis's journey across our continent to the Pacific has added a number of new plants to our former stock. Some of them are curious, some ornamental, some useful, and some may by culture be made acceptable on our tables. I have growing, which I destine for you, a very handsome little shrub of the size of a currant bush. Its beauty consists in a great produce of berries of the size of currants, and literally as white as snow, which remain on the bush through the winter, after its leaves have fallen, and make it an object as singular as it is beautiful. We call it the snow-berry bush.

# On Napoleon

## TO THOMAS LEIPER.

MONTICELLO, *January 1, 1814.*

That Bonaparte is an unprincipled tyrant, who is deluging the continent of Europe with blood, there is not a human being, not even the wife of his bosom, who does not see; nor can there, I think, be a doubt as to the line we ought to wish drawn between his successes and those of Alexander. Surely none of us wish to see Bonaparte conquer Russia, and lay thus at his feet the whole continent of Europe. This done, England would be but a breakfast; and, although I am free from the visionary fears which the votaries of England have affected to entertain, because I believe he cannot effect the conquest of Europe; yet put all Europe into his hands, and he might spare such a force, to be sent in British ships, as I would as leave not have to encounter, when I see how much trouble a handful of British soldiers in Canada has given us. No. It cannot be to our interest that all Europe should be reduced to a single monarchy. . . .

But is our particular interest to make us insensible to all sentiments of morality? Is it then become criminal, the moral wish that the torrents of blood this man is shedding in Europe, the sufferings of so many human beings, good as ourselves, on whose necks he is trampling, the burnings of ancient cities, devastations of great countries, the destruction of law and order, and demoralization of the world, should be arrested, even if it should place our peace a little further distant? No. You and I cannot differ in wishing that Russia, and Sweden, and Denmark, and Germany, and Spain, and Portugal, and Italy, and even England, may retain their independence.

# On Washington

## TO DR. WALTER JONES.

MONTICELLO, *January 2, 1814.*

I deplore, with you, the putrid state into which our newspapers have passed, and the malignity, the vulgarity, and mendacious spirit of those who write for them . . . These ordures are rapidly depraving the public taste, and lessening its relish for sound food. As vehicles of information, and a curb on our functionaries, they have rendered themselves useless, by forfeiting all title to belief. That this has, in a great degree, been produced by the violence and malignity of party spirit, I agree with you; and I have read with great pleasure the paper you enclosed me on that subject. There was but a single passage where I wished a little more development of a very sound and catholic idea; a single intercalation to rest it solidly on true bottom. It is near the end of the first page, where you make a statement of genuine republican maxims; saying, "that the people ought to possess as much political power as can possibly exist with the order and security of society." Instead of this, I would say, "that the people, being the only safe depository of power, should exercise in person every function which their qualifications enable them to exercise, consistently with the order and security of society; that we now find them equal to the election of those who shall be invested with their executive and legislative powers, and to act themselves in the judiciary, as judges in questions of fact; that the range of their powers ought to be enlarged," etc. This gives both the reason and exemplification of the maxim you express, "that they ought to possess as much political power," etc. I see nothing to correct either in your facts or principles.

I think I knew General Washington intimately and thoroughly; and were I called on to delineate his character, it should be in terms like these.

His mind was great and powerful, without being of the very first order; his penetration strong, though not so acute as that of a Newton, Bacon, or Locke; and as far as he saw, no judgment was ever sounder. It was slow in operation, being little aided by invention or imagination, but sure in conclusion. Hence the common remark of his officers, of the advantage he derived from councils of war, where hearing all suggestions, he selected whatever was best; and certainly no general ever planned his battles more judiciously. But if deranged during the course of the action, if any member of his plan was dislocated by sudden circumstances, he was slow in re-adjustment. The consequence was, that he often failed in the field, and rarely against an enemy in station, as at Boston and York. He was incapable of fear, meeting personal dangers with the calmest unconcern. Perhaps the strongest feature in his character was prudence, never acting until every circumstance, every consideration, was maturely weighed; refraining if he saw a doubt, but, when once decided, going through with his purpose, whatever obstacles opposed. His integrity was most pure, his justice the most inflexible I have ever known, no motives of interest or consanguinity, of friendship or hatred, being able to bias his decision. He was, indeed, in every sense of the words, a wise, a good, and a great man. His temper was naturally irritable and high toned; but reflection and resolution had obtained a firm and habitual ascendency over it. If ever, however, it broke its bonds, he was most tremendous in his wrath. In his expenses he was honorable, but exact; liberal in contributions to whatever promised utility; but frowning and unyielding on all visionary projects, and all unworthy calls on his charity. His heart was not warm in its affections; but he exactly calculated every man's value, and gave him a solid esteem proportioned to it. His person, you know, was fine, his stature exactly what one would wish, his deportment easy, erect and noble; the best horseman of his age, and the most graceful figure that could be seen on horseback. Although in the circle of his friends, where he might be unreserved with safety, he took a free share in conversation, his colloquial talents were not above mediocrity, possessing neither copiousness of ideas, nor fluency of words. In public, when called on for a sudden opinion, he was unready, short and embarrassed. Yet he wrote readily, rather diffusely, in an easy and correct style. This he had acquired by conversation with the world, for his education was merely reading, writing and common arithmetic, to which he added surveying at a later day. His time was employed in action chiefly, reading little, and that only in agriculture and English history. His correspondence became necessarily extensive, and, with journalizing his agricultural proceedings, occupied most of his leisure hours within doors. On the whole, his character was, in its mass, perfect, in nothing bad, in few points indifferent; and it may truly be said, that never did nature and fortune combine more perfectly to make a man great, and to place him in the same constellation with whatever worthies have merited from man an everlasting remembrance. For his was the singular destiny and merit, of leading the armies of his country successfully through an arduous war, for the establishment of its independence; of conducting its councils through the birth of a government, new in its forms and principles, until it had settled down into a quiet and orderly train; and of scrupulously obeying the laws through the whole of his career, civil and military, of which the history of the world furnishes no other example.

He has often declared to me that he considered our new Constitution as an experiment on the practicability of republican government, and with what dose of liberty man could be trusted for his own good; that he was determined the experiment should have a fair trial, and would lose the last drop of his blood in support of it. And these declarations he repeated to me the oftener and more pointedly, because he knew my suspicions of Colonel Hamilton's views, and probably had heard from him the same declarations which I had, to wit, "that the British constitution, with its unequal representation, corruption and other existing abuses, was the most perfect government which had ever been established on earth, and that a reformation of those abuses would make it an impracticable government." I do believe that General Washington had not a firm confidence in the durability of our government. He was naturally distrustful of men, and inclined to gloomy apprehensions; and I was ever persuaded that a belief that we must at length end in something like a British constitution, had some weight in his adoption of the ceremonies of levees, birthdays, pompous meetings with Congress, and other forms of the same character, calculated to prepare us gradually for a change which he believed possible, and to let it come on with as little shock as might be to the public mind.

## Occupational Hazards

### TO HORATIO G. SPAFFORD.

MONTICELLO, *March 17, 1814.*

I join in your reprobation of our merchants, priests, and lawyers, for their adherence to England and monarchy, in preference to their own country and its Constitution. But merchants have no country. The mere spot they stand on does not constitute so strong an attachment as that from which they draw their gains. In every country and in every age, the priest has been hostile to liberty. He is always in alliance with the despot, abetting his abuses in return for protection to his own. It is easier to acquire wealth and power by this combination than by deserving them, and to effect this, they have perverted the purest religion ever preached to man into mystery and jargon, unintelligible to all mankind, and therefore the safer engine for their purposes. With the lawyers it is a new thing. They have, in the Mother country, been generally the firmest supporters of the free principles of their constitution. But there too they have changed. . . .

## Indignant Protest

TO MONSIEUR N. G. DUFIEF.

MONTICELLO, *April 19, 1814.*

DEAR SIR,—Your favor of the 6th instant is just received, and I shall with equal willingness and truth, state the degree of agency you had, respecting the copy of M. de Becourt's book, which came to my hands. That gentleman informed me, by letter, that he was about to publish a volume in French, "Sur la Création du Monde, un Système d'Organisation Primitive," which, its title promised to be, either a geological or astronomical work. I subscribed; and, when published, he sent me a copy; and as you were my correspondent in the book line in Philadelphia, I took the liberty of desiring him to call on you for the price, which, he afterwards informed me, you were so kind as to pay him for me, being, I believe, two dollars. But the sole copy which came to me was from himself directly, and, as far as I know, was never seen by you.

I am really mortified to be told that, *in the United States of America,* a fact like this can become a subject of inquiry, and of criminal inquiry too, as an offence against religion; that a question about the sale of a book can be carried before the civil magistrate. Is this then our freedom of religion? and are we to have a censor whose imprimatur shall say what books may be sold, and what we may buy? And who is thus to dogmatize religious opinions for our citizens? Whose foot is to be the measure to which ours are all to be cut or stretched? Is a priest to be our inquisitor, or shall a layman, simple as ourselves, set up his reason as the rule for what we are to read, and what we must believe? It is an insult to our citizens to question whether they are rational beings or not, and blasphemy against religion to suppose it cannot stand the test of truth and reason. If M. de Becourt's book be false in its facts, disprove them; if false in its reasoning, refute it. But, for God's sake, let us freely hear both sides, if we choose. I know little of its contents, having barely glanced over here and there a passage, and over the table of contents. From this, the Newtonian philosophy seemed the chief object of attack, the issue of which might be trusted to the strength of the two combatants; Newton certainly not needing the auxiliary arm of the government, and still less the holy Author of our religion, as to what in it concerns Him. I thought the work would be very innocent, and one which might be confided to the reason of any man; not likely to be much read if let alone, but, if persecuted, it will be generally read. Every man in the United States will think it a duty to buy a copy, in vindication of his right to buy, and to read what he pleases. I have been just reading the new constitution of Spain. One of its fundamental bases is expressed in these words: "The *Roman Catholic* religion, the only true one, is, and always shall be, that of the Spanish nation. The government protects it by wise and just laws, and prohibits the exercise of any other whatever." Now I wish this presented to those who question what you may sell, or we may buy, with a request to strike out the words, "Roman Catholic," and to insert the denomination of their own religion. This would ascertain the code of dogmas which each wishes should domineer over the opinions of all others, and be taken, like the Spanish religion, under the "protection of wise and just laws." It would show to what they wish to reduce the liberty for which one generation has sacrificed life and happiness. It would present our boasted freedom of religion as a thing of theory only, and not of practice, as what would be a poor exchange for the theoretic thraldom, but practical freedom of Europe. But it is impossible that the laws of Pennsylvania, which set us the first example of the wholesome and happy effects of religious freedom, can permit the inquisitorial functions to be proposed to their courts. Under them you are surely safe.

## "Seven-fold Wonders"

### TO JOHN ADAMS.

Monticello, *July 5, 1814.*

Shall you and I last to see the course the seven-fold wonders of the times will take? The Attila of the age dethroned, the ruthless destroyer of ten millions of the human race, whose thirst for blood appeared unquenchable, the great oppressor of the rights and liberties of the world, shut up within the circle of a little island of the Mediterranean, and dwindled to the condition of an humble and degraded pensioner on the bounty of those he had most injured. How miserably, how meanly, has he closed his inflated career! What a sample of the bathos will his history present! He should have perished on the swords of his enemies, under the walls of Paris. . . .

But Bonaparte was a lion in the field only. In civil life, a cold-blooded, calculating, unprincipled usurper, without a virtue; no statesman, knowing nothing of commerce, political economy, or civil government, and supplying ignorance by bold presumption. I had supposed him a great man until his entrance into the Assembly *des cinq cens,* eighteen Brumaire (an 8). From that date, however, I set him down as a great scoundrel only. To the

wonders of his rise and fall, we may add that of a Czar of Muscovy, dictating, *in Paris,* laws and limits to all the successors of the Cæsars, and holding even the balance in which the fortunes of this new world are suspended.
. . . Our post-revolutionary youth are born under happier stars than you and I were. They acquire all learning in their mother's womb, and bring it into the world ready made. The information of books is no longer necessary; and all knowledge which is not innate, is in contempt, or neglect at least. Every folly must run its round; and so, I suppose, must that of self-learning and self-sufficiency; of rejecting the knowledge acquired in past ages, and starting on the new ground of intuition. When sobered by experience, I hope our successors will turn their attention to the advantages of education. I mean of education on the broad scale, and not that of the petty *academies,* as they call themselves, which are starting up in every neighborhood, and where one or two men, possessing Latin and sometimes Greek, a knowledge of the globes, and the first six books of Euclid, imagine and communicate this as the sum of science. They commit their pupils to the theatre of the world, with just taste enough of learning to be alienated from industrious pursuits, and not enough to do service in the ranks of science.

## On the Caste System

### TO DR. THOMAS COOPER.

MONTICELLO, *September 10, 1814.*

A comparison of the conditions of Great Britain and the United States, which is the subject of your letter of August 17th, would be an interesting theme indeed. . . . The population of England is composed of three descriptions of persons (for those of minor note are too inconsiderable to affect a general estimate). These are, 1. The aristocracy, comprehending the nobility, the wealthy commoners, the high grades of priesthood, and the officers of government. 2. The laboring class. 3. The eleemosynary class, or paupers, who are about one-fifth of the whole. The aristocracy, which have the laws and government in their hands, have so managed them as to reduce the third description below the means of supporting life, even by labor; and to force the second, whether employed in agriculture or the arts, to the maximum of labor which the construction of the human body can endure, and to the minimum of food, and of the meanest kind, which will preserve it in life, and in strength sufficient to perform its functions. To obtain food enough, and clothing, not only their whole strength must be unremittingly exerted, but the utmost dexterity also which they can acquire; and those of great dexterity only can keep their ground, while those of less must sink into the class of paupers. Nor is it manual dexterity alone, but the acutest resources of the mind also which are impressed into this struggle for life; and such as have means a little above the rest, as the master-workmen, for instance, must strengthen themselves by acquiring as much of the philosophy of their trade as will enable them to compete with their rivals, and keep themselves above ground. Hence the industry and manual dexterity of their journeymen and day-laborers, and the science of their master-workmen, keep them in the foremost ranks of competition with those of other nations; and the less dexterous individuals, falling into the eleemosynary ranks, furnish materials for armies and navies to defend their country, exercise piracy on the ocean, and carry conflagration, plunder and devastation, on the shores of all those who endeavor to withstand their aggressions. A society thus constituted possesses certainly the means of defence. But what does it defend? The pauperism of the lowest class, the abject oppression of the laboring, and the luxury, the riot, the domination and the vicious happiness of the aristocracy. In their hands, the paupers are used as tools to maintain their own wretchedness, and to keep down the laboring portion by shooting them whenever the desperation produced by the cravings of their stomachs drives them into riots. Such is the happiness of scientific England; now let us see the American side of the medal.

And, first, we have no paupers, the old and crippled among us, who possess nothing and have no families to take care of them, being too few to merit notice as a separate section of society, or to affect a general estimate. The great mass of our population is of laborers; our rich, who can live without labor, either manual or professional, being few, and of moderate wealth. Most of the laboring class possess property, cultivate their own lands, have families, and from the demand for their labor are enabled to exact from the rich and the competent such prices as enable them to be fed abundantly, clothed above mere decency, to labor moderately and raise their families. They are not driven to the ultimate resources of dexterity and skill, because their wares will sell although not quite so nice as those of England. The wealthy, on the other hand, and those at their ease, know nothing of what the Europeans call luxury. They have only somewhat more of the comforts and decencies of life than those who furnish them. Can any condition of society be more desirable than this? Nor in the class of laborers do I mean to withhold from the comparison that portion whose color has condemned them, in certain parts of our Union, to a subjection to the will of others. Even these are better fed in these States, warmer clothed, and labor less than the journeymen or day-laborers of England. They have the comfort, too, of numerous families, in the midst of whom they live without want, or fear of it; a solace which few of the laborers of England possess. They are subject, it is true, to bodily coercion; but are not the hundreds of thousands of British soldiers and seamen subject to the same, without seeing, at the end of their career, when age and accident shall have rendered them unequal to labor, the certainty, which the other has, that he will never want? And has not the British seaman, as much as the African, been reduced to this bondage by force, in flagrant violation of his own consent, and of his natural right in his own person? and with the laborers of England generally, does not the moral coercion of want subject their will as despotically to that of their employer, as the physical constraint does the soldier, the seaman, or the slave?

But do not mistake me. I am not advocating slavery. I am not justifying the wrongs we have committed on a foreign people, by the example of another nation committing equal wrongs on their own subjects. On the contrary, there is nothing I would not sacrifice to a practicable plan of abolishing every vestige of this moral and political depravity. But I am at present comparing the condition and degree of suffering to which oppression has reduced the man of one color, with the condition and degree of suffering to which oppression has reduced the man of another color; equally condemning both. Now let us compute by numbers the sum of happiness of the two countries. In England, happiness is the lot of the aristocracy only; and the proportion they bear to the laborers and paupers, you know better than I do. Were I to guess that they are four in every hundred, then the happiness of the nation would be to its misery as one in twenty-five. In the United States it is as eight millions to zero, or as all to none. But it is said they possess the means of defence, and that we do not. How so? Are we not men? Yes; but our men are so happy at home that they will not hire themselves to be shot at for a shilling a day. Hence we can have no standing armies for defence, because we have no paupers to furnish the materials. The Greeks and Romans had no standing armies, yet they defended themselves. The Greeks by their laws, and the Romans by the spirit of their people, took care to put into the hands of their rulers no such engine of oppression as a standing army. Their system was to make every man a soldier, and oblige him to repair to the standard of his country whenever that was reared. This made them invincible; and the same remedy will make us so. In the beginning of our government we were willing to introduce the least coercion possible on the will of the citizen. Hence a system of military duty was established too indulgent to his indolence. This is the first opportunity we have had of trying it, and it has completely failed; an issue foreseen by many, and for which remedies have been proposed. That of classing the militia according to age, and allotting each age to the particular kind of service to which it was competent, was proposed to Congress in 1805, and subsequently; and, on the last trial was lost, I believe, by a single vote only. Had it prevailed, what has now happened would not have happened. . . .

With this force properly classed, organized, trained, armed and subject to tours of a year of military duty, we have no more to fear for the defence of our country than those who have the resources of despotism and pauperism.

But, you will say, we have been devastated in the meantime. True, some of our public buildings have been burnt, and some scores of individuals on the tide-water have lost their movable property and their houses. I pity them, and execrate the barbarians who delight in unavailing mischief. But these individuals have their lands and their hands left. They are not paupers, they have still better means of subsistence than $24\frac{4}{25}$ of the people of England. Again, the English have burnt our Capitol and President's house by means of their force. We can burn their St. James' and St. Paul's by means of our money, offered to their own incendiaries, of whom there are thousands in London who would do it rather than starve. But it is against the laws of civilized warfare to employ secret incendiaries. Is it not equally so to destroy the works of art by armed incendiaries? Bonaparte, possessed at times of almost every capital of Europe, with all his despotism and power, injured no monument of art. If a nation, breaking through all the restraints of civilized character, uses its means of destruction (power, for example) without distinction of objects, may we not use our means (*our* money and *their* pauperism) to retaliate their barbarous ravages? Are we obliged to use for resistance exactly the weapons chosen by them for aggression? When they destroyed Copenhagen by superior force, against all the laws of God and man, would it have been unjustifiable for the Danes to have destroyed their ships by torpedoes? Clearly not; and they and we should now be justifiable in the conflagration of St. James' and St. Paul's. And if we do not carry it into execution, it is because we think it more moral and more honorable to set a good example, than follow a bad one.

## Religious Test

### TO MR. MILES KING.

MONTICELLO, *September 26, 1814.*

I must ever believe that religion substantially good which produces an honest life, and we have been authorized by One whom you and I equally respect, to judge of the tree by its fruit. Our particular principles of religion are a subject of accountability to our God alone. I inquire after no man's, and trouble none with mine; nor is it given to us in this life to know whether yours or mine, our friends or our foes, are exactly the right. Nay, we have heard it said that there is not a Quaker or a Baptist, a Presbyterian or an Episcopalian, a Catholic or a Protestant in heaven; that, on entering that gate, we leave those badges of schism behind, and find ourselves united in those principles only in which God has united us all. Let us not be uneasy then about the different roads we may pursue, as believing them the shortest, to that our last abode; but, following the guidance of a good conscience, let us be happy in the hope that by these different paths we shall all meet in the end.

## Second Country

### TO WILLIAM SHORT, ESQ.

MONTICELLO, *November 28, 1814.*

You intimate a possibility of your return to France, now that Bonaparte is put down. I do not wonder at it; France, freed from that monster, must again become the most agreeable country on earth. It would be the second choice of all whose ties of family and fortune give a preference to some other one, and the first of all not under those ties. Yet I doubt if the tranquillity of France is entirely settled. If her Pretorian bands are not furnished with employment on her external enemies, I fear they will recall the old, or set up some new cause.

God bless you and preserve you in bodily health. Tranquillity of mind depends much on ourselves, and greatly on due reflection "how much pain have cost us the evils which have never happened." Affectionately adieu.

## On Finance

### TO COLONEL JAMES MONROE.

MONTICELLO, *January 1, 1815.*

DEAR SIR,—Your letters of November the 30th and December the 21st have been received with great pleasure. A truth now and then projecting into the ocean of newspaper lies, serves like headlands to correct our course. Indeed, my scepticism as to everything I see in a newspaper, makes me indifferent whether I ever see one.

Although a century of British experience has proved to what a wonderful extent the funding on specific redeeming taxes enables a nation to anticipate in war the resources of peace, and although the other nations of Europe have tried and trodden every path of force or folly in fruitless quest of the same object, yet *we* still expect to find in juggling tricks and banking dreams, that money can be made out of nothing, and in sufficient quantity to meet the expenses of a heavy war by sea and land. It is said, indeed, that money cannot be borrowed from our merchants as from those of England. But it can be borrowed from our people. They will give you all the necessaries of war they produce, if, instead of the bankrupt trash they now are obliged to receive for want of any other, you will give them a paper promise funded on a specific pledge, and of a size for common circulation. But you say the merchants will not take this paper. What the people take, the merchants must take, or sell nothing. All these doubts and fears prove only the extent of the dominion which the banking institutions have obtained over the minds of our citizens, and especially of those inhabiting cities or other banking places; and this dominion must be broken, or it will break us. But here, as in the other case, we must make up our minds to suffer yet longer before we can get right. The misfortune is, that in the meantime we shall plunge ourselves in unextinguishable debt, and entail on our posterity an inheritance of eternal **taxes, which** will bring our government and people into the condition of those of England, a nation of pikes and gudgeons, the latter bred merely as food for the former.

# On Hierarchies

TO CHARLES CLAY, ESQ.

MONTICELLO, *January 29, 1815.*

I should as soon think of writing for the reformation of Bedlam, as of the world of religious sects. Of these there must be, at least, ten thousand, every individual of every one of which believes all wrong but his own. To undertake to bring them all right, would be like undertaking, single-handed, to fell the forests of America. . . . I abuse the priests, indeed, who have so much abused the pure and holy doctrines of their Master, and who have laid me under no obligations of reticence as to the tricks of their trade. The genuine system of Jesus, and the artificial structures they have erected, to make them the instruments of wealth, power, and preëminence to themselves, are as distinct things in my view as light and darkness; and while I have classed them with soothsayers and necromancers, I place Him among the greatest reformers of morals, and scourges of priest-craft that have ever existed. They felt Him as such, and never rested until they had silenced Him by death.

Government, as well as religion, has furnished its schisms, its persecutions, and its devices for fattening idleness on the earnings of the people. It has its hierarchy of emperors, kings, princes, and nobles, as that has of popes, cardinals, archbishops, bishops, and priests. In short, cannibals are not to be found in the wilds of America only, but are reveling on the blood of every living people.

# State of the Union

TO THE MARQUIS DE LA FAYETTE.

MONTICELLO, *February 14, 1815.*

The British ministers . . . found some hopes on the state of our finances. . . . They have hoped more in their Hartford convention. Their fears of republican France being now done away, they are directed to republican America, and they are playing the same game for disorganization here, which they played in your country. The Marats, the Dantons and Robespierres of Massachusetts are in the same pay, under the same orders, and making the same efforts to anarchise us, that their prototypes in France did there.

I do not say that all who met at Hartford were under the same motives of money, nor were those of France. Some of them are Outs, and wish to be Ins; some the mere dupes of the agitators, or of their own party passions, while the Maratists alone are in the real secret; but they have very different materials to work on. The yeomanry of the United States are not the *canaille* of Paris. We might safely give them leave to go through the United States recruiting their ranks, and I am satisfied they could not raise one single regiment (gambling merchants and silk-stocking clerks excepted) who would support them in any effort to separate from the Union. The cement of this Union is in the heart-blood of every American. I do not believe there is on earth a government established on so immovable a basis. Let them, in any State, even in Massachusetts itself, raise the standard of separation, and its citizens will rise in mass, and do justice themselves on their own incendiaries. . . . Have then no fears for us, my friend. The grounds of these exist only in English newspapers, edited or endowed by the Castlereaghs or the Cannings, or some other such models of pure and uncorrupted virtue. Their military heroes, by land and sea, may sink our oyster boats, rob our hen roosts, burn our negro huts, and run off. But a campaign or two more will relieve them from further trouble or expense in defending their American possessions.

P. S. *February 26th.* My letter had not yet been sealed, when I received news of our peace. I am glad of it, and especially that we closed our war with the eclat of the action at New Orleans.

## Isolation vs. Trade

### TO JEAN BATISTE SAY.

MONTICELLO, *March 2, 1815.*

The question proposed in my letter of February 1st, 1804, has since become quite a "question viseuse." I had then persuaded myself that a nation, distant as we are from the contentions of Europe, avoiding all offences to other powers, and not over-hasty in resenting offence from them, doing justice to all, faithfully fulfilling the duties of neutrality, performing all offices of amity, and administering to their interests by the benefits of our commerce, that such a nation, I say, might expect to live in peace, and consider itself merely as a member of the great family of mankind; that in such case it might devote itself to whatever it could best produce, secure of a peaceable exchange of surplus for what could be more advantageously furnished by others, as takes place between one county and another of France. But experience has shown that continued peace depends not merely on our own justice and prudence, but on that of others also; that when forced into war, the interception of exchanges which must be made across a wide ocean, becomes a powerful weapon in the hands of an enemy domineering over that element, and to the other distresses of war adds the want of all those necessaries for which we have permitted ourselves to be dependent on others, even arms and clothing. This fact, therefore, solves the question by reducing it to its ultimate form, whether profit or preservation is the first interest of a State?

## "Peace, God Bless It!"

### TO JOHN ADAMS.

MONTICELLO, *June 10, 1815.*

It is long since we have exchanged a letter, and yet what volumes might have been written on the occurrences even of the last three months. In the first place, peace, God bless it! has returned to put us all again into a course of lawful and laudable pursuits; a new trial of the Bourbons has proved to the world their incompetence to the functions of the station they have occupied. . . .

And have our commercial citizens merited from their country its encountering another war to protect their gambling enterprises? That the persons of our citizens shall be safe in freely traversing the ocean, that the transportation of our own produce, in our own vessels, to the markets of our choice, and the return to us of the articles we want for our own use, shall be unmolested, I hold to be fundamental, and the gauntlet that must be for ever hurled at him who questions it. But whether we shall engage in every war of Europe, to protect the mere agency of our merchants and ship-owners in carrying on the commerce of other nations, even were these merchants and ship-owners to take the side of their country in the contest, instead of that of the enemy, is a question of deep and serious consideration, with which, however, you and I shall have nothing to do; so we will leave it to those whom it will concern.

I thank you for making known to me Mr. Ticknor and Mr. Gray. They are fine young men, indeed, and if Massachusetts can raise a few more such, it is probable she would be better counseled as to social rights and social duties. Mr. Ticknor is, particularly, the best bibliograph I have met with, and very kindly and opportunely offered me the means of reprocuring some part of the literary treasures which I have ceded to Congress, to replace the devastations of British vandalism at Washington. I cannot live without books. But fewer will suffice, where amusement, and not use, is the only future object.

## On Moral Progress

### TO MONSIEUR CORREA DE SERRA.

MONTICELLO, *June 28, 1815.*

Europe has been a second time turned topsy-turvy since we were together; and so many things have happened there that I have lost my compass. As far as we can judge from appearances, Bonaparte, from being a mere military usurper, seems to have become the choice of his nation;

and the allies in their turn, the usurpers and spoliators of the European world. The right of nations to self-government being my polar star, my partialities are steered by it, without asking whether it is a Bonaparte or an Alexander towards whom the helm is directed. Believing that England has enough on her hands without us, and therefore has by this time settled the question of impressment with Mr. Adams, I look on this new conflict of the European gladiators, as from the higher forms of the amphitheatre, wondering that man, like the wild beasts of the forest, should permit himself to be led by his keeper into the arena, the spectacle and sport of the lookers on. Nor do I see the issue of this tragedy with the sanguine hopes of our friend M. Dupont. I fear, from the experience of the last twenty-five years, that morals do not of necessity advance hand in hand with the sciences.

# On Foreign Wars

## TO MADAME LA BARONNE DE STAËL-HOLSTEIN.

MONTICELLO, *July 3, 1815.*

DEAR MADAM,—I considered your letter of November 10th, 12th, as an evidence of the interest you were so kind as to take in the welfare of the United States, and I was even flattered by your exhortations to avoid taking any part in the war then raging in Europe, because they were a confirmation of the policy I had myself pursued, and which I thought and still think should be the governing canon of our republic. Distance, and difference of pursuits, of interests, of connections and other circumstances, prescribe to us a different system, having no object in common with Europe, but a peaceful interchange of mutual comforts for mutual wants. But this may not always depend on ourselves; and injuries may be so accumulated by an European power, as to pass all bounds of wise forbearance.

I learned with great pleasure your return to your native country. It is the only one which offers elements of society analogous to the powers of your mind, and sensible of the flattering distinction of possessing them. It is true that the great events which made an opening for your return, have been reversed. But not so, I hope, the circumstances which may admit its continuance. On these events I shall say nothing. At our distance, we hear too little truth and too much falsehood to form correct judgments concerning them; and they are moreover foreign to our umpirage. We wish the happiness and prosperity of every nation; we did not believe either of these promoted by the former pursuits of the present ruler of France, and hope that his return, if the nation wills it to be permanent, may be marked by those changes which the solid good of his own country, and the peace and well-being of the world, may call for. But these things I leave to whom they belong; the object of this letter being only to convey to you a vindication of my own country, and to have the honor on a new occasion of tendering you the homage of my great consideration, and respectful attachment.

# Distinguished Refugee

### TO J. CORREA DE SERRA.

MONTICELLO, *January 1, 1816.*

I learned, my dear Sir, with inexpressible concern on my arrival at home, that my detention in Bedford had lost me the pleasure of your visit here. Having heard nothing from you since our parting on the Natural Bridge, I had supposed your return longer delayed than you had expected, and that even, possibly, your course might be so shaped as to take Poplar Forest in your way. I hungered for your observations on the country you had passed over, and should not probably have been mistaken in your estimate of it.

I am ashamed to ask whether your observations or information as to the cisterns of Charlestown can facilitate the perfecting of those I have constructed because by some accident which I cannot ascertain, I lost the paper you were so kind as to give me at Dowthwaites. You recollect our situation there; I was shaving, changing my linen, opening and doing up my baggage on the bed when you put that paper into my hands. I thought it certain that I put it into my pocket, but when I got back to Poplar Forest I could not find it. Whether it was lost out of my pocket, or laid and left on the bed I cannot say, but being lost I am thrown again on your goodness to replace it if you can.

What effect will the apparent restoration of the Bourbons have on your movements? Will it tempt your return? I do not see in this a restoration of quiet; on the contrary I consider France as in a more volcanic state than at any preceding time, there must be an explosion and one of the most destructive character. I look forward to crimes more fierce and pitiless than those which have already distinguished that bloody revolution. These are not scenes, my dear friend, for you to be thrown into. They have no analogies with the tranquillity of your character. True, we cannot offer you the scientific society of Paris, but who can enjoy science, or who think of it in the midst of insurrection, madness and massacre? Besides, you possess all science within yourself; from others you can get nothing new, and the pleasure of communicating it should be greatest where it is most wanting. Stay then with us, become our instructor, help us on in the paths of that science which is wanting to our ripening character. You know how much you are beloved and desired everywhere, welcome everywhere, but nowhere so cordially as at Monticello. Come and make it your home then, the place of rest and tranquillity, from which, as your pre-des-tal, you can make what excursions you please. You will find its summers as moderate as those of Philadelphia, and its winters more so. Had I arrived before your departure I should have pressed your trial of it for the present winter. A comfortable room in a country of fuel, for retirement when you chose it, and a sociable family full of affection and respect for you, when tired of being alone, would have made you forget the suspension of the season for botanical rambling. Turn this subject in your mind, my good friend, and let us have as much of the benefit of the result as shall be consistent with your own happiness, and in all cases be assured of my warm affection and respect.

## Experience Teaches

### TO BENJAMIN AUSTIN, ESQ.

MONTICELLO, *January 9, 1816.*

You tell me I am quoted by those who wish to continue our dependence on England for manufactures. There was a time when I might have been so quoted with more candor, but within the thirty years which have since elapsed, how are circumstances changed! . . . Experience has taught me that manufactures are now as necessary to our independence as to our comfort. If it shall be proposed to go beyond our own supply, the question of '85 will then recur, will our *surplus* labor be then most beneficially employed in the culture of the earth, or in the fabrications of art? We have time yet for consideration, before that question will press upon us; and the maxim to be applied will depend on the circumstances which shall then exist; for in so complicated a science as political economy, no one axiom can be laid down as wise and expedient for all times and circumstances, and for their contraries. Inattention to this is what has called for this explanation, which reflection would have rendered unnecessary with the candid.[1]

## On the State of Europe

### TO JOHN ADAMS.

MONTICELLO, *January 11, 1816.*

I agree with you in . . . eulogies on the eighteenth century. It certainly witnessed the sciences and arts, manners and morals, advanced to a higher degree than the world had ever before seen. . . . With some exceptions only, through the seventeenth and eighteenth centuries, morality occupied an honorable chapter in the political code of nations. . . . How then has it happened that these nations, France especially and England, so great, so dignified, so distinguished by science and the arts, plunged all at once into

[1] Granting permission to publish this letter, Jefferson wrote "There is perhaps a degree of duty to avow a change of opinion called for by a change of circumstances, and especially on a point now become peculiarly interesting."

all the depths of human enormity, threw off suddenly and openly all the restraints of morality, all sensation to character, and unblushingly avowed and acted on the principle that power was right? I say France and not Bonaparte; for, although he was the head and mouth, the nation furnished the hands which executed his enormities. England, although in opposition, kept full pace with France, not indeed by the manly force of her own arms, but by oppressing the weak and bribing the strong. At length the whole choir joined and divided the weaker nations among them. Your prophecies to Dr. Price proved truer than mine; and yet fell short of the fact, for instead of a million, the destruction of eight or ten millions of human beings has probably been the effect of these convulsions. I did not, in '89, believe they would have lasted so long, nor have cost so much blood. But although your prophecy has proved true so far, I hope it does not preclude a better final result. That same light from our west seems to have spread and illuminated the very engines employed to extinguish it. It has given them a glimmering of their rights and their power. The idea of representative government has taken root and growth among them. Their masters feel it, and are saving themselves by timely offers of this modification of their powers. Belgium, Prussia, Poland, Lombardy, etc., are now offered a representative organization; illusive probably at first, but it will grow into power in the end. Opinion is power, and that opinion will come. Even France will yet attain representative government. . . . The idea then is rooted, and will be established, although rivers of blood may yet flow between them and their object. The allied armies now couching upon them are first to be destroyed, and destroyed they will surely be. A nation united can never be conquered. We have seen what the ignorant, bigoted and unarmed Spaniards could do against the disciplined veterans of their invaders. What then may we not expect from the power and character of the French nation? The oppressors may cut off heads after heads, but like those of the Hydra they multiply at every stroke. The recruits within a nation's own limits are prompt and without number; while those of their invaders from a distance are slow, limited, and must come to an end. I think, too, we perceive that all these allies do not see the same interest in the annihilation of the power of France. There are certainly some symptoms of foresight in Alexander that France might produce a salutary diversion of force were Austria and Prussia to become her enemies. France, too, is the neutral ally of the Turk, as having no interfering interests, and might be useful in neutralizing and perhaps turning that power on Austria. That a re-acting jealousy, too, exists with Austria and Prussia, I think their late strict alliance indicates; and I should not wonder if Spain should discover a sympathy with them. Italy is so divided as to be nothing. Here then we see new coalitions in embryo, which, after France shall in turn have suffered a just punishment for her crimes, will not only raise her from the earth on which she is prostrate, but give her an opportunity to establish a government of as much liberty as she can bear—enough to ensure her happiness and prosperity. When insurrection begins, be it where it will, all the partitioned countries will rush to arms, and Europe again become an arena of gladiators. And what is the definite object they will propose? A restoration certainly of the *status quo prius*, of the state of possession of '89. I see no other principle on which Europe can ever again settle down in lasting peace.

## Beginning of Revolution

### TO DABNEY CARR.

MONTICELLO, *January 19, 1816.*

While Mr. Girardin was in this neighborhood writing his continuation of Burke's history, I had suggested to him a proper notice of the establishment of the committee of correspondence here in 1773. . . . The transaction took place in the session of Assembly of March, 1773. Patrick Henry, Richard Henry Lee, Frank Lee, your father and myself, met by agreement, one evening, about the close of the session, at the Raleigh Tavern, to consult on the measures which the circumstances of the times seemed to call for. We agreed, in result, that concert in the operations of the several colonies was indispensable; and that to produce this, some channel of correspondence between them must be opened; that therefore, we would propose to our House the appointment of a committee of correspondence, which should be authorized and instructed to write to the Speakers of the House of Representatives of the several colonies, recommending the appointment of similar committees on their part, who, by a communication of sentiment on the transactions threatening us all, might promote a harmony of action salutary to all. I remember that Mr. Carr and myself, returning home together, and conversing on the subject by the way, concurred in the conclusion that that measure must inevitably beget the meeting of a Congress of Deputies from all the colonies, for the purpose of uniting all in the same principles and measures for the maintenance of our rights. I am certain I remember also, that a similar proposition, and nearly cotemporary, was made by Massachusetts, and that our northern messenger passed theirs on the road.

## On Local Government

### TO JOSEPH C. CABELL.

MONTICELLO, *February 2d, 1816.*

My letter of the 24th ultimo conveyed to you the grounds of the two articles objected to in the College bill. Your last presents one of them in a new point of view, that of the commencement of the ward schools as likely to render the law unpopular to the country. It must be a very inconsiderate and rough process of execution that would do this. My idea of the mode of carrying it into execution would be this: Declare the county *ipso facto* divided into wards for the present, by the boundaries of the militia captaincies; somebody attend the ordinary muster of each company, having first desired the captain to call together a full one. There explain the object of the law to the people of the company, put to their vote whether they will have a school established, and the most central and convenient place for it; get them to meet and build a log school-house; have a roll taken of the children who would attend it, and of those of them able to pay. These would probably be sufficient to support a common teacher, instructing gratis the few unable to pay. If there should be a deficiency, it would require too trifling a contribution from the county to be complained of; and especially as the whole county would participate, where necessary, in the same resource. Should the company, by its vote, decide that it would have no school, let them remain without one. The advantages of this proceeding would be that it would become the duty of the alderman elected by the county, to take an active part in pressing the introduction of schools, and to look out for tutors. If, however, it is intended that the State government shall take this business into its own hands, and provide schools for every county, then by all means strike out this provision of our bill. I would never wish that it should be placed on a worse footing than the rest of the State. But if it is believed that these elementary schools will be better managed by the Governor and Council, the commissioners of the literary fund, or any other general authority of the government, than by the parents within each ward, it is a belief against all experience. Try the principle one step further, and amend the bill so as to commit to the Governor and Council the management of all our farms, our mills, and merchants' stores. No, my friend, the way to have good and safe government, is not to trust it all to one, but to divide it among the many, distributing to every one exactly the functions he is competent to. Let the national government be entrusted with the defence of the nation, and its foreign and federal relations; the State governments with the civil rights, laws, police, and administration of what concerns the State generally; the counties with the local concerns of the counties, and each ward direct the interests within itself. It is by dividing and subdividing these republics from the great national one down through all its subordinations, until it ends in the administration of every man's farm by himself; by placing under every one what his own eye may superintend, that all will be done for the best. What has destroyed liberty and the rights of man in every government which has ever existed under the sun? The generalizing and concentrating all cares and powers into one body, no matter whether of the autocrats of Russia or France, or of the aristocrats of a Venetian senate. And I do believe that if the Almighty has not decreed that man shall never be free, (and it is a blasphemy to believe it,) that the secret will be found to be in the making himself the depository of the powers respecting himself, so far as he is competent to them, and delegating only what is beyond his competence by a synthetical process, to higher and higher orders of functionaries, so as to trust fewer and fewer powers in proportion as the trustees become more and more oligarchical. The elementary republics of the wards, the county republics, the State republics, and the republic of the Union, would form a gradation of authorities, standing each on the basis of law, holding every one its delegated share of powers, and constituting truly a system of fundamental balances and checks for the government. Where every man is a sharer in the direction of his ward-republic, or of some of the higher ones, and feels that he is a participator in the government of affairs, not merely at an election one day in the year, but every day; when there shall not be a man in the State who will not be a member of some one of its councils, great or small, he will let the heart be torn out of his body sooner than his power be wrested from him by a Cæsar or a Bonaparte. How powerfully did we feel the energy of this organization in the case of embargo? I felt the foundations of the government shaken under my feet by the New England townships. There was not an individual in their States whose body was not thrown with all its momentum into action; and although the whole of the other States were known to be in favor of the measure, yet the organization of this little selfish minority enabled it to overrule the Union. What would the unwieldy counties of the Middle, the South, and the West do? Call a county meeting, and the drunken loungers at and about the court-houses would have collected, the distances being too great for the good people and the industrious generally to attend. The character of those who really met would have been the measure of the weight they would have had in the scale of public opinion. As Cato, then, concluded every speech with the words, "*Carthago delenda est*," so do I every opinion, with the injunction, "divide the counties into wards." Begin them only for a single purpose; they will soon show for what others they are the best instruments. God bless you, and all our rulers, and give them the wisdom, as I am sure they have the will, to fortify us against the degeneracy of our government, and the concentration of all its powers in the hands of the one, the few, the wellborn or the many.

## On the Census

### TO THOMAS W. MAURY.

MONTICELLO, *February 3, 1816.*

For the articles of a statistical table, I think the last census of Congress presented what was proper, as far as it went, but did not go far enough. It required detailed accounts of our manufactures, and an enumeration of our people, according to ages, sexes, and colors. But to this should be added an enumeration according to their occupations. We should know what proportion of our people are employed in agriculture, what proportion are carpenters, smiths, shoemakers, tailors, bricklayers, merchants, sea-

men, etc. No question is more curious than that of the distribution of
society into occupations, and none more wanting. I have never heard of
such tables being effected but in the instance of Spain, where it was first
done under the administration, I believe, of Count D'Aranda, and a second
time under the Count de Florida Blanca, and these have been considered
as the most curious and valuable tables in the world. The combination of
callings with us would occasion some difficulty, many of our tradesmen
being, for instance, agriculturists also; but they might be classed under
their principal occupation.

On the geographical branch I have reflected occasionally. I suppose a
person would be employed in every county to put together the private
surveys, either taken from the surveyors' books or borrowed from the
proprietors, to connect them by supplementary surveys, and to survey
the public roads, noting towns, habitations, and remarkable places, by
which means a special delineation of water-courses, roads, etc., will be
obtained. But it will be further indispensable to obtain the latitudes and
longitudes of principal points in every county, in order to correct the
errors of the topographical surveys, to bring them together, and to assign
to each county its exact space on the map. These observations of latitude
and longitude might be taken for the whole State, by a single person well
qualified, in the course of a couple of years. I could offer some ideas on that
subject to abridge and facilitate the operations, and as to the instruments
to be used; but such details are probably not within the scope of your
inquiries.

## Good Neighbor Policy

### TO JAMES MONROE.

MONTICELLO, *February 4, 1816.*

From forty years' experience of the wretched guess-work of the newspapers of what is not done in open daylight, and of their falsehood even
as to that, I rarely think them worth reading, and almost never worth
notice. A ray, therefore, now and then, from the fountain of light, is like
sight restored to the blind. It tells me where I am; and that to a mariner
who has long been without sight of land or sun, is a rallying of reckoning
which places him at ease.

The ground you have taken with Spain is sound in every part. It is the
true ground, especially, as to the South Americans. When subjects are
able to maintain themselves in the field, they are then an independent
power as to all neutral nations, are entitled to their commerce, and to protection within their limits. Every kindness which can be shown the South
Americans, every friendly office and aid within the limits of the law of
nations, I would extend to them, without fearing Spain or her Swiss auxiliaries. For this is but an assertion of our own independence. But to join in

their war, as General Scott proposes, and to which even some members of Congress seem to squint, is what we ought not to do as yet. On the question of our interest in their independence, were that alone a sufficient motive of action, much may be said on both sides. When they are free, they will drive every article of our produce from every market, by underselling it, and change the condition of our existence, forcing us into other habits and pursuits. We shall, indeed, have in exchange some commerce with them, but in what I know not, for we shall have nothing to offer which they cannot raise cheaper; and their separation from Spain seals our everlasting peace with her. On the other hand, so long as they are dependent, Spain, from her jealousy, is our natural enemy, and always in either open or secret hostility with us. These countries, too, in war, will be a powerful weight in her scale, and, in peace, totally shut to us. Interest then, on the whole, would wish their independence, and justice makes the wish a duty. They have a right to be free, and we a right to aid them, as a strong man has a right to assist a weak one assailed by a robber or murderer.

## Dictator's Promises

### TO BENJAMIN AUSTIN, ESQ.

MONTICELLO, *February 9, 1816.*

I am in general extremely unwilling to be carried into the newspapers, no matter what the subject . . . With respect, however, to so much of my letter of January 9th as relates to manufactures, I have less repugnance, because there is perhaps a degree of duty to avow a change of opinion called for by a change of circumstances, and especially on a point now become peculiarly interesting.

What relates to Bonaparte stands on different ground. . . . I have grieved to see even good republicans so infatuated as to this man, as to consider his downfall as calamitous to the cause of liberty. In their indignation against England which is just, they seem to consider all *her* enemies as *our* friends, when it is well known there was not a being on earth who bore us so deadly a hatred. In fact, he saw nothing in this world but himself, and looked on the people under him as his cattle, beasts for burden and slaughter. Promises cost him nothing when they could serve his purpose. On his return from Elba, what did he not promise? But those who had credited them a little, soon saw their total insignificance, and, satisfied they could not fall under worse hands, refused every effort after the defeat of Waterloo. Their present sufferings will have a term; his iron despotism would have had none. France has now a family of fools at its head, from whom, whenever it can shake off its foreign riders, it will extort a free Constitution, or dismount them and establish some other on the solid basis of national right.

# University Buildings

## TO GOVERNOR WILSON C. NICHOLAS.

MONTICELLO, *April 2, 1816.*

I would strongly recommend . . . instead of one immense building, to have a small one for every professorship, arranged at proper distances around a square, to admit extension, connected by a piazza, so that they may go dry from one school to another. This village form is preferable to a single great building for many reasons, particularly on account of fire, health, economy, peace and quiet. Such a plan had been approved in the case of the Albemarle College, which was the subject of the letter above mentioned; and should the idea be approved by the Board, more may be said hereafter on the opportunity these small buildings will afford, of exhibiting models in architecture of the purest forms of antiquity, furnishing to the student examples of the precepts he will be taught in that art.

# "A Good World"

## TO JOHN ADAMS.

MONTICELLO, *April 8, 1816.*

You ask, if I would agree to live my seventy or rather seventy-three years over again? To which I say, yea. I think with you, that it is a good world on the whole; that it has been framed on a principle of benevolence, and more pleasure than pain dealt out to us. There are, indeed, (who might say nay) gloomy and hypochondriac minds, inhabitants of diseased bodies, disgusted with the present, and despairing of the future; always counting that the worst will happen, because it may happen. To these I say, how much pain have cost us the evils which have never happened! My temperament is sanguine. I steer my bark with Hope in the head, leaving Fear astern. My hopes, indeed, sometimes fail; but not oftener than the forebodings of the gloomy. There are, I acknowledge, even in the happiest life, some terrible convulsions, heavy set-offs against the opposite page of the account. I have often wondered for what good end the sensations of grief could be intended. All our other passions, within proper bounds, have an useful object. And the perfection of the moral character is, not in a stoical apathy, so hypocritically vaunted, and so untruly too, because impossible, but in a just equilibrium of all the passions. I wish the pathologists then would tell us what is the use of grief in the economy, and of what good it is the cause, proximate or remote.

# Power of the People

## TO MONSIEUR DUPONT DE NEMOURS.

POPLAR FOREST, *April 24, 1816.*

I received, my dear friend, your letter covering the Constitution for your Equinoctial republics, just as I was setting out for this place. I brought it with me, and have read it with great satisfaction. I suppose it well formed for those for whom it was intended, and the excellence of every government is its adaptation to the state of those to be governed by it. For us it would not do. Distinguishing between the structure of the government and the moral principles on which you prescribe its administration, with the latter we concur cordially, with the former we should not. We of the United States, you know, are constitutionally and conscientiously democrats. We consider society as one of the natural wants with which man has been created; that he has been endowed with faculties and qualities to effect its satisfaction by concurrence of others having the same want; that when, by the exercise of these faculties, he has procured a state of society, it is one of his acquisitions which he has a right to regulate and control, jointly indeed with all those who have concurred in the procurement, whom he cannot exclude from its use or direction more than they him. We think experience has proved it safer, for the mass of individuals composing the society, to reserve to themselves personally the exercise of all rightful powers to which they are competent, and to delegate those to which they are not competent to deputies named, and removable for unfaithful conduct, by themselves immediately. . . . You first set down as zeros all individuals not having lands, which are the greater number in every society of long standing. Those holding lands are permitted to manage in person the small affairs of their commune or corporation, and to elect a deputy for the canton; in which election, too, every one's vote is to be an unit, a plurality, or a fraction, in proportion to his landed possessions. The assemblies of cantons, then, elect for the districts; those of districts for circles; and those of circles for the national assemblies. Some of these highest councils, too, are in a considerable degree self-elected, the regency partially, the judiciary entirely, and some are for life. Whenever, therefore, an *esprit de corps*, or of party, gets possession of them, which experience shows to be inevitable, there are no means of breaking it up, for they will never elect but those of their own spirit. Juries are allowed in criminal cases only. I acknowledge myself strong in affection to our own form, yet both of us act and think from the same motive, we both consider the people as our children, and love them with parental affection. But you love them as infants whom you are afraid to trust without nurses; and I as adults whom I freely leave to self-government.

# On Direct Action

TO JOHN TAYLOR.

MONTICELLO, *May 28, 1816.*

Indeed, it must be acknowledged, that the term *republic* is of very vague application in every language. Witness the self-styled republics of Holland, Switzerland, Genoa, Venice, Poland. Were I to assign to this term a precise and definite idea, I would say, purely and simply, it means a government by its citizens in mass, acting directly and personally, according to rules established by the majority; and that every other government is more or less republican, in proportion as it has in its composition more or less of this ingredient of the direct action of the citizens. Such a government is evidently restrained to very narrow limits of space and population. I doubt if it would be practicable beyond the extent of a New England township. . . . The further the departure from direct and constant control by the citizens, the less has the government of the ingredient of republicanism.

The purest republican feature in the government of our own State, is the House of Representatives. The Senate is equally so the first year, less the second, and so on. . . . And add, also, that one-half of our brethren who fight and pay taxes, are excluded, like Helots, from the rights of representation, as if society were instituted for the soil, and not for the men inhabiting it; or one-half of these could dispose of the rights and the will of the other half, without their consent.

If, then, the control of the people over the organs of their government be the measure of its republicanism, and I confess I know no other measure, it must be agreed that our governments have much less of republicanism than ought to have been expected; in other words, that the people have less regular control over their agents, than their rights and their interests require. And this I ascribe, not to any want of republican dispositions in those who formed these Constitutions, but to a submission of true principle to European authorities, to speculators on government, whose fears of the people have been inspired by the populace of their own great cities, and were unjustly entertained against the independent, the happy, and therefore orderly citizens of the United States. Much I apprehend that the golden moment is past for reforming these heresies. The functionaries of public power rarely strengthen in their dispositions to abridge it, and an unorganized call for timely amendment is not likely to prevail against an organized opposition to it. We are always told that things are going on well; why change them? *"Chi sta bene, non si muove,"* said the Italian, "let him who stands well, stand still." This is true; and I verily believe they would go on well with us under an absolute monarch, while our present character remains, of order, industry and love of peace, and restrained, as he would be, by the proper spirit of the people. But it is while it remains such, we should provide against the consequences of its deterioration. And let us rest in the hope that it will yet be done . . .

On this view of the import of the term *republic,* instead of saying, as has been said, "that it may mean anything or nothing," we may say with truth and meaning, that governments are more or less republican, as they have more or less of the element of popular election and control in their composition; and believing, as I do, that the mass of the citizens is the safest depository of their own rights and especially, that the evils flowing from the duperies of the people, are less injurious than those from the egoism of their agents, I am a friend to that composition of government which has in it the most of this ingredient. And I sincerely believe, with you, that banking establishments are more dangerous than standing armies.

## On Changing the Constitution

### TO SAMUEL KERCHEVAL.

MONTICELLO, *July 12, 1816.*

Where then is our republicanism to be found? Not in our Constitution certainly, but merely in the spirit of our people. That would oblige even a despot to govern us republicanly. Owing to this spirit, and to nothing in the form of our Constitution, all things have gone well. But this fact, so triumphantly misquoted by the enemies of reformation, is not the fruit of our Constitution, but has prevailed in spite of it. Our functionaries have done well, because generally honest men. If any were not so, they feared to show it.

But it will be said, it is easier to find faults than to amend them. I do not think their amendments so difficult as is pretended. Only lay down true principles, and adhere to them inflexibly. Do not be frightened into their surrender by the alarms of the timid, or the croakings of wealth against the ascendency of the people. . . . I am not among those who fear the people. They, and not the rich, are our dependence for continued freedom.

Some men look at constitutions with sanctimonious reverence, and deem them like the ark of the covenant, too sacred to be touched. They ascribe to the men of the preceding age a wisdom more than human, and suppose what they did to be beyond amendment. I knew that age well; I belonged to it, and labored with it. It deserved well of its country. It was very like the present, but without the experience of the present; and forty years of experience in government is worth a century of book-reading; and this they would say themselves, were they to rise from the dead. I am certainly not an advocate for frequent and untried changes in laws and constitutions. I think moderate imperfections had better be borne with; because, when once known, we accommodate ourselves to them, and find practical means of correcting their ill effects. But I know also, that laws and institutions must go hand in hand with the progress of the human mind. As that becomes more developed, more enlightened, as new discoveries are made, new truths disclosed, and manners and opinions change with the change of circumstances, institutions must advance also, and keep pace with the times. We might as well require a man to wear still the coat which fitted him when a boy, as civilized society to remain ever under the regimen of their barbarous ancestors. It is this preposterous idea which has lately deluged Europe in blood. Their monarchs, instead of wisely yielding to the gradual change of circumstances, of favoring progressive accommodation to progressive improvement, have clung to old abuses, entrenched themselves behind steady habits, and obliged their subjects to seek through blood and violence rash and ruinous innovations, which, had they been referred to the peaceful deliberations and collected wisdom of the nation, would have been put into acceptable and salutary forms. Let us follow no such examples, nor weakly believe that one generation is not as capable as another of taking care of itself, and of ordering its own affairs. Let us, as our sister States have done, avail ourselves of our reason and experience, to correct the crude essays of our first and unexperienced, although wise, virtuous, and well-meaning councils. And lastly, let us provide in our Constitution for its revision at stated periods. What these periods should be, nature herself indicates. By the European tables of mortality, of the adults living at any one moment of time, a majority will be dead in about nineteen years. At the end of that period then, a new majority is come into place; or, in other words, a new generation. Each generation is as independent of the one preceding, as that was of all which had gone before. It has then, like them, a right to choose for itself the form of government it believes most promotive of its own happiness; consequently, to accommodate to the circumstances in which it finds itself, that received from its predecessors; and it is for the peace and good of mankind, that a solemn opportunity of doing this every nineteen or twenty years, should be provided by the Constitution; so that it may be handed on, with periodical repairs, from generation to generation, to the end of time, if anything human can so long endure.

This corporeal globe, and everything upon it, belong to its present corporeal inhabitants, during their generation. They alone have a right to direct what is the concern of themselves alone, and to declare the law of that direction; and this declaration can only be made by their majority. That majority, then, has a right to depute representatives to a convention, and to make the Constitution what they think will be the best for themselves.

## On War Hatred

TO THE SECRETARY OF STATE (JAMES MONROE).

MONTICELLO, *October 16, 1816.*

DEAR SIR,—If it be proposed to place an inscription on the capitol, the lapidary style requires that essential facts only should be stated:

FOUNDED 1791.—BURNT BY A BRITISH ARMY 1814.—RESTORED BY CONGRESS 1817.

No passion can be imputed to this inscription, every word being justifiable from the most classical examples.

But a question of more importance is whether there should be one at all? Should not our wise men, lifted above the passions of the ordinary citizen, begin to contemplate what *will be* the interests of our country? I think it would be better . . . to prepare the minds of our citizens for a corresponding change of disposition, by acts of comity towards England rather than by commemoration of hatred.

## On Friendly Visiting

TO MRS. ABIGAIL ADAMS.

MONTICELLO, *January 11, 1817.*

My grand-daughter, Ellen Randolph, is justly sensible of, and flattered by your kind notice of her. Could I, in the spirit of your wish, count backwards a score of years, it would not be long before Ellen and myself would pay our homage personally to Quincy. But those twenty years! Alas! where are they? With those beyond the flood. Our next meeting must then be in the country to which they have flown,—a country for us not now very distant. For this journey we shall need neither gold nor silver in our purse, nor scrip, nor coats, nor staves. Nor is the provision for it more easy than the preparation has been kind. I heard once a very old friend, who had troubled himself with neither poets nor philosophers, say the same thing in plain prose, that he was tired of pulling off his shoes and stockings at night, and putting them on again in the morning. The wish to stay here is thus gradually extinguished; but not so easily that of returning once, in awhile, to see how things have gone on. Perhaps, however, one of the elements of future felicity is to be a constant and unimpassioned view of what is passing here. If so, this may well supply the wish of occasional visits.

## Private Belief

TO JOHN ADAMS.

MONTICELLO, *January 11, 1817.*

The result of your fifty or sixty years of religious reading, in the four words, "Be just and good," is that in which all our inquiries must end; as the riddles of all the priesthoods end in four more, "*ubi panis, ibi deus.*" What all agree in, is probably right. What no two agree in, most probably wrong. One of our fan-coloring biographers, who paints small men as very great, inquired of me lately, with real affection too, whether he might consider as authentic, the change in my religion much spoken of in some circles. Now this supposed that they knew what had been my religion before, taking for it the word of their priests, whom I certainly never made the confidants of my creed. My answer was, "say nothing of my religion. It is known to my God and myself alone. Its evidence before the world is to be sought in my life; if that has been *honest and dutiful* to society, the religion which has regulated it cannot be a bad one."

## Personal Mention

TO JOSEPH DELAPLAINE.

MONTICELLO, *April 12, 1817.*

DEAR SIR,—My repugnance is so invincible to be saying anything of my own history as if worthy to occupy the public attention that I have suffered your letter of March 17, but not received till March 28, to lie thus long without resolution enough to take it up. . . . The number of names and ages of my children, grandchildren, great-grandchildren, etc., would produce fatigue and disgust to your readers of which I would be an unwilling instrument, it will certainly be enough to say that from one daughter living and another deceased, I have a numerous family of grandchildren and an increasing one of great-grandchildren.

I was married on New Year's day of 1772, and Mrs. J. died in the autumn of 1782. I was educated at William and Mary College, in Williamsburg. I read Greek, Latin, French, Italian, Spanish and English of course, with something of its radics, the Anglo-Saxon. I became a member of the legislature of Virginia in 1769 at the accession of Lord Botetourt to our government. I could not readily make a statement of the literary societies of which I am a member, they are many and would be long to enumerate and would savor too much of vanity and pedantry. Would it not be better to say merely that I am a member of many literary societies in Europe and America.

Your statements of the corrections of the Declaration of Independence by Dr. Franklin and Mr. Adams are neither of them at all exact. I should think it better to say generally that the rough draft was communicated to those two gentlemen, who each of them made two or three short and verbal alterations only, but even this is laying more stress on mere composition than it merits, for that alone was mine. The sentiments were of all America.

## True Religion

TO JOHN ADAMS.

MONTICELLO, *May 5, 1817.*

. . . If by *religion* we are to understand *sectarian dogmas*, in which no two of them agree, then your exclamation on that hypothesis is just, "that this would be the best of all possible worlds, if there were no religion in it." But if the moral precepts, innate in man, and made a part of his physical constitution, as necessary for a social being, if the sublime doctrines of philanthropism and deism taught us by Jesus of Nazareth, in which all agree, constitute true religion, then, without it, this would be, as you again say, "something not fit to be named even, indeed, a hell."

## The Erie Canal

TO BARON ALEXANDER VON HUMBOLDT.

MONTICELLO, *June 13, 1817.*

In our America we are turning to public improvements. Schools, roads, and canals are everywhere either in operation or contemplation. The most gigantic undertaking yet proposed, is that of New York, for drawing the waters of Lake Erie into the Hudson. The distance is 353 miles, and the height to be surmounted 661 feet. The expense will be great, but its effect incalculably powerful in favor of the Atlantic States. Internal navigation by steamboats is rapidly spreading through all our States, and that by sails and oars will ere long be looked back to as among the curiosities of antiquity. We count much, too, on its efficacy for harbor defence; and it will soon be tried for navigation by sea. We consider the employment of the contributions which our citizens can spare, after feeding, and clothing, and lodging themselves comfortably, as more useful, more moral, and even more splendid than that preferred by Europe, of destroying human life, labor and happiness.

# On Civil Rights

### TO ALBERT GALLATIN.

MONTICELLO, *June 16, 1817.*

Three of our papers have presented us the copy of an act of the legislature of New York, which, if it has really passed, will carry us back to
the times of the darkest bigotry and barbarism, to find a parallel. Its pur-
port is, that all those who shall *hereafter* join in communion with the
religious sect of Shaking Quakers, shall be deemed civilly dead, their marriages dissolved, and all their children and property taken out of their
hands. This act being published nakedly in the papers, without the usual
signatures, or any history of the circumstances of its passage, I am not
without a hope it may have been a mere abortive attempt. It contrasts
singularly with a cotemporary vote of the Pennsylvania legislature, who,
on a proposition to make the belief in God a necessary qualification for
office, rejected it by a great majority, although assuredly there was not a
single atheist in their body. And you remember to have heard, that when
the act for religious freedom was before the Virginia Assembly, a motion
to insert the name of Jesus Christ before the phrase, "the author of our
holy religion," which stood in the bill, was rejected, although that was the
creed of a great majority of them.

# Progress of Plans

### TO ALBERT GALLATIN.

MONTICELLO, *February 15, 1818.*

DEAR SIR,—I take the liberty of putting under the protection of your
cover a letter to Cardinal Dugnani at Rome, in the hope that through the
Nuncio resident at Paris it may find a sure conveyance to him. In return
for this trouble I wish I could give you any news which would interest
you, but withdrawn entirely from all attention to public affairs, I neither
know nor enquire what Congress are doing. You will probably know this
better than myself from the newspapers, which I have ceased to read in a
great degree.

A single measure in my own State has interested me much. Our legislature some time ago appropriated a fund of a million and a half dollars
to a system of general education. After two or three projects proposed
and put by I ventured to offer one which, although not adopted, is printed
and published for general consideration to be taken up at the next session.
It provides an elementary school in every neighborhood of fifty or sixty
families, a college for the languages, mensuration, navigation and geography

within a day's ride of every man's house, and a central university of the sciences for the whole State of eight, ten or twelve professors. But it has to encounter ignorance, malice, egoism, fanaticism, religious, political and local perversities.

## Almanac

### TO JACOB BIGELOW.

MONTICELLO, *April 11, 1818.*

I thank you, Sir, for the comparative statement of the climates of the several States as deduced from observations on the flowering of trees in the same year. It presents a valuable view and one which it is much to be desired could be extended through a longer period of years and embrace a greater number of those circumstances which indicate climate.

I closed the year before last a seven years' course of observations intended to characterize the climate of this State, which though very various in its various parts may be considered as reduced to a mean at this place nearly central to the whole. In return for your favor I transcribe the heads of observation which I thought requisite and some of the general results with the assurance of my high respect and esteem.

1. The greatest and least height of the thermometer every day.
2. The greatest, least and mean height of the thermometer in every month, with the mean of each year and the mean of the seven years which last was 55½°.
3. The minimum and maximum of the whole term, to wit: 5½° and 94½°.
4. The number of freezing nights in a winter (50) and of freezing days (10).
5. How long fires are necessary in our apartments, to wit: 4 months constant, and on evening and morning of month before and after that time.
6. The earliest frost in autumn Oct. 7–26, and the latest in spring Mar. 19–May 1.
7. The earliest ice in autumn Oct. 24–Nov. 15, and latest in spring Mar. 8–Apr. 10.
8. The quantity of water falling in a year, average 47.218.
9. The number of rains in the year, 89.
10. The number of fair days average 5 to the week.
11. The number of snow 22½ inches average covers the ground 22 days.
12. The number of days each wind prevailed through the year.
13. The flowering of plants, ripening of their fruit and coming to table of the products of the garden, arrival of birds, insects, etc.
14. The temperature of the springs 54½°, the winter air being at 75°.
15. The latitude of the place of observation (Monticello) 37° 57′ 51″–26″.

Extract from Number 13:
The peach blossoms Mar. 9–Apr. 4.
The tick appears Mar. 15–Apr. 2.
The house martin Mar. 18–Apr. 9.
Asparagus comes to table Mar. 23–Apr. 14.
The lilac blooms Apr. 1–Apr. 28.

The red bud blooms Apr. 2–19.
The whip-poor-will is heard Apr. 2–21.
The dogwood blossoms Apr. 3–22.
The locust blossoms Apr. 25–May 17.
Garden pea comes to table (unforced) May 3–25.
Strawberries ripe May 3–25.
Fireflies appear May 8.
Cherries ripe May 18–25.
Wheat harvest begins June 21–29.
Cucumbers at table (unforced) June 22–25.
Peaches ripe July 7–21.
Katydids or sawyers heard July 14–20.

| | AVERAGE OF EVERY MONTH. | | Prevalence of the several winds stated in days of year. |
|---|---|---|---|
| | Therm. | Rain. | |
| Jan. | 36 | 3.66 | |
| Feb. | 40 | 3.47 | N. 61 |
| Mar. | 46 | 2.92 | N. E. 29 |
| Apr. | 56½ | 3.59 | E. 15 |
| May | 61½ | 5.60 | S. E. 16 |
| June | 72 | 3.47 | S. 60 |
| July | 75 | 6.56 | S. W. 66 |
| Aug. | 73 | 4.06 | W. 47 |
| Sept. | 67 | 5.96 | N. W. 71 |
| Oct. | 57 | 3.40 | —— |
| Nov. | 45½ | 2.92 | 365 |
| Dec. | 37 | 1.56 | |

## Chinese Alphabet

### TO CHARLES JARED INGERSOLL.

MONTICELLO, *July 20, 1818.*

SIR,—On my return the day before yesterday after a long absence from this place, I found here your favor of July 4 with the two Chinese works from Mr. Wilcox which accompanied it. I pray you to accept my thanks for the trouble you have taken in forwarding them, and if you are in correspondence with Mr. Wilcox and should have other occasion to write to him I must request you to express to him my sense of his kind attention in sending me these works.

They are real curiosities and give us a better idea of the state of science in China than the relations of travellers have effected. It is surely impossible that they can make much progress with characters so complicated, so voluminous and inadequate as these are. It must take a life to learn the characters only and then their expression of ideas must be very imperfect. I imagine that some fortuitous circumstances will some day call their attention to the simple alphabets of Europe, which with proper improvements may be made to express the sounds of their language as well as of others, and that then they may enter on the field of science. I think missionaries to instruct them in our alphabets would be more likely to take good effect and lead them to the object of our religious missionaries than an abrupt introduction of new doctrines for which their minds are in no wise prepared.

## University Site

### TO NATHANIEL BOWDITCH.

MONTICELLO, *October 26, 1818.*

DEAR SIR,—I have for some time owed you a letter of thanks for your learned pamphlet on Dr. Stewart's formula for obtaining the sun's distance from the motion of the moon's apsides, a work, however, much above my mathematical stature. This delay has proceeded from a desire to address you on an interest much nearer home, and on the subject of which I must make a long story.

On a private subscription of about fifty or sixty thousand dollars we began the establishment of what we called the Central College, about a mile from the village of Charlottesville and four miles from this place, and have made some progress in the buildings. The legislature at their last session took up the subject and passed an act establishing an University, endowing it for the present with an annuity of fifteen thousand dollars and directing commissioners to meet to recommend a site, a plan of buildings, the professorships necessary for teaching all the branches of science at this day deemed useful, etc.

The commissioners by a vote of sixteen for the Central College, two for a second place and three for a third adopted that for the site of the University. They approved by an unanimous vote the plan of building begun at that place, and agreed on such a distribution of the sciences as it was thought might bring them all within the competence of ten professors; and no doubt is entertained of a confirmation by the legislature at their meeting in December. The plan of building is not to erect one single magnificent building to contain everybody, and everything, but to make of it an academical village, in which every professor should have his separate house, containing his lecturing room with two, three or four rooms for his own accommodation according as he may have a family or no family, with kitchen, garden, etc., distinct dormitories for the students, not more than two in a room and separate boardinghouses for dieting them by private housekeepers. We concluded to employ no professor who is not of the first order of the science he professes, that when we can find such in our own country we shall prefer them and when we cannot we will procure them wherever else to be found.

## Non-Aggression

TO THE MARQUIS DE LA FAYETTE.

MONTICELLO, *November 23, 1818.*

Here all is well. Our government is now so firmly put on its republican tack that it will not be easily monarchised by forms. You have made a mighty noise in Europe about our taking possession of some posts in Florida. The President's message delivered a few days ago will set you right on that subject, and show that no wrong was contemplated for a single moment. And what shows an honorable and comfortable trait in our nation was the universal uproar of our own people in the first moment of the apparent aggression and until they saw that their government had no such thing in view. I was delighted with this proof of moral principle in our citizens as to the conduct of their foreign relations and considered it as a pledge that they would never as a nation approve of any measure swerving from justice.

## Report on Franklin

TO ROBERT WALSH.

MONTICELLO, *December 4, 1818.*

DEAR SIR,—Yours of November the 8th has been some time received; but it is in my power to give little satisfaction as to its inquiries. Dr. Franklin had many political enemies, as every character must, which, with decision enough to have opinions, has energy and talent to give them effect on the feelings of the adversary opinion. These enmities were chiefly in Pennsylvania and Massachusetts. In the former, they were merely of the proprietary party. In the latter, they did not commence till the Revolution, and then sprung chiefly from personal animosities, which spreading by little and little, became at length of some extent. Dr. Lee was his principal calumniator, a man of much malignity, who, besides enlisting his whole family in the same hostility, was enabled, as the agent of Massachusetts with the British government, to infuse it into that State with considerable effect. Mr. Izard, the Doctor's enemy also, but from a pecuniary transaction, never countenanced these charges against him. Mr. Jay, Silas Deane, Mr. Laurens, his colleagues also, ever maintained towards him unlimited confidence and respect. That he would have waived the formal recognition of our independence, I never heard on any authority worthy notice. As to the fisheries, England was urgent to retain them exclusively, France neutral, and I believe, that had they been ultimately made a *sine qua non*, our commissioners (Mr. Adams excepted) would have relinquished them, rather than have broken off the treaty. To Mr. Adams' perseverance alone, on that point, I have always understood we were indebted for their reservation. As to the charge of subservience to France, besides the evidence of his friendly colleagues before named, two years of my own service with him at Paris, daily visits, and the most friendly and confidential conversation, convince me it had not a shadow of foundation. He possessed the confidence of that government in the highest degree, insomuch, that it may truly be said, that they were more under his influence, than he under theirs. The fact is, that his temper was so amiable and conciliatory, his conduct so rational, never urging impossibilities, or even things unreasonably inconvenient to them, in short, so moderate and attentive to their difficulties, as well as our own, that what his enemies called subserviency, I saw was only that reasonable disposition, which, sensible that advantages are not all to be on one side, yielding what is just and liberal, is the more certain of obtaining liberality and justice. Mutual confidence produces, of course, mutual influence, and this was all which subsisted between Dr. Franklin and the government of France.

I state a few anecdotes of Dr. Franklin, within my own knowledge, too much in detail for the scale of Delaplaine's work . . .

Our revolutionary process, as is well known, commenced by petitions, memorials, remonstrances, etc., from the old Congress. These were followed by a non-importation agreement, as a pacific instrument of coercion. While that was before us, and sundry exceptions, as of arms, ammunition, etc., were moved from different quarters of the house, I was sitting by Dr. Franklin and observed to him that I thought we should except books; that we ought not to exclude science, even coming from an enemy. He thought so too, and I proposed the exception, which was agreed to. Soon after it occurred that medicine should be excepted, and I suggested that also to the Doctor. "As to that," said he, "I will tell you a story. When I was in London, in such a year, there was a weekly club of physicians, of which Sir John Pringle was president, and I was invited by my friend Dr. Fothergill to attend when convenient. Their rule was to propose a thesis one week and discuss it the next. I happened there when the question to be considered was whether physicians had, on the whole, done most good or harm? The young members, particularly, having discussed it very learnedly and eloquently till the subject was exhausted, one of them observed to Sir John Pringle, that although it was not usual for the President to take part in a debate, yet they were desirous to know his opinion on the question. He said they must first tell him whether, under the appellation of physicians, they meant to include *old women*, if they did he thought they had done more good than harm, otherwise more harm than good."...

When Dr. Franklin went to France, on his revolutionary mission, his eminence as a philosopher, his venerable appearance, and the cause on which he was sent, rendered him extremely popular. For all ranks and conditions of men there, entered warmly into the American interest. He was, therefore, feasted and invited into all the court parties. At these he sometimes met the old Duchess of Bourbon, who, being a chess player of about his force, they very generally played together. Happening once to put her king into prize, the Doctor took it. "Ah," said she, "we do not take kings so." "We do in America," said the Doctor.

At one of these parties the Emperor Joseph III, then at Paris, incog., under the title of Count Falkenstein, was overlooking the game in silence, while the company was engaged in animated conversations on the American question. "How happens it, M. le Comte," said the Duchess, "that while we all feel so much interest in the cause of the Americans, you say nothing for them?" "I am a king by trade," said he.

When the Declaration of Independence was under the consideration of Congress, there were two or three unlucky expressions in it which gave offence to some members. The words "Scotch and other foreign auxiliaries" excited the ire of a gentleman or two of that country. Severe strictures on the conduct of the British king, in negotiating our repeated repeals of the law which permitted the importation of slaves, were disapproved by some Southern gentlemen, whose reflections were not yet matured to the full abhorrence of that traffic. Although the offensive expressions were immediately yielded these gentlemen continued their depredations on other parts of the instrument. I was sitting by Dr. Franklin, who perceived that I was not insensible to these mutilations. "I have made it a rule," said he, "whenever in my power, to avoid becoming the draughtsman of papers to be reviewed by a public body. I took my lesson from an incident which I will relate to you. When I was a journeyman printer, one of my companions, an apprentice hatter, having served out his time, was about to open shop for himself. His first concern was to have a handsome signboard, with a proper inscription. He composed it in these words, 'John Thompson, *Hatter*, *makes* and *sells hats* for ready money,' with a figure of a hat subjoined; but he thought he would submit it to his friends for their amendments. The first he showed it to thought the word '*Hatter*' tautologous, because followed by the words 'makes hats,' which show he was a hatter. It was struck out. The next observed that the word '*makes*' might as well be omitted, because his customers would not care who made the hats. If good and to their mind, they would buy, by whomsoever made. He struck it out. A third said he thought the words '*for ready money*' were useless, as it was not the custom of the place to sell on credit. Every one who purchased expected to pay. They were parted with, and the inscription now stood, 'John Thompson sells hats.' '*Sells hats!*' says his next friend. Why nobody will expect you to give them away, what then is the use of that word? It was stricken out, and '*hats*' followed it, the rather as there was one painted on the board. So the inscription was reduced ultimately to 'John Thompson' with the figure of a hat subjoined."

The Doctor and Silas Deane were in conversation one day at Passy, on the numerous errors in the Abbé's *Histoire des deux Indes*, when he happened to step in. After the usual salutations, Silas Deane said to him, "The Doctor and myself, Abbé, were just speaking of the errors of fact into which you have been led in your history." "Oh, no Sir," said the Abbé, "that is impossible. I took the greatest care not to insert a single fact, for which I had not the most unquestionable authority." "Why," says Deane, "there is the story of Polly Baker, and the eloquent apology you have put into her mouth, when brought before a court of Massachusetts to suffer punishment under a law which you cite, for having had a bastard. I know there never was such a law in Massachusetts." "Be assured," said the Abbé, "you are mistaken, and that that is a true story. I do not immediately recollect indeed the particular information on which I quote it; but I am certain that I had for it unquestionable authority." Doctor Franklin, who had been for some time shaking with unrestrained laughter at the Abbé's confidence in his authority for that tale, said, "I will tell you, Abbé, the origin of that story. When I was a printer and editor of a newspaper, we were sometimes slack of news, and to amuse our customers, I used to fill up our vacant columns with anecdotes and fables, and fancies of my own, and this of Polly Baker is a story of my making, on one of these occasions." The Abbé, without the least disconcert, exclaimed with a laugh, "Oh, very well, Doctor, I had rather relate your stories than other men's truths."

## Personal Report

### TO DOCTOR VINE UTLEY.

MONTICELLO, *March 21, 1819.*

SIR,—Your letter of February the 18th came to hand on the 1st instant; and the request of the history of my physical habits would have puzzled me not a little, had it not been for the model with which you accompanied it, of Doctor Rush's answer to a similar inquiry. I live so much like other people, that I might refer to ordinary life as the history of my own. Like my friend the Doctor, I have lived temperately, eating little animal food, and that not as an aliment, so much as a condiment for the vegetables, which constitute my principal diet. I double however, the Doctor's glass and a half of wine, and even treble it with a friend; but halve its effects by drinking the weak wines only. The ardent wines I cannot drink, nor do I use ardent spirits in any form. Malt liquors and cider are my table drinks, and my breakfast, like that also of my friend, is of tea and coffee. I have been blest with organs of digestion which accept and concoct, without ever murmuring, whatever the palate chooses to consign to them, and I have not yet lost a tooth by age. I was a hard student until I entered on the business of life, the duties of which leave no idle time to those disposed to fulfil them; and now, retired, and at the age of seventy-six, I am again a hard student. Indeed, my fondness for reading and study revolts me from the drudgery of letter-writing. And a stiff wrist, the consequence of an early dislocation, makes writing both slow and painful. I am not so regular in my sleep as the Doctor says he was, devoting to it from five to eight hours, according as my company or the book I am reading interests me; and I never go to bed without an hour, or half hour's previous reading of something moral, whereon to ruminate in the intervals of sleep. But whether I retire to bed early or late, I rise with the sun. I use spectacles at night, but not necessarily in the day, unless in reading small print. My hearing is distinct in particular conversation, but confused when several voices cross each other . . . I enjoy good health; too feeble, indeed, to walk much, but riding without fatigue six or eight miles a day, and sometimes thirty or forty. I may end these egotisms, therefore, as I began, by saying that my life has been so much like that of other people, that I might say with Horace, to every one *"nomine mutato, narratur fabula de te."* I must not end, however, without due thanks for the kind sentiments of regard you are so good as to express towards myself; and with my acknowledgments for these, be pleased to accept the assurances of my respect and esteem.

## Stuart Portrait

### TO HENRY DEARBORN.

MONTICELLO, *July 5, 1819.*

With respect to Mr. Stuart, it was in May, 1800, I got him to draw my picture and immediately after the last sitting I paid him his price, one hundred dollars. He was yet to put the last hand on it, so it was left with him. When he came to Washington in 1805 he told me he was not satisfied with it, and therefore begged me to sit again, and he drew another which he was to deliver me instead of the first, but begged permission to keep it until he could get an engraving from it. I soon after got him to sketch me in the medallion form, which he did on paper with crayons. Although a slight thing I gave him another hundred dollars, probably the treble of what he would have asked. This I have; it is a very fine thing, although very perishable.

I cannot say I am anxious about the Spanish treaty; in giving up the province of Texas, we gave up a sugar country sufficient for the supply of the United States. I would rather keep that and trust to the inevitable falling of Florida into our mouths. It is true, however, that present peace is secured by the exchange.

## Powers of the Supreme Court

### TO JUDGE SPENCER ROANE.

POPLAR FOREST, *September 6, 1819.*

I go further than you do, if I understand rightly your quotation from the Federalist, of an opinion that "the judiciary is the last resort in relation *to the other departments* of the government, but not in relation to the rights of the parties to the compact under which the judiciary is derived." If this opinion be sound, then indeed is our Constitution a complete *felo de se.* For intending to establish three departments, co-ordinate and independent, that they might check and balance one another, it has given, according to this opinion, to one of them alone, the right to prescribe rules for the government of the others, and to that one too, which is unelected by, and independent of the nation. For experience has already shown that the impeachment it has provided is not even a scare-crow; that such opinions as the one you combat, sent cautiously out, as you observe also, by detachment, not belonging to the case often, but sought for out of it, as if to rally the public opinion beforehand to their views, and to indicate the line they are to walk in, have been so quietly passed over as never to have excited animadversion, even in a speech of any one of the body entrusted with impeachment. The Constitution, on this hypothesis, is a mere thing of wax in the hands of the judiciary, which they may twist and shape into any form they please. It should be remembered, as an axiom of eternal truth in politics, that whatever power in any government is independent, is absolute also; in theory only, at first, while the spirit of the people is up, but in practice, as fast as that relaxes. Independence can be trusted nowhere but with the people in mass. They are inherently independent of all but moral law. My construction of the Constitution is very different from that you quote. It is that each department is truly independent of the others, and has an equal right to decide for itself what is the meaning of the Constitution in the cases submitted to its action; and especially, where it is to act ultimately and without appeal.

## Threat of Civil War

### TO WILLIAM SHORT.

MONTICELLO, *April 13, 1820.*

Although I had laid down as a law to myself, never to write, talk, or even think of politics, to know nothing of public affairs, and therefore had ceased to read newspapers, yet the Missouri question aroused and filled me with alarm. The old schism of federal and republican threatened nothing, because it existed in every State, and united them together by the fraternism of party. But the coincidence of a marked principle, moral and political, with a geographical line, once conceived, I feared would never more be obliterated from the mind; that it would be recurring on every occasion and renewing irritations, until it would kindle such mutual and mortal hatred, as to render separation preferable to eternal discord. I have been among the most sanguine in believing that our Union would be of long duration. I now doubt it much, and see the event at no great distance, and the direct consequence of this question; not by the line which has been so confidently counted on; but by the laws of nature control this; but by the Potomac, Ohio and Missouri, or more probably, the Mississippi upwards to our northern boundary. My only comfort and confidence is, that I shall not live to see this; and I envy not the present generation the glory of throwing away the fruits of their fathers' sacrifices of life and fortune, and of rendering desperate the experiment which was to decide ultimately whether man is capable of self-government?

## Fire-Bell in the Night

TO JOHN HOLMES.

MONTICELLO, *April 22, 1820.*

I thank you, dear Sir, for the copy you have been so kind as to send me of the letter to your constituents on the Missouri question. It is a perfect justification to them. I had for a long time ceased to read newspapers, or pay any attention to public affairs, confident they were in good hands, and content to be a passenger in our bark to the shore from which I am not distant. But this momentous question, like a fire-bell in the night, awakened and filled me with terror. I considered it at once as the knell of the Union. It is hushed, indeed, for the moment. But this is a reprieve only, not a final sentence. A geographical line, coinciding with a marked principle, moral and political, once conceived and held up to the angry passions of men, will never be obliterated; and every new irritation will mark it deeper and deeper. I can say, with conscious truth, that there is not a man on earth who would sacrifice more than I would to relieve us from this heavy reproach, in any *practicable* way. The cession of that kind of property, for so it is misnamed, is a bagatelle which would not cost me a second thought, if, in that way, a general emancipation and *expatriation* could be effected; and, gradually, and with due sacrifices, I think it might be. But as it is, we have the wolf by the ears, and we can neither hold him, nor safely let him go. . . .

I regret that I am now to die in the belief, that the useless sacrifice of themselves by the generation of 1776, to acquire self-government and happiness to their country, is to be thrown away by the unwise and unworthy passions of their sons, and that my only consolation is to be, that I live not to weep over it. If they would but dispassionately weigh the blessings they will throw away, against an abstract principle more likely to be effected by union than by scission, they would pause before they would perpetrate this act of suicide on themselves, and of treason against the hopes of the world. To yourself, as the faithful advocate of the Union, I tender the offering of my high esteem and respect.

## University Plan

TO JOHN ADAMS.

MONTICELLO, *August 15, 1820.*

Our University, four miles distant, gives me frequent exercise, and the oftener, as I direct its architecture. Its plan is unique, and it is becoming an object of curiosity for the traveler. I have lately had an opportunity of reading a critique on this institution in your North American Review of January last, having been not without anxiety to see what that able work would say of us; and I was relieved on finding in it much coincidence of opinion, and even where criticisms were indulged, I found they would have been obviated had the developments of our plan been fuller.

## Bulwark of the Nation

TO WILLIAM CHARLES JARVIS.

MONTICELLO, *September 28, 1820.*

. . . You seem . . . to consider the judges as the ultimate arbiters of all constitutional questions; a very dangerous doctrine indeed, and one which would place us under the despotism of an oligarchy. Our judges are as honest as other men, and not more so. They have, with others, the same passions for party, for power, and the privilege of their corps. Their maxim is *"boni judicis est ampliare jurisdictionem,"* and their power the more dangerous as they are in office for life, and not responsible, as the other functionaries are, to the elective control. The Constitution has erected no such single tribunal, knowing that to whatever hands confided, with the corruptions of time and party, its members would become despots. It has more wisely made all the departments co-equal and co-sovereign within themselves. The judges certainly have more frequent occasion to act on constitutional questions, because the laws of *meum* and *tuum* and of criminal action, forming the great mass of the system of law, constitute their particular department. When the legislative or executive functionaries act unconstitutionally, they are responsible to the people in their elective capacity. The exemption of the judges from that is quite dangerous enough. I know no safe depository of the ultimate powers of the society but the people themselves; and if we think them not enlightened enough to exercise their control with a wholesome discretion, the remedy is not to take it from them, but to inform their discretion by education. This is the true corrective of abuses of constitutional power. Pardon me, Sir, for this difference of opinion. My personal interest in such questions is entirely extinct, but not my wishes for the longest possible continuance of our government on its pure principles; if the three powers maintain their mutual independence on each other it may last long, but not so if either can assume the authorities of the other.

## "Unchangeable Friend"

### TO MARIA COSWAY.

MONTICELLO, *December 27, 1820.*

I rejoice in the first place that you are well; for your silence on that subject encourages me to presume it. And next, that you have been so usefully and pleasingly occupied in preparing the minds of others to enjoy the blessings you have yourself derived from the same source, a cultivated mind. Of Mr. Cosway I fear to say anything, such is the disheartening account of the state of his health given in your letter. But here or wherever, I am sure he has all the happiness which an honest life ensures. Nor will I say anything of the troubles of those among whom you live. I see they are great, and wish them happily out of them, and especially that you may be safe and happy, whatever be their issue. I will talk about Monticello, then, and my own country, as is the wish expressed in your letter. My daughter[1] Randolph, whom you knew in Paris a young girl, is now the mother of eleven living children, the grandmother of about half a dozen others, enjoys health and good spirits, and sees the worth of her husband attested by his being at present Governor of the State in which we live. Among these, I live like a patriarch of old. Our friend Trumbull is well, and profitably and honorably employed by his country in commemorating with his pencil some of its revolutionary honors. Of Mrs. Cruger I hear nothing, nor for a long time of Madame de Corny. Such is the present state of our former coterie: dead, diseased, and dispersed. But "tout ce qui est differé n'est pas perdu," says the French proverb, and the religion you so sincerely profess tells us we shall meet again; and we have all so lived as to be assured it will be in happiness. Mine is the next turn, and I shall meet it with good will, for after one's friends are all gone before them, and our faculties leaving us, too, one by one, why wish to linger in mere vegetation,—as a solitary trunk in a desolate field, from which all its former companions have disappeared? You have many good years remaining yet to be happy yourself and to make those around you happy. May these, my dear friend, be as many as yourself may wish, and all of them filled with health and happiness, will be among the last and warmest wishes of an unchangeable friend.

[1]Martha Jefferson (Mrs. Thomas Mann Randolph).

# Notes for an Autobiography

MONTICELLO, *January 6, 1821.*

The tradition in my father's family was, that their ancestor came to this country from Wales, and from near the mountain of Snowdon, the highest in Great Britain. . . . The first particular information I have of any ancestor was of my grandfather, who lived at the place in Chesterfield called Ozborne's, and owned the lands afterwards the glebe of the parish. He had three sons; Thomas who died young, Field who settled on the waters of Roanoke and left numerous descendants, and Peter, my father, who settled on the lands I still own, called Shadwell, adjoining my present residence. He was born February 29, 1707–8, and intermarried 1739, with Jane Randolph, of the age of 19, daughter of Isham Randolph, one of the seven sons of that name and family, settled at Dungeoness in Goochland. They trace their pedigree far back in England and Scotland, to which let every one ascribe the faith and merit he chooses.

My father's education had been quite neglected; but being of a strong mind, sound judgment, and eager after information, he read much and improved himself, insomuch that he was chosen, with Joshua Fry, Professor of Mathematics in William and Mary college, to continue the boundary line between Virginia and North Carolina, which had been begun by Colonel Byrd; and was afterwards employed with the same Mr. Fry, to make the first map of Virginia which had ever been made, that of Captain Smith being merely a conjectural sketch. They possessed excellent materials for so much of the country as is below the Blue Ridge; little being then known beyond that ridge. He was the third or fourth settler, about the year 1737, of the part of the country in which I live. He died, August 17th, 1757, leaving my mother a widow, who lived till 1776, with six daughters and two sons, myself the elder. To my younger brother he left his estate on James River, called Snowdon, after the supposed birth-place of the family: to myself, the lands on which I was born and live.

He placed me at the English school at five years of age; and at the Latin at nine, where I continued until his death. My teacher, Mr. Douglas, a clergyman from Scotland, with the rudiments of the Latin and Greek languages, taught me the French; and on the death of my father, I went to the Reverend Mr. Maury, a correct classical scholar, with whom I continued two years; and then, to wit, in the spring of 1760, went to William and Mary college, where I continued two years. It was my great good fortune, and what probably fixed the destinies of my life, that Dr. William Small of Scotland, was then Professor of Mathematics, a man profound in most of the useful branches of science, with a happy talent of communication, correct and gentlemanly manners, and an enlarged and liberal mind. He, most happily for me, became soon attached to me, and made me his daily companion when not engaged in the school; and from his conversation I got my first views of the expansion of science, and of the system of things in which we are placed. Fortunately, the philosophical chair became vacant soon after my arrival at college, and he was appointed to fill it *per interim:* and he was the first who ever gave, in that college, regular lectures in Ethics, Rhetoric and Belles Lettres. He returned to Europe in 1762, having previously filled up the measure of his goodness to me, by procuring for me, from his most intimate friend, George Wythe, a reception as a student of law, under his direction, and introduced me to the acquaintance and familiar table of Governor Fauquier, the ablest man who had ever filled that office. With him, and at his table, Dr. Small and Mr. Wythe, his *amici omnium horarum,* and myself, formed a *partie quarrée,* and to the habitual conversations on these occasions I owed much instruction. Mr. Wythe continued to be my faithful and beloved mentor in youth, and my most affectionate friend through life. In 1767, he led me into the practice of the law at the bar of the General court, at which I continued until the Revolution shut up the courts of justice.

In 1769, I became a member of the legislature by the choice of the county in which I live, and so continued until it was closed by the Revolution. I made one effort in that body for the permission of the emancipation of slaves, which was rejected: and indeed, during the regal government, nothing liberal could expect success. Our minds were circumscribed within narrow limits, by an habitual belief that it was our duty to be subordinate to the mother country in all matters of government, to direct all our labors in subservience to her interests, and even to observe a bigoted intolerance for all religions but hers. The difficulties with our representatives were of habit and despair, not of reflection and conviction. Experience soon proved that they could bring their minds to rights, on the first summons of their attention. But the King's Council, which acted as another house of legislature, held their places at will, and were in most humble obedience to that will: the Governor too, who had a negative on our laws, held by the same tenure, and with still greater devotedness to it: and, last of all, the Royal negative closed the last door to every hope of amelioration.

On the 1st of January, 1772, I was married to Martha Skelton, widow of Bathurst Skelton, and daughter of John Wayles, then twenty-three years old. Mr. Wayles was a lawyer of much practice, to which he was introduced more by his great industry, punctuality, and practical readiness, than by eminence in the science of his profession. He was a most agreeable companion, full of pleasantry and good humor, and welcomed in every society. He acquired a handsome fortune, and died in May, 1773, leaving three daughters: the portion which came on that event to Mrs. Jefferson, after the debts should be paid, which were very considerable, was about equal to my own patrimony, and consequently doubled the ease of our circumstances.

When the famous Resolutions of 1765, against the Stamp-act, were proposed, I was yet a student of law in Williamsburg. I attended the debate, however, at the door of the lobby of the House of Burgesses, and heard the splendid display of Mr. Henry's talents as a popular orator. They were great indeed; such as I have never heard from any other man. He appeared to me to speak as Homer wrote. Mr. Johnson, a lawyer, and member from the Northern Neck, seconded the resolutions, and by him the learning and the logic of the case were chiefly maintained. My recollections of these transactions may be seen page 60 of the life of Patrick Henry, by Wirt, to whom I furnished them.

In May, 1769, a meeting of the General Assembly was called by the Governor, Lord Botetourt. I had then become a member; and to that meeting became known the joint resolutions and address of the Lords and Commons, of 1768-9, on the proceedings in Massachusetts. Counter-resolutions, and an address to the King by the House of Burgesses, were agreed to with little opposition, and a spirit manifestly displayed itself of considering the cause of Massachusetts as a common one. The Governor dissolved us: but we met the next day in the Apollo[1] of the Raleigh tavern, formed ourselves into a voluntary convention, drew up articles of association against the use of any merchandise imported from Great Britain, signed and recommended them to the people, repaired to our several counties, and were re-elected without any other exception than of the very few who had declined assent to our proceedings.

Nothing of particular excitement occurring for a considerable time, our countrymen seemed to fall into a state of insensibility to our situation; the duty on tea, not yet repealed, and the declaratory act of a right in the British Parliament to bind us by their laws in all cases whatsoever, still suspended over us. But a court of inquiry held in Rhode Island in 1762, with a power to send persons to England to be tried for offences committed here, was considered, at our session of the spring of 1773, as demanding attention. Not thinking our old and leading members up to the point of forwardness and zeal which the times required, Mr. Henry, Richard Henry Lee, Francis L. Lee, Mr. Carr and myself agreed to meet in the evening, in a private room of the Raleigh, to consult on the state of things. There may have been a member or two more whom I do not recollect. We were all sensible that the most urgent of all measures was that of coming to an understanding with all the other colonies, to consider the British claims as a common cause to all, and to produce a unity of action: and, for this purpose, that a committee of correspondence in each colony would be the best instrument for intercommunication: and that their first measure would probably be, to propose a meeting of deputies from every colony, at some central place, who should be charged with the direction of the measures which should be taken by all.

. . . The origination of these committees of correspondence between the colonies has been since claimed for Massachusetts . . .

The Boston port bill, by which that port was to be shut up on the 1st of June, 1774, arrived while we were in session in the spring of that year. The lead in the House, on these subjects, being no longer left to the old members, Mr. Henry, R. H. Lee, Fr. L. Lee, three or four other members, whom I do not recollect, and myself, agreeing that we must boldly take an un-

[1] [A public room in the Raleigh.]

equivocal stand in the line with Massachusetts, determined to meet and consult on the proper measures, in the council-chamber, for the benefit of the library in that room. We were under conviction of the necessity of arousing our people from the lethargy into which they had fallen, as to passing events; and thought that the appointment of a day of general fasting and prayer would be most likely to call up and alarm their attention. No example of such a solemnity had existed since the days of our distresses in the war of '55, since which a new generation had grown up. With the help, therefore, of Rushworth, whom we rummaged over for the revolutionary precedents and forms of the Puritans of that day, preserved by him, we cooked up a resolution, somewhat modernizing their phrases, for appointing the 1st day of June, on which the port-bill was to commence, for a day of fasting, humiliation, and prayer, to implore Heaven to avert from us the evils of civil war, to inspire us with firmness in support of our rights, and to turn the hearts of the King and Parliament to moderation and justice. . . .

The Governor dissolved us, as usual. We retired to the Apollo, as before, agreed to an association, and instructed the committee of correspondence to propose to the corresponding committees of the other colonies, to appoint deputies to meet in Congress at such place, *annually*, as should be convenient, to direct, from time to time, the measures required by the general interest: and we declared that an attack on any one colony, should be considered as an attack on the whole. This was in May. We further recommended to the several counties to elect deputies to meet at Williamsburg, the 1st of August ensuing, to consider the state of the colony, and particularly to appoint delegates to a general Congress, should that measure be acceded to by the committees of correspondence generally. It was acceded to; Philadelphia was appointed for the place, and the 5th of September for the time of meeting. We returned home, and in our several counties invited the clergy to meet assemblies of the people on the 1st of June, to perform the ceremonies of the day, and to address to them discourses suited to the occasion. The people met generally, with anxiety and alarm in their countenances, and the effect of the day, through the whole colony, was like a shock of electricity, arousing every man, and placing him erect and solidly on his centre. They chose, universally, delegates for the convention. Being elected one for my own county, I prepared a draught of instructions to be given to the delegates whom we should send to the Congress, which I meant to propose at our meeting.

. . . I set out for Williamsburg some days before that appointed for our meeting, but was taken ill of a dysentery on the road, and was unable to proceed. I sent on, therefore, to Williamsburg, two copies of my draught, the one under cover to Peyton Randolph, who I knew would be in the chair of the convention, the other to Patrick Henry. Whether Mr. Henry disapproved the ground taken, or was too lazy to read it (for he was the laziest man in reading I ever knew) I never learned: but he communicated it to nobody. Peyton Randolph informed the convention he had received such a paper from a member. prevented by sickness from offering it in his place, and he laid it on the table for perusal. It was read generally by the members, approved by many, though thought too bold for the present state of things; but they printed it in pamphlet form, under the title of "A Summary View of the Rights of British America." It found its way to England, was taken up by the opposition, interpolated a little by Mr. Burke so as to make it answer opposition purposes, and in that form ran rapidly through several editions. This information I had from Parson Hurt, who happened at the time to be in London, whither he had gone to receive clerical orders; and I was informed afterwards by Peyton Randolph, that it had procured me the honor of having my name inserted in a long list of proscriptions, enrolled in a bill of attainder commenced in one of the Houses of Parliament, but suppressed in embryo by the hasty step of events, which warned them to be a little cautious. . . .

The convention met on the 1st of August, renewed their association, appointed delegates to the Congress, gave them instructions very temperately and properly expressed, both as to style and matter; and they repaired to Philadelphia at the time appointed. The splendid proceedings of that Congress, at their first session, belong to general history, are known to every one, and need not therefore be noted here. They terminated their session on the 26th of October, to meet again on the 10th of May ensuing. I took my seat with them on the 21st of June. On the 24th, a committee which had been appointed to prepare a declaration of the causes of taking up arms, brought in their report (drawn I believe by J. Rutledge) which, not being liked, the House recommitted it, on the 26th, and added Mr. Dickinson and myself to the committee. On the rising of the House, the committee having not yet met, I happened to find myself near Governor W. Livingston, and proposed to him to draw the paper. He excused himself and proposed that I should draw it. On my pressing him with urgency, "we are as yet but new acquaintances, sir," said he, "why are you so earnest for my doing it?" "Because," said I, "I have been informed that you drew the Address to the people of Great Britain, a production, certainly, of the finest pen in America." "On that," says he, "perhaps, sir, you may not have been correctly informed." I had received the information in Virginia from Colonel Harrison on his return from that Congress. Lee, Livingston, and Jay had been the committee for that draught. The first, prepared by Lee, had been disapproved and recommitted. The second was drawn by Jay, but being presented by Governor Livingston, had led Colonel Harrison into the error. The next morning, walking in the hall of Congress, many members being assembled, but the House not yet formed, I observed Mr. Jay speaking to R. H. Lee, and leading him by the button of his coat to me. "I understand, sir," said he to me, "that this gentleman informed you, that Governor Livingston drew the Address to the people of Great Britain." I assured him, at once, that I had not received that information from Mr. Lee, and that not a word had ever passed on the subject between Mr. Lee and myself; and after some explanations the subject was dropped. These gentlemen had had some sparrings in debate before, and continued ever very hostile to each other.

I prepared a draught of the declaration committed to us. It was too strong for Mr. Dickinson. He still retained the hope of reconciliation with the mother country, and was unwilling it should be lessened by offensive statements. He was so honest a man, and so able a one, that he was greatly indulged even by those who could not feel his scruples. We therefore requested him to take the paper, and put it into a form he could approve. He did so, preparing an entire new statement, and preserving of the former only the last four paragraphs and half of the preceding one. We approved and reported it to Congress, who accepted it. Congress gave a signal proof of their indulgence to Mr. Dickinson, and of their great desire not to go too fast for any respectable part of our body, in permitting him to draw their second petition to the King according to his own ideas, and passing it with scarcely any amendment. The disgust against this humility was general; and Mr. Dickinson's delight at its passage was the only circumstance which reconciled them to it. . . .

On the 15th of May, 1776, the convention of Virginia instructed their delegates in Congress, to propose to that body to declare the colonies independent of Great Britain . . .

It appearing in the course of . . . debates, that the colonies of New York, New Jersey, Pennsylvania, Delaware, Maryland, and South Carolina were not yet matured for falling from the parent stem, but that they were fast advancing to that state, it was thought most prudent to wait a while for them, and to postpone the final decision to July 1st; but, that this might occasion as little delay as possible, a committee was appointed to prepare a Declaration of Independence. The committee were John Adams, Dr. Franklin, Roger Sherman, Robert R. Livingston, and myself. Committees were also appointed, at the same time, to prepare a plan of confederation for the colonies, and to state the terms proper to be proposed for foreign alliance. The committee for drawing the Declaration of Independence, desired me to do it. It was accordingly done, and being approved by them, I reported it to the House on Friday, the 28th of June, when it was read, and ordered to lie on the table. On Monday, the 1st of July, the House resolved itself into a committee of the whole . . . The pusillanimous idea that we had friends in England worth keeping terms with, still haunted the minds of many. For this reason, those passages which conveyed censures on the people of England were struck out, lest they should give them offence. The clause too, reprobating the enslaving the inhabitants of Africa, was struck out in complaisance to South Carolina and Georgia, who had never attempted to restrain the importation of slaves, and who, on the contrary, still wished to continue it. Our northern brethren also, I believe, felt a little tender under those censures; for though their people had very few slaves themselves, yet they had been pretty considerable carriers of them to others. The debates, having taken up the greater parts of the 2d, 3d, and 4th days of July, were, on the evening of the last, closed; the Declaration was reported by the committee, agreed to by the House, and signed by every member present, except Mr. Dickinson.

On Friday, July 12, the committee appointed to draw the articles of Confederation reported them, and, on the 22d, the House resolved themselves into a committee to take them into consideration. On the 30th and 31st of that month, and 1st of the ensuing, those articles were debated which determined the proportion, or quota, of money which each state should furnish to the common treasury, and the manner of voting in Congress. . . .

Mr. Chase moved that the quotas should be fixed, not by the number of inhabitants of every condition, but by that of the "white inhabitants." He admitted that taxation should be always in proportion to property, that this was, in theory, the true rule; but that, from a variety of difficulties, it was a rule which could never be adopted in practice. The value of the property in every State, could never be estimated justly and equally. Some other measure for the wealth of the State must therefore be devised, some standard referred to, which would be more simple. He considered the number of inhabitants as a tolerably good criterion of property, and that this might always be obtained. He therefore thought it the best mode which we could adopt, with one exception only: he observed that negroes are property, and as such, cannot be distinguished from the lands or personalities held in those States where there are few slaves; that the surplus of profit which a Northern farmer is able to lay by, he invests in cattle, horses, &c., whereas a Southern farmer lays out the same surplus in slaves. There is no more reason, therefore, for taxing the Southern States on the farmer's head, and on his slave's head, than the Northern ones on their farmer's heads and the heads of their cattle; that the method proposed would, therefore, tax the Southern States according to their numbers and their wealth conjunctly, while the Northern would be taxed on numbers only: that negroes, in fact, should not be considered as members of the State, more than cattle, and that they have no more interest in it.

Mr. John Adams observed, that the numbers of people were taken by this article, as an index of the wealth of the State, and not as subjects of taxation; that, as to this matter, it was of no consequence by what name you called your people, whether by that of freemen or of slaves; that in some countries the laboring poor were called freemen, in others they were called slaves; but that the difference as to the state was imaginary only. . . . That the condition of the laboring poor in most countries, that of the fishermen particularly of the Northern States, is as abject as that of slaves. It is the number of laborers which produces the surplus for taxation, and numbers, therefore, indiscriminately, are the fair index of wealth; that it is the use of the word "property" here, and its application to some of the people of the State, which produces the fallacy. How does the Southern farmer procure slaves? Either by importation or by purchase from his neighbor. If he imports a slave, he adds one to the number of laborers in his country, and proportionably to its profits and abilities to pay taxes; if he buys from his neighbor, it is only a transfer of a laborer from one farm to another, which does not change the annual produce of the State, and therefore, should not change its tax. . . .

Mr. Harrison proposed, as a compromise, that two slaves should be counted as one freeman. He affirmed that slaves did not do as much work as freemen, and doubted if two effected more than one; that this was proved by the price of labor; the hire of a laborer in the Southern colonies being from £8 to £12, while in the Northern it was generally £24.

Mr. Wilson said, that if this amendment should take place, the Southern colonies would have all the benefit of slaves, whilst the Northern ones would bear the burthen: that slaves increase the profits of a State, which the Southern States mean to take to themselves; that they also increase the burthen of defence, which would of course fall so much the heavier on the Northern: that slaves occupy the places of freemen, and eat their food. Dismiss your slaves, and freemen will take their places. It is our duty to lay every discouragement on the importation of slaves; but this amendment would give the *jus trium liberorum* to him who would import slaves: that other kinds of property were pretty equally distributed through all the colonies: there were as many cattle, horses and sheep, in the North as the South, and South as the North; but not so as to slaves: that experience has shown that those colonies have been always able to pay most, which have the most inhabitants, whether they be black or white; and the practice of the Southern colonies has always been to make every farmer pay poll taxes upon all his laborers, whether they be black or white. He acknowledges, indeed, that freemen work the most; but they consume the most also. They do not produce a greater surplus for taxation. The slave is neither fed nor clothed so expensively as a freeman. Again, white women are exempted from labor generally, but negro women are not. In this, then, the Southern States have an advantage as the article now stands. . . .

I moved and presented a bill for the revision of the laws, which was passed on the 24th of October; and on the 5th of November, Mr. Pendleton, Mr. Wythe, George Mason, Thomas L. Lee, and myself, were appointed a committee to execute the work. We agreed to meet at Fredericksburg to settle the plan of operation, and to distribute the work. We met there accordingly, on the 13th of January, 1777.

I proposed to abolish the law of primogeniture, and to make real estate descendible in parcenary to the next of kin, as personal property is, by the statute of distribution. Mr. Pendleton wished to preserve the right of primogeniture, but seeing at once that that could not prevail, he proposed we should adopt the Hebrew principle, and give a double portion to the elder son. I observed, that if the eldest son could eat twice as much, or do double work, it might be a natural evidence of his right to a double portion; but being on a par in his powers and wants, with his brothers and sisters, he should be on a par also in the partition of the patrimony; and such was the decision of the other members.

The bill for establishing religious freedom, the principles of which had, to a certain degree, been enacted before, I had drawn in all the latitude of reason and right. It still met with opposition; but, with some mutilations in the preamble, it was finally passed; and a singular proposition proved that its protection of opinion was meant to be universal. Where the preamble declares, that coercion is a departure from the plan of the holy author of our religion, an amendment was proposed, by inserting the word "Jesus Christ," so that it should read, "a departure from the plan of Jesus Christ, the holy author of our religion"; the insertion was rejected by a great majority, in proof that they meant to comprehend, within the mantle of its protection, the Jew and the Gentile, the Christian and Mahometan, the Hindoo, and Infidel of every denomination.

We thought that . . . a systematical plan of general education should be proposed, and I was requested to undertake it. I accordingly prepared three bills for the Revisal, proposing three distinct grades of education, reaching all classes. 1st. Elementary schools, for all children generally, rich and poor. 2d. Colleges, for a middle degree of instruction, calculated for the common purposes of life, and such as would be desirable for all who were in easy circumstances. And, 3d, an ultimate grade for teaching the sciences generally, and in their highest degree. The first bill proposed to lay off every county into Hundreds, or Wards, of a proper size and population for a school, in which reading, writing, and common arithmetic should be taught; and that the whole State should be divided into twenty-four districts, in each of which should be a school for classical learning, grammar, geography, and the higher branches of numerical arithmetic. The second bill proposed to amend the constitution of William and Mary college, to enlarge its sphere of science, and to make it in fact a University. The third was for the establishment of a library. These bills were not acted on until the same year, '96, and then only so much of the first as provided for elementary schools. . . . And in the Elementary bill, they inserted a provision which completely defeated it; for they left it to the court of each county to determine for itself, when this act should be carried into execution, within their county. One provision of the bill was, that the expenses of these schools should be borne by the inhabitants of the county, every one in proportion to his general tax rate. This would throw on wealth the education of the poor; and the justices, being generally of the more wealthy class, were unwilling to incur that burden, and I believe it was not suffered to commence in a single county. I shall recur again to this subject, towards the close of my story, if I should have life and resolution enough to reach that term; for I am already tired of talking about myself.

The bill on the subject of slaves, was a mere digest of the existing laws respecting them, without any intimation of a plan for a future and general emancipation. It was thought better that this should be kept back, and attempted only by way of amendment, whenever the bill should be brought on. The principles of the amendment, however, were agreed on, that is to say, the freedom of all born after a certain day, and deportation at a proper age. But it was found that the public mind would not yet bear the proposition, nor will it bear it even at this day. Yet the day is not distant when it must bear and adopt it, or worse will follow. Nothing is more certainly written in the book of fate, than that these people are to be free . . .

On the 1st of June, 1779, I was appointed Governor of the Commonwealth, and retired from the legislature. Being elected, also, one of the Visitors of William and Mary college, a self-electing body, I effected, during my residence in Williamsburg that year, a change in the organization of that institution, by abolishing the Grammar school, and the two professorships of Divinity and Oriental languages, and substituting a professorship of Law and Police, one of Anatomy, Medicine and Chemistry, and one of Modern languages; and the charter confining us to six professorships, we added the Law of Nature and Nations, and the Fine Arts to the duties of the Moral professor, and Natural History to those of the professor of Mathematics and Natural Philosophy.

Being now, as it were, identified with the Commonwealth itself, to write my own history, during the two years of my administration, would be to write the public history of that portion of the revolution within this State. This has been done by others . . .

Soon after my leaving Congress, in September, '76, to wit, on the last day of that month, I had been appointed, with Dr. Franklin, to go to France, as a Commissioner, to negotiate treaties of alliance and commerce with that government. Silas Deane, then in France, acting as agent for procuring military stores, was joined with us in commission. But such was the state of my family that I could not leave it, nor could I expose it to the dangers of the sea, and of capture by the British ships, then covering the ocean. I saw, too, that the laboring oar was really at home, where much was to be done, of the most permanent interest, in new modelling our governments, and much to defend our fanes and fire-sides from the desolations of an invading enemy, pressing on our country in every point. I declined, therefore, and Mr. Lee was appointed in my place. On the 15th of June, 1781, I had been appointed, with Mr. Adams, Mr. Franklin, Mr. Jay, and Mr. Laurens, a Minister Plenipotentiary for negotiating peace, then expected to be effected through the mediation of the Empress of Russia. The same reasons obliged me still to decline; and the negotiation was in fact never entered on. But, in the autumn of the next year, 1782, Congress receiving assurances that a general peace would be concluded in the winter and spring, they renewed my appointment on the 13th of November of that year. I had, two months before that, lost the cherished companion of my life, in whose affections, unabated on both sides, I had lived the last ten years in unchequered happiness. With the public interests, the state of my mind concurred in recommending the change of scene proposed; and I accepted the appointment, and left Monticello on the 19th of December, 1782, for Philadelphia, where I arrived on the 27th. The Minister of France, Luzerne, offered me a passage in the Romulus frigate, which I accepted; but she was then lying a few miles below Baltimore, blocked up in the ice. I remained, therefore, a month in Philadelphia, looking over the papers in the office of State, in order to possess myself of the general state of our foreign relations, and then went to Baltimore, to await the liberation of the frigate from the ice. After waiting there nearly a month, we received information that a Provisional treaty of peace had been signed by our Commissioners on the 3d of September, 1782, to become absolute, on the conclusion of peace between France and Great Britain. Considering my proceeding to Europe as now of no utility to the public, I returned immediately to Philadelphia, to take the orders of Congress, and was excused by them from further proceeding. I, therefore, returned home, where I arrived on the 15th of May, 1783.

On the 6th of the following month, I was appointed by the legislature a delegate to Congress, the appointment to take place on the 1st of November ensuing, when that of the existing delegation would expire. . . .

Congress had now become a very small body, and the members very remiss in their attendance on its duties. . . .

The remissness of Congress, and their permanent session, began to be a subject of uneasiness; and even some of the legislatures had recommended to them intermissions, and periodical sessions. As the Confederation had made no provision for a visible head of the government, during vacations of Congress, and such a one was necessary to superintend the executive business, to receive and communicate with foreign ministers and nations, and to assemble Congress on sudden and extraordinary emergencies, I proposed, early in April, the appointment of a committee, to be called the "Committee of the States," to consist of a member from each State, who should remain in session during the recess of Congress: that the functions of Congress should be divided into executive and legislative, the latter to be reserved, and the former, by a general resolution, to be delegated to that Committee. This proposition was afterwards agreed to; a Committee appointed, who entered on duty on the subsequent adjournment of Congress, quarrelled very soon, split into two parties, abandoned their post, and left the government without any visible head, until the next meeting in Congress. We have since seen the same thing take place in the Directory of France; and I believe it will forever take place in any Executive consisting of a plurality. Our plan, best, I believe, combines wisdom and practicability, by providing a plurality of Counsellors, but a single Arbiter for ultimate decision.

I was in France when we heard of this schism, and separation of our Committee, and, speaking with Dr. Franklin of this singular disposition of men to quarrel, and divide into parties, he gave his sentiments, as usual, by way of Apologue. He mentioned the Eddystone lighthouse, in the British channel, as being built on a rock, in the mid-channel, totally inaccessible in winter, from the boisterous character of that sea, in that season; that, therefore, for the two keepers employed to keep up the lights, all provisions for the winter were necessarily carried to them in autumn, as they could never be visited again till the return of the milder season; that, on the first practicable day in the spring, a boat put off to them with fresh supplies. The boatmen met at the door one of the keepers, and accosted him with a "How goes it, friend? Very well. How is your companion? I do not know. Don't know? Is not he here? I can't tell. Have not you seen him to-day? No. When did you see him? Not since last fall. You have killed him? Not I, indeed."

They were about to lay hold of him, as having certainly murdered his companion; but he desired them to go up stairs and examine for themselves. They went up, and there found the other keeper. They had quarrelled, it seems, soon after being left there, had divided into two parties, assigned the cares below to one, and those above to the other, and had never spoken to, or seen, one another since.

But to return to our Congress at Annapolis. The definitive treaty of peace which had been signed at Paris on the 3d of September, 1783, and received here, could not be ratified without a House of nine States. On the 23d of December, therefore, we addressed letters to the several Governors, stating the receipt of the definitive treaty; that seven States only were in attendance, while nine were necessary to its ratification; and urging them to press on their delegates the necessity of their immediate attendance.

Our body was little numerous, but very contentious. Day after day was wasted on the most unimportant questions. A member, one of those afflicted with the morbid rage of debate, of an ardent mind, prompt imagination, and copious flow of words, who heard with impatience any logic which was not his own, sitting near me on some occasion of a trifling but wordy debate, asked me how I could sit in silence, hearing so much false reasoning, which a word should refute? I observed to him, that to refute indeed was easy, but to silence was impossible; that in measures brought forward by myself, I took the laboring oar, as was incumbent on me; but that in general, I was willing to listen; that if every sound argument or objection was used by some one or other of the numerous debaters, it was enough; if not, I thought it sufficient to suggest the omission, without going into a repetition of what had been already said by others: that this was a waste and abuse of the time and patience of the House, which could not be justified. And I believe, that if the members of deliberate bodies were to observe this course generally, they would do in a day, what takes them a week; and it is really more questionable, than may at first be thought, whether Bonaparte's dumb legislature, which said nothing, and did much, may not be preferable to one which talks much, and does nothing. I served with General Washington in the legislature of Virginia, before the revolution, and, during it, with Dr. Franklin in Congress. I never heard either of them speak ten minutes at a time, nor to any but the main point, which was to decide the question. They laid their shoulders to the great points, knowing that the little ones would follow of themselves. If the present Congress errs in too much talking, how can it be otherwise, in a body to which the people send one hundred and fifty lawyers, whose trade it is to question everything, yield nothing, and talk by the hour? That one hundred and fifty lawyers should do business together, ought not to be expected. . . .

On the 7th of May Congress resolved that a Minister Plenipotentiary should be appointed, in addition to Mr. Adams and Dr. Franklin, for negotiating treaties of commerce with foreign nations, and I was elected to that duty. I accordingly left Annapolis on the 11th, took with me my eldest daughter, then at Philadelphia (the two others being too young for the voyage), and proceeded to Boston, in quest of a passage. While passing through the different States, I made a point of informing myself of the state of the commerce of each; went on to New Hampshire with the same view, and returned to Boston. Thence I sailed on the 5th of July, in the Ceres, a merchant ship of Mr. Nathaniel Tracey, bound to Cowes. He was himself a passenger, and, after a pleasant voyage of nineteen days, from land to land, we arrived at Cowes on the 26th. I was detained there a few days by the indisposition of my daughter. On the 30th, we embarked for Havre, arrived there on the 31st, left it on the 3d of August, and arrived at Paris on the 6th. I called immediately on Dr. Franklin, at Passy, communicated to him our charge, and we wrote to Mr. Adams, then at the Hague, to join us at Paris.

Mr. Adams being appointed Minister Plenipotentiary of the United States, to London, left us in June, and in July, 1785, Dr. Franklin returned to America, and I was appointed his successor at Paris. . . .

Celebrated writers of France and England had already sketched good principles on the subject of government; yet the American Revolution seems first to have awakened the thinking part of the French nation in general, from the sleep of despotism in which they were sunk. The officers too, who had been to America, were mostly young men, less shackled by habit and prejudice, and more ready to assent to the suggestions of common sense, and feeling of common rights, than others. They came back with new ideas and impressions. The press, notwithstanding its shackles, began to disseminate them; conversation assumed new freedoms; Politics became the theme of all societies, male and female, and a very extensive and zealous party was formed, which acquired the appellation of the Patriotic party, who, sensible of the abusive government under which they lived, sighed for occasions of reforming it. This party comprehended all the honesty of the kingdom, sufficiently at leisure to think, the men of letters, the easy Bourgeois, the young nobility, partly from reflection, partly from mode; for these sentiments became matter of mode, and as such, united most of the young women to the party. . . .

Our first essay, in America, to establish a federative government had fallen, on trial, very short of its object. During the war of Independence, while the pressure of an external enemy hooped us together, and their enterprises kept us necessarily on the alert, the spirit of the people, excited by danger, was a supplement to the Confederation, and urged them to zealous exertions, whether claimed by that instrument or not; but, when peace and safety were restored, and every man became engaged in useful and profitable occupation, less attention was paid to the calls of Congress. The fundamental defect of the Confederation was, that Congress was not authorized to act immediately on the people, and by its own officers. Their power was only requisitory, and these requisitions were addressed to the several Legislatures, to be by them carried into execution, without other coercion than the moral principle of duty. This allowed, in fact, a negative to every

Legislature, on every measure proposed by Congress; a negative so frequently exercised in practice, as to benumb the action of the Federal government, and to render it inefficient in its general objects, and more especially in pecuniary and foreign concerns. The want, too, of a separation of the Legislative, Executive, and Judiciary functions, worked disadvantageously in practice. Yet this state of things afforded a happy augury of the future march of our Confederacy, when it was seen that the good sense and good dispositions of the people, as soon as they perceived the incompetence of their first compact, instead of leaving its correction to insurrection and civil war, agreed, with one voice, to elect deputies to a general Convention, who should peaceably meet and agree on such a Constitution as "would ensure peace, justice, liberty, the common defense and general welfare."

This Convention met at Philadelphia on the 25th of May, '87. It sat with closed doors, and kept all its proceedings secret, until its dissolution on the 17th of September, when the results of its labors were published all together. I received a copy, early in November, and read and contemplated its provisions with great satisfaction. As not a member of the Convention, however, nor probably a single citizen of the Union, had approved it in all its parts, so I, too, found articles which I thought objectionable. The absence of express declarations ensuring freedom of religion, freedom of the press, freedom of the person under the uninterrupted protection of the Habeas corpus, and trial by jury in Civil as well as in Criminal cases, excited my jealousy; and the re-eligibility of the President for life, I quite disapproved. I expressed freely, in letters to my friends, and most particularly to Mr. Madison and General Washington, my approbations and objections. How the good should be secured and the ill brought to rights, was the difficulty. To refer it back to a new Convention might endanger the loss of the whole. My first idea was, that the nine States first acting, should accept it unconditionally, and thus secure what in it was good, and that the four last should accept on the previous condition, that certain amendments should be agreed to; but a better course was devised, of accepting the whole, and trusting that the good sense and honest intentions of our citizens, would make the alterations which should be deemed necessary. Accordingly, all accepted, six without objection, and seven with recommendations of specified amendments. Those respecting the press, religion, and juries, with several others, of great value, were accordingly made . . .

I found Paris . . . in high fermentation. . . . Nor should we wonder at this pressure, when we consider the monstrous abuses of power under which this people were ground to powder; when we pass in review the weight of their taxes, and the inequality of their distribution; the oppressions of the tithes, the tailles, the corvees, the gabelles, the farms and the barriers; the shackles on commerce by monopolies; on industry by guilds and corporations; on the freedom of conscience, of thought, and of speech; on the freedom of the press by the Censure; and of the person by Lettres de Cachet; the cruelty of the Criminal code generally; the atrocities of the Rack; the venality of the Judges, and their partialities to the rich; the

monopoly of Military honors by the Noblesse; the enormous expenses of
the Queen, the Princes and the Court; the prodigalities of pensions; and
the riches, luxury, indolence and immorality of the Clergy. Surely under
such a mass of misrule and oppression, a people might justly press for a
thorough reformation, and might even dismount their rough-shod riders,
and leave them to walk on their own legs. . . .

For, while laboring under the want of money for even ordinary purposes, in a government which required a million of livres a day, and driven
to the last ditch by the universal call for liberty, there came on a winter
of such severe cold, as was without example in the memory of man, or in
the written records of history. The Mercury was at times 50° below the
freezing point of Fahrenheit, and 22° below that of Reaumur. All out-
door labor was suspended, and the poor, without the wages of labor, were,
of course, without either bread or fuel. The government found its necessities
aggravated by that of procuring immense quantities of fire-wood, and of
keeping great fires at all the cross streets, around which the people gathered
in crowds, to avoid perishing with cold. Bread, too, was to be bought, and
distributed daily, gratis, until a relaxation of the season should enable the
people to work; and the slender stock of bread stuff had for some time
threatened famine, and had raised that article to an enormous price. So
great, indeed, was the scarcity of bread, that, from the highest to the lowest citizen, the bakers were permitted to deal but a scanty allowance per
head, even to those who paid for it; and, in cards of invitation to dine in
the richest houses, the guest was notified to bring his own bread. To eke
out the existence of the people, every person who had the means, was called
on for a weekly subscription, which the Curés collected, and employed in
providing messes for the nourishment of the poor, and vied with each
other in devising such economical compositions of food, as would subsist
the greatest number with the smallest means. This want of bread had been
foreseen for some time past, and M. de Montmorin had desired me to
notify it in America, and that, in addition to the market price, a premium
should be given on what should be brought from the United States. Notice
was accordingly given, and produced considerable supplies. . . .

Hitherto no acts of popular violence had been produced by the struggle
for political reformation. Little riots, on ordinary incidents, had taken
place as at other times, in different parts of the kingdom, in which some
lives, perhaps a dozen or twenty had been lost; but in the month of April,
a more serious one occurred in Paris, unconnected, indeed, with the
Revolutionary principle, but making part of the history of the day. The
Fauxbourg St. Antoine is a quarter of the city inhabited entirely by the
class of day laborers and journeymen in every line. A rumor was spread
among them, that a great paper manufacturer, of the name of Reveillon,
had proposed, on some occasion, that their wages should be lowered to
fifteen sous a day. Inflamed at once into rage, and without inquiring into
its truth, they flew to his house in vast numbers, destroyed everything in
it, and in his magazines and work-shops, without secreting, however, a

pin's worth to themselves, and were continuing this work of devastation, when the regular troops were called in. Admonitions being disregarded, they were of necessity fired on, and a regular action ensued, in which about one hundred of them were killed, before the rest would disperse. There had rarely passed a year without such a riot, in some part or other of the Kingdom; and this is distinguished only as cotemporary with the Revolution, although not produced by it.

The States General were opened on the 5th of May, '89 . . .

The objects for which this body was convened being of the first order of importance, I felt it very interesting to understand the views of the parties of which it was composed, and especially the ideas prevalent as to the organization contemplated for their government. I went, therefore, daily from Paris to Versailles, and attended their debates, generally till the hour of adjournment. Those of the Noblesse were impassioned and tempestuous. They had some able men on both sides, actuated by equal zeal. The debates of the Commons were temperate, rational, and inflexibly firm. As preliminary to all other business, the awful questions came on, shall the State sit in one, or in distinct apartments? And shall they vote by heads or houses? The opposition was soon found to consist of the Episcopal order among the clergy, and two-thirds of the Noblesse; while the Tiers État were, to a man, united and determined. After various propositions of compromise had failed, the Commons undertook to cut the Gordian knot. . . . Concluding that their dissolution was now to take place, they repaired to a building called the "Jeu de paume" (or Tennis court) and there bound themselves by oath to each other, never to separate, of their own accord, till they had settled a constitution for the nation, on a solid basis, and, if separated by force, that they would reassemble in some other place. The next day they met in the church of St. Louis, and were joined by a majority of the clergy. The heads of the Aristocracy saw that all was lost without some bold exertion. The King was still at Marly. Nobody was permitted to approach him but their friends. He was assailed by falsehoods in all shapes. He was made to believe that the Commons were about to absolve the army from their oath of fidelity to him, and to raise their pay. The court party were now all rage and desperation. . . .

The soldiery had not yet indicated which side they should take, and that which they should support would be sure to prevail. I considered a successful reformation of government in France, as insuring a general reformation through Europe, and the resurrection, to a new life, of their people, now ground to dust by the abuses of the governing powers. I was much acquainted with the leading patriots of the Assembly. Being from a country which had successfully passed through a similar reformation, they were disposed to my acquaintance, and had some confidence in me. I urged, most strenuously, an immediate compromise; to secure what the government was now ready to yield, and trust to future occasions for what might still be wanting.

Violent ferment . . . gained the soldiery, first of the French guards, extended to those of every other denomination, except the Swiss, and even to the body guards of the King. They began to quit their barracks, to assemble in squads, to declare they would defend the life of the King, but would not be the murderers of their fellow-citizens. They called themselves the soldiers *of the nation*, and left now no doubt on which side they would be, in case of rupture. Similar accounts came in from the troops in other parts of the kingdom, giving good reason to believe they would side with their fathers and brothers, rather than with their officers.

The Assembly now entered on the business of their mission, and first proceeded to arrange the order in which they would take up the heads of their constitution, as follows:

First, and as Preliminary to the whole, a general Declaration of the Rights of Man. Then, specifically, the Principles of the Monarchy; Rights of the Nation; Rights of the King; Rights of the Citizens; Organization and Rights of the National Assembly; Forms necessary for the enactment of Laws; Organization and Functions of the Provincial and Municipal Assemblies; Duties and Limits of the Judiciary power; Functions and Duties of the Military power.

A Declaration of the Rights of Man, as the preliminary of their work, was accordingly prepared and proposed by the Marquis de La Fayette.

But the quiet of their march was soon disturbed by information that troops, and particularly the foreign troops, were advancing on Paris from various quarters. The King had probably been advised to this, on the pretext of preserving peace in Paris. But his advisers were believed to have other things in contemplation. The Marshal de Broglio was appointed to their command, a high-flying aristocrat, cool and capable of everything. Some of the French guards were soon arrested, under other pretexts, but really, on account of their dispositions in favor of the National cause. The people of Paris forced their prison, liberated them, and sent a deputation to the Assembly to solicit a pardon. The Assembly recommended peace and order to the people of Paris, the prisoners to the King, and asked from him the removal of the troops. His answer was negative and dry, saying they might remove themselves, if they pleased, to Noyons or Soissons. In the meantime, these troops, to the number of twenty or thirty thousand, had arrived, and were posted in, and between Paris and Versailles. The bridges and passes were guarded. . . .

The King was now completely in the hands of men, the principal among whom had been noted, through their lives, for the Turkish despotism of their characters, and who were associated around the King, as proper instruments for what was to be executed. The news of this change began to be known at Paris, about one or two o'clock. In the afternoon, a body of about one hundred German cavalry were advanced, and drawn up in the Place Louis XV., and about two hundred Swiss posted at a little distance in their rear. This drew people to the spot, who thus accidentally found themselves in front of the troops, merely at first as spectators; but, as their numbers increased, their indignation rose. They retired a few steps, and posted themselves on and behind large piles of stones, large and small, collected in that place for a bridge, which was to be built adjacent to it. In this position, happening to be in my carriage on a visit, I passed through the lane they had formed, without interruption. But the moment after I had passed, the people attacked the cavalry with stones. They charged, but the advantageous position of the people, and the showers of stones, obliged the horse to retire, and quit the field altogether, leaving one of their number on the ground, and the Swiss in the rear not moving to their aid. This was the signal for universal insurrection, and this body of cavalry, to avoid being massacred, retired towards Versailles. The people now armed themselves with such weapons as they could find in armorers' shops, and private houses, and with bludgeons; and were roaming all night, through all parts of the city, without any decided object. The next day (the 13th,) the Assembly pressed on the King to send away the troops, to permit the Bourgeoisie of Paris to arm for the preservation of order in the city, and offered to send a deputation from their body to tranquillize them; but their propositions were refused. A committee of magistrates and electors of the city were appointed by those bodies, to take upon them its government. The people, now openly joined by the French guards, forced the prison of St. Lazare, released all the prisoners, and took a great store of corn, which they carried to the cornmarket. Here they got some arms, and the French guards began to form and train them. The city-committee determined to raise forty-eight thousand Bourgeoise, or rather to restrain their numbers to forty-eight thousand. On the 14th, they sent one of their members (Monsieur de Corny) to the Hotel des Invalides, to ask arms for their Garde Bourgeoise. He was followed by, and he found there, a great collection of people. The Governor of the Invalides came out, and represented the impossibility of his delivering arms, without the orders of those from whom he received them. De Corny advised the people then to retire, and retired himself; but the people took possession of the arms. It was remarkable, that not only the Invalides themselves made no opposition, but that a body of five thousand foreign troops, within four hundred yards, never stirred. M. de Corny, and five others, were then sent to ask arms of M. de Launay, Governor of the Bastile. They found a great collection of people already before the place, and they immediately planted a flag of truce, which was answered by a like flag hoisted on the parapet. The deputation prevailed on the people to fall back a little, advanced themselves to make their demand of the Governor, and in that instant, a discharge from the Bastile killed four persons of those nearest to the deputies. The deputies retired. I happened to be at the house of M. de Corny, when he returned to it, and received from him a narrative of these transactions. On the retirement of the deputies, the people rushed forward, and almost in an instant, were in possession of a fortification of infinite strength, defended by one hundred men, which in other times had stood several regular sieges, and had never been taken. How they forced their entrance has never been explained. They took all the arms, discharged the prisoners, and such of the garrison as were not killed in the first moment of fury, carried the Governor and Lieutenant Governor, to the Place de Grève, (the place of public execution,) cut off their heads, and sent them through the city, in triumph, to the Palais royal.

The decapitation of de Launay worked powerfully through the night on the whole Aristocratic party; insomuch, that in the morning, those of the greatest influence on the Count d'Artois, represented to him the absolute necessity that the King should give up everything to the Assembly. . . .

In the evening of August the 4th, and on the motion of the Viscount de Noailles, brother in law of La Fayette, the Assembly abolished all titles of rank, all the abusive privileges of feudalism, the tithes and casuals of the Clergy, all Provincial privileges, and, in fine, the Feudal regimen generally. . . . Many days were employed in putting into the form of laws, the numerous demolitions of ancient abuses; which done, they proceeded to the preliminary work of a Declaration of Rights. There being much concord of sentiment on the elements of this instrument, it was liberally framed, and passed with a very general approbation. They then appointed a Committee for the "reduction of a projet" of a constitution, at the head of which was the Archbishop of Bordeaux. I received from him, as chairman of the Committee, a letter of July 20th, requesting me to attend and assist at their deliberations; but I excused myself, on the obvious considerations, that my mission was to the King as Chief Magistrate of the nation, that my duties were limited to the concerns of my own country, and forbade me to intermeddle with the internal transactions of that, in which I had been received under a specific character only.

Their plan of a constitution was discussed in sections, and so reported from time to time, as agreed to by the Committee. The first respected the general frame of the government; and that this should be formed into three departments, Executive, Legislative and Judiciary, was generally agreed. But when they proceeded to subordinate developments, many and various shades of opinion came into conflict, and schism, strongly marked, broke the Patriots into fragments of very discordant principles. . . .

The Aristocracy was cemented by a common principle, of preserving the ancient regime, or whatever should be nearest to it. Making this their polar star, they moved in phalanx, gave preponderance on every question to the minorities of the Patriots, and always to those who advocated the least change. The features of the new constitution were thus assuming a fearful aspect, and great alarm was produced among the honest Patriots by these dissensions in their ranks.

In this uneasy state of things, I received one day a note from the Marquis de La Fayette, informing me that he should bring a party of six or eight friends to ask a dinner of me the next day. I assured him of their welcome. When they arrived, they were La Fayette himself, Duport, Barnave, Alexander la Meth, Blacon, Mounier, Maubourg, and Dagout. These were leading Patriots, of honest but differing opinions, sensible of the necessity of effecting a coalition by mutual sacrifices, knowing each other, and not afraid, therefore, to unbosom themselves mutually. This last was a material principle in the selection. With this view, the Marquis had invited the conference, and had fixed the time and place inadvertently, as to the embarrassment under which it might place me. The cloth being removed, and wine set on the table, after the American manner, the Marquis introduced the objects of the conference, by summarily reminding them of the state of things in the Assembly, the course which the principles of the Constitution were taking, and the inevitable result, unless checked by more concord among the Patriots themselves. He observed, that although he also had his opinion, he was ready to sacrifice it to that of his brethren of the same cause; but that a common opinion must now be formed, or the Aristocracy would carry everything, and that, whatever they should now agree on, he, at the head of the National force, would maintain. The discussions began at the hour of four, and were continued till ten o'clock in the evening; during which time, I was a silent witness to a coolness and candor of argument, unusual in the conflicts of political opinion; to a logical reasoning, and chaste eloquence, disfigured by no gaudy tinsel of rhetoric or declamation, and truly worthy of being placed in parallel with the finest dialogues of antiquity, as handed to us by Xenophon, by Plato and Cicero. The result was, that the King should have a suspensive veto on the laws, that the legislature should be composed of a single body only, and that to be chosen by the people. This Concordat decided the fate of the constitution. The Patriots all rallied to the principles thus settled, carried every question agreeably to them, and reduced the Aristocracy to insignificance and impotence. But duties of exculpation were now incumbent on me. I waited on Count Montmorin the next morning, and explained to him, with truth and candor, how it had happened that my house had been made the scene of conferences of such a character. He told me, he already knew everything which had passed, that so far from taking umbrage at the use made of my house on that occasion, he earnestly wished I would habitually assist at such conferences, being sure I should be useful in moderating the warmer spirits, and promoting a wholesome and practicable reformation only. I told him, I knew too well the duties I owed to the King, to the nation, and to my own country, to take any part in councils concerning their internal government, and that I should persevere, with care, in the character of a neutral and passive spectator, with wishes only, and very sincere ones, that those measures might prevail which would be for the greatest good of the nation.

Here I discontinue my relation of the French Revolution. The minuteness with which I have so far given its details, is disproportioned to the general scale of my narrative. But I have thought it justified by the interest which the whole world must take in this Revolution. As yet, we are but in the first chapter of its history. The appeal to the rights of man, which had been made in the United States, was taken up by France, first of the European nations. From her, the spirit has spread over those of the

South. The tyrants of the North have allied indeed against it; but it is irresistible. Their opposition will only multiply its millions of human victims; their own satellites will catch it, and the condition of man through the civilized world, will be finally and greatly ameliorated. This is a wonderful instance of great events from small causes. So inscrutable is the arrangement of causes and consequences in this world, that a two-penny duty on tea, unjustly imposed in a sequestered part of it, changes the condition of all its inhabitants. I have been more minute in relating the early transactions of this regeneration, because I was in circumstances peculiarly favorable for a knowledge of the truth. Possessing the confidence and intimacy of the leading Patriots, and more than all, of the Marquis Fayette, their head and Atlas, who had no secrets from me, I learned with correctness the views and proceedings of that party; while my intercourse with the diplomatic missionaries of Europe at Paris, all of them with the court, and eager in prying into its councils and proceedings, gave me a knowledge of these also. My information was always, and immediately committed to writing, in letters to Mr. Jay, and often to my friends, and a recurrence to these letters now insures me against errors of memory.

These opportunities of information ceased at this period, with my retirement from this interesting scene of action. I had been more than a year soliciting leave to go home, with a view to place my daughters in the society and care of their friends, and to return for a short time to my station at Paris. But the metamorphosis through which our government was then passing from its Chrysalid to its Organic form suspended its action in a great degree; and it was not till the last of August, that I received the permission I had asked. And here, I cannot leave this great and good country, without expressing my sense of its pre-eminence of character among the nations of the earth. A more benevolent people I have never known, nor greater warmth and devotedness in their select friendships. Their kindness and accommodation to strangers is unparalleled, and the hospitality of Paris is beyond anything I had conceived to be practicable in a large city. Their eminence, too, in science, the communicative dispositions of their scientific men, the politeness of the general manners, the ease and vivacity of their conversation, give a charm to their society, to be found nowhere else. In a comparison of this, with other countries, we have the proof of primacy, which was given to Themistocles, after the battle of Salamis. Every general voted to himself the first reward of valor, and the second to Themistocles. So, ask the travelled inhabitant of any nation, in what country on earth would you rather live?—Certainly, in my own, where are all my friends, my relations, and the earliest and sweetest affections and recollections of my life. Which would be your second choice? France.

On the 26th of September I left Paris for Havre, where I was detained by contrary winds until the 8th of October. On that day, and the 9th, I crossed over to Cowes, where I had engaged the Clermont, Capt. Colley, to touch for me. She did so; but here again we were detained by contrary winds, until the 22d, when we embarked, and landed at Norfolk on the

23d of November. On my way home, I passed some days at Eppington, in Chesterfield, the residence of my friend and connection, Mr. Eppes; and, while there, I received a letter from the President, General Washington, by express, covering an appointment to be Secretary of State. I received it with real regret. My wish had been to return to Paris, where I had left my household establishment, as if there myself, and to see the end of the Revolution, which I then thought would be certainly and happily closed in less than a year. I then meant to return home, to withdraw from political life, into which I had been impressed by the circumstances of the times, to sink into the bosom of my family and friends, and devote myself to studies more congenial to my mind. In my answer of December 15th, I expressed these dispositions candidly to the President, and my preference of a return to Paris; but assured him, that if it was believed I could be more useful in the administration of the government, I would sacrifice my own inclinations without hesitation, and repair to that destination; this I left to his decision. I arrived at Monticello on the 23d of December, where I received a second letter from the President, expressing his continued wish that I should take my station there, but leaving me still at liberty to continue in my former office, if I could not reconcile myself to that now proposed. This silenced my reluctance, and I accepted the new appointment.

In the interval of my stay at home, my eldest daughter had been happily married to the eldest son of the Tuckahoe branch of Randolphs, a young gentleman of genius, science, and honorable mind, who afterwards filled a dignified station in the General Government, and the most dignified in his own State. I left Monticello on the first of March, 1790, for New York. At Philadelphia I called on the venerable and beloved Franklin. . . .

I arrived at New York on the 21st of March, where Congress was in session.

(Here the notes end.)

## For the New Generation

### TO JOHN ADAMS.

MONTICELLO, *September 12, 1821.*

Are we to surrender the pleasing hopes of seeing improvement in the moral and intellectual condition of man? The events of Naples and Piedmont cast a gloomy cloud over that hope, and Spain and Portugal are not beyond jeopardy. And what are we to think of this northern triumvirate, arming their nations to dictate despotisms to the rest of the world? And the evident connivance of England, as the price of secret stipulations for continental armies, if her own should take side with her malcontent and pulverized people? And what of the poor Greeks, and their small chance of amelioration even if the hypocritical Autocrat should take them under the iron cover of his Ukazes. Would this be lighter or safer than that of the Turk? These, my dear friend, are speculations for the new generation. . . . Yet I will not believe our labors are lost. I shall not die without a hope that light and liberty are on steady advance. We have seen, indeed, once within the records of history, a complete eclipse of the human mind continuing for centuries. And this, too, by swarms of the same northern barbarians, conquering and taking possession of the countries and governments of the civilized world. Should this be again attempted, should the same northern hordes, allured again by the corn, wine, and oil of the south, be able again to settle their swarms in the countries of their growth, the art of printing alone, and the vast dissemination of books, will maintain the mind where it is, and raise the conquering ruffians to the level of the conquered, instead of degrading these to that of their conquerors. And even should the cloud of barbarism and despotism again obscure the science and liberties of Europe, this country remains to preserve and restore light and liberty to them. In short, the flames kindled on the 4th of July, 1776, have spread over too much of the globe to be extinguished by the feeble engines of despotism; on the contrary, they will consume these engines and all who work them.

# New University

## TO ————.[1]

MONTICELLO, *November 24, 1821.*

DEAR SIR,—Your welcome favor of the 12th came to hand two days ago. I was just returned from Poplar Forest, which I have visited four times this year. I have an excellent house there, inferior only to Monticello, am comfortably fixed and attended, have a few good neighbors, and pass my time there in a tranquillity and retirement much adapted to my age and indolence. . . . I am very little able to walk, but ride freely without fatigue. No better proof than that on a late visit to the Natural Bridge I was six days successively on horseback from breakfast to sunset. You enquire also about our University. All its buildings except the Library will be finished by the ensuing spring. It will be a splendid establishment, would be thought so in Europe, and for the chastity of its architecture and classical taste leaves everything in America far behind it. But the Library, not yet begun, is essentially wanting to give it unity and consolidation as a single object. It will have cost in the whole but 250,000 dollars. The library is to be on the principle of the Pantheon, a sphere within a cylinder of 70 feet diameter,— to wit, one-half only of the dimensions of the Pantheon, and of a single order only. When this is done you must come and see it. I do not admire your Canada speculation. I think, with Mr. Rittenhouse, that it is altogether

[1] Address missing; probably to William Short.

unaccountable how any man can stay in a cold country who can find room in a warm one, and should certainly prefer, to polar regions of ice and snow, lands as fertile and cheap which may be covered with groves of olives and oranges. I envy M. Chaumont nothing but his French cook and cuisine. These are luxuries which can neither be forgotten nor possessed in our country.

## Russian Enigma

### TO LEVETT HARRIS.

MONTICELLO, *December 12, 1821.*

I am afraid our quondam favorite Alexander has swerved from the true faith. His becoming an accomplice of the soi-disant Holy Alliance, the antinational principles he has separately avowed, and his becoming the very leader of a combination to chain mankind down eternally to oppressions of the most barbarous ages, are clouds on his character not easily to be cleared away. But these are problems for younger heads than mine. You will see their solution and tell me of it in another world. I salute you with great friendship and respect.

## Party System

### TO WILLIAM T. BARRY.

MONTICELLO, *July 2, 1822.*

I was only of a band devoted to the cause of independence, all of whom exerted equally their best endeavors for its success, and have a common right to the merits of its acquisition. So also is the civil revolution of 1801. Very many and very meritorious were the worthy patriots who assisted in bringing back our government to its republican tack. To preserve it in that, will require unremitting vigilance. Whether the surrender of our opponents, their reception into our camp, their assumption of our name, and apparent accession to our objects, may strengthen or weaken the genuine principles of republicanism, may be a good or an evil, is yet to be seen. I consider the party division of Whig and Tory the most wholesome which can exist in any government, and well worthy of being nourished, to keep out those of a more dangerous character.

# Liberty, Neutrality and Spain

## TO THE PRESIDENT OF THE UNITED STATES (JAMES MONROE).

MONTICELLO, *June 11, 1823.*

On the question you propose, whether we can, in any form, take a bolder attitude than formerly in favor of liberty, I can give you but commonplace ideas. They will be but the widow's mite, and offered only because requested. The matter which now embroils Europe, the presumption of dictating to an independent nation the form of its government, is so arrogant, so atrocious, that indignation, as well as moral sentiment, enlists all our partialities and prayers in favor of one, and our equal execrations against the other. I do not know, indeed, whether all nations do not owe to one another a bold and open declaration of their sympathies with the one party, and their detestation of the conduct of the other. But farther than this we are not bound to go; and indeed, for the sake of the world, we ought not to increase the jealousies, or draw on ourselves the power of this formidable confederacy. I have ever deemed it fundamental for the United States, never to take active part in the quarrels of Europe. Their political interests are entirely distinct from ours. Their mutual jealousies, their balance of power, their complicated alliances, their forms and principles of government, are all foreign to us. They are nations of eternal war. All their energies are expended in the destruction of the labor, property and lives of their people. On our part, never had a people so favorable a chance of trying the opposite system, of peace and fraternity with mankind, and the direction of all our means and faculties to the purposes of improvement instead of destruction.

While no duty, therefore, calls on us to take part in the present war of Europe, and a golden harvest offers itself in reward for doing nothing, peace and neutrality seem to be our duty and interest. We may gratify ourselves, indeed, with a neutrality as partial to Spain as would be justifiable without giving cause of war to her adversary . . . And I expect daily and confidently to hear of a spark kindled in France, which will employ her at home, and relieve Spain from all further apprehensions of danger.

That England is playing false with Spain cannot be doubted. Her government is looking one way and rowing another. It is curious to look back a little on past events. During the ascendency of Bonaparte, the word among the herd of kings, was "*sauve qui peut.*" Each shifted for himself, and left his brethren to squander and do the same as they could. After the battle of Waterloo, and the military possession of France, they rallied and combined in common cause, to maintain each other against any similar and future danger. . . . There can be no doubt that the allies are bound by treaty to aid England with their armies, should insurrection take place among her people.

This war is evidently that of the general body of the aristocracy, in which England is also acting her part. "Save but the nobles and there shall be no war," says she, masking her measures at the same time under the form of friendship and mediation, and hypocritically, while a party, offering herself as a judge, to betray those whom she is not permitted openly to oppose. A fraudulent neutrality, if neutrality at all, is all Spain will get from her. And Spain, probably, perceives this, and willingly winks at it rather than have her weight thrown openly into the other scale.

## On the Declaration

### TO JAMES MADISON.

MONTICELLO, *August 30, 1823.*

You have doubtless seen Timothy Pickering's Fourth of July observations on the Declaration of Independence. If his principles and prejudices, personal and political, gave us no reason to doubt whether he had truly quoted the information he alleges to have received from Mr. Adams, I should then say, that in some of the particulars, Mr. Adams' memory has led him into unquestionable error. At the age of eighty-eight, and forty-seven years after the transactions of Independence, this is not wonderful. Nor should I, at the age of eighty, on the small advantage of that difference only, venture to oppose my memory to his, were it not supported by written notes, taken by myself at the moment and on the spot. He says, "the committee of five, to wit, Dr. Franklin, Sherman, Livingston, and ourselves, met, discussed the subject, and then appointed him and myself to make the draught; that we, as a sub-committee, met, and after the urgencies of each on the other, I consented to undertake the task; that the draught being made, we, the sub-committee, met, and conned the paper over, and he does not remember that he made or suggested a single alteration." Now these details are quite incorrect. The committee of five met; no such thing as a sub-committee was proposed, but they unanimously pressed on myself alone to undertake the draught. I consented; I drew it; but before I reported it to the committee, I communicated it *separately* to Dr. Franklin and Mr. Adams, requesting their corrections, because they were the two members of whose judgments and amendments I wished most to have the benefit, before presenting it to the committee; and you have seen the original paper now in my hands, with the corrections of Dr. Franklin and Mr. Adams interlined in their own handwritings. Their alterations were two or three only, and merely verbal. I then wrote a fair copy, reported it to the committee, and from them, unaltered, to Congress. This personal communication and consultation with Mr. Adams, he has misremembered into the actings of a sub-committee. Pickering's observations, and Mr. Adams' in addition, "that it contained no new ideas, that it is a commonplace compilation, its sentiments hackneyed in Congress for two years before, and its essence contained in Otis' pamphlet," may all be true. Of that I am not to be the judge. Richard Henry Lee charged it as copied from Locke's treatise on government. Otis' pamphlet I never saw, and whether I had gathered my ideas from reading or reflection I do not know. I know only that I turned to neither book nor pamphlet while writing it. I did not consider it as any part of my charge to invent new ideas altogether, and to offer no sentiment which had ever been expressed before. Had Mr. Adams been so restrained, Congress would have lost the benefit of his bold and impressive advocations of the rights of Revolution. For no man's confident and fervid addresses, more than Mr. Adams', encouraged and supported us through the difficulties surrounding us, which, like the ceaseless action of gravity, weighed on us by night and by day. Yet, on the same ground, we may ask what of these elevated thoughts was new, or can be affirmed never before to have entered the conceptions of man?

Whether, also, the sentiments of Independence, and the reasons for declaring it, which make so great a portion of the instrument, had been hackneyed in Congress for two years before the 4th of July, '76, or this dictum also of Mr. Adams be another slip of memory, let history say. This, however, I will say for Mr. Adams, that he supported the Declaration with zeal and ability, fighting fearlessly for every word of it. As to myself, I thought it a duty to be, on that occasion, a passive auditor of the opinions of others, more impartial judges than I could be, of its merits or demerits. During the debate I was sitting by Doctor Franklin, and he observed that I was writhing a little under the acrimonious criticisms on some of its parts; and it was on that occasion, that by way of comfort, he told me the story of John Thompson, the hatter, and his new sign.

Timothy thinks the instrument the better for having a fourth of it expunged. He would have thought it still better, had the other three-fourths gone out also, all but the single sentiment (the only one he approves), which recommends friendship to his dear England, whenever she is willing to be at peace with us. His insinuations are, that although "the high tone of the instrument was in unison with the warm feelings of the times, this sentiment of habitual friendship to England should never be forgotten, and that the duties it enjoins should *especially* be borne in mind on every celebration of this anniversary." In other words, that the Declaration, as being a libel on the government of England, composed in times of passion, should now be buried in utter oblivion, to spare the feelings of our English friends and Angloman fellow citizens. But it is not to wound them that we wish to keep it in mind; but to cherish the principles of the instrument in the bosoms of our own citizens: and it is a heavenly comfort to see that these principles are yet so strongly felt, as to render a circumstance so trifling as this little lapse of memory of Mr. Adams, worthy of being solemnly announced and supported at an anniversary assemblage of the nation on its birthday.

# The Light Will Spread

TO JOHN ADAMS.

MONTICELLO, *September 4, 1823.*

DEAR SIR,—Your letter of August the 15th was received in due time, and with the welcome of everything which comes from you. With its opinions on the difficulties of revolutions from despotism to freedom, I very much concur. The generation which commences a revolution rarely completes it. Habituated from their infancy to passive submission of body and mind to their kings and priests, they are not qualified when called on to think and provide for themselves; and their inexperience, their ignorance and bigotry make them instruments often, in the hands of the Bonapartes and Iturbides, to defeat their own rights and purposes. This is the present situation of Europe and Spanish America. But it is not desperate. The light which has been shed on mankind by the art of printing, has eminently changed the condition of the world. As yet, that light has dawned on the middling classes only of the men in Europe. The kings and the rabble, of equal ignorance, have not yet received its rays; but it continues to spread, and while printing is preserved, it can no more recede than the sun return on his course. A first attempt to recover the right of self-government may fail, so may a second, a third, etc. But as a younger and more instructed race comes on, the sentiment becomes more and more intuitive, and a fourth, a fifth, or some subsequent one of the ever renewed attempts will ultimately succeed.

# Monroe Doctrine

TO THE PRESIDENT OF THE UNITED STATES
(JAMES MONROE).

MONTICELLO, *October 24, 1823.*

DEAR SIR,—The question presented by the letters you have sent me, is the most momentous which has ever been offered to my contemplation since that of Independence. That made us a nation, this sets our compass and points the course which we are to steer through the ocean of time opening on us. And never could we embark on it under circumstances more auspicious. Our first and fundamental maxim should be, never to entangle ourselves in the broils of Europe. Our second, never to suffer Europe to intermeddle with cis-Atlantic affairs. America, North and South, has a set of interests distinct from those of Europe, and peculiarly her own. She should therefore have a system of her own, separate and apart from that of Europe. While the last is laboring to become the domicile of despotism, our endeavor should surely be, to make our hemisphere that of freedom. One nation, most of all, could disturb us in this pursuit; she now offers to lead, aid, and accompany us in it. By acceding to her proposition, we detach her from the bands, bring her mighty weight into the scale of free government, and emancipate a continent at one stroke, which might otherwise linger long in doubt and difficulty. Great Britain is the nation which can do us the most harm of any one, or all on earth; and with her on our side we need not fear the whole world. With her then, we should most sedulously cherish a cordial friendship; and nothing would tend more to knit our affections than to be fighting once more, side by side, in the same cause. Not that I would purchase even her amity at the price of taking part in her wars. But the war in which the present proposition might engage us, should that be its consequence, is not her war, but ours. Its object is to introduce and establish the American system, of keeping out of our land all foreign powers, of never permitting those of Europe to intermeddle with the affairs of our nations. It is to maintain our own principle, not to depart from it. And if, to facilitate this, we can effect a division in the body of the European powers, and draw over to our side its most powerful member, surely we should do it. But I am clearly of Mr. Canning's opinion, that it will prevent instead of provoking war. With Great Britain withdrawn from their scale and shifted into that of our two continents, all Europe combined would not undertake such a war. For how would they propose to get at either enemy without superior fleets? Nor is the occasion to be slighted which this proposition offers, of declaring our protest against the atrocious violations of the rights of nations, by the interference of any one in the internal affairs of another, so flagitiously begun by Bonaparte, and now continued by the equally lawless Alliance, calling itself Holy.

But we have first to ask ourselves a question. Do we wish to acquire to our own confederacy any one or more of the Spanish provinces? I candidly confess, that I have ever looked on Cuba as the most interesting addition which could ever be made to our system of States. The control which, with Florida Point, this island would give us over the Gulf of Mexico, and the countries and isthmus bordering on it, as well as all those whose waters flow into it, would fill up the measure of our political well-being. Yet, as I am sensible that this can never be obtained, even with her own consent, but by war; and its independence, which is our second interest, (and especially its independence of England,) can be secured without it, I have no hesitation in abandoning my first wish to future chances, and accepting its independence, with peace and the friendship of England, rather than its association, at the expense of war and her enmity.

I could honestly, therefore, join in the declaration proposed, that we aim not at the acquisition of any of those possessions, that we will not stand in the way of any amicable arrangement between them and the Mother country; but that we will oppose, with all our means, the forcible interposition of any other power, as auxiliary, stipendiary, or under any other form or pretext, and most especially, their transfer to any power by conquest, cession, or acquisition in any other way. I should think it, therefore, advisable, that the Executive should encourage the British government to a continuance in the dispositions expressed in these letters, by an assurance of his concurrence with them as far as his authority goes; and that as it may lead to war, the declaration of which requires an act of Congress, the case shall be laid before them for consideration at their first meeting, and under the reasonable aspect in which it is seen by himself.

## On Party Names

### TO THE MARQUIS DE LA FAYETTE.

MONTICELLO, *November 4, 1823.*

In truth, the parties of Whig and Tory are those of nature. They exist in all countries, whether called by these names, or by those of Aristocrats and Democrats, Coté Droite and Coté Gauche, Ultras and Radicals, Serviles, and Liberals. The sickly, weakly, timid man fears the people, and is a Tory by nature. The healthy, strong and bold, cherishes them, and is formed a Whig by nature.

## Soldiers' Vote

### TO JOHN HAMBDEN PLEASANTS.

MONTICELLO, *April 19, 1824.*

DEAR SIR,—I received in due time your favor of the 12th, requesting my opinion on the proposition to call a convention for amending the constitution of the State. That this should not be perfect cannot be a subject of wonder. . . . The basis of our constitution is in opposition to the principle of equal political rights, refusing to all but freeholders any participation in the natural right of self-government. It is believed, for example, that a very great majority of the militia, on whom the burden of military duty was imposed in the late war, were men unrepresented in the legislation which imposed this burden on them. However nature may by mental or physical disqualifications have marked infants and the weaker sex for the protection, rather than the direction of government, yet among the men who either pay or fight for their country, no line of right can be drawn. The exclusion of a majority of our freemen from the right of representation is merely arbitrary, and an usurpation of the minority over the majority; for it is believed that the non-freeholders compose the majority of our free and adult male citizens.

## Washington's Politics

### TO MARTIN VAN BUREN.

MONTICELLO, *June 29, 1824.*

General Washington was himself sincerely a friend to the republican principles of our Constitution. His faith, perhaps, in its duration, might not have been as confident as mine; but he repeatedly declared to me, that he was determined it should have a fair chance for success, and that he would lose the last drop of his blood in its support, against any attempt which might be made to change it from its republican form. He made these declarations the oftener, because he knew my suspicions that Hamilton had other views, and he wished to quiet my jealousies on this subject. For Hamilton frankly avowed that he considered the British Constitution, with all the corruptions of its administration, as the most perfect model of government which had ever been devised by the wit of man; professing however, at the same time, that the spirit of this country was so fundamentally republican, that it would be visionary to think of introducing monarchy here, and that, therefore, it was the duty of its administrators to conduct it on the principles their constituents had elected.

I had meant to have added some views on the amalgamation of parties, to which your favor of the 8th has some allusion; an amalgamation of name, but not of principle. Tories are Tories still, by whatever name they may be called.

## Natural Division

### TO HENRY LEE.

MONTICELLO, *August 10, 1824.*

Men by their constitutions are naturally divided into two parties: 1. Those who fear and distrust the people, and wish to draw all powers from them into the hands of the higher classes. 2. Those who identify themselves with the people, have confidence in them, cherish and consider them as the most honest and safe, although not the most wise depository of the public interests. In every country these two parties exist, and in every one where they are free to think, speak, and write, they will declare themselves. Call them, therefore, Liberals and Serviles, Jacobins and Ultras, Whigs and Tories, Republicans and Federalists, Aristocrats and Democrats, or by whatever name you please, they are the same parties still, and pursue the same object. The last appellation of Aristocrats and Democrats is the true one expressing the essence of all.

## Progress of Society

TO WILLIAM LUDLOW.

MONTICELLO, *September 6, 1824.*

SIR,—The idea which you present in your letter of July 30th, of the progress of society from its rudest state to that it has now attained, seems conformable to what may be probably conjectured. Indeed, we have under our eyes tolerable proofs of it. Let a philosophic observer commence a journey from the savages of the Rocky Mountains, eastwardly towards our seacoast. These he would observe in the earliest stage of association living under no law but that of nature, subsisting and covering themselves with the flesh and skins of wild beasts. He would next find those on our frontiers in the pastoral state, raising domestic animals to supply the defects of hunting. Then succeed our own semi-barbarous citizens, the pioneers of the advance of civilization, and so in his progress he would meet the gradual shades of improving man until he would reach his, as yet, most improved state in our seaport towns. This, in fact, is equivalent to a survey, in time, of the progress of man from the infancy of creation to the present day. I am eighty-one years of age, born where I now live, in the first range of mountains in the interior of our country. And I have observed this march of civilization advancing from the seacoast, passing over us like a cloud of light, increasing our knowledge and improving our condition, insomuch as that we are at this time more advanced in civilization here than the seaports were when I was a boy. And where this progress will stop no one can say.

## Collective Mind

TO HENRY LEE.

MONTICELLO, *May 8, 1825.*

With respect to our rights, and the acts of the British government contravening those rights, there was but one opinion on this side of the water. All American Whigs thought alike on these subjects. When forced, therefore, to resort to arms for redress, an appeal to the tribunal of the world was deemed proper for our justification. This was the object of the Declaration of Independence. Not to find out new principles, or new arguments, never before thought of, not merely to say things which had never been said before; but to place before mankind the common sense of the subject, in terms so plain and firm as to command their assent, and to justify ourselves in the independent stand we are compelled to take. Neither aiming at originality of principle or sentiment, nor yet copied from any particular and previous writing, it was intended to be an expression of the American mind, and to give to that expression the proper tone and spirit called for by the occasion. All its authority rests then on the harmonizing sentiments of the day, whether expressed in conversation, in letters, printed essays, or in the elementary books of public right, as Aristotle, Cicero, Locke, Sidney, etc.

## Peaceful Progress

### TO ELLEN W. COOLIDGE.

MONTICELLO, *August 27, 1825.*

I am glad you took the delightful tour which you describe in your letter. It is almost exactly that which Mr. Madison and myself pursued in May and June, 1791. Setting out from Philadelphia, our course was to New York, up the Hudson to Albany, Troy, Saratoga, Fort Edward, Fort George, Lake George, Ticonderoga, Crown Point, penetrated into Lake Champlain, returned the same way to Saratoga, thence crossed the mountains to Bennington, Northampton, along Connecticut River to its mouth, crossed the Sound into Long Island, and along its northern margin to Brooklyn, re-crossed to New York, and returned. But from Saratoga till we got back to Northampton was then mostly desert. Now it is what thirty-four years of free and good government have made it. It shows how soon the labor of men would make a paradise of the whole earth, were it not for misgovernment, and a diversion of all his energies from their proper object—the happiness of man, —to the selfish interests of kings, nobles, and priests.

Our University goes on well. We have passed the limit of 100 students some time since. As yet it has been a model of order and good behavior, having never yet had occasion for the exercise of a single act of authority. We studiously avoid too much government. We treat them as men and gentlemen, under the guidance mainly of their own discretion. They so consider themselves, and make it their pride to acquire that character for their institution. In short, we are as quiet on that head as the experience of six months only can justify. Our professors, too, continue to be what we wish them. Mr. Gilmer accepts the Law chair, and all is well.

## Historic Gift

### TO ELLEN W. COOLIDGE.

MONTICELLO, *November 14, 1825.*

We have heard of the loss of your baggage, with the vessel carrying it, and sincerely condole with you on it. It is not to be estimated by its pecuniary value, but by that it held in your affections,—the documents of your childhood, your letters, correspondencies, notes, books, etc., etc., all gone! and your life cut in two, as it were, and a new one to begin, without any records of the former. John Hemmings was the first who brought me the news. He had caught it accidentally from those who first read the letter from Colonel Peyton announcing it. He was *au desespoir!* That beautiful writing desk he had taken so much pains to make for you! everything else seemed as nothing in his eye, and that loss was everything. Virgil could not have been more afflicted had his Aeneid fallen a prey to the flames. I asked him if he could not replace it by making another. No; his eyesight had failed him too much, and his recollection of it was too imperfect. It has occurred to me, however, that I can replace it, not, indeed, to you, but to Mr. Coolidge, by a substitute, not claiming the same value from its decorations, but from the part it has *borne* in our history and the events with which it has been associated. I received a letter from a friend in Philadelphia lately, asking information of the house, and room of the house there, in which the Declaration of Independence was written, with a view to future celebrations of the Fourth of July in it, another enquiring whether a paper given to the Philosophical Society there, as a rough draught of that Declaration was genuinely so. A society is formed there lately for an annual celebration of the advent of Penn to that place. It was held in his ancient mansion, and the chair in which he actually sat when at his writing table was presented by a lady owning it, and was occupied by the president of the celebration. Two other chairs were given them, made of the elm under the shade of which Penn had made his first treaty with the Indians. If then things acquire a superstitious value because of their connection with particular persons, surely a connection with the great Charter of our Independence may give a value to what has been associated with that; and such was the idea of the enquirers after the room in which it was written. Now I happen still to possess the writing-box on which it was written. It was made from a drawing of my own by Ben. Randall, a cabinetmaker in whose house I took my first lodgings on my arrival in Philadelphia in May, 1776, and I have used it ever since. It claims no merit of particular beauty. It is plain, neat, convenient, and, taking no more room on the writing table than a moderate quarto volume, it yet displays itself sufficiently for any writing. Mr. Coolidge must do me the favor of accepting this. Its imaginary value will increase with years, and if he lives to my age, or another half-century, he may see it carried in the procession of our nation's birthday, as the relics of the saints are in those of the Church. I will send it through Colonel Peyton, and hope with better fortune than that for which it is to be a substitute.

# Last Letter

## TO ROGER C. WEIGHTMAN.

MONTICELLO, *June 24, 1826.*

RESPECTED SIR,—The kind invitation I receive from you, on the part of the citizens of the city of Washington, to be present with them at their celebra-

tion on the fiftieth anniversary of American Independence, as one of the sur-
viving signers of an instrument pregnant with our own, and the fate of the
world, is most flattering . . . I should, indeed, with peculiar delight, have
met and exchanged there congratulations personally with the small band, the
remnant of that host of worthies, who joined with us on that day, in the
bold and doubtful election we were to make for our country, between submission or the sword; and to have enjoyed with them the consolatory fact,
that our fellow citizens, after half a century of experience and prosperity,
continue to approve the choice we made. May it be to the world, what I
believe it will be, (to some parts sooner, to others later, but finally to all,)
the signal of arousing men to burst the chains under which monkish ignorance and superstition had persuaded them to bind themselves, and to assume
the blessings and security of self-government. That form which we have
substituted, restores the free right to the unbounded exercise of reason and
freedom of opinion. All eyes are opened, or opening, to the rights of man.
The general spread of the light of science has already laid open to every
view the palpable truth, that the mass of mankind has not been born with
saddles on their backs, nor a favored few booted and spurred, ready to ride
them legitimately, by the grace of God.